P9-BHV-122

Guide to
Western Canada

Sixth Edition

edited by
Ann Carroll Burgess

The
Globe
Pequot
Press

Guilford, Connecticut

Copyright © 1987, 1990, 1993, 1996, 1998, 2001 by The Globe Pequot Press

All rights reserved. No part of this book may be reproduced or transmitted in any form by any means, electronic or mechanical, including photocopying and recording, or by any information storage and retrieval system, except as may be expressly permitted by the 1976 Copyright Act or by the publisher. Requests for permission should be made in writing to The Globe Pequot Press, P.O. Box 480, Guilford, Connecticut 06437.

Photo credits: pp. 50, 54, 98, and 109 © Brain A. Gauvin, courtesy British Columbia Convention and Visitors Bureau; p. 211 © Mel Bruschert, courtesy Calgary Convention and Visitors Bureau; and p. 299 A. Carroll Burgess. All other photographs courtesy of the tourism services of Alberta, British Columbia, Manitoba, the Northwest Territories, Saskatchewan, and the Yukon Territory and of the federal tourism-promotion department of the govenment of Canada.

Cover photo: T. Dietrich/H. Armstrong Roberts
Maps created by Mary Ballachino

Library of Congress Cataloging-in-Publication Data

Guide to western Canada / edited by Ann Carroll Burgess. — 6th ed.
    p. cm.
    Rev ed. of: Guide to western Canada / by Frederick Pratson. 5th ed. c1998.
    Includes index.
    ISBN 0-7627-0649-X
    1. Canada, Western—Guidebooks.   I. Burgess, Ann Carroll.
II. Pratson, Frederick John. Guide to western Canada.

F1060.4 .G85 2001
917.1204'3—dc21

                                  2001023074

Manufactured in the United States of America
Sixth Edition/First Printing

CHAPTER 1

The Special Allure of Western Canada

Western Canada in Brief

Tales of adventure are etched into the landscape of Western Canada. From the windswept plains of Manitoba and Saskatchewan to the snow-covered slopes of the Rockies and northern Pacific coast, the stories of settlers, prospectors, trappers, and fortune seekers form an integral part of the wild and majestic region.

Western Canada epitomizes the appeal of the great outdoors combined with the pizzazz of modern, cosmopolitan cities. You'll discover rugged crags, lush rain forests, and the world's largest indoor shopping mall. You'll behold untamed wilderness in harmony with industrialization.

Within this vast region are some of the highest mountains on the North American continent; sprawling glaciers and giant trees; scores of wild rivers and thousands of unnamed lakes; seacoasts, richly described in Indian legend; sprawling prairies thick with golden wheat; and the mysterious Arctic region, itself inhabited by the First Nations of the Western Hemisphere.

You will also find cosmopolitan cities and quaint towns that bespeak bygone times and values; major expositions and international sports events, ethnic festivals, and authentic rodeos; and magnificent resorts and charming inns.

In Western Canada you can go helicopter skiing, white-water rafting, and trail riding; play golf surrounded by the Rocky Mountains; canoe, sailboard, hunt, and fish; photograph the beauty all around you; hike or camp; ride on top of a glacier; attend plays,

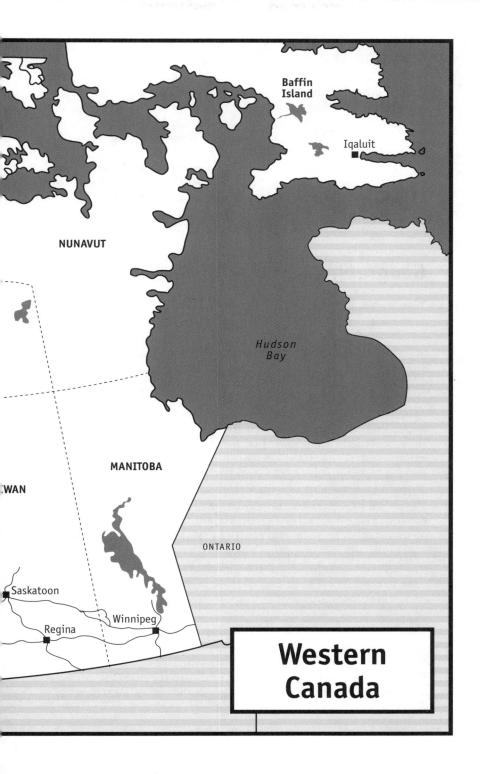

Baffin
Island

Iqaluit

NUNAVUT

*Hudson
Bay*

MANITOBA

:WAN

ONTARIO

Saskatoon

Regina

Winnipeg

Western
Canada

operas, and symphonies; stay at some of the finest hotels in the world and dine at superior gourmet restaurants; see unusual exhibits of art and science; and thrill to the sight of orcas (killer whales), eagles, bears, moose, caribou, elk, and mountain sheep.

Western Canada is no stranger to tourism. The great hotels of the railway lines, such as the Banff Springs Hotel and Chateau Lake Louise, began bringing visitors to Western Canada in the late nineteenth century.

In the twentieth century visitors were attracted to Western Canada by events such as the Calgary Stampede, Edmonton's Klondike Days, the Olympics in Calgary, and Expo 86 in Vancouver. The twenty-first century promises even more reasons to explore and experience the grandeur that is Western Canada.

Geography

Western Canada forms its southern border with the United States at the forty-ninth parallel. The southeastern section of Vancouver Island—facing the Pacific Ocean, with the capital city of Victoria at its tip—dips below the forty-ninth parallel and nears the forty-eighth. This section of Vancouver Island is in the area of the Strait of Juan de Fuca and the San Juan Islands, and it is pointed toward Seattle, Washington. Along the forty-ninth parallel, from west to east, are the provinces of British Columbia, Alberta, Saskatchewan, and Manitoba. South of the border, from west to east, are the states of Washington, Idaho, Montana, North Dakota, and Minnesota. To the north of British Columbia is the Yukon Territory, which borders eastern Alaska and the western Northwest Territories. The Yukon also has a small coast along Mackenzie Bay, which is part of the Beaufort Sea and thence the Arctic Ocean. The Northwest Territories and Nunavut span much of northern Canada, from the Yukon to Davis Strait, which separates Canada from Greenland.

Let's look at the varied topography of Western Canada, from west to east. The Pacific coastline of British Columbia is indented with long fjords and broken into hundreds of islands, the largest of which are Vancouver Island and the Queen Charlotte Islands. Queen Charlotte Strait and the Strait of Georgia separate Vancouver Island from mainland British Columbia. Most of the people in the province live in its extreme southwestern part. The Fraser River, a great waterway of Canada, flows through the province and empties into the Strait of Georgia at the city of Vancouver.

Canada—Did You Know?

- From its southernmost point where Pelee Island rises out of Lake Erie to Ellesmere Island in the Arctic Ocean, Canada stretches about 4,800 km/2,982 mi, or more than five times the length of Japan.

- Canada is one of the least populated countries in the world: There are fewer than thirty million people in the nation. More than three-quarters of these people live in urban centers, and two-thirds are concentrated within 200 km/125 mi of the U.S. border.

- There are more than a million rivers, streams, and lakes, which together make up a quarter of the world's freshwater supply. The Great Lakes, which Canada shares with the United States, are the world's largest body of fresh water.

British Columbia is essentially a province of mountain ranges: the Vancouver Island Ranges, Coast Mountains, Columbia Mountains, Monashee Mountains, Selkirk Mountains, Purcell Mountains, and Rocky Mountains.

The Japan Current helps create a mild climate along the Pacific coast. The Coast Mountains trap most of the storms moving east, and a great deal of rain is dumped along the coast, creating extremely lush forests of giant trees and a relatively long growing season. As a result, this area supports thriving lumber, agricultural, and allied industries, with much of the product exported to other countries, particularly those on the Pacific Rim. Fisheries, especially those that catch and process salmon, are also vital to the economic life of the province.

Just east of the Coast Mountains, however, the landscape is very arid, similar to that of the southwestern United States. This region is also one of the most productive agricultural areas in the province because of intensive irrigation.

North-central British Columbia is a rugged plateau with many lakes and dense forests. The cordillera (system of mountain ranges) continues through much of the Yukon and Alaska. Mount Logan (5,955 m/19,850 ft) in the Yukon is Canada's highest mountain. The famous goldfields of the Klondike are also in the

Yukon; mining is a principal economic activity in both the Yukon and British Columbia.

The Northwest Territories is primarily tundra with many lakes, including Great Bear Lake and Great Slave Lake, two of the largest in North America. The Mackenzie River, running north from Great Slave Lake to the Beaufort Sea, is one of Canada's most important and longest waterways.

The border between British Columbia and Alberta is formed by the impressive Rocky Mountains. Here, too, is the Great (Continental) Divide, where rivers and streams on the west side flow toward the Pacific and those on the east side flow toward the Atlantic and Hudson Bay. Recreation (national parks, resorts, skiing, trail riding, and hiking), mining, ranching, and forestry are the chief economic activities in the Rockies. The Rockies form only the western edge of Alberta; the rest of the province is flat or rolling terrain, known as the Interior Plains and also as the Prairies of Canada.

The Interior Plains/Prairies stretch across the rest of western Canada—Saskatchewan and Manitoba—to the Ontario border. Much of the land is devoted to growing wheat and other grains and to raising beef cattle. Alberta has large deposits of oil, oil-bearing materials (tar sands), and natural gas. Because of its intense petroleum production, this province is often referred to as the Texas of Canada. Saskatchewan is one of the world's leading producers of potash, used as fertilizer in agriculture.

Located in the interior of Manitoba is Lake Winnipeg, almost 5,200 sq km/2,000 sq mi and larger than Lake Ontario. The northeastern portion of this province also has shoreline on Hudson Bay, the largest inland sea in the Western Hemisphere. The Churchill River, a favorite haunt of naturalists and explorers, flows through northeastern Manitoba into Hudson Bay, where there is a major polar bear population.

Northern Alberta, Saskatchewan, and Manitoba are primarily wilderness areas of countless lakes, which are attractive to the serious angler. All the principal cities, towns, and transportation routes in these three provinces are located in the south, where the land is more suited to agriculture and the winter climate is less severe.

History

In 1885 the last spike of the Canadian Pacific Railroad was driven into place. Canada was at last linked, from coast to coast, by a modern transportation system that would greatly increase the human settlement and economic progress of this vast area of North America. The completion of this railroad was one of the great engineering accomplishments of the nineteenth century—in its time similar in complexity, effort, and investment to that required to land people on the moon in more recent years.

The completion of the railway came at a tremendous cost of both human life and bison—there was a mass extinction of herds—yet was of enormous symbolic importance to national unity. The railway transformed the sleeping trading post of Winnipeg and log fort at Calgary into cities, while the Pacific terminus turned the little township of Granville into the great port city of Vancouver. The railway's own hotels opened up the tourist industry from Québec City's Château Frontenac to Banff Springs Hotel and Chateau Lake Louise in the Rockies and Victoria's Empress Hotel on Vancouver Island.

Prior to the completion of the railroad, Canada was a confederation of seven provinces: Ontario, Québec, New Brunswick, Nova Scotia, Prince Edward Island, Manitoba, and British Columbia. British Columbia joined the confederation with the strict stipulation that it be connected to the rest of the country by rail; otherwise, it might choose to remain a colony of Great Britain, join the United States, or become independent. At that time Canada was fortunate enough to have had Sir John A. Macdonald as its first prime minister under the British North America Act, the instrument that created the confederation. Macdonald goaded Parliament into moving ahead with the railroad in order to keep British Columbia in the confederation and, as a result, forge a new country.

During the building of the railway in 1885, construction ran up against an ongoing armed struggle for land rights in Manitoba for the Métis—descendants of Indians and French fur traders. Led by the fiery Louis Riel, the fight, which at first enjoyed the support of Anglo-Saxon farmers, was also for cultural equality of French and English schools and churches. After the death of a Northwest Mounted Police officer from Toronto, troops were sent by train to quash the rebellion. Riel was captured, put on trial, found guilty, and hanged. To this day the rebellion remains a controversial episode in an otherwise peaceful Canadian history.

Despite this and other setbacks, the railway was completed and the nation was united. But the saga of Western Canada's history actually begins eons earlier. Historians speculate that the first group to inhabit the upper reaches of Western Canada arrived there from somewhere in Asia by means of a now-nonexistent land bridge during the last ice age. No one knows for certain what climatic changes and food shortages were responsible for this migration, but enough people crossed over to spread throughout the Western Hemisphere.

European arrivals centuries later would refer to these people as Indians or Eskimos. Neither is accurate. Native Canadians prefer to refer to themselves in their own languages simply as the People—undisputed first inhabitants of the land.

Today the Inuit, the descendants of these ancient peoples, continue to live and develop their cultures in Western Canada. The creation of Nunavut—Canada's newest territory, formed in 1999—recognizes the unique culture of these people. The ability to self-govern will help ensure the preservation of their history and future.

It is not known exactly who the first Europeans to come to America were, but legends—and some recently unearthed artifacts—indicate that the Norsemen of Scandinavia landed on the East Coast of North America (including Newfoundland) long before the arrival of Christopher Columbus.

However, it was not until the early European colonizers arrived that Canada would become a prize much sought after. French explorers, and, later, English ones, initially came in pursuit of furs for the demanding European market. As a result, men such as Samuel de Champlain and Pierre Gaultier de la Varennes Vérendrye became the first Europeans to investigate the interior of Canada. The British were not far behind, and in 1660 the Company of Gentlemen Adventurers into Hudson Bay (later known as the Hudson's Bay Company) was created under the auspices of King Charles II. The rivalry between the English and the French, which has pervaded most of Canadian history, began in earnest.

Over time, because of its strategically located trading posts throughout the North and West, Hudson's Bay came to control much of the territory of what is Canada today. In 1868, however, Britain's Parliament made the company turn over its immense holdings to the relatively new government of Canada, although the company continued with its business dealings throughout much of these lands. Today the Hudson's Bay Company is familiar to all Canadians, and to visitors, as a chain of excellent department stores known as the Bay. Yet if you travel to the remote reaches of northern Canada, you will likely make a stop for supplies at a Hudson's Bay Company trading post, because they are often the only source for hundreds of miles. At these trading posts,

The Mounties

Western Canada is different from the western United States in a fundamental way: It was not as wild in the gun-shooting, Indian-chasing sense. Law and order came to Western Canada in the form of tough, disciplined men wearing the red tunics and blue pants of the Northwest Mounted Police—the world-famous and legendary Mounties, established in 1874. This glowing legend generally contains more truth than falsehood. The Mounties came to Western Canada as the federal government's strong arm and to provide assistance to provincial and territorial governments that had few if any law-enforcement services of their own. The Mounties protected the rights of both Natives and settlers in a fair and just manner—not every time, but often enough to win respect.

After the battle of the Little Big Horn, thousands of U.S. Indians, including Sitting Bull, knowing that their victory was a prelude to attack by U.S. soldiers, moved across the border into lower Alberta, seeking refuge ensured by a shield of compassion and resolve provided by the Mounties. One Mountie legend says that a Mountie always gets his man. In case after case the Mounties have indeed pursued lawbreakers, often under extremely harsh conditions of weather and terrain, refusing to give up the chase until the fugitive has been captured—preferably alive. Their record in this regard isn't perfect, but it and the quality of the men and women themselves do serve as a deterrent to crime. Today's Mounties are officially known as the Royal Canadian Mounted Police, or RCMP. Their major training center is at Regina, Saskatchewan.

you can experience a bit of the atmosphere and heritage of the seventeenth century.

The early history of Western Canada is replete with the immortal names of important explorers. Some historians speculate that Sir Francis Drake could have seen the coast of British Columbia from his ship in the sixteenth century, but they are sure that Captain James Cook landed on what would later be called Vancouver Island in 1778. Captain George Vancouver, from whom the island and the chief city of the province would derive their name, mapped British Columbia's coast from 1792 to 1794.

Around the same time, in 1793, Sir Alexander Mackenzie, a Scot working for the North West Company (a rival of the Hudson's Bay Company), reached the Pacific after crossing much of the continent. He accomplished this amazing feat, including crossing the Rockies and the other mountain ranges of British Columbia, about thirteen years before Lewis and Clark stood at the shores of the Pacific. Mackenzie was also the explorer of the 1,792-km/1,120-mi river bearing his name that runs north from Great Slave Lake through the Northwest Territories (near eastern Alaska) to Mackenzie Bay and the Beaufort Sea above the Arctic Circle.

Western Canada also saw countless trading company explorers, trappers, mountain people, French Jesuit priests, and others keen on adventure and staking territorial claims for their patrons. Still, much of its northern reaches remain unexplored even today.

To adventuresome souls in the nineteenth century, the big news coming out of Western Canada was not the creation of a railroad but the discovery of gold. The coast of British Columbia and the interior regions of the Yukon were flooded by thousands of men with wild dreams of fabulous wealth. The sandbars of the lower Fraser River and the Klondike region became famous and have been immortalized in folklore. These gold seekers, whether successful or not, infused Western Canada with a bullish philosophy that anything is possible with a lot of pluck. Much of this individualistic, entrepreneurial spirit still exists in Western Canada and motivates its people, be they progeny of several generations or the most recent immigrant.

Confederation and completion of the railway yielded another significant milestone in Western Canadian development. At long last the vast empty lands that stretched between Manitoba and the Pacific coast of British Columbia had become accessible from the east and so could be populated.

A concentrated effort was made to attract new settlers from outside the country, most specifically in eastern Europe and Ukraine, to fill this new and still-desolate land. A massive publicity campaign promising free farmland to those who established themselves in Canada attracted immigrants from all over Europe. They were taken westward on special trains run along the newly completed Canadian Pacific transcontinental line.

"O Canada!"

Scholars claim that Canada got its name when the sixteenth-century French explorer Jacques Cartier heard an Iroquois word, *kanata,* meaning "town" or "dwelling." Another explanation suggests that early Spanish explorers returned from a fruitless quest for gold and declared, *"Aca Nada"*—"there is nothing there."

Although many of the newcomers gave up and went home, the descendants of many of the original settlers still farm the same prairie land today.

Eventually, this massive influx of new settlers resulted in the formation of the new provinces of Saskatchewan and Alberta in 1905. During the next century the map of Canada would change only twice—with the inclusion of Newfoundland in 1949 and creation of Nunavut in 1999.

In the twentieth century the prairie population continued to expand, with Manitoba attracting large numbers of eastern European immigrants, who today constitute 11 percent of Canada's population. Edmonton, the supply center for the Klondike gold rush of the late 1890s, also boomed.

But following World War I, a surplus of wheat followed by seasons of drought and bad harvests set the scene for Canada's share of the Great Depression. World War II and the discovery of major oil fields in northern Alberta in 1947 helped put Canada back on economic track. In the last quarter of the twentieth century, Western Canada truly began to shine. Expo 86 in Vancouver and the 1988 Calgary Winter Olympics focused global attention on these areas and opened a floodgate of tourism.

Canada will begin the twenty-first century as a strong and united country. Its basic traits of tolerance and understanding have made it not only a world leader in conflict resolution, but also a gracious host to many visitors.

The Great Cities of Western Canada

It is hard to believe that just over a hundred years ago the great cities of Western Canada—Vancouver, Victoria, Calgary, Edmonton, Saskatoon, Regina, Winnipeg—were little more than trading posts, frontier police garrisons, or logging towns. When you glimpse their gleaming, impressive skylines today, all the marks of a progressive, contemporary society are there. You see commercial and industrial activities of all kinds, a wide variety of cultural and entertainment attractions, fine universities and medical centers, and wonderful hotels and restaurants. You see, too, a broad diversity of people representing just about all ethnic, racial, and religious groups inhabiting this planet. In the cities of Eastern Canada, great emphasis is placed on the two founding cultures— French and British. In Western Canadian cities, however, the second most important culture, after English, might be Ukrainian or Chinese.

Although Western Canadian cities can't boast long, dramatic histories—except in the case of Native tribes—a dynamic "We can do it!" spirit is here that is often lacking in more established areas. These cities have had their boom-and-bust times, particularly in the commodities they produce and ship—oil, minerals, lumber, fish, and grain. Regardless, they have always bounced back bigger and better than before.

The quality of urban life the people here have created and continue to refine is the envy of cities centuries old. Here, there is always a sense of anticipation, of becoming, of something new around the bend. On a more mundane but nonetheless important level, Western Canadian cities are kept as clean as cities can be. The crime rates are also low enough that most people are not afraid.

These cities are on the threshold of the great Canadian wilderness, where you can travel hundreds of miles over a rugged, magnificent landscape and meet hardly another soul. After you've visited some of the great cities of Western Canada and toured their countryside, you won't return home wondering when you'll be back for another visit. You will, most likely, be planning to return to stay for good.

CHAPTER 2

General Information

Free Information for Travelers

The following national, provincial, and territorial tourism agencies will supply you with free information, maps, and brochures. For the quickest response, use toll-free (800) telephone numbers, accessible throughout the continental United States and Canada, or visit the Web site provided.

Canadian Tourism Commission
235 Queen Street
Ottawa, Ontario, Canada K1A 0H6
Toll-free (877) 8–CANADA
www.canadatourism.com

British Columbia
Ministry of Tourism and Provincial Secretary
Parliament Buildings
Victoria, British Columbia
Canada V8V 1X4
Toll-free (800) 663–6000
www.HelloBC.com

Alberta
Travel Alberta
10025 Jasper Avenue
Edmonton, Alberta
Canada T5J 3Z3
Toll-free (800) 661–8888
www.exploreAlberta.com

Saskatchewan
Tourism Saskatchewan
1919 Saskatchewan Drive
Regina, Saskatchewan
Canada S4P 3V7
Toll-free (800) 667–7191
www.sasktourism.com

Manitoba
Travel Manitoba
155 Carlton Street
Winnipeg, Manitoba
Canada R3C 3H8
Toll-free (800) 665–0040
www.travelmanitoba.com

Yukon
Tourism Yukon
P.O. Box 2703
Whitehorse, Yukon
Canada Y1A 2C6
(867) 667–5340
www.touryukon.com

Northwest Territories
Northwest Territories Tourism
Box 1320
Yellowknife, Northwest Territories
Canada X1A 2L9
Toll-free (800) 661–0788
www.nwtravel.nt.ca

Nunavut Tourism
P.O. Box 1450
Iqaluit, Nunavut
Canada X0A 0H0
Toll-free (800) 491–7910
www.nunatour.nt.ca

VIA Rail Canada (coast-to-coast rail travel)
Toll-free (888) 842–7245
www.viarail.ca

Air Canada
Toll-free (888) 247–2262
www.aircanada.ca

Free tourism information about Western Canada can also be obtained by contacting Canadian Consulates General in the United States.

Atlanta
1175 Peachtree Street, N.E.
Suite 1700
Atlanta, GA 30361–6205
(404) 532–2000

Boston
Three Copley Place, Suite 400
Boston, MA 02116
(617) 262–3760

Buffalo
1 Marine Midland Center, Suite 3000
Buffalo, NY 14203–2884
(716) 858–9500

Chicago
180 North Stetson Avenue, Twenty-Fourth Floor
Chicago, IL 60601
(312) 616–1860

Dallas
750 North St. Paul Street, Suite 1700
Dallas, TX 75201
(214) 922–9806

Detroit
600 Renaissance Center, Suite 1100
Detroit, MI 48243
(313) 567–2340

Los Angeles
California Plaza
500 South Hope, Ninth Floor
Los Angeles, CA 90071–2627
(213) 346–2700

Miami
200 South Biscayne Boulevard, Suite 1600
Miami, FL 33131
(305) 579–1600

Minneapolis
701 Fourth Avenue South
Minneapolis, MN 55415
(612) 332–7486

New York City
Exxon Building
1251 Avenue of the Americas
New York, NY 10020
(212) 596–1600

San Juan
107 Cereipo Street, Alt. de Santa Maria, Guaynabo
San Juan, PR 00969
(787) 790–2210
Fax: (787) 790–2205

Seattle
412 Plaza 600 Building
Sixth and Stewart Avenue
Seattle, WA 98101
(206) 443–1777

Washington, D.C.
Canadian Embassy
501 Pennsylvania Avenue N.W.
Washington, DC 20001
(202) 682–1740

Calculating Costs

Canada is an exceptional travel bargain due to the difference in the value between Canadian and U.S. dollars. At the time of this writing, the U.S. dollar is worth more than 45 percent of the Canadian dollar (the actual exchange rate varies from day to day).

Like the United States, Canada uses the decimal system and the dollar. However, Canadian bills, like most European currencies, are colored according to their value. Canada has replaced its

$1.00 and $2.00 bills with coins. The $1.00 coin is nicknamed the loonie for the loon on one side, and the $2.00 coin is referred to as a toonie.

Rather than publishing specific prices that are subject to change, this guide uses a scale of relative prices to indicate costs for accommodations and restaurant meals: *expensive, moderate,* and *inexpensive.*

Accommodations

An *expensive* double room in Vancouver, Victoria, Calgary, or Edmonton is likely to cost $175 and up a night in Canadian dollars. Be sure to ask about special discounts such as weekend rates, senior-citizen rates, and special rates for second rooms for children.

Discount rates may be difficult to find in Vancouver during the Alaska cruise season (May through September), because many of the hotels have devoted blocks of space to cruise-ship passengers. Rooms just outside the city may be more likely to offer bargains.

Accommodations rated *moderate* cost $75 to $175 a night in Canadian dollars. It is important to know that the quality of a moderately priced accommodation in a smaller city or town in Western Canada may be equal to (if not better than) that of some *expensive* places in the large metropolitan areas.

An accommodation rated *inexpensive* costs less than $75 a night in Canadian dollars.

Dining

Prices for restaurant meals are about the same throughout Western Canada, with the exception of remote areas and communities in the Yukon, the Northwest Territories, and Nunavut, where expensive transportation raises the price of goods. This means that a simple meal costs about the same in Winnipeg as it does in Vancouver, but a similar meal tends to cost more in Yellowknife and Whitehorse.

An *expensive* meal for two at a top restaurant in a big city can cost $90 and up. A *moderate* dinner for two can range from $40 to $90. An *inexpensive* meal costs less than $40 in Canadian dollars.

Although the restaurants designated *expensive* in this guide generally offer excellent ingredients, preparation, ambience, and service, those marked *moderate* and *inexpensive* have been selected with regard to their high quality and value to customers as well. This guide's emphasis is on diversity—presenting a wide choice of dining opportunities.

Western Canada, in general, is not a gourmet's paradise, but there is no denying the exceptional quality of its seafood from the Pacific and beef from Alberta. In the major cities of Vancouver, Edmonton, Calgary, and Winnipeg, you'll fine a wide array of fine Chinese, Japanese, Italian, and even French restaurants. And don't hesitate to try a wine from British Columbia to accompany your meal. Many of the vineyards are producing excellent wines to rival those from Bordeaux and Burgundy.

If you want to save money when staying at a big-city hotel, avoid making frequent use of room service. Have breakfast at a nearby coffee shop or diner, where meals are served faster and cost less. Also, consider bringing to your room a deli sandwich, pizza, or carton of chicken wings.

Attractions

Admission to many of the attractions described in this book is *free*. Others are designated *admission is charged* or *donations are accepted*. Major attractions usually have several price categories—adults, children, seniors, groups, and so forth. During the peak summer vacation season, from the end of June to Canada's Labour Day (first Monday in September), most attractions are open from 10:00 A.M. to 5:30 P.M. Some major attractions (amusement parks, historical villages, fairs, expositions) extend their hours into the evening during the peak season.

Food and Lodging in Western Canada

Accommodations

Accommodations in Western Canada—hotels, motels, resorts, bed-and-breakfast places, hunting or fishing camps, farm and country houses, inns, tourist homes, and so on—are comparable in quality and diversity to those in the United States and in any other highly developed, industrialized country. You'll find that accommodation standards—housekeeping, safety, amenities—are exceptionally high in Canada.

Both the federal and the provincial governments have done a fine job in providing roadside and park camping areas. Many of these include power hookups, safe drinking water, toilet and bathing facilities, fireplaces, picnic tables, and various recreational offerings.

Canada offers country home/farm vacations (including bed-and-breakfast places). Here you enjoy the best in Canadian rural life, including superb home-cooked meals, for a reasonable cost. The hosts even invite you to take part in the chores.

Tips on Tipping

A service charge is not automatically added to bills in Canada. It is customary, however, to give a tip of 15 percent of the total amount on a bill, excluding sales tax, to the people who serve you. Excellent service warrants an additional 5 percent or more. Taxi drivers receive 10 to 15 percent of the meter's total. People who handle your bags receive $1.00 per piece of luggage. Don't forget the person who tidies your room, makes your bed, and cleans the bath; $1.00 to $2.00 a night shows appreciation for his or her efforts. And note, as part of the tipping bottom line, that indifferent or poor service warrants the usual—an empty plate.

From May through August most Canadian universities and other schools welcome overnight guests. For a nominal charge you can have a room on campus; some offer a private bath, cafeteria services, and recreational facilities. Contact the various tourism promotion agencies listed at the beginning of this chapter for more information.

Dining

Dining out in Western Canada can range from the sublime to the mundane; from fine cuisine to mass-produced fast food. Incorporate local foods, such as fresh salmon in British Columbia and beef in Alberta, into your travel experience. Those waving wheat fields of Saskatchewan and Manitoba have raised bread making to high art that will make your visit to Canada's heartland even more memorable. You'll also discover a vast array of ethnic restaurants to sample—Ukrainian, Japanese, Portuguese, Chinese, Greek, and Italian. At first glance the prices on menus may give you sticker shock, so remember to calculate in the difference in currency.

Alcohol and Drug Laws

The legal drinking age in British Columbia, Saskatchewan, the Northwest Territories, the Yukon, and Nunavut is nineteen; in Alberta and Manitoba, eighteen.

Bottled liquor is sold through stores operated by the provincial governments. Selling hours vary from province to province.

Liquor can also be purchased in licensed restaurants and bars. Hours for sale at these establishments also vary.

Canada has strict drug laws, sharp enforcement, and tough penalties. It would be prudent to abstain while in the country.

Provincial Sales Taxes

All Canadian provinces except Alberta, the Northwest Territories, and the Yukon apply a sales tax to purchases of most goods, food in restaurants, and accommodations. In some provinces a sales tax refund is available when the goods you buy are taken out of the country. You should inquire about sales tax rebates when you make purchases.

Canada also has a national Goods and Services Tax, which is currently 7 percent. It is applied on all sales of hard goods and of services in addition to provincial sales taxes. Tax rebates are available when purchases total more than $100. Pick up a rebate form at the nearest Travel InfoCentre, or telephone (800) 668–4748 (613–991–3346 from outside Canada) for further details.

Weather

The best time for most vacation travel in Western Canada is during the warm-weather months—from mid-May to the end of September. July and August are the peak summer months. Spring and fall, in terms of seasonal transitions, are relatively short periods, except for coastal British Columbia, where the weather is mild throughout much of the year. The mountain regions, of course, get snow early, and some peaks are white year-round. June can be a tricky month in the high mountains—at Banff, for instance, where one day it can be shirtsleeves warm and the next a surprise snowstorm can drop a few inches. In winter the mountains offer some of the best skiing in the world. The prairies region of Alberta, Saskatchewan, and Manitoba is like a corridor down from the Arctic, whence high winds and cruel temperatures flow. During summer, however, it can get hot enough to fry eggs on the Trans-Canada Highway. During late fall and winter along British Columbia's coast, a great deal of rain falls, and people wonder if they'll ever see the sun again; it's much like the weather in Seattle. But the heavy rains help grow the lush forests and profusion of lovely flowers, some blossoming through winter. Very little snow

falls along the southern coast, and what does quickly melts. Overall, during the primary months of vacation travel, the weather throughout Western Canada is nearly perfect.

How should you dress for the weather? Tailor your wardrobe to the season and the kinds of outdoor activities you'll want to do. A windbreaker, warm sweater, and basic rain gear should be standard, even in summer. In case you forget something, all these items can be purchased virtually anywhere in Canada. There are some good values in English and Scottish woolens, in just about every form of clothing (weavings, patterns, colors) you want. Unless you are going up to the Arctic reaches of the Northwest Territories, Yukon, and Nunavut, the clothing you bring should be no different from what you would take if you were going to northern California, Oregon, Washington, or the coast of Maine.

Time Zones

Western Canada is divided into three time zones: Central Standard Time (Manitoba, Saskatchewan, and Nunavut), Mountain Standard Time (northwest Saskatchewan, Alberta, eastern British Columbia, the Northwest Territories), and Pacific Standard Time (British Columbia and Yukon); Nunavut also spans Eastern Standard Time and Atlantic Standard Time. There is a one-hour difference between time zones (12:00 noon Mountain Standard Time in Calgary is 11:00 A.M. Pacific Standard Time in Vancouver).

Telephone Area Codes

Telephone area codes for Western Canada are as follows:

Alberta	403, 780
British Columbia	604, 250
Manitoba	204
Northwest Territories (Yellowknife)	867
Saskatchewan	306
Yukon (Whitehorse)	867
Nunavut	867

Toll-free 800 numbers are in common use throughout Canada, and you should use them, if possible, before making a toll call. This book lists toll-free numbers wherever possible.

How to Get to Western Canada

Your Travel Agent

Travel anywhere these days has become so complicated and costly that even the most sophisticated traveler needs help to get through the maze of details and figures. For such assistance, you need go no farther than your local travel agent. He or she can book your accommodations, meal plans, transportation, tours, rental cars, and many other aspects of your trip; everything will be arranged to fit the budget you specify. In addition, your travel agent will give advice based on his or her own familiarity with popular places and special programs in Western Canada.

Your Cyber Agent

The World Wide Web provides extensive travel information at the touch of a dot com. This marvel of technology is a boon to do-it-yourself travelers, because Web sites are available twenty-four hours a day, seven days a week. All the provinces and territories have Web sites that provide information on airlines, rail services, bus lines, tour companies, attractions, hotels, and restaurants.

Be careful not to rely solely on the information provided by individual sites, which will have a healthy bias for what they are promoting. Whenever possible, check a second source.

Discount Fares

Travelers over sixty-five years of age are eligible to receive discounts on air, rail, and bus fares in some provinces. You must show proof of age when tickets are purchased. Get full details on these money-saving arrangements from your local travel agent or the transportation company's ticket clerk.

Package Tours, Cruises, and Vacations

Through your local travel agent, you can book many different kinds of package tours and vacations to Western Canada—for example, bus tours of every kind, fly-and-drive packages, ski and resort packages, big-city tours, hunting and fishing packages, railroad and cruise packages. Many escorted tours include accommodations, meals, sight-seeing, transportation, tour managers and guides, entertainment, and special events.

Major Canadian Transportation Companies

Air Canada, (888) 247–2262 or www.aircanada.ca, is the national airline of Canada. Air Canada's regularly scheduled flights provide service to most urban centers in the country and direct flights to Canadian destinations from several U.S. cities. This carrier also works with a number of leading package-tour operators, providing travelers with a wide variety of package tours to Western Canada—touring, skiing, big-city holidays, and so on.

Canadian Airlines, (800) 426–7000 or www.cdnair.ca, which has recently merged with Air Canada, provides regularly scheduled service to Western Canada destinations from most centers in Canada and the United States.

VIA Rail, (888) 842–7245 or www.viarail.ca, the national rail service of Canada, provides regularly scheduled passenger rail service throughout much of Canada, including one of the world's great rail trips—from Halifax, Nova Scotia, on the Atlantic to Vancouver, British Columbia, on the Pacific. Departures for Western Canada are from most major cities—Halifax, Québec, Montréal, Ottawa, Toronto, Winnipeg, Calgary, Vancouver. Sleeping accommodations and dining cars are on board. Western Canada package tours are also available.

Direct Flights from U.S. Cities

Vancouver is served by direct flights from these U.S. cities: Chicago, Dallas, Denver, Honolulu, Los Angeles, Minneapolis, New York, Phoenix, Portland, Reno, San Diego, San Jose, and Seattle.

Calgary has direct service from Boise, Chicago, Dallas, Denver, Houston, Las Vegas, Los Angeles, New York, Palm Springs, Phoenix, San Diego, and San Francisco.

Edmonton is directly served from Chicago, Dallas, Denver, Houston, Las Vegas, Miami, Minneapolis, Phoenix, San Francisco, and Seattle.

Winnipeg can be reached directly from Chicago, Denver, Fort Lauderdale, Los Angeles, Miami, Minneapolis, New York, Phoenix, San Francisco, Seattle, and Tampa.

Travelers from other U.S. locations can reach any Western Canada destination through connecting flights. For the convenience of many eastern-seaboard U.S. travelers, Western Canada flight connections are made through airports in Toronto or Montréal.

Airport Services

Major airports providing international services in Western Canada are in Vancouver, Victoria, Calgary, Edmonton, Regina, and Winnipeg. These airports provide foreign currency exchange, lockers, telephones, duty-free shops, bars, restaurants, newsstands, bookstores, drugstores, and various other shops and services. Hotels and motels are conveniently located near all international airports.

These airports also offer ground transportation to city centers by bus, taxi, or limousine. The major car-rental companies have facilities at the airports as well.

All these terminals have special facilities for the handicapped, including ramps, washrooms, and automatic doors.

Primary Gateways from the United States and Eastern Canada by Car

You can enter Western Canada through the following gateways:

From Eastern Canada, eastern United States (New York, Pennsylvania, New Jersey, New England, Washington, D.C.), Toronto, or other Ontario cities: via the Trans-Canada Highway, through the gateway of Winnipeg, Manitoba. The Trans-Canada Highway runs across the country, from sea to sea, essentially east–west, connecting most of the major cities.

From Detroit, Cleveland, other midwestern, mid-Atlantic, or southern U.S. cities: via I–75 to Sault Sainte Marie, to the Trans-Canada, thence to Winnipeg.

From Chicago, Saint Paul/Minneapolis, other midwestern, or southern U.S. cities: via I–94 to Fargo, North Dakota, then I–29 to Manitoba Highway 75, to Winnipeg.

From U.S. cities in the Rocky Mountain and southwestern states: to I–15, which runs north–south through Montana, to Alberta Highway 4 leading to Lethbridge, thence to Highway 2 to Calgary and Edmonton.

From U.S. cities in California and the Pacific Northwest: to Vancouver via I–5; to British Columbia, Highway 99; also from Port Angeles on Washington's Olympic Peninsula to Victoria, British Columbia, via ferry.

There are a number of other access routes into Western Canada from the United States. Consult your atlas to find the routing and entry points most convenient for you.

Road Distances from Selected North American Cities

The following charts give driving distances from major North American cities to various destinations in Western Canada.

Eastern Canada

Toronto, Ontario, to Winnipeg = 2,099 km/1,259 mi
Ottawa, Ontario, to Winnipeg = 2,218 km/1,331 mi
Montréal, Québec, to Winnipeg = 2,408 km/1,445 mi
Québec City, Québec, to Winnipeg = 2,678 km/1,607 mi
Halifax, Nova Scotia, to Winnipeg = 3,656 km/2,199 mi

Western Canada

Winnipeg to Regina = 571 km/343 mi
Winnipeg to Calgary = 1,336 km/802 mi
Winnipeg to Edmonton = 1,357 km/814 mi
Winnipeg to Vancouver = 2,232 km/1,339 mi
Winnipeg to Victoria = 2,337 km/1,402 mi

United States

Fairbanks, Alaska, to Edmonton = 1,840 mi/2,962 km
Fairbanks, Alaska, to Vancouver = 2,207 mi/3,553 km
Los Angeles, California, to Vancouver = 1,437 mi/2,314 km
San Francisco, California, to Vancouver = 1,013 mi/1,631 km
Seattle, Washington, to Vancouver = 144 mi/232 km
Washington, D.C., to Winnipeg = 1,641 mi/2,642 km
Chicago, Illinois, to Winnipeg = 895 mi/1,441 km
Saint Paul/Minneapolis, Minnesota, to Winnipeg = 436 mi/702 km
Detroit, Michigan, to Winnipeg = 1,182 mi/1,903 km
Philadelphia, Pennsylvania, to Winnipeg = 1,630 mi/2,624 km
New York, New York, to Winnipeg = 1,854 mi/2,985 km
Boston, Massachusetts, to Winnipeg = 1,835 mi/2,954 km

Services and Safety Tips

Rules of the Road

Everyone in your vehicle should wear seat belts when driving in Canada. Strict seat-belt laws are in effect throughout Canada,

with the exception of Alberta, the Yukon, the Northwest Territories, and Nunavut.

U.S. drivers should remember that maximum speed limits in Canada are posted in kilometers per hour (km/h). Distances are also given in kilometers (e.g., Vancouver 1,244 km; 771 mi). One hundred km/h equals 60 miles per hour, the maximum speed on many major highways.

Studded tires are permitted without seasonal limitation in Saskatchewan, the Northwest Territories, the Yukon, and Nunavut, but only during winter in the other provinces.

Use of radar-detection devices is illegal in Alberta, Manitoba, the Northwest Territories, the Yukon, and Nunavut, and in some of the eastern provinces. If you are driving across the country, pack the device away in a suitcase.

Safe Driving on Gravel Roads

Throughout most of your travels in Western Canada, if you are driving you will find that the hard-surface roads are well engineered and constructed for various terrain and climatic conditions, with escape roads for runaways and plenty of scenic overlooks and rest areas. Roads are well maintained during periods of bad weather, such as snow and ice, and directional, warning, and destination signs are well placed and easy to read. Service stations, restaurants, and accommodations are found along most routes. If, however, you plan to do some off-the-main-highway exploring, which will usually place you on gravel roads, the following safe-driving tips will make your touring adventure more secure and enjoyable.

Gravel sections of the Alaska Highway (most of the Alaska Highway is now paved) and major roads in northern British Columbia, Alberta, the Yukon, the Northwest Territories, and Nunavut are generally safe and well maintained. They are paved with loose gravel because of harsh climatic conditions during certain times of the year. The rapid deterioration of asphalt or concrete surfaces during severe weather (freezing and thawing), for example, causes road hazards and difficult maintenance; gravel surfaces, in contrast, provide better, safer traction in snow, ice, and mud. Further, be careful of slippery road conditions after heavy rains or thaws. A four-wheel-drive vehicle is ideal for

Emergencies

In an emergency simply dial 0 on the telephone and ask the operator for the police, who have been specially trained to handle all types of emergencies. In major cities dial 911 for emergencies.

If someone has an urgent need to get in touch with you but does not know where or how, he or she should contact the RCMP (Royal Canadian Mounted Police) in the area where you are traveling (leave your itinerary with a friend or relative back home). Several times each day, many of the CBC (Canadian Broadcasting Company) radio outlets broadcast the names of individuals traveling in their areas of Canada, requesting them to contact the nearest RCMP office for an emergency message. This excellent service should be used only for genuine emergencies.

north-country driving. Studded tires are recommended for ice and hard-packed snow.

Make sure your vehicle is in top mechanical condition. Repair shops are scarce on long stretches of road, and bills for work performed are high. Take some spare parts and tools with you—a spare tire in prime condition, a fan belt, spark plugs, wrenches, and so on. Take a container of extra gas, a jug of coolant, some extra motor oil, and plenty of windshield washer fluid.

Protect your gas tank from being punctured by loose gravel by fastening a rubber mat to the surface that faces the road. Protect your headlights from rocks by attaching plastic shields and your radiator from swarms of bugs by using an appropriate screen. Most of this auto equipment can be bought at your local supply store or at stores in Western Canada. Many garages located near major gravel roads can help equip your vehicle.

Take the following personal gear in the event that you get stranded for a while: sleeping bags, warm coats, sweaters, hats and mittens, insect repellent, basic pots and pans, drinking water, enough food for a couple of days, fuel and fire-making tools, first-aid materials, emergency flares, and, if possible, a citizens band radio. If you have to spend a night off the road, the best bet is to sleep in your vehicle. Doing so will save your skin from insects and your hide from bears. Be alert to animals suddenly getting in your way on the road. Hitting an elk at 100 km/h (60mi/h) is not much different from smashing into a brick wall.

Keep a good distance between your vehicle and the one in front—a strategy that will help keep rocks from spinning up and cracking your windshield. Anticipate that you may very well have bits and pieces of gravel hitting the glass and metal of your vehicle when trucks and cars, which travel at high speeds on these roads, pass you. Most travelers get through their journey without any damage occurring, but don't be surprised if it happens. It's part of the way of travel in these areas, and your insurance policy should help set things right again when you're back home. During dry periods, moving cars and trucks send up thick plumes of dust—another reason to keep a healthy distance between you and the next car. Keep your headlights on at all times—whether it's dusty or not—while traveling the gravel roads. Keep your windshield washer filled with fluid and use it frequently. When being overtaken by a truck, pull over to the shoulder and let it pass, but don't stop—keep moving.

Don't let your gas tank go below half full. Top it off at frequent intervals. Know how far it is to the next gas station, and don't let yourself come up short.

Don't drive when tired. Take plenty of rest stops and enjoy the scenery. Share the wheel with your partner. Be alert at all times.

Do, though, enjoy the country you're passing through—it's among the great adventures of a lifetime.

Auto Clubs

The Canadian Automobile Association (CAA) extends full services to the American Automobile Association (AAA), Alliance Internationale de Tourisme (AIT), Fédération Internationale de l'Automobile (FIA), Federation of Interamerican Touring and Automobile Clubs (FITAC), and Commonwealth Motoring Conference (CMC). These services, obtainable upon presentation of your membership card, include travel information, itineraries, maps, tour books, information on road and weather conditions, accommodation reservations, and emergency road and travel agency services.

Wildlife and Forest Safety

The rugged mountain and wilderness areas of Western Canada, in British Columbia and Alberta, are home to North America's kings of beasts—the bears. This is their natural and legitimate place; you are merely a guest in their territory. Grizzly and black bears are most common, and many have been spoiled by well-meaning humans with handouts of food. Forget about how cute your teddy

How to Speak Canadian

When you initially cross the border, you won't hear much English that's different from what you hear in the United States. You will soon discover, however, that some words and phrases are distinctly Canadian.

Muskeg. If you travel to the Far North, you'll certainly come across this swampy, marshy land that goes on for miles.

Pemmican or bannock. A treat you'll find in the Far North, after you've extricated yourself from the muskeg. The first is dried meat, often tough and stringy. The second is the traditional flour-and-water pancake guaranteed to keep your hunger at bay.

Chinook. A dry, warm wind that blows from the southwest. In winter it often causes sharply changing temperatures that can rise by 40 degrees within a few hours, changing snow to slush.

Toque (pronounced "toook"). A knitted woolen cap, absolutely indispensable for keeping your head warm in January or February.

Hydro. Used to describe both the electricity supply and the company that provides it.

Medicare. The government health insurance plan.

Chesterfield. Some folks call it a sofa or couch.

Snowbirds. A term used to describe the human relatives of the snow goose who migrate in their recreational vehicles or on the planes of Air Canada, to warmer temperatures during winter months.

Humongous. Big, huge, gigantic—a good word for describing the vastness of the country.

Tad. At the other end of the scale, try using *tad* to describe something that's just a little bit of whatever, such as being "a tad out of line."

bear is back home—here you're dealing with dynamite that can maim and kill. You can assume that these magnificent animals, especially mothers with cubs, are always unpredictable and very dangerous. Most people never come close enough to a bear to fear an attack. Nevertheless, when you are hiking, make enough noise on the trail so that bears will avoid you. Never get between a mother and her cub. When you spot a bear, keep a safe distance between you and it—the bear is considerably faster than you and is about as powerful an animal as exists. Resist moving in closer for a better camera shot.

When camping, keep your area clean. This means wrapping all food items in airtight packages and placing the supply caches away from your tent. Clean up all traces and scents of food that can attract bears. Avoid bringing any food, such as a sandwich or snack, into your tent before going to sleep. If you have problems with a bear, make a report to the nearest wildlife officer. When entering a national or provincial park, be sure to get the latest information on bear sightings and advice on what to do should you have a problem.

The forests of Western Canada are among the great riches of the continent. Enjoy them and protect them from destruction by fire. Be careful in the use of matches and lighting instruments. Make sure that anything that was burning (match, campfire) is out cold. Do not dispose of your smoking material until you are certain it is no longer burning. Build your campfires on hard, clear ground and away from vegetation, leaves, pine needles, and other materials that can accidentally catch fire and spread flames throughout the forest. When entering a national or provincial park, be sure to get current information on fire regulations, use of wood, and safe campfire locations.

Staying in Touch While on the Road

One of the best treats while touring Western Canada by auto is tuning in to a CBC (Canadian Broadcasting Company) radio station. A federal-government-operated network, CBC provides some of the finest news, discussion, cultural, and entertainment programming in the English- and French-speaking worlds. Its broadcasts of classical music are outstanding in variety and number.

Hunting and Fishing Regulations

Hunting is regulated by federal, provincial, and territorial laws. You must obtain a license from that province or territory in which you plan to hunt. A federal permit for hunting migratory game birds is required for such species, and available at most Canadian post offices. Many of Canada's provincial parks, reserves, and adjacent areas prohibit entry with any type of weapon. Both the

Northwest Territories and Nunavut require an export permit for all unprocessed wildlife that is taken out.

Fishing is also regulated by law. You must obtain a nonresident license for the province in which you wish to try your luck.

In British Columbia you need a license for tidal-water sport fishing. Also, in British Columbia you cannot export salmon or other game fish beyond the possession limit without obtaining written authorization from a fisheries officer. No more than 40 kg/88 lb gross weight of canned salmon, taken by sport fishing, can be exported from the province in any year.

A special fishing permit is needed in all national parks and can be obtained at any national park site for a nominal fee; these permits are valid throughout Canada.

Non-Canadian fishing guides cannot work in Canada without approval from the Canada Employment and Immigration Commission, and such approval must be obtained *before* you come to Canada (contact your nearest Canadian consulate listed earlier in this chapter).

For more information on parks, reserves, hunting and fishing laws, licenses, and wildlife conditions, contact provincial and territorial tourism agencies (listed earlier in this chapter).

CHAPTER 3

Canada for Non-Canadians

The Canadian Nation

Canadians are governed by a parliamentary form of democracy, in contrast to the republican form in the United States. Elizabeth II, queen of the United Kingdom, is also queen of Canada. The governor-general, a noteworthy Canadian citizen appointed by the prime minister and approved by the queen, is her representative. When the queen is not present in the country, the governor-general acts as the symbolic chief of state. The prime minister, who is also a member of Parliament and the leader of the political party having a majority of members in Parliament, is the chief executive officer of Canada. Unlike the U.S. system, which separates the executive and legislative branches, the Canadian political system combines both, similar to the United Kingdom's method. There are four major political parties in Canada: the Reform party, the Québec-based Bloc Québecois, the New Democratic party (NDP), and the Liberal party. All members of a prime minister's cabinet must be elected members of Parliament—another difference from the U.S. system, in which a president's cabinet members are appointed and cannot hold elective office. Ottawa, in the province of Ontario—between Toronto and Montréal—is Canada's federal capital.

Canada is a member of the United Nations, NATO, and the Commonwealth of Nations. Because of its generosity to people in need everywhere around the globe and its reasonable position on many key international issues, Canada is one of the most respected nations in the world.

Inventive Canada

Before you think that the only inventions to come out of Canada are refinements of hockey sticks and better ways of processing salmon, take a look at Canada's inventive and ingenious nature.

Basketball—yes, basketball—was invented by Canadian Dr. James Naismith, who was an instructor at a Massachusetts school. The need for a competitive indoor team sport led him to devise this game played under thirteen basic rules with a ball and round hoop.

Ice hockey was invented by a group of soldiers in Kingston, Ontario, who tied blades to their boots and used field hockey sticks and an old lacrosse ball to chase away the boredom on Christmas Day in 1855.

The electron microscope was developed by members of the physics department of the University of Toronto. The team was headed by Professor E. F. Burton, and C. E. Howe, Ely Berton, and James Hillier. Although the basic concept of the microscope came from Germany, Burton's team made it work as a practical device.

Instant mashed potatoes came from Dr. W. H. Cook at the National Research Council. He was responsible for developing a new way of making frozen dried food.

The gas mask, which saved so many lives of Allied soldiers during World War I, was developed by Canadian doctor Cluny McPhereson in 1915.

The first precooked, vitamin-enriched baby cereal was developed by Drs. Frederick Tisdall, Theodore Drake, and Alan Brown at the Hospital for Sick Children in Toronto in the 1930s. It was first marketed by Mead Johnston as Pablum.

The humble paint roller revolutionized the painting and decorating industry and certainly helped launch the do-it-yourself era. It was invented by Norman Breakey of Toronto in 1940.

The snowmobile—or "skidoo," as it was called—was the brainchild of Québec manufacturer Joseph-Armand Bombardier in 1922.

The discovery of insulin for the treatment of diabetes was the work of four medical researchers at the University of Toronto—Frederick J. Banting, Charles H. Best, J. B. Collip, and J. J. R. MacLeod. Banting and MacLeod were awarded the 1923 Nobel Prize for Chemistry, which they shared with their colleagues.

And let's not forget Trivial Pursuit, the game that launched a thousand arguments. It was the brainchild of Chris Haney, photo editor of the *Montréal Gazette*, and Scott Abbott, a sportswriter for Canadian Press.

The following are the provinces of Canada and their capitals (provinces are similar in concept to states but possess far more powers for self-governance): Newfoundland/Labrador (St. John's), Prince Edward Island (Charlottetown), Nova Scotia (Halifax), New Brunswick (Fredericton), Québec (Québec City), Ontario (Toronto), Manitoba (Winnipeg), Saskatchewan (Regina), Alberta (Edmonton), and British Columbia (Victoria). Canada also has three vast land areas in the north that are awaiting designation as provinces: the Yukon Territory (Whitehorse), the Northwest Territories (Yellowknife), and Nunavut (Iqaluit). On the provincial level the queen of Canada is represented by lieutenant governors-general, whose functions are chiefly ceremonial. These officials are outstanding citizens of their respective provinces. When the queen and members of the royal family visit the provinces of Canada, the lieutenant governors-general are their chief hosts. Political power in the provinces lies with the legislative assemblies and with the premiers who hold dominant power both in the executive and legislative branches and within the majority political party. The operational form of government here is similar to what it is on the federal level.

Canada has a population of about thirty million. Close to two-thirds of Canadians reside in the provinces of Ontario and Québec, and about two-thirds of all Canadians live within 200 km/125 mi of the U.S. border. (Most of the important urban centers of Canada are near the border.) About 30 percent of all Canadians are French; more than 40 percent are of British stock (English, Irish, Scottish, Welsh); and the remainder are of various groups, among them Ukrainians, Poles, Japanese, Germans, Italians, Chinese, West Indians, and Greeks. Unlike the United States, which thinks of itself as a "melting pot" in which groups are assimilated into the dominant Anglo-Saxon culture, Canada considers itself a "cultural mosaic" whose citizens can be equally proud of their ethnic and Canadian heritages. This concept of a cultural mosaic has become institutionalized in most aspects of Canadian life and is the official cultural policy of every level of government throughout the country. Although a majority of Canadians are Christians of various denominations, the country is also home to large concentrations of Jews, Muslims, and numerous other religious groups.

Canadians enjoy one of the highest standards of living in the world. For example, through government subsidies, low-cost medical care is available to all citizens. Moreover, through government subsidization, the cost of higher education is considerably lower in Canada than in the United States.

In April 1982 Canadians witnessed a historic event when Elizabeth II, queen of Canada, sat before a crowded assembly of the House of Commons and Senate of the Parliament of Canada in Ottawa and presided over the proclamation of the Constitution Act of 1982. This great moment in history marked a number of significant changes in Canada's constitution and is a milestone in this country's political evolution. With the proclamation of the Constitution Act, Canada repatriated from the British Parliament its constitution and shed an outmoded vestige of its colonial past.

Entry into Canada

Canada Customs clears foreign visitors for entry into Canada. Its checkpoints are located on all highways that cross the border between the United States and Canada and at international airports and seaports. The French word for customs is *douane,* and it is part of the official bilingual signature of this vital federal department.

Citizens or permanent residents of the United States do not require passports or visas and can usually cross the U.S.–Canadian border without difficulty or delay. It is strongly recommended, however, that you carry some form of valid personal identification, such as proof of residence and citizenship (birth certificate or other document that provides legal evidence). Naturalized U.S. citizens should carry their naturalization certificate or other evidence of citizenship. Permanent residents who are not citizens should carry their alien registration receipt card. Those under the age of eighteen who travel to Canada without an adult must have a letter of permission from a parent or guardian. U.S. citizens can also enter Canada from third countries without a passport or visa.

All other people—with the exception of U.S. citizens or legal residents, citizens of France residing on the islands of Saint Pierre and Miquelon, and residents of Greenland—require a valid passport, visa, or other acceptable travel document to gain entry into Canada. If you are entering Canada from the United States, make sure that your travel documents are acceptable to the U.S. Immigration Service before you leave the United States so that you won't have trouble reentering.

Employment and Study

If you want to study in Canada—and thousands of non-Canadians do so every year—you must obtain a student authorization before coming to Canada. You will also need an authorization for working in Canada. Employment authorizations are usually not issued if qualified Canadians or permanent residents are available for the kind of work you are seeking.

Clearing Canada Customs

By Car

The entry of vehicles and trailers into Canada for touring purposes, for periods of up to twelve months, is generally a quick, routine matter that does not require the payment of duty. Motor vehicle registration forms should be carried, as should a copy of the contract if you are driving a rented vehicle. If you are driving a vehicle registered to someone else, you must carry that person's authorization to use the vehicle. All national driver's licenses, as well as the International Driver's Permit, are valid in Canada.

By Private Boat

If you're planning to come to Canada on your own boat, contact the regional Canada Customs office nearest to where you intend to enter Canadian waters for a list of ports of entry that provide

---

Special Auto Insurance Identification

All provinces in Canada require motorists to produce evidence of financial responsibility in case of an accident. The minimum liability insurance requirement in Canada is $200,000 (in the Northwest Territories, $50,000). U.S. motorists are advised to obtain from their insurance agents a Canadian Nonresident Interprovincial Liability Insurance Card, which is issued free of charge. If you have an accident in Canada and don't have this card, your vehicle can be impounded and other serious legal action can be taken against you. *Don't leave home without it.*

customs facilities and their hours of operation. If you have an emergency, report your arrival, as soon as possible, to the nearest regional customs office or to the local detachment of the RCMP (Royal Canadian Mounted Police).

By Private Plane

Visiting aviators should plan to land at an airport that provides customs clearance. You must report to Canada Customs immediately and complete all documentation. In emergencies you can land at other fields, but then you must, as soon as possible, report your arrival to the nearest regional customs office or the nearest detachment of the RCMP (Royal Canadian Mounted Police). For more details on flying your own plane to Canada, contact your nearest Canadian Consulate General (see Chapter 2).

Personal Exemptions

Everything you bring into Canada must be declared and is subject to inspection by Canada Customs. The following are commonsense rules and should present no real burden to the average traveler.

Tobacco. If you are sixteen years of age or older, you can bring in duty-free fifty cigars, 200 cigarettes, and 4.4 kg/2 lb of processed tobacco.

Alcoholic beverages. You can bring into Canada duty-free 1.2 l/40 oz of liquor or wine or twenty-four cans or bottles of beer or ale. You must be at least nineteen years of age in British Columbia, the Northwest Territories, Saskatchewan, the Yukon, and Nunavut; at least eighteen in Alberta and Manitoba.

Gifts. You can bring in duty-free gifts for friends and relatives provided that the value of each gift does not exceed $100 (Canadian) and that the item is not tobacco, liquor, advertising material, or any good that does not qualify as a gift under customs definitions. You must declare currency exceeding $5,000 Canadian. Contact your nearest Canadian consulate (see Chapter 2) if you have any questions.

Business equipment and materials. Printed materials, commercial samples, blueprints, charts, audiovisual materials, convention and exhibit displays, and the like brought into Canada may be subject to the full rate of duty and tax or a portion thereof, or they may be duty- and tax-free. Contact the Commercial and Trade Division at your nearest Canadian Consulate General for answers and information (see Chapter 2).

Pets. Canada is a pet-loving nation. You can bring your dogs and cats into Canada provided that each animal has a certificate from a licensed veterinarian confirming vaccination against rabies within the preceding thirty-six months. Puppies and kittens under three months and Seeing Eye dogs accompanied by their owners can enter Canada without certification or restriction.

Pet birds, songbirds, and birds of the parrot family can be brought into Canada provided that the owner accompanies the birds and declares on arrival that they have been in his or her possession during the preceding ninety days and have not been in contact with other birds during that period. There is a limit of two birds per family.

Endangered species. The importation of endangered species of animals, plants, and their products is restricted and may require the prior issuance of an import permit. This restriction also applies to certain animal skins and to mounted animals and trophies.

Fruits and vegetables. You can bring most fruits and vegetables into Canada; however, there are restrictions regarding certain types, and these stipulations change from time to time. Contact your nearest Canadian Consulate General for current information (see Chapter 2).

Recreational boats and vehicles. You can bring in your boats, motors, trailers, snowmobiles, and other types of recreational vehicles duty- and tax-free under a temporary entry permit, issued by Canada Customs when you arrive, on the condition that such vehicles are for personal use only and will be taken out of the country at the end of your visit.

Recreational equipment. You can bring in the following items duty- and tax-free provided that they are for your personal use only: fishing tackle; camping, golf, tennis, scuba, and skiing equipment; radios, television sets, computers, and typewriters; camera equipment with a reasonable amount of film; and other recreational or hobby items.

Firearms. Firearms having no legitimate sporting or recreational use (e.g., handguns) are not permitted entry into Canada. Canada has strong handgun laws, and they are enforced to the limit. Don't even try to bring such a weapon into the country.

If you are traveling through Canada to get to Alaska, you must ship your prohibited or restricted weapons by commercial carrier; you cannot bring them in with you. If you are discovered in possession of a restricted weapon, it can be legally taken away from you.

If you plan to bring in a handgun for a shooting competition, you must obtain a permit in advance from a local Canadian registrar of firearms.

Canadian or American?

Quick! How many famous Canadians can you name? Probably more than you think, but most may think these people are American. To name just a few:

John Kenneth Galbraith—former presidential adviser

Saul Bellow, Arthur Hailey, Jack Kerouac, and Margaret Atwood—authors

Mary Pickford, Raymond Burr, Raymond Massey, Lorne Greene, Christopher Plummer, Donald Sutherland, William Shatner, Margot Kidder, John Candy, Dan Ackroyd, and Michael J. Fox—actors

Peter Jennings—newscaster

Paul Anka—singer

Elizabeth Arden—cosmetics queen

Long guns—those used for hunting and competition shooting—can be brought into Canada and used without a permit by visitors sixteen years of age and older. Nonresident hunters may bring in 200 rounds of ammunition (per person) duty-free. Nonresident sharpshooters competing in meets recognized by the Amateur Trap Shooting Association, the Shooting Federation of Canada, the Dominion of Canada Rifle Association, or the National Skeet Shooting Association may bring in 1,000 rounds of ammunition (per person) as personal baggage. For more information contact your nearest Canadian Consulate General (see Chapter 2) and your hunting/shooting organization, such as the National Rifle Association in the United States.

Reentry into the United States

U.S. citizens and residents must satisfy U.S. Immigration and Naturalization Service (INS) authorities as to their right to return to the United States. You can do this by presenting some form of identification or proof of citizenship. (Preferable is your passport or a copy of your birth certificate; driver's licenses are generally not good forms of identification at border crossings.)

Make a list of all the Canadian purchases that you plan to take across the border, keeping sales slips ready for inspection. Pack these purchases separately for easy inspection.

You can take out of and bring into the United States up to $10,000 in U.S. currency. You must report amounts above this limit to U.S. Customs.

Items of cultural, historical, or scientific value to the heritage of Canada that are more than fifty years old (e.g., antique furniture and paintings) cannot be taken out of the country without official permission.

Exemptions

By staying in Canada for at least forty-eight hours, you can bring into the United States up to $400 (U.S. dollars) of purchases duty-free.

Regardless of age, every member of your family is entitled to this exemption. Members of the same family can pool their exemptions into a larger duty-free total.

You can also bring home duty-free one hundred cigars, as long as they have not been made in Cuba; 200 duty-free cigarettes; and one liter of liquor (the minimum age to bring in alcohol is twenty-one).

Duty-free gifts can be sent from Canada to friends and relatives in the United States if the value of each gift does not exceed $50. The package should be marked UNSOLICITED GIFT.

Your Health While Traveling

Unexpected health problems may happen on a trip. The best way financially to protect yourself and members of your family is to make sure your health insurance plan provides the coverage you might need while traveling—adequate to pay for the costs of treatment. Daily rates for hospital care vary from hospital to hospital and from province to province. Charges for adult inpatient care can start at $800 per day. Before you come to Canada, seek advice on your present health care benefits and ascertain what additional coverage you might need. Also be sure to bring copies of your prescriptions in the event that they need to be renewed by a Canadian doctor.

Put on stout hiking boots and what you need on your back and experience the wonder of the Canadian Rockies by being close to the boundless land and sky.

Canadian Holidays

Many services—banks, government offices, factories, business offices, and so on—are closed during the national and provincial holidays listed here. Places of accommodation, many restaurants, and some services, however, are open for the convenience of travelers.

National Holidays
New Year's Day
Good Friday
Easter Monday
Victoria Day, third Monday in May
Canada Day (formerly Dominion Day), July 1
Labour Day, first Monday in September
Thanksgiving Day, second Monday in October
Remembrance Day (memorial for Canadian men and women who served in the military), November 11
Christmas Day, December 25
Boxing Day, December 26

Provincial Holidays
Alberta
Heritage Day, first Monday in August

British Columbia
British Columbia Day, first Monday in August

Manitoba, Saskatchewan, Northwest Territories
Civic Holiday, first Monday in August

Yukon
Discovery Day, third Monday in August

The Metric System

All measurements in Canada follow the metric system, which is commonplace in most countries outside the United States.

Temperature is given in degrees Celsius (C); gas is sold by the liter, groceries by grams and kilograms; and road speeds are posted in kilometers per hour.

If you are not already familiar with the metric system, the following measurements will be helpful during your travels in Canada:

Speed
15 miles per hour = approximately 24 kilometers (km) per hour
30 miles per hour = approximately 48 kilometers (km) per hour
50 miles per hour = approximately 80 kilometers (km) per hour
60 miles per hour = approximately 96 kilometers (km) per hour

Length
1 inch = 2.54 centimeters (cm)
1 foot = 0.3 meter (m) or 30 centimeters (cm)
1 yard = 0.9 meter (m) or 90 centimeters (cm)
1 mile = 1.6 kilometers (km) or 1,600 meters (m)

Mass
1 ounce = 28 grams (g)
1 pound = 0.45 kilogram (kg) or 450 grams (g)

Volume
1 fluid ounce = 28 milliliters (ml)
1 Imperial pint = 0.57 liter (l) or 570 milliliters (ml)
1 Imperial quart = 1.14 liters (l) or 1,140 milliliters (ml)
1 Imperial gallon = 4.5 liters (l) or 4,500 milliliters (ml)

When buying gasoline in Canada, remember that the Imperial gallon is close to one liter larger than the U.S. gallon. The Imperial gallon will at first seem to cost more, but the price tends to equal out in the total purchase price.

Temperature
86°F = approximately 30°C (a hot summer day)
68°F = approximately 20°C (room temperature)
32°F = approximately 0°C (water freezes)
−6°F = approximately −20°C

The following is a formula for temperature conversion; it may, however, be useful only to mathematicians:

To convert Celsius to Fahrenheit $(C \times 9/5) + 32 = F$
To convert Fahrenheit to Celsius $(F - 32) \times 5/9 = C$

Money Matters

The Canadian System

The monetary system of Canada, like that of the United States, is based on dollars and cents. The denominations of coins and paper bills are the same. In addition, each denomination of Canadian paper money is of a different color, which makes it easier to tell a $5.00 bill from a $10.00 bill. The $1.00 denomination is a coin known as the loonie, because of the loon featured on its face. Canada also has a $2.00 coin.

The value of the Canadian dollar has averaged between 25 cents and 40 cents *below* the U.S. dollar, depending on prevailing market values—which means more value for your travel dollars.

Where to Convert to Canadian Money

U.S. currency, including major traveler's checks and credit cards, is widely accepted throughout Canada for the purchase of goods and services.

It's a good idea to convert some of your money into Canadian currency at your hometown bank (about $100 for initial expenses, such as cabs, tips, and fast food). The larger U.S. banks usually handle Canadian currency. You can also buy traveler's checks in Canadian denominations before you leave on your trip. Both your local banks and traveler's-check-issuing companies must give you the benefit of the prevailing exchange rate.

Canadian banks are usually the best places in which to convert your money to Canadian currency (that is, if you want to get the best rate of exchange). Canadian banking hours are usually from 10:00 A.M. to 4:00 P.M. Monday through Friday. Almost all banks have extended hours of operation (set by individual banks) on certain days of the week, such as Saturday.

Automatic Teller Machines (ATMs)

Need cash? Various automatic teller machines (ATMs) are located in most cities in British Columbia, Alberta, Saskatchewan, and Manitoba. Consult your bank card company to find out which ATMs in the Western Canada provinces will provide the instant-cash services you might need.

Many ATMs will make cash advances on major credit cards as well; be sure that before leaving home, you inquire at your credit card company about the availability of this option in Canada.

Credit Cards

All major national and international credit cards (such as American Express, Visa, and MasterCard) are widely accepted throughout Canada. Major credit cards are necessary for renting automobiles and are used as a form of identification when checking into places of accommodation. In hotels, restaurants, shops, and other business establishments, be sure to check beforehand that your card will be accepted.

Postal Services

Canadian postage stamps must be used on all mail sent from Canadian locations. First-class letters sent from Canada to a U.S. address must have a first-class Canadian stamp. Goods and Services Tax (GST) is added to the price of a stamp.

Electricity and Water

Travelers from the United States can use their electric appliances—shavers, hair dryers and curlers, irons, and so on—as they would at home. Special adapters are not needed.

Drinking water throughout Western Canada is safe to use from the tap.

Business Hours

Business hours in Canada are similar to those in the United States. Most offices are in full operation by 9:00 A.M., and work for most people usually ends by 5:00 P.M. Most stores are open from 10:00 A.M. to 6:00 P.M., and late-hour drugstores and newsstands can be found in most large cities. The hourly routine of everyday life is not very different in Canada from what it is in the United States.

Touring Spectacular British Columbia

British Columbia in Brief

British Columbia is Canada's third largest province, after Québec and Ontario. It is also the third most populous, with more than three million inhabitants. More than 90 percent of its people speak English as their first language. Most British Columbians are of British stock—English, Scottish, Welsh, Irish—and this is Canada's most British province, not just in name but also in attitudes and lifestyle, although a burgeoning Chinese population is gaining clout, especially in Vancouver and Victoria. British Columbia also contains large populations whose ethnic roots are Germanic, Scandinavian, Slavic, and Asian. In fact, almost all the world's ethnic, racial, and religious groups are represented in British Columbian society. The vast majority of British Columbians reside in the southern part of the province, close to the U.S.–Canadian border along the forty-ninth parallel.

The capital of British Columbia (the province is known most typically in Canada as B.C.) is Victoria, named in honor of the "Great Queen" and empress of what was once a significant empire. Victoria is located on the southern tip of Vancouver Island, well below the forty-ninth parallel. The largest city in British Columbia is Vancouver, third in economic importance after Toronto and Montréal. Other large B.C. cities are Prince George, Kamloops, Kelowna, Nanaimo, and Penticton.

Fine dining is available throughout Western Canada.

B.C. entered the Canadian Confederation in 1871, about four years after Upper Canada, Lower Canada, Nova Scotia, and New Brunswick came together as a united country. British Columbia has always felt itself far removed from the centers of economic and political power represented by Toronto, Ottawa, and Montréal. The linking of B.C. with the rest of Canada through the transcontinental railroad in the nineteenth century ended some of this isolation, as did the Trans-Canada Highway and the advent of transcontinental air travel.

In recent years B.C. has turned its attention toward the thriving nations of the Pacific Rim, and its future growth and prosperity will depend increasingly on the Far East, especially Japan, Taiwan, Singapore, and South Korea. The province also has a close affinity with the nearby states of Alaska, Washington, Oregon, and California, and the majority of American tourists who visit B.C. come from these states. The actual borders of British Columbia are the Yukon and Northwest Territories to the north; Alberta to the east; the states of Montana, Idaho, and Washington to the south; and the Pacific Ocean to the west.

The climate along the Pacific coast throughout the year is mild: dry and sunny during summer, rainy and foggy during winter. Coastal areas receive little if any snow during winter, except in the high mountains. It is not unusual to see delicate, colorful flowers blooming in Victoria throughout winter. On Vancouver Island you can see many trees that are hundreds of years old and have grown to incredible heights. The heavy rainfall here has created lush vegetation, such as giant ferns and thick moss. From the Coast Mountains to the Rockies on its far eastern border, British Columbia is rippled with mountain range after mountain range. All these ranges and valleys are thickly forested, except for the southern part of the Okanagan region, where the terrain is desert-like, similar in many respects to that of Arizona or New Mexico. The north-central interior flattens out into a rolling plateau. Throughout the interior are countless lakes, rivers, streams, waterfalls, and glaciers. Some of the great national parks of Canada, such as Yoho, Glacier, and Kootenay, are in eastern British Columbia. Near the Alberta border is Mount Robson, the highest point in the Canadian Rockies (Mount Fairweather, however, at 4,663 m/15,300 ft, is the highest in the province). In contrast to

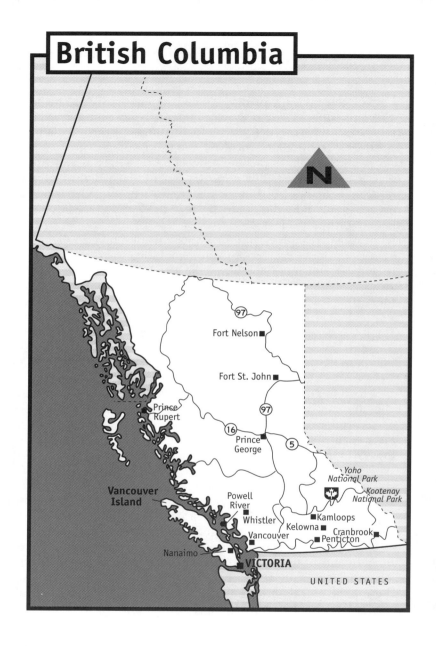

British Columbia

N

97

Fort Nelson ■

Fort St. John ■

97

Prince
Rupert ■

16

Prince ■
George

5

Yoho
National Park

Kootenay
National Park

Vancouver
Island

Powell
River ■

Whistler ■

Kamloops ■

Kelowna ■

Cranbrook ■
Penticton ■

Vancouver ■

Nanaimo ■

VICTORIA ■

UNITED STATES

the coast, which is either sunny or rainy, the climate of the interior is more typical of North America, with four distinct seasons.

A substantial part of British Columbia's economy is based on developing and processing natural resources—lumber, minerals, food (cattle, fruits and vegetables, and, of course, fish). Travelers to British Columbia dine on such treats as Pacific salmon and province-grown fruits and vegetables of almost every kind.

In the 1800s the province was a center for the fur-trading operations of the Hudson's Bay Company and for the discovery of gold in the Northwest. The city of Vancouver today is an important North American business center, with banking, investment ventures, motion picture and television production, tourism, and insurance leading the way.

British Columbians enjoy an exceptionally high standard of living. There is affluence as well as a high level of culture. The educational system is superb, particularly the major universities, such as the University of British Columbia, Victoria, and Simon Fraser.

Tourism is the second most important economic sector, and its infrastructure—accommodations, restaurants, shops, parks, transportation, attractions, entertainment—is generally excellent in all parts of the province, especially in the prime vacation areas: Vancouver, Victoria, Whistler, the Okanagan, and the Rockies.

No other province in Canada has such a diverse range of magnificent scenery that is largely accessible to most visitors. In the end, it is this glorious spectacle of nature that is most memorable about British Columbia. B.C.'s motto—concerning its beauty and quest for excellence—is therefore most apt: *Splendor Sine Occasu* ("splendor without diminishment").

Note: See chapter 5 for information on the city of Vancouver and its environs, the Whistler resort area, and the Gulf Islands; see chapter 6 for information on the city of Victoria, Vancouver Island, the Inside Passage, and traveling from Prince Rupert to Prince George.

The Sunshine Coast Tour

Exploring British Columbia's Sunshine Coast brings you into a magnificent area of islands, mountains, and sea, all close to the city of Vancouver. You can take a one-day trip here or undertake a major touring adventure. Because of its great beauty and relative

Tourism British Columbia

For free information (maps, brochures, etc.) and touring advice, contact:

> Ministry of Tourism and Provincial Secretary
> Parliament Buildings
> Victoria, British Columbia, Canada V8V 1X4
> or call toll-free in North America (800) 663–6000

Tourism BC also has a wonderful Web site that connects with all of the regional tourism associations in the province: www.hellobc.com. This comprehensive site covers attractions and hotels along with dining, recreational, cultural, and sight-seeing opportunities.

closeness to Vancouver, the Sunshine Coast is home to many writers, craftspeople, and those who wish to live a more independent life a bit removed from the hassles of civilization. In addition to tourism, this region offers sport fishing, camping, hiking, canoeing, wild-bird and -animal photography, beach walking, heritage museums, Canadian cultural displays, fishing and sight-seeing charters, horseback riding, golf, tennis, and local festivals.

It's easy to get to the Sunshine Coast. Take Highway 99 north to the ferry terminal at Horseshoe Bay. From here take a B.C. ferry (in Vancouver call 604–685–1027 for information or 604–669–1211 for recorded information twenty-four hours a day; in Victoria call 250–656–0757) across Horseshoe Bay, passing between Bowen and Gambier Islands, to Langdale, the beginning of the Sunshine Coast tour. From Langdale follow Highway 101 up the coast to Gibsons, Sechelt, Secret Cove, Madeira Park, Pender Harbour, Irvines Landing, Garden Bay, and Earls Cove. At Earls Cove take another ferry across Jervis Inlet to Saltery Bay, Lang Bay, and Powell River. The ferries running from Powell River can take you across the Strait of Georgia to Comox on Vancouver Island. From Comox head north to Port Hardy and the Inside Passage trip on the B.C. ferry; head south to Qualicum Beach, which will take you to Highway 4 and thence to the west coast of the island, facing the open Pacific, and the Pacific Rim National Park; or go farther south to the city of Victoria (see chapter 6). At Powell River take the ferry to Texada Island, or stay on the mainland and keep driving north on Highway 101 to the end of the road at

Lund (the communities north of Lund to Prince Rupert are served by ferries and airplanes).

Accommodations and Attractions

Gibsons. Visit the Elphinstone Pioneer Museum and the Captain Vancouver Cairn, or stroll along the sea walk. Sea Cavalcade and jazz festivals take place in July.

Sunshine Lodge is 4 km/2.4 mi west of the ferry terminal, (604) 886–3321. Moderate.

Bonniebrook Lodge, 1532 Ocean Beach Esplanade, (604) 886–2887, is a romantic inn with the charm of yesteryear. Steps from the beach, it offers ocean views and a restaurant with fine dining. Moderate.

Sechelt. Visit the Sunshine Coast Arts Centre, featuring paintings, graphics, sculpture, and crafts by local area artists; open Wednesday through Sunday; (604) 885–5412. There is a Sunshine Coast Golf Course in this town.

Driftwood Inn, on Highway 101, (604) 885–5811, has a restaurant and a swimming beach. Moderate.

Garden Bay. Sundowner Inn is a bed-and-breakfast at a historic site, (604) 883–9676. Moderate.

Powell River. Visit Willington Beach, Valentine Mountain lookout, the archaeological display, and the salmon hatchery. There are canoe circle routes from here and a ferry to Texada Island. Try the Powell River Golf Course.

Beach Gardens Resort Hotel, on Highway 101, (604) 485–6267, has a restaurant and landscaped grounds; the rooms offer views of water and mountains. Moderate to expensive.

Lund. On Highway 101 the **Lund Hotel,** (604) 483–3187, has a dining room. Inexpensive.

Metro Vancouver to Lake Louise, Alberta, via Trans-Canada Highway 1

Trans-Canada Highway 1 heads across lower British Columbia and over some of the most varied topography in North America. Beginning your trip in Vancouver, travel through the sprawling eastern suburbs of the city: Burnaby, Port Coquitlam, New Westminster, and Surrey. From the Langley area to the town of Hope, you'll be paralleling the Fraser River as you move through the

Fraser Valley. The Fraser Valley is broad, flat, rich agricultural land, with many fruit, vegetable, grain, and livestock farms and pretty communities that serve them. The Fraser River along this stretch meanders toward its delta in a leisurely fashion and empties into the Strait of Georgia just below Vancouver city center.

As you travel east, the valley narrows, with the walls of mountains pulling closer to the road. The road begins climbing and the Fraser River flows through rock gorges in angry torrents. At Hope there is a junction of the Trans-Canada and Crowsnest Highway 3. The Crowsnest dips south and then moves east, hugging the U.S.–Canadian border (see page 76 for a description of this route to Banff, Alberta). From Hope the Trans-Canada goes north until it reaches Cache Creek then heads east. Here you move away from the eastern slopes of the Coast Mountains and enter a more arid, almost desertlike region. The Trans-Canada and Highway 97 meet at Cache Creek. Highway 97 takes you north through the Cariboo-Chilcotin region and eventually to the Alaska Highway, which leads to the Yukon, the Northwest Territories, and the state of Alaska.

At the city of Kamloops, the Trans-Canada heads in an easterly direction toward the Canadian Rockies, Lake Louise, and Banff. Along the way you will cross several mountain ranges, such as the Monashees, the Selkirks, the Purcells, and the Great Divide at the Canadian Rockies themselves. Kamloops is the gateway to the Okanagan region, one of the province's prime four-season vacation areas. The Okanagan is also famous for its many fruit orchards, vineyards, and wineries. Once you pass the Okanagan Valley and begin moving toward Revelstoke, the topography becomes alpine, with high, snowcapped mountains; lush forests; long lakes; and such attractions as Rogers Pass and Glacier National Park.

The distance between Vancouver and Banff, Alberta, is 858 km/515 mi. The drive along the Trans-Canada is not only the most direct road route between these two points but also one of the most scenic and interesting drives in Canada. There are plenty of accommodations, restaurants, parks, recreational opportunities, and gas/repair stations along the way.

New Westminster

As you head east out of Vancouver via Highway 1A, you may want to take a side trip to New Westminster to see these interesting attractions:

Westminster Quay and Public Market, on the waterfront at the foot of Eighth Street. This is the heart of New Westminster's waterfront redevelopment. Open daily with shops, dining, and a walkway along the Fraser River. The Inn at Westminster Quay is an exciting concept: It is built on pillars and reaches out over the river.

Museum of the Royal Westminster Regiment, the Armoury, 530 Queen's Avenue; call (604) 526–5116 for hours and visiting information. Displays of the regiment's history from 1863.

Fort Langley and Abbotsford

Beyond New Westminster are several small, historical communities, including Fort Langley and Abbotsford.

Fort Langley National Historic Park (site of the birthplace of British Columbia) is reached via Highway 10, off the Trans-Canada, about 75 km/45 mi from Vancouver city center; call (250) 888–4424. Open daily except Christmas Day, Boxing Day, and New Year's Day. Admission is charged. A restored Hudson's Bay Company post, with one building dating back to 1840. All buildings are furnished in the mid-nineteenth-century period, and costumed inhabitants are engaged in the crafts and chores of the fur-trading pioneers and those who worked provisioning the company's Columbia District.

Abbotsford is famous for its **International Air Show,** held annually in early August at the airport on Highway 401; call (604) 852–8511 for information.

For accommodations, try the following, which have dining rooms and other amenities:

Holiday Inn Express Abbotsford, 2073 Clearbrook Road, (604) 859–6211. Moderate.

Best Western Bakerview Motor Inn, 1821 Sumas Road, (604) 859–1341. Moderate.

Best Western Regency Inn and Conference Centre, 32110 Marshall Road, (604) 853–3111; (800) 771–3077. Full amenities, including Jacuzzis, fitness center, conference facilities, free movie channel, two indoor pools. Moderate.

Mission/Hatzic Area

In the Mission/Hatzic area, via Highways 11 North to 7 East, **Westminster Abbey,** a community of Benedictine monks, provides a place of natural beauty for rest and prayer; call (604) 826–8975 for visiting hours.

Take the Lougheed Highway (Highway 7) east from Mission City and you'll come to Morris Valley Road. There you'll find **Rowena's Inn on the River** (604) 796–0234; (800) 661–5108. This grand private estate is one of the most spectacular inns in the province, with guest cottages on the property to supplement the in-house rooms. Set on 65 ha/160 acres, the private-estate-turned-inn is luxurious and includes a 21-m/70-foot swimming pool. Expensive.

Harrison Hot Springs Resort Area

This area can be reached via the Trans-Canada to Bridal Falls, then north across the Fraser to Highway 7 (the Sasquatch Highway); turn left on 7 and then right on 9 North. Harrison Hot Springs is on Lake Harrison. It is in the deep woods of this area that the human/ape creature known as Sasquatch (Big Foot) is supposed to roam. So far no one has been able to get near it, although some have taken photos of a strange being purported to be Sasquatch; perhaps it is better for both the creature and us that Sasquatch remain a mystery. Within this popular vacation area are hot springs for bathing, golf courses, and the Sasquatch Provincial Park, with hiking trails and camping.

While in Harrison take time to shake off your shoes and play in the sandy beach along the shores of the lake. We all built sand castles as children—now imagine the best master sculptors in the world turning a fun pastime into an art form. It happens every September. These talented silica architects gather at Harrison Hot Springs to compete in the World Championship Sand Sculpture Competition. For more information visit www.harrisand.org.

Accommodations in the Harrison Hot Springs Resort Area include the following:

Harrison Hot Springs Hotel, (604) 796–2244; (800) 663–2266. Lake/mountain setting, golf, pools, boating, tennis, restaurant for fine dining, dancing, and entertainment. Expensive.

Harrison Village Motel, (604) 796–2616. Overlooking the lake; some rooms have patios; heated pool. Moderate.

Campgrounds. Call the chamber of commerce, (604) 796–3425, for information.

Hope

Originally a Hudson's Bay Company post, Hope was laid out by royal engineers in 1858. Later, gold seekers came here to find their fortunes in the sandbars of the Fraser River. The Dewdney Trail, the first pack trail, was opened here in 1860. In 1965 the side of a mountain (a hundred-million-ton slide of mud, rock, and snow) broke away and crashed down on many homes in an area near town; the people, homes, and autos remain buried in a common grave under the rubble. Also near Hope is the Hell's Canyon Airtram (see below); a doll museum and minigolf are in the area. Crowsnest Highway 3 joins the Trans-Canada at Hope.

All accommodations have dining rooms and other amenities:

Quality Inn, 350 Hope/Princeton Highway, (604) 869–9951. Moderate.

Maple Leaf Motor Inn, 377 Hope/Princeton Highway, (604) 869–7107. Moderate.

Skagit Motel, 655 Third Avenue, (604) 869–5220. Moderate.

Yale

Yale was once known as Fort Yale, in its Hudson's Bay Company days. St. John the Divine, located here, is B.C.'s oldest Anglican church. Visit the Pioneer Cemetery, Spirit Cave Hiking Trail, the National Monument to Chinese Pioneers (those who helped build the transcontinental railroad), and the Cariboo Wagon Road National Monument. During August the Fraser River Barrel Race takes place.

Hell's Canyon Airtram, on the Trans-Canada, is just northeast of Yale, (250) 867–9277. Open April through October. Admission is charged. A pair of twenty-five-passenger airtrams takes you high above the Fraser Canyon, through which the mighty Fraser River surges. This facility also has floral gardens, landscaped grounds, a gift shop featuring British Columbian jade items, and a restaurant serving grilled salmon and salmon chowder.

Cache Creek

Cache Creek, at the junction of the Trans-Canada and Highway 97, is the gateway to the Thompson-Okanagan region and on the route to the Alaska Highway (see pages 66–71 for accommodations). For on-line information visit www.thompsonokanagan.com.

Kamloops

Kamloops, with a population of about 73,000, is one of the province's largest cities and is strategically located at the junction of three major highways and two railways. Just four hours east of Vancouver, along the Coquihalla Highway (longer along scenic Fraser Canyon/Thompson Valley routes of the Trans-Canada Highway), it's the entryway into Jasper National Park in Alberta along Highways 5 and 16 (Yellowhead) and into southern Alberta and Banff (along Highway 1, the Trans-Canada). The route to Jasper eventually takes you past Mount Robson, the highest point in the Rockies (3,954 m/12,972 ft) and through Yellowhead Pass (1,146 m/3,717 ft), for which the highway is named.

The city, known as the tournament capital of British Columbia, attracts sporting events from around the country, and its golf courses are among the finest in the province. The Kamloops Wildlife Park allows visitors to see native animals in their natural settings; the Secwepemc Native Heritage Park provides insight into the culture of the Shuswap people. Sitting at the confluence of the North and South Arms of the Thompson River, the city combines a sense of city living with rustic country charm. Nearby Sun Peaks Resort at Tod Mountain, with fifty-six runs, has developed into one of the province's major ski destinations.

Attractions in Kamloops include the following:

Kamloops Museum and Archives, 207 Seymour Street, (250) 828–3576. Closed Monday and holidays. Free. Displays of local history, Native cultures, fur trading, ranching, and railroading.

Kamloops Waterslide and R.V. Park, east of city center on the Trans-Canada, (250) 573–3789. Admission is charged. Six water slides, minigolf, hot tubs, a children's playground, and facilities for recreational vehicles (RVs).

Kamloops Wildlife Park, east of city center on the Trans-Canada, (250) 573–3242. Admission is charged. Displays of live wild animals, minitrain rides, and a nature trail.

All accommodations have restaurants and other amenities:

The Ramada Inn Kamloops, 555 West Columbia Street, (250) 374–0358. Moderate.

South Thompson Inn Guest Ranch, 610 West Columbia Street, (250) 573–3777. Moderate to expensive.

Hospitality Inn, 500 West Columbia Street, (250) 374–4164. Moderate.

Sandman Inn, 550 Columbia Street at Sixth Avenue, (250) 374–1218. Moderate.

Coast Canadian Inn, 339 St. Paul Street and Third Avenue, (250) 372–5201. Moderate to expensive.

Riverland Motel, 1530 River Street, (250) 374–1530. Inexpensive to moderate.

Best Western Kamloops, 1250 Rogers Way, (250) 828–6660. Moderate to expensive.

Courtesy Inn Motel, 1773 Trans-Canada, east of the city, (250) 372–8533. Moderate.

Okanagan Valley

Highway 97 South joins the Trans-Canada at Kamloops. It leads to one of British Columbia's top vacation areas: the Okanagan Valley region, frequented by travelers from the west coast of the province, Americans from south of the border, and those from Alberta who want to relax and have fun in an environment different from their own.

Whether you are traveling east or west along the Trans-Canada (or on Crowsnest Highway 3 to the south), you will probably want to take a side trip through the Okanagan region, even for a day or two. Okanagan Lake, a long stretch of warm water, is perfect for swimming, sailboarding, boating, fishing, and waterskiing. It even has its own resident monster—affectionately called Ogopogo—that is supposed to be a cousin of "Nessie" in Scotland's Loch Ness.

This is a prime fruit-producing area, and you'll find fruit and vegetable stands selling freshly picked crops throughout the region. Accommodations, from bed-and-breakfasts to resorts, are plentiful, and the golf is excellent, as are tennis, trail riding, skiing, and just about any other sports activity you enjoy. Be sure to visit the vineyards and their wineries, many of which offer free samples at the end of tours.

The key vacation cities in the Okanagan are Vernon, Kelowna, and Penticton. Smaller communities, such as Enderby, Armstrong, Westbank, Peachland, Summerland, Keremeos, Oliver, and Osoyoos, though a bit quieter, also offer most of the vacation features and attractions of the three main cities.

Okanagan Festivals

Okanagan Wine Festivals, late January, early May, and late October
Highland Games, Penticton, mid-July
Peach Festival, Penticton, end of July
Square Dancers Jamboree, Penticton, early August
Iron Man Canada, Penticton, August
Air Fair, Penticton, August

Vernon

A prominent vacation center in northern Okanagan, Vernon offers every kind of water sport, as well as fine entertainment, culture, accommodations, dining, and shopping. Three lakes and five mountains are close by—and so are golf, skiing at Silver Star Mountain, hot-spring bathing, hunting, and trail riding. This is a friendly and relaxing place to stop during your travels across the province. Attractions in Vernon include the following:

Vernon Museum, 3009 Thirty-second Avenue at the Civic Centre, (250) 542–3142. Open Monday through Saturday. Free. Exhibits on the lifestyle of the early settlers and on the paddle-wheel boats that sailed on the lake.

Historic O'Keefe Ranch, on Highway 97, (250) 542–7868. Open mid-May to Canadian Thanksgiving. Admission charged. Established in 1867, this ranch, consisting of about 8,100 ha/ 20,000 acres, was once the biggest cattle empire in the Okanagan. You can visit the ranch buildings and see the mansion and furnishings of the O'Keefe family as well as St. Ann's Church.

Topham Brown Art Gallery, 3009 Thirty-second Avenue in the Civic Centre; call (250) 545–3173 for hours and fees. Exhibitions by local artists and traveling shows.

Accommodations are varied. Below are some possibilities to consider:

Village Green Inn, junction of Highway 97 and Silver Star Road, (250) 542–3321. Excellent accommodations and dining, indoor and outdoor pools, championship tennis courts; near the lake, beaches, golf courses, and skiing. Moderate.

Best Western Vernon Lodge, 3914 Thirty-second Street, (250) 545–3385. Indoor pool, dining room, nightclub. Moderate.

Best Western Villager Motor Inn, 5121 Twenty-sixth Street, (250) 549–2224. Moderate.

Vernon Sandman Inn, 4201 Thirty-second Street, (250) 542–4325. Indoor pool, dining room. Moderate.

Swiss Hotel Silver Lode Inn, at Silver Star Mountain Ski Area, (250) 549–5105. At the base of the lifts; Swiss-style dining room, sauna, and swimming pool. Moderate to expensive.

Silver Star Club Resort, at Silver Star Mountain Ski Area, (250) 549–5191. At the base of the lifts; dining room, lounge, rooftop hot tubs. Moderate to expensive.

Kelowna

Kelowna is in the middle of the Okanagan vacation region. It boasts thirty-one parks, with nine of them on Okanagan Lake.

Hot Sands Beach, for example, perfect for sunbathing and swimming, is right in city center. Kelowna's cultural life includes the Okanagan Symphony and the Sunshine Theatre for live drama and comedy. Knox Mountain offers hiking, mountain biking, and terrific views of the city and surrounding landscape. There are excellent accommodations, restaurants, and shops in Kelowna. It prides itself on treating vacationers well—and it succeeds.

Listed below are some of the main attractions in Kelowna:

Father Pandosy Mission, Benvoulin Road, (250) 860–8369. Founded in 1859, this mission was the first permanent European settlement in the Okanagan Valley. There are several restored log buildings and displays of equipment.

Guisachan Heritage Park, 1060 Cameron Avenue. Part of one of Kelowna's earliest ranches and the onetime home of Lord Aberdeen, governor-general of Canada, 1893–98. You'll find a perennial garden and a restaurant.

Kasugai Gardens. Tucked behind Bennett on Queen Street, this Japanese garden is complete with a boulder-ringed pond, waterfall, and stone garden. Kasugai, in Japan, is Kelowna's sister city.

Centennial Museum, 470 Queensway Avenue. Call (250) 763–2417. Open daily during summer. Free. Displays about local history include a Chinese house and store, McDougal's Trading Post, a 1910 street scene, the first Kelowna radio station, and the interior of a Salish Amerindian home.

Accommodations abound. Here are several suggestions:

Lake Okanagan Resort, on the lake near Kelowna, (250) 769–3511; (800) 663–3273. This is one of the finest resort hotels in central British Columbia. It has been awarded the AAA four-diamond award for excellence. The resort is located on more than 120 ha/300 acres and includes 1.6 km/1 mi of shoreline on the lake. Excellent rooms and dining facilities, seven championship tennis courts, par-3 golf, swimming, horseback riding, and hiking. Moderate to expensive.

Coast Capri Hotel, 1171 Harvey Avenue, (250) 860–6060. Modern hotel, nicely appointed rooms; suites available. Swimming pool, restaurants, grills, and lounges. Convenient to all recreational attractions in the area. Moderate to expensive.

Accent Inns, 1140 Harvey Avenue, (250) 862–8888; (800) 663–0298. Family restaurant, pool, sauna, opposite shopping mall, nonsmoking units, housekeeping units. Inexpensive to moderate.

Holiday Inn Express, 2429 Highway 97 North, (250)

763–0500; (800) 465–0200. Indoor pool, complimentary breakfast buffet, near golf and family attractions. Moderate to expensive.

Grand Okangan Lakefront Resort, 1310 Water Street, (250) 763–4500; (800) 465–4651. Heated pools, all amenities, fourteen meeting rooms, located on the lakeshore in downtown Kelowna. Moderate to expensive.

Super 8 Motel, 2592 Highway 97 North, (250) 762–8222. Seasonal outdoor heated pool, year-round hot tub, family plan, off-season rates. Inexpensive to moderate.

Sandman Hotel Kelowna, 2130 Harvey Avenue, (250) 860–6409. Centrally located, twenty-four-hour family restaurant, senior-citizen discount, sports bar. Inexpensive to moderate.

Manted Resort, Lakeshore Road, (250) 860–1031. Expensive.

Big White Mountain Ski Area Central Reservations. Call (250) 765–8888 to book hotel rooms and condo units at this popular ski area.

Best Western Inn Kelowna, Highway 97, (250) 860–1212. Moderate.

Peachland

Between Kelowna and Penticton, on Highway 97, is the community of Peachland. When passing through, stop and visit the **Peachland Museum** at 5890 Beach Avenue, (250) 767–3441; open June through August. Call for hours and fees. The museum is housed in the former Peachland Baptist Church, a unique, eight-sided wooden structure built in 1910. Its collection tells about some of the first orchards in the Okanagan, which were planted in this area.

Penticton

Penticton, on Lake Okanagan, is encircled by mountains, and located nearby are many beaches, orchards, and vineyards. You might call it Eden, and for those who stay a while, it is. What could be better than attending the Peach Festival, sailing on the lake, dining on schnitzel at Karl's restaurant, or playing golf on lush fairways? All vacation amenities are here. Some of Penticton's attractions are listed below:

The Okanagan Summer School of the Arts offers classes in music, the visual arts, drama, dance, creative writing, and voice; call (250) 493–0390 for information.

Tin Whistle Brewery, 954 West Echkhardt Avenue, (250) 770–1112. You can taste three types of British ale here as well as

Wineries in the Okanagan

In addition to being one of British Columbia's leading vacation regions, the Okanagan is the province's wine-producing country. Botanist G. W. Henry was the first to plant grapevines in B.C., in 1899. In 1926 J. W. Hughes, a Kelowna rose grower, planted the first vineyard in the Okanagan on the same site that Father Charles Pandosy planted the region's first apple orchard in 1862. Both men knew that the soil and climate were suitable for fruit growing and that the growing season was long (five and a half months), considering the region's northern location. Dr. Eugene Rittich, a Hungarian with extensive experience in wine making in France, Germany, and Austria, came into the Okanagan in the early 1930s, and the region's involvement in this most enjoyable industry began because of his know-how and efforts.

Today the Okanagan has more than three dozen wineries producing a wide variety of wines. Some are excellent, though others have a way to go in terms of acceptance by connoisseurs. What is impressive is that through scientific research and advanced agriculture, Okanagan wines are improving and winning awards around the world. If you are in the region from late September to mid-October, be sure to attend the Okanagan Wine Festival, featuring various events and the tasting of the region's best wines; call (250) 861-6654 for more information. You can also discover the wines of the Okanagan by taking the Okanagan Wine Country Tour, (250) 868-9463. Leisurely half-day tours take you to a selection of vineyards between Penticton and Kelowna and include lunch. The wineries listed below welcome visitors:

Calona Wines, 1125 Richter Street in Kelowna. Tours from the end of May to the end of October; (250) 762-9144.

Mission Hills Vineyard, off Highway 97, Westbank; (250) 768-7611.

Cedar Creek Winery, Lakeshore Road, Kelowna. Tours from May to the end of October; (250) 764-8866.

Quail's Gate Estate Winery, Boucherie Road, Kelowna; (250) 769-4451.

Gray Monk Estate Cellars, Camp Road in Okanagan Centre. Tours from May to end the of October; (250) 766-3168.

Tin Horn Creek Vineyards, off Highway 97, Oliver; (250) 498-3743.

Sumac Ridge Estate Winery, Highway 97 North. Tours from the end of May to Canadian Thanksgiving; (250) 494-0451.

a special Peaches and Cream brew that's available only May through September.

Art Gallery of the South Okanagan, 11 Ellis Street at Front Street, next to the Lakeside resort; call (250) 493–2928 for hours and fees. Changing exhibitions of painting, photography, pottery, and drawings. World's first art gallery operating on passive solar energy.

Dominion Radio Astrophysical Observatory, Whitelake Road off Highway 97, (250) 497–5321. Open Monday through Friday. Free. A visitor center has displays on the scientific work being conducted at this facility. There are both radio and optical telescopes, and astronomers are on hand to explain their science.

Reg Atkinson Museum, 785 Main Street, (250) 492–6025. Open Monday through Saturday. Free. Collection of Salish and local archaeological artifacts, natural history specimens, the Braun collection of mounted animals, military memorabilia, and pioneer tools.

For accommodations and dining in the Penticton area, try the following:

Penticton Lakeside Resort, Convention Centre, and Casino, 21 Lakeshore Drive, (250) 493–8221. One of the premier resorts in the Okanagan, the Lakeside fronts on Okanagan Lake and has its own sandy beach for sunbathing and swimming. The spacious rooms have balconies; there are fine restaurants, saunas, a health club, an indoor pool, and tennis courts. Arrangements for skiing, snowmobiling, skating, ice sailing, and trail riding can be made through the hotel. Expensive.

Best Western Inn at Penticton, 3180 Skaha Lake Road, (250) 493–0311. Near the beach; indoor and outdoor pools, restaurant. Moderate.

Sandman Hotel Penticton, 939 Burnaby Avenue, (250) 493–7151. Moderate.

Penticton Travelodge, 950 Westminster Avenue, (250) 492–0225. Moderate.

Rochester Resort, 970 Lakeshore Drive, (250) 493–1128. Moderate.

Ramada Courtyard Inn, 1050 Eckhardt Avenue West, (250) 492–8926; (800) 665–4966. Near the convention center, shopping, and airport. Adjacent to a golf course. Laundry, kitchenettes. Inexpensive to moderate.

Executive Inn & Suites, 333 Main, (250) 492–3600; (800) 665–2221. City center, all amenities, licensed restaurant, ski and golf packages. Moderate to expensive.

Days Inn Penticton, Riverside Drive, (888) 999–6616. Moderate.

Hostelling International Penticton, downtown, (250) 492–3992.

Apex Alpine Ski Resort, c/o 160–1636 Main Street, (250) 493–3200; (877) 777–2739. Moderate to expensive condominium units.

Revelstoke

After a time in the Okanagan, if you wish to continue east on the Trans-Canada, follow Highway 97 to 97A North, which connects with the Trans-Canada at Revelstoke. (If you are traveling west, take 97 North to the Trans-Canada and Kamloops; if you want to take the Crowsnest Highway 3 East, follow 97 South.)

Situated on the source waters of the Columbia River and between the Selkirk and Monashee Mountains, Revelstoke was named in honor of Lord Revelstoke, head of a British bank that helped finance the transcontinental railroad at a critical time in its development. In the late 1800s the town became the mountain divisional center for the Canadian Pacific Railroad (CPR), and it continues to function as an important transportation and supply center for its mountain region. While in Revelstoke, visit the following:

Railway Museum, Victoria Road, (250) 837–6060. Call for hours. Check out Canadian Pacific's large Mikado-class steam engine, business car, and other rolling stock.

Revelstoke Museum, 315 West First Street, (250) 837–3067. Housed in the stately old brick post office building, the museum has an impressive collection of historic artifacts, displays, and information dating back to the founding of Revelstoke in the 1880s. Call for hours. Free.

All of the following accommodations have restaurants and other amenities:

Three Valley Lake Chateau, 19 km/11.4 mi west of town, (250) 837–2109. Moderate.

Hillcrest Resort Hotel, 2100 Oak Drive, (250) 837–3322. Revelstoke's newest deluxe hotel, with seventy-five rooms.

Sandman Inn, off the Trans-Canada, (250) 837–5271. Moderate.

Best Western Wayside Inn, 1901 Laforme Boulevard, (250) 837–6161. Moderate.

Swiss Chalet Motel, 1101 Victoria Road, (250) 837–4650. Inexpensive to moderate.

Other attractions in the area include **Naksup Hot Springs** on Highway 23, south from the Trans-Canada at Revelstoke, (250) 265–4528, which offers natural hot springs bathing at 44°C/100°–107°F; waterskiing; helicopter skiing; golf.

Access to **Mount Revelstoke National Park** is off the Trans-Canada in the Revelstoke area. The 260 sq km/100 sq mi park is located on the western slope of the Selkirk Mountains. There are wonderful views of mountain peaks, glaciers, alpine meadows, and lakes. Hiking trails (65 km/40 mi of them), such as Skunk Cabbage, Giant Cedars, and Mountain Meadows, take you into the interior of the park. A road off the Trans-Canada heads to Mount Revelstoke and its alpine meadows. Also in this area is Balsam Lake. From Mount Revelstoke a hiking trail, along which the natural beauty of the wilderness is both poetic and awesome, heads farther into the park to Eva Lake. Campgrounds are located at Mountain Creek, Loop Brook, and Illecillewaet. The interpretive or information center is at Rogers Pass. For more information contact Mount Revelstoke National Park, 301B Third Street, Box 350, Dept. K, Revelstoke, British Columbia V0E 2S0; (250) 837–7500, operator 129.

Rogers Pass

Glacier National Park (same address and telephone number as Mount Revelstoke National Park, described above) can be reached from the Trans-Canada. The community of Rogers Pass is at the center of the park. There are over 400 glaciers in this national park, as well as dense stands of hemlock and cedar. During the winter and thawing seasons, this is avalanche country, and the frequent plunge of millions of tons of ice and snow down the slopes made the Rogers Pass area one of the most difficult obstacles to overcome in the building of the transcontinental railroad and the Trans-Canada Highway. Today howitzers are used to break up the snow and prevent avalanches from becoming a danger to travelers.

Guided hikes begin at the Illecillewaet Campground and move through diverse ecological zones. If you are interested in hiking on the glaciers themselves, check for full details with your local mountaineering club or with the Sierra Club branch in your area. Among the trails in Glacier National Park (140 km/93 mi of them) are Trestle, Loop, Meeting of the Waters, and Abandoned Rails. Campgrounds in the area include Illecillewaet (fifty-eight sites) and Loop Brook (twenty sites). They're open mid-June to the end

Rogers Pass Information Centre

April 1–June 14	9:00 A.M.–5:00 P.M.
June 15–September 15	8:00 A.M.–8:30 P.M.
September 16–October 31	9:00 A.M.–5:00 P.M.
November	9:00 A.M.–5:00 P.M. (Thursday through Monday)
December 1–March 31	7:00 A.M.–5:00 P.M.

of August, unserviced, and primitive (pit toilets and pump water). The fee includes firewood.

In 1882, A. B. Rogers, an employee of the CPR, found a pass through the Selkirk Range (later named in his honor) so that one of the final links in the transcontinental railroad could be built. The railroad was put through **Rogers Pass** (elevation 1,323 m/ 4,302 ft) at great effort and expense in 1885 and 1886. Because the area was subject to frequent avalanches, the 8-km/4.8-mi Connaught Tunnel was built in 1916 to protect lives and the passage of trains. The Trans-Canada Highway came through here in 1962. Avalanches are still a problem, but an excellent safety program protects travelers moving through this area.

Rogers Pass Information Centre is on the Trans-Canada, (250) 837–6274. For hours of operation see the sidebar. Free. This information center, operated by Parks Canada, is located at the top of Rogers Pass. It provides information on the building and operation of the transcontinental railroad through this rugged part of the country and on the natural history of the area—glaciers, avalanches, caves, alpine meadows, and wildlife—and shows a movie on the secrets of the Nakimu Cave System. The center is well worth the stop to understand the magnificent landscape you are passing through.

For accommodations, try the **Best Western Glacier Park Lodge,** off the Trans-Canada, (250) 837–2126. Great location; dining room and lounge. Moderate.

Golden

The town of Golden, on the Trans-Canada between the Selkirk Mountains and Glacier National Park and the Rockies and Yoho

National Park, was once known as Kicking Horse Flats. You'll find golf, hunting, fishing, wild-river rafting, hiking, and access to some of the top national parks in Canada here. The **Golden Rim Motor Inn**, off the Trans-Canada, (250) 344–2216, has saunas, an indoor pool, and a dining room. Moderate.

Yoho and Kootenay National Parks

Yoho and Kootenay are "Siamese twin" parks in that they join each other at the B.C.–Alberta border. Yoho, the northern park, runs along the spine of the Canadian Rockies, and Kootenay is the southern park. There's no mistaking that you are in high mountain country here, with a landscape of deep forests, icy glaciers, wild rivers, pure lakes, and an abundance of wildlife. Within its shale area—particularly Burgess, now a World Heritage Site—are fossils from prehistory. They're protected and not for collecting, but you can see the remains of ancient creatures by hiking into the shale zone.

The main access to **Yoho National Park** is off the Trans-Canada Highway, and the park's office is in the community of Field. Among the many features of the park are the Spiral Tunnels Viewpoint, Kicking Horse Pass, Kicking Horse River, Lake O'Hara (the Alpine Club of Canada has a shelter here), Emerald Lake, Takakkaw Falls, the Yoho River, Twin Falls, Laughing Falls, Point Lace Falls, Angel's Staircase Falls, Yoho Glacier, Hamilton Falls and Lake, and Natural Bridge. There are numerous hiking trails (360 km/225 mi of them), such as the Deer Lodge Trail and the Avalanche Trail, and the following campgrounds: Kicking Horse, Hoodoo Creek, Chancellor Peak, Takakkaw Falls, and Lake O'Hara. Trout fishing is allowed in Yoho, but you have to get a permit from park authorities; canoeing is possible on Lake O'Hara and Emerald Lake; and you can go trail riding from a stable at Emerald Lake. For more information contact Superintendent, Yoho National Park, Box 99, Field, British Columbia V0A 1G0; (250) 343–6783.

In addition to its impressively high mountains, **Kootenay National Park** is famous for its wild rivers, glaciers, canyons, and hot springs. Access is from many points along Banff-Windermere Highway 93 and from the Trans-Canada and Highway 95. The southern end of the park, Radium Hot Springs, is slightly more arid than the northern part at Vermilion Pass (Lake Louise and Banff can be reached from here). These dual climate zones make for diverse vegetation and animal and bird life. Kootenay is a naturalist's paradise, and when the naturalist gets through trekking and observing, there are natural hot springs to soak away fatigue and reestablish a more complete tranquility. The many hiking trails (200 km/125 mi of them), such as Marble Canyon, Paint Pots, Fireweed, Valley View, and Juniper, lead throughout the park. Paint Pots is a bed of ocher that was used in long-past days by the local Native peoples. A suspension bridge, reached via the Paint Pots Trail, crosses the powerful Vermilion River.

The hot springs at Radium (noted later in this chapter) are world famous, and people come from all over North America and many foreign countries to seek a cure for what ails them. A soak in these hot mineral waters is the perfect ending to a long day's drive or hours spent on nearby ski slopes.

Camping with facilities for recreational vehicles is available at Redstreak, off Highway 95 near the Trans-Canada; McLeod Meadows, to the north of Radium Hot Springs; and Marble Canyon. Kootenay also offers fishing (permit required) and canoeing on the Kootenay and Vermilion Rivers.

For more information, contact Superintendent, Kootenay National Park, Box 220, Box K, Radium Hot Springs, British Columbia V0A 1M0; (250) 347–9615.

Highly recommended for accommodation in this area is **Emerald Lake Lodge,** near Field, off the Trans-Canada, about thirty minutes from Lake Louise, Alberta; (403) 343–6321. This is a historic, chalet-type lodge in Yoho National Park. For more than eighty-five years it has been popular with sophisticated travelers seeking tranquility, and it has been recently restored and renovated to contemporary standards. The outstanding setting takes advantage of the essential beauty of the Canadian Rockies. Within the Emerald Lake area you can hunt for fossils or go canoeing, fishing, trail riding, cross-country skiing, or dogsledding. Nearby are Lake O'Hara, Takakkaw Falls, and Yoho Glacier. The main lodge has a dining room and an 1890s Yukon saloon. Entertainers (singers, musicians, dancers, comics) are brought in from Banff. Expensive.

The Canadian Rockies: The B.C.–Alberta Border

The Trans-Canada Highway crosses the **Continental Divide** and enters the province of Alberta through **Kicking Horse Pass** (1,647 m/5,402 ft). Just a few miles past the border, near the Trans-Canada, is Lake Louise. If you head north on Highway 93, you'll reach Jasper (connecting with the Yellowhead Highway 16 East to Edmonton). Highway 93 South leads to Banff and Calgary.

Metro Vancouver to Banff, Alberta, via Crowsnest Highway 3

Crowsnest Highway 3 (and Rocky Mountain Trench Highway 93/95 East in the Kootenay region) takes you through or near towns with familiar- and odd-sounding names alike: Princeton, Osoyoos, Greenwood, Trail, Castlegar, Creston, Yahk, Kitchener, Cranbrook, Wasa, Skookumchuck, Fairmont Hot Springs, Invermere, and Radium Hot Springs. You travel over several mountain ranges, through thickly forested valleys, arid ones, and those lush with fruit orchards, until you come to the Kootenays and the Canadian Rockies. View after view of gorgeous alpine scenery and fields of wild mountain flowers are breathtaking. All along the way are museums, historical sites, and places for swimming, fishing, camping, boating, skiing, tennis, hiking, trail riding, wild-river rafting, and golf. The accommodations in the towns are fine; some of the resorts are as outstanding as those you'll find anywhere in the world. Although there are few gourmet restaurants as such, most places serve good, honest cooking—both North American and ethnic cuisines—that will satisfy travelers' appetites. If you've previously traveled across B.C. along the Trans-Canada, you'll find this southern route a nice change and see new aspects of this beautiful province. U.S. travelers coming from eastern Washington, Idaho, and western Montana will also find this an enjoyable route to Vancouver.

Osoyoos

Osoyoos is the southern gateway to the Okanagan vacation region. In architecture and style Osoyoos is reminiscent of a town in Arizona or New Mexico—in fact, it's called the Spanish capital of Canada. Although the hills around the town are almost desertlike, the land in the valley is irrigated to support extensive orchards and vegetable crops. In July the folks here hold a **Cherry Festival** to honor the fruit they grow in such abundance. Just to the south of town is **Osoyoos Lake,** a perfect place for swimming, sunbathing, boating, fishing, and windsurfing. The **Osoyoos Museum,** (250) 495–6723, welcomes visitors who want to learn about the history of this pleasant community. Osoyoos is just a stone's throw from the B.C.–Washington border, and U.S. travelers can enter the province via U.S. Highway 97.

The following accommodations have restaurants and other amenities:

Desert Motor Inn, on Highway 3, (250) 495–6525. Moderate.

Holiday Sunspree Resort, Highway 3, (250) 495–7223; (800) 216–6246. This waterfront complex, which opened in May 1997, has all the amenities plus golf packages, a marina, and boat rentals. Moderate to expensive.

Grand Forks

Grand Forks is right on the B.C.–Washington border, and U.S. Highways 21 and 395 give access to the province at this point. Within the town are a local history museum, a Doukhobor museum and an art gallery. **Grand Forks Motor Inn,** in town, (250) 442–2127, has a restaurant and a pool. Moderate.

Trail

Both gold and copper were discovered in the Trail area in the late 1800s. Today the primary economic activity is smelting minerals (zinc, lead, and silver) from the region's mines. U.S. travelers coming from Washington can take Washington Highway 25 to B.C. Highway 22. In the city are the Birchbank eighteen-hole golf course, Beaver Creek Provincial Park, Wright Public Pool, Gyro Park, and Seven Mile Dam. Also in Trail is the **City of Trail Museum,** in city hall. Open weekdays June through August. Free. Exhibits of local history.

Rossland

Rossland Historical Museum. Open from mid-May to mid-September, 9:00 A.M. to 5:00 P.M., (250) 362–7722. Admission is charged. Displays on the geological history of the area. Le Roi Gold Mine underground tour is here. Home of B.C. Ski Hall of Fame.

Also in the Rossland area are the **Nancy Greene Lake Provincial Park,** with campsites, hiking, and fishing, and the **Red Mountain Ski Area,** with thirty downhill runs, a vertical drop of 850 m/ 2,789 ft, and cross-country trails.

The following accommodations have restaurants and other amenities:

Ram's Head Inn, Red Mountain Road, (250) 362–9577. In a forest setting 3 km/2 mi from Rossland on Highway 3B. Fireside lounge; at the base of the Red Mountain Ski Area. Moderate.

Uplander Hotel, 1919 Columbia Avenue, (250) 362–7375. Family restaurant, cable TV, dining room, lounge, and conference facilities. Just five minutes from Red Mountain ski facilities.

Castlegar

Castlegar is well worth the side trip on Highway 22 North from Trail. The Doukhobors, a unique community of people who live here, came from the steppes of czarist Russia, where they were persecuted for their strong religious beliefs. They were pacifists and refused to serve in the military; they lived in a highly structured communal society; they were vegetarians; and their religious practices were simple and basic in comparison with those of the Byzantine Russian Orthodox.

The writer Leo Tolstoy and the North American Society of Friends (the Quakers, whom the Doukhobors resemble in attitudes and religious practices) helped the Doukhobors leave Russia and settle in Canada. They originally settled in Alberta and Saskatchewan, carving out farms on the prairies. Because of disputes with the provincial governments, they had to move on again and, at last, found refuge in south-central British Columbia. The Doukhobors are famous for their choirs, which have performed to enthusiastic audiences throughout Canada, the United States, and other countries. Visit the Zuckerberg Island Heritage Park, the Kootenay Indian Pit House, the Russian Chapel House, the Doukhobor Bridge, and Verigin's Tomb. Peter Lordly Verigin was the Doukhobor spiritual leader who brought them to Canada. Castlegar is also the gateway to the Arrow Lakes—reached via Highway 6—with great opportunities for fishing, swimming, camping, hiking, and sunbathing. While in Castlegar, be sure to see the following:

Doukhobor Village Museum, across from Castlegar Airport. Open May through September; (250) 365–6622. Admission is charged. Buildings show the communal character and lifestyle of the Doukhobors and tell of their history in Russia and Canada. Sample Russian culinary specialties, such as borscht and pierogi (spelled perogie in western Canada), at the Doukhobor Restaurant, where all dishes are vegetarian.

Kootenay Gallery of Art, History & Science, next to the Doukhobor museum. Open daily; (250) 365–3337; free. One of twenty-three national exhibition centers in Canada. Exhibits from local and international cultures.

The following inns have restaurants and other amenities:

Sandman Hotel, 1944 Columbia Avenue, (250) 365–8444. Moderate.

Best Western Fireside Inn, 1810 Eighth Avenue, (250) 365–2128. Moderate.

Creston

Creston, on the Kootenay River on Highway 3, is famous for its fruit orchards and fields (strawberries, raspberries, cherries, apricots, peaches, plums, pears, and most kinds of apples). A visit here in spring, when the blossoms are out, or in summer, when apples are ripening, is a memorable experience in human-cultivated beauty set against a backdrop of magnificent nature.

If you have extra time for exploring, take Highway 3A North to the **Kootenay Lake** area, where there are several fishing resorts and an 18-hole golf resort. At Kootenay Bay you can take a ferry to Balfour and then Highway 3A to the hot springs at **Ainsworth**. This area can also be visited by taking Highway 3A North from Castlegar to Nelson, or Highway 6 to Nelson and then Highway 3A. U.S. citizens coming to Creston from Idaho should take U.S. Highway 95 to Idaho Highway 1 to the border, and then B.C. Highway 21 to Creston.

The annual **Blossom Festival** is held in May. There's a golf course in town. Other attractions include the following:

Creston Valley Museum, off Highway 3, (250) 428–9262. Call for hours. Admission is charged. Housed in the old Stone House; depicts the town's agricultural heritage.

Creston Valley Wildlife Management Area, outside the downtown district. Open throughout the year. Free. You'll find almost 7,000 ha/17,000 acres of lakes, streams, and marshes supporting a wide variety of wildlife; guided walks, canoe trips, films, talks, gift shop, and snack bar. For campgrounds call (250) 428–3260.

Wayside Garden and Aboretum, on Highway 3. Open May through October, (250) 428–2062. Admission is charged. Beautiful floral displays: rose garden, rhododendron dell, water lily and fish ponds, perennial borders, rock garden and lily beds, teahouse, and gift shop.

Recommended accommodations are as follows:

Skimmerhorn Inn, on Highway 3, (250) 428–4009. Moderate.

The Hacienda Inn, in town, (250) 428–2224, has a dining room. Inexpensive to moderate.

City Centre Motel, in town, (250) 428–2257. Moderate.

Downtowner Motor Inn, 1218 Canyon Road, (250) 428–2238. Senior discount, golf packages, adjacent to licensed restaurants, conference rooms, complimentary in-room coffee.

Cranbrook

U.S. travelers entering British Columbia in the Cranbrook region can take Montana Highway 93 or Idaho Highway 95. Both these highways come into the city of Cranbrook and continue north through the eastern part of the province to Banff, Alberta; the Trans-Canada; and Lake Louise. If you are headed for Banff and then Calgary, leave the Crowsnest Highway at Cranbrook and continue on Highway 93/95 North.

Cranbrook was developed in the late 1800s when the railroad serving the region selected it over Fort Steele as the terminal point. Today Cranbrook is one of the major commercial and transportation centers for the lower Kootenay region. There are fine accommodations, restaurants, shops, and services in this city.

Don't miss **Sam Steele Days** in June, and if you're interested in the railroads visit the **Canadian Museum of Rail Travel,** in downtown Cranbrook, (250) 489–3918. This is the only national museum of its kind and is dedicated to the restoration and conservation of several Canadian Pacific Railway train sets of different eras. Experience the elegance of a bygone era. Open year-round; admission is charged.

All of the following accommodations have restaurants and other amenities:

Sandman Inn, 405 Cranbrook Street, (250) 426–4236. Moderate.

Heritage Estate Motel, 362 South Van Horne Street, (250) 426–3862. Inexpensive.

Town and Country Motor Inn, 600 Cranbrook Street, (250) 426–6683. Moderate.

Heritage Inn, 803 Cranbrook Street, (250) 489–4301. Moderate.

Prestige Rocky Mountain Resort and Convention Center, 910 Cranbrook Street South, (250) 417–0444. A full-service resort with restaurant, lounge, and meeting rooms. Moderate.

Best Western Coach House Motor Inn, 1417 Cranbrook Street, (250) 426–7236, (800) 528–1234. Moderate.

From Cranbrook to the Alberta Border

From Cranbrook, Crowsnest Highway 3 continues east to the Alberta border, where, at Pincher Creek, Alberta, it forms a junction with Highway 6. By heading south on 6 you come to Waterton Lakes National Park (see Chapter 7). Just below Waterton—actually, adjoining it—is Glacier National Park in Montana. Between Cranbrook and the Alberta border is the Fernie Alpine Resort, and just past the town of Sparwood, you go through Crowsnest Pass (elevation 1,396 m/4,533 ft) at the border of the two provinces.

This region of British Columbia (between Cranbrook and the Alberta border) has numerous resort areas offering everything from skiing and white-water rafting to horseback riding and golf. While you're in the area, be sure to visit the following:

Fort Steele Heritage Town, 13 km/7 mi north of Cranbrook on Rocky Mountain Trench Highway 93/95; (250) 426–7352. Open daily. Free. Fort Steele is the main historical attraction in the Kootenay region and should not be missed. A canny fellow by the name of John Galbraith—no relation to the famous economist—saw the potential of this site as settlers, miners, and merchants began moving in, and he started a ferry line. Then there came disputes between the whites and local Natives. In 1887 Superintendent Samuel B. Steele and seventy-five Northwest Mounted Police (D Division) arrived aboard Galbraith's Ferry to establish law and order, and here they built the first Northwest Mounted Police post in British Columbia. Fort Steele, on the bank of the Kootenay River, became a transportation, commercial, and social center for this area. In 1898, however, after the B.C. Southern Railway chose Cranbrook as its divisional point, Fort Steele declined into oblivion. It was brought back to life as a historical park, and today you can stroll Fort Steele's streets and visit its buildings as they were in the 1800s. You can step into the millinery shop; the blacksmith shop; Bleasdell's drugstore; Dr. Watt's office; the Kershaw family store; Coventry's opera house; the Presbyterian, Anglican, and Roman Catholic churches; the Windsor Hotel; and numerous private residences from the Victorian period. Vaudeville shows are performed at the Wild Horse Theatre. You'll also find a tea room for snacks and an interesting museum of local lore.

Kimberley

The city of Kimberley, a highly recommended side trip via Highway 95A that is tucked away in the Purcell Mountains, is Bavaria in Canada. Its architecture is a mix of southern German, Austrian, Swiss, and English Tudor.

The Platzl (a downtown pedestrian mall) draws people to shops, restaurants serving schnitzel, outdoor cafes, and the sight of Happy Hans (the city's mascot) jumping out of North America's largest cuckoo clock. Residents wearing lederhosen and dirndls are a common sight during summer.

One of Kimberley's main attractions is **Trickle Creek,** an eighteen-hole, par-71 Canadian Professional Golfers Association (CPGA) golf course set in the midst of magnificent scenery. The **Alpine Slide,** an 823-m/2,700-ft thrilling run down the side of a mountain, is in operation from July to Labour Day.

Kimberley's annual festivals include the **International Old-Time Accordion Festival** in July. The **Bavarian City Mining Railway** gives rides from the end of June until Labour Day. Be sure to visit the **Kimberley Heritage Museum**, located above the public library in the Platzl, and the Cominco Gardens, with its 50,000 blooms per year.

The following accommodations are highly recommended:

Top of the World Ranch, off Highway 93/95, north of Fort Steele, (250) 426–6306. Top of the World is a family-owned ranch high in the Canadian Rockies (Kootenay region). It takes guests year-round and offers the authentic western ranch experience: trail rides, campfires, hearty home-cooked food, comfortable accommodations, the panorama of changing seasons, the sight of wild animals and birds, the glory of the mountains, barbecues, fishing, and the knowledge that you have escaped civilization and are enjoying it. Moderate.

Fairmont Hot Springs Resort, in Fairmont Hot Springs on Highway 93/95; (250) 345–6311. The largest natural mineral hot pools in Canada are at this resort, which has been a favorite with families since 1922. In addition to swimming and hot-spring bathing, it features two championship eighteen-hole golf courses, deluxe hotel and villas, and excellent facilities for camping at its RV park. Its natural hot-spring pools have a clear, odorless water with temperatures of 35° to 45°C/90° to 106°F.

The resort also offers tennis, racquetball, squash, trail riding, hiking, and helicopter sight-seeing; a game room for children; and canoeing, fishing, and windsurfing on nearby Columbia Lake. In winter it operates its own ski center with 16-km/10-mi runs (see page 91). The resort is located at the base of the Kootenay section of the Canadian Rockies, and the alpine and lake scenery is fantastic. Fairmont, considered one of Canada's top family resorts, is worth a visit or a prolonged stay. Reservations are essential during peak summer and winter seasons. Moderate to expensive.

Invermere

Invermere, a small resort community, is at the northern end of Windermere Lake, which flows into Columbia Lake, the source of the mighty Columbia River. The lakes in this area are good for swimming, canoeing, fishing, and windsurfing. There are a number of places with accommodations (such as the Fairmont and Panorama resorts), restaurants, and stores in this scenic area. Be sure to visit the following:

Windermere Valley Pioneer Museum, in town, (250) 342–9769. Open June through August. Admission is charged. Museum in the old railroad station; pioneer log cabins, old schoolhouse; copy of the journal of David Thompson (an early explorer, fur trader, surveyor, and mapmaker who helped establish the border between Canada and the United States); pleasant park setting.

Accommodations in Kimberley include:

Chicamon Springs Lodge, Kimberley Alpine Resort (250) 427–1888. Moderate to expensive.

Inn West/Kirkwood Inn, Kimberley Alpine Resort (250) 427–7616. Moderate.

Purcell-Rocky Mountain Condos, Kimberley Alpine Resort (250) 427–5385. Moderate.

Quality Inn of the Rockies, 300 Wallinger Avenue (250) 427–2266. Moderate.

Within the area the following accommodations are recommended.

Panorama Mountain Village, in the Invermere area; (250) 342–6941. Panorama is one of Canada's finest alpine resorts. It's actually a self-contained village of deluxe hotel and inn rooms and condos. Grocery, liquor, sports equipment, and gift shops are within the Panorama complex. The resort offers trail rides, wild-river rafting trips, guided treks through the rugged wilderness, tennis, and winter sports. Swimming is nearby in Columbia and Windermere Lakes. In late August the resort is the host site for the **Annual Scottish Gathering.** Moderate to expensive.

Radium Hot Springs

Radium Hot Springs, at the junction of Highways 93 and 95 bordering Kootenay National Park, (250) 347–9331, is one of the world's most famous hot springs. Before the coming of the Europeans, Natives sought to cure their ills in these baths (40°C/ 102°F). So did Winston Churchill during one of his trips to Canada. Thousands of people believe that these odorless, clear waters heal; many have experienced relief. The Aquacourt accommodates both bathers and swimmers; it is open to all, every day of the year, with summer hours from 8:30 A.M. to 11:00 P.M.

At the **Springs at Radium Golf Resort,** an eighteen-hole golf course as well as facilities for squash, racquetball, and tennis are available. Also in the area are water slides, wild-river rafting trips, hiking trails (some reached by helicopter), and trail rides. Other places to visit are the nearby Bugaboo Park and Our Lady of Peace Shrine.

White Water Trips, Glacier Raft Company, (250) 344–6521, provides thrilling wild-river raft trips on the Vermilion and Kootenay Rivers; horseback trips through Yoho National Park, the Continental Divide, and Top of the World Provincial Park; and other trips on the Alberta side of the Rockies.

Accommodations in the area are listed below:

The Springs at Radium Golf Resort (see above); (250) 347–9311. Moderate to expensive.

Motel Bavaria, (250) 347–9915. Moderate.

Alpen Motel, (250) 347–9823. Moderate.

Crystal Springs Motel, Radium Boulevard, (250) 347–9759. Moderate.

Mount Assiniboine Lodge, in Mount Assiniboine Provincial Park, bordering Kootenay and Banff National Parks; (403) 678–2883. Access by hiking trail, helicopter, or cross-country skiing. Log lodge overlooks Magog Lake. Reservations essential. Expensive.

The Canadian Rockies: The B.C.–Alberta Border

If you are heading for the Canadian Rockies in Alberta, take Highway 93 East through Kootenay National Park, which crosses the Great Divide at Vermilion Pass (1,639 m/5,367 ft) and enters Banff National Park. The highway joins the Trans-Canada in Alberta just south of Lake Louise. Highway 95 splits off from 93 and continues north until it joins the Trans-Canada at Golden, B.C. From here you can head east, entering Alberta through Kicking Horse Pass, just a few miles north of Lake Louise or south of Jasper National Park.

Metro Vancouver to the Yukon and Alaska via Highway 97

Cache Creek Area

Cache Creek, at the junction of the Trans-Canada and Highway 97 North, might be a good place to stop for the night if you have come up nonstop from Vancouver and intend to go north on Highway 97. The following accommodations have restaurants and other amenities:

Sandman Inn, (250) 457–6284. Moderate.

Cache Creek Motor Inn, (250) 457–6224. Moderate.

Cariboo Country Annual Festivals

Western Days, May
South Cariboo Square Dance Jamboree, June
Great Cariboo Ride, August

Clinton Area

The old gold town of Clinton is 40 km/25 mi beyond Cache Creek. Here, there's the pleasant feeling that not much has changed. In town, real-life Dr. Frank Cambell's office has a sign outside that dates from the 1800s. It reads: BONES SET, BLOOD LET, HOLES PATCHED, BABIES HATCHED.

Eighty km/50 mi west of Clinton, at the base of Mount Bowman, is the spectacular **Echo Valley Ranch Resort,** (250) 459–2386; (800) 253–8831. Combining the rolling grazing lands of the Cariboo with down-home luxury, the resort offers a 791-sq-km/ 8,500 sq-ft log ranch house with six themed bedrooms, two private cabins, and a honeymoon cabin. Horse rides, pack trips, whitewater rafting, Native feast, and tepee accommodation. Moderate to expensive.

100 Mile House Area

In the 1860s, this part of British Columbia—near 100 Mile House—attracted people in quest of furs and gold. The 100 Mile House is 161 km/100 mi from the town of Lillooet, which is at "mile 0" on the Cariboo Wagon Road.

For fun and adventure try the following:

The Great Cariboo Ride Society, (250) 395–4096. A nine-day horseback trek across the Fraser Plateau to Gang Ranch; great meals; fishing and dips in waterfalls.

Accommodations include the following:

Red Coach Inn, in the village, (250) 395–2266. Moderate.

Imperial Motel, in the village, (250) 395–2471. Moderate.

Best Western 108 Resort, 108 Ranch, (250) 791–5211. Moderate to expensive resort with an eighteen-hole golf course.

The Hills Health and Guest Ranch, Highway 97, (250) 791–5225. Moderate to expensive with a new lodge.

Williams Lake

Williams Lake is named for Chief William of the Sugar Cane Reserve. Its Indian name is *Colunetza*, which means "gathering place of the lordly ones." Williams Lake serves the many cattle ranches in the area. Lumbering and mining are also important economic activities. While in town visit the Bullion Gold Mine, see the downtown murals, and tour the Gibralter mines.

The **Williams Lake Golf and Tennis Club**, (250) 392–6026, has an eighteen-hole golf course, three tennis courts, and a restaurant.

All of the following accommodations have restaurants and other amenities:

Sandman Inn, 664 Oliver Street, (250) 392–6557. Moderate.

Fraser Inn, 285 Donald Road, (250) 398–7055. Moderate.

Bella Coola Side Trip

From Williams Lake take Highway 20 to Bella Coola on the coast, a long journey of 465 km/279 mi. The first fourth of the way, up to Hanceville, is paved road, and the rest of the way is gravel. If your vehicle is in good condition and prepared for some rough spots, this trip could be a nice adventure from the interior of the province to the coast. The scenery along the way is beautiful. You pass through several small towns and **Tweedsmuir Park.** You can camp and enjoy the wilderness along the way. If you are bringing along a canoe, all the better. The paved road picks up again at the western end of Tweedsmuir Park and takes you to Bella Coola, which is at the Labouchere, Dean, and Burke Channels just east of the Inside Passage (see page 182). There are accommodations, supplies, gas, and food in the villages and in Bella Coola.

Quesnel Area

In the old days Quesnel, on Highway 97, was a supply center and steamboat landing for the gold-mining town of Bakersville, which is now a historical park. Today Quesnel continues as a transportation center for the local mining and lumbering industries. Both natural gas and oil potential have been found here, and Quesnel may be important to our future as a source of energy.

Barkerville Historic Park, at the end of Highway 26 East, is 82 km/49 mi from Quesnel. Open daily, (250) 994–3332. Free. A restored village, it dates from the gold rush period in the late 1800s. During summer there are stage shows and demonstrations of how people lived and worked in those days. The buildings include a blacksmith shop, saloon, miner's cabin, churches, Chinese herbal shop, general store, and many more. Barkerville does a good job of telling its story.

The Alexander Mackenzie Heritage Trail, between Quesnel in Cariboo's interior and Bella Coola on the coast, is a demanding but immensely satisfying hiking trek through beautiful and historic country; for more information call Heritage Properties Branch in Victoria, (250) 387–1619, or write Alexander Mackenzie Trail Association, P.O. Box 425, Kelowna, British Columbia V1Y 7P1.

For accommodations try the following:

Cascade Inn, 383 St. Laurent Avenue, (250) 992–5575. Moderate.

Talisman Inn, 753 Front Street, (250) 922–7247. Moderate.

As you travel north from Quesnel, you'll pass through Prince George (described in Chapter 6), the next major city along Highway 97. From here you can take a few routes. If you are still headed for the Alaska Highway, continue on Highway 97 North until you come to Chetwynd. At the junction take Highway 29 North, which reconnects with Highway 97 just above the town of Fort St. John. This loop will save you a great deal of time and mileage. Once you commit yourself to the Alaska Highway going north, your only other option (should you decide to turn south) is to take Highway 37 (above Watson Lake in the Yukon) to Prince Rupert; otherwise, you have to backtrack until you reach Prince George.

Yellowhead Highway 16 bisects Highway 97 in Prince George, and at this point, if you wish to turn east, take the Yellowhead to Jasper and then to Edmonton. From Jasper you can go south on Highway 93 through Jasper National Park and to the Trans-Canada to Lake Louise, Banff, and Calgary. Near the British Columbian border, the Yellowhead passes through Mount Robson Provincial Park, where Mount Robson, the highest point in the Canadian Rockies, and Mount Terry Fox, named in honor of the brave Canadian cross-country runner, are located.

Fort St. John

On the banks of the Peace River, once a link in a chain of fur-trading posts, Fort St. John became in recent times a center for exploring and developing oil and natural gas in this part of the province. Attractions here include a monument to Alexander Mackenzie, the North Peace Museum of local history, and the North Peace Art Gallery.

The following accommodations have restaurants and other amenities:

Cedar Lodge Motor Inn, 9824 Ninety-ninth Avenue, (250) 785–8107; (800) 661–2210. Full amenities, free airport pickup. Inexpensive to moderate.

Alexander Mackenzie Inn, 9223 One Hundredth Street, (250) 785–8364; (800) 663–8313. Indoor pool, sports lounge. Inexpensive to moderate.

Fort Nelson

In 1800 the North West Company established a trading post in Fort Nelson (408 km/246 mi north of Fort St. John), and the Hudson's Bay Company took over in 1865. Exploration for oil and natural gas has improved the economy here. Lumbering is a principal activity.

Accommodations are available at the **Coachhouse Inn,** 4711 Fiftieth Avenue, (250) 774–3911. Dining room and lounge. Moderate.

To the B.C.–Yukon Border

The distance between Fort St. John and the Yukon border is 940 km/564 mi. The only community of any size en route is Fort Nelson, which is about halfway, although there are some small villages. Your best bet is to make sure, while you are in Fort St. John, that your vehicle is fit for the trip—the town is a good place for getting supplies, gas, and whatever else you need. The Alaska Highway going through B.C. is paved, except for a stretch just before the Yukon border. Take advantage of the accommodations and hot meals available in Fort Nelson. It's a good stopping point if you're there in the afternoon; night driving can be hazardous because of the wild animals that cross the road. Two provincial parks with facilities—Muncho Lake and Stone Mountain—are located on the highway north of Fort Nelson. After you enter the Yukon, the first town of any size is Watson Lake, where there are accommodations, food, and auto and other services.

Winter Sports in British Columbia

British Columbia has more opportunities for enjoying winter sports than almost any other of the provinces in Western Canada. Within B.C. you can ski downhill or cross country, be dropped off on virgin powder from helicopters or snowcats, or go ice skating, snowshoeing, ice climbing, or fishing. The province's infrastructure of resorts, hotels, restaurants, transportation systems, après-ski activities, shops, and ski schools is among the best on the continent. If you haven't yet enjoyed winter in B.C., you've got a cornucopia of treats and thrills waiting for you.

Downhill Skiing

Mount Washington, in the Courtney area of Vancouver Island, (250) 338–1386. Twenty downhill runs; lodges and condos; ski school; après-ski dining and entertainment; by-the-week packages; equipment rentals.

Grouse, in North Vancouver, a few minutes from city center (see Chapter 5), (604) 984–0661. All runs are lighted until 11:00 P.M.; Bavarian beer garden; snowmaking; Canadian Ski Instructor's Alliance (CSIA) ski school; 1,110-m/3,641-ft summit; close to city accommodations and restaurants.

Whistler/Blackcomb, one of the top ski resort areas in Western Canada; more than sixty marked runs for every level of expertise (see Chapter 5 for more details); call (604) 932–4222 or (800) 944–7853 for information on packages and hotel reservations.

Hemlock Valley, in Hemlock Valley, two hours from Vancouver city center via Highway 7, (604) 797–4411. More than 200 ha/ 500 acres of skiing terrain; Winter Carnival; helicopter skiing; Hemlock Inn; ski school; night skiing.

Apex Alpine, in the Okanagan region (Penticton area), (250) 493–2880; (800) 387–2739. Thirty-six runs; 610-m/2,000-ft vertical drop; ski school; ice rink; hot tubs; condos.

Big White Ski Resort, in the Okanagan region (Kelowna area), (250) 765–8888; (800) 663–2772. Forty-one runs; 579-m/1,900-ft vertical drop; ski packages; ski school; day-care facility.

Silver Star Mountain Resort, in the Okanagan region (Vernon area), (250) 542–0224; (800) 663–4431. Thirty-two runs; accommodations; equipment rentals; ski school.

Sun Peaks Resort, in the Okanagan region (Kamloops area), (250) 578–7222; (800) 663–2838. There's a 945-m/3,100-ft vertical drop; forty-six runs; ski school. Several new mountaintop hotels have been constructed in recent years.

White Water, in the southeastern corner of the province, the Selkirk Range of the Canadian Rockies, (250) 354–4944. Eighteen runs; helicopter skiing on virgin powder; accommodations in Nelson.

Red Mountain, in the Trail area, (250) 362–7700. You'll find an 853-m/2,800-ft vertical drop; powdery alpine meadows; hot racing slopes; ski school; equipment rentals; helicopter skiing.

Panorama Resort, located south of the Bugaboos, (250) 342–6941; (800) 663–2929. There's a 1,158-m/3,800-ft vertical drop; cross-country trails; helicopter skiing; luxury accommodations; outdoor hot tubs.

Fairmont Hot Springs, in the heart of the Canadian Rockies, (250) 345–6311. Runs for all levels of expertise; cross-country trails; excellent accommodations; ski packages.

Kimberley Resort, which in the Rockies is called Little Bavaria because of German-style architecture in the town and restaurants, (250) 427–4881; (800) 667–0871. Seven-hundred-meter/2,300-ft vertical drop; longest night skiing run in North America; ski school; plenty of accommodations, entertainment, and restaurants.

Fernie Snow Valley, in the Canadian Rockies near Cranbrook, (250) 423–9221. You'll find a 732-m/2,400-ft vertical drop; excellent accommodations, restaurants, and entertainment in the area; ski school.

Helicopter Skiing

Helicopters take you to mountaintops where there are unlimited runs of virgin powder. Top professional guides show you the way down, and the safety standards in equipment and on the runs are among the best in the world. Helicopter skiing in the Canadian Rockies is one of the thrilling wonders of this world. The following organizations offer helicopter skiing in the mountain ranges of British Columbia:

Kootenay Helicopter Skiing, the Selkirks and Monashees; (250) 265–3121 or (800) 663–0100.

Heli-Ski Panorama, the Purcells; (250) 342–3889 or (800) 661–6060.

Selkirk Wilderness Skiing, the Selkirks and Monashees; (250) 366–4424 or (800) 799–3499.

Snowcat Skiing

A twelve-passenger snowcat vehicle will take a group to the top of a virgin powder run—no lifts, no crowds, the mountain mostly to yourselves. This type of skiing offers all the advantages of helicopter skiing without the helicopter.

Selkirk Wilderness Skiing, five-day, all-inclusive packages; (250) 366–4424 or (800) 799–3499.

Nordic and Cross-Country Skiing

British Columbia has some of the most spectacular ski-touring areas in North America. Within or near the national and provincial parks are bed-and-breakfasts, ranches, motels, and resorts. A number of resorts have their own cross-country skiing trails.

National parks. Yoho, Kootenay, and Glacier.

Provincial parks. Assiniboine, Garibaldi, Manning, Alice Lake, Brandywine Falls, Champion Lakes, Kokanee Creek, Maclure Lake, Nancy Greene, Strathcona, Top of the World, Wells Gray, Whiteswan, Beaton, Bugaboo Glacier, Cypress, Kitsumkalum Mountain, Kokanee Glacier, Mount Seymour, Stageleap, Ten Mile Lake, Wasa, West Lake, and Mount Robson.

Call Tourism British Columbia at (800) 663–6000 for more information on recreation in these parks.

CHAPTER 5

Vancouver: Camelot by the Pacific

Gulf Islands · Whistler Resort Area

Vancouver in Brief

You will lose your heart to Vancouver with just one look. The spectacular setting—blue ocean surrounded by snowcapped mountains that rush to the water's edge—is simply breathtaking.

The largest city in Western Canada, Vancouver is a transportation, manufacturing, financial, and media hub that has grown to international importance in the Pacific Rim. All this activity might lend the impression that the city has an all-work-and-no-play mentality. Nothing could be further from the truth. The boat-filled marinas, long sandy beaches, and outdoor cafes explain why so many people come to Vancouver to work *and* play.

Vancouver has a mild climate most of the year, although it gets bountiful doses of rain from time to time, as does nearby Seattle. The hazards of snow and ice rarely plague drivers here.

Vancouver offers skiing and sailing, both within an hour of each other. Its backyard sprawls over millions of acres of thick forests, tall mountains, wild rivers, and pure lakes. Some, such as Native healers and scientists, say the legendary but shy Big Foot lives nearby in the deep woods.

Among the noteworthy people who have lived in the Vancouver area are the artist/writer Emily Carr; Malcolm Lowry, author of *Under the Volcano;* and Ayn Rand, the famous writer and promoter of rugged individualism. The best of contemporary Canadian architecture has its roots here through such talented designers as Arthur Erickson.

Vancouver is a city of opera, symphony, rock and roll, live theater, motion picture and television production, gourmet restaurants, diverse museums, and folk arts and crafts. Among the TV shows shot on location here have been *The X-Files, Millennium, The Commish, Stargate-1,* and a host of made-for-TV movies and feature films such as *Stakeout, Rambo,* and *Runaway.* Vancouverites love sports—hockey, soccer, lawn bowling, golf, sailing, cricket. They are prime candidates for a major-league baseball team. They are fanatical about sports oddities also, and in a nearby suburb, during summer, there is an annual belly-flopping contest in which men weighing in the 160-kg/350-lb range jump into a pool to determine who can make the biggest splash.

To learn what really makes Vancouver special, you must return to the water. Boats are the lifeblood of the city, and sightseers can hop on and off the passenger ferries that cross the harbor and the little water taxis that ply False Creek. You can take harbor cruises, rent a sea kayak or sailboat for a day, walk the seawall of Stanley Park, or roll your blanket onto one of the many beaches and gaze at the vast grandeur of the Pacific Ocean.

Attractions you must not miss include the historic buildings and shops of Gastown, where Vancouver was born in 1876; Granville Island, with its yachts, houseboats, boutiques, cafes, art galleries, and lively market; and Stanley Park, a 405-ha/1,000-acre urban rain forest crisscrossed with walking and cycling paths. The Stanley Park Aquarium, Canada's largest, has 8,000 aquatic creatures including beluga whales. A perimeter seawall is regularly filled with pedestrians and cyclists.

If it's panoramas you seek, take the ski lift, Canada's largest tramway, to the top of Grouse Mountain in North Vancouver. Or drive the Seaview Highway that weaves along Howe Sound, a spectacularly beautiful fjord north of the city.

But the true panorama of Vancouver is found on the streets. The city's diverse mix of cultures offers a vast array of tastes, smells, and sounds—the quiet classical Chinese garden in the heart of bustling Chinatown, the carnival atmosphere of Granville Island, the Greek taverns on Broadway that abut natural food stores, and the Italian trattorias on Commercial Avenue. Vancouver is a thriving, exuberant international city.

One of Vancouver's quirks is its highways—or lack of them. This is the only major city in North America that does not have a freeway running through the city. Trans-Canada Highway 1 skirts it to the north; Highway 99 from the south becomes a two-lane road when it crosses Oak Street Bridge and enters the city.

What's a tourist to do? Do as the locals. If you drive, be patient. Traffic moves at a glacial pace. Take the bus, the Seabus, the Sky Train, or walk. Vancouver is one of the most walkable cities in North America. From your downtown hotel location, you'll be within walking distance of almost all the major attractions, including Stanley Park, the Vancouver Art Gallery, Granville Island, and Robson Street (or Robsonstrasse, as the locals call it).

If time allows, take a day trip (or two) to visit Whistler Resort, situated at the base of Blackcomb and Whistler Mountains. In summer you can hike, canoe, cycle, play golf, or indulge in a spa day at Chateau Whistler. In winter it's a skier's paradise.

Take a drive into the Fraser River Valley, east of the city, to visit Fort Langley, a reconstructed Hudson's Bay Company trading post furnished in 1850s style. Sentries in period costume patrol the palisades. The Trans-Canada Highway follows the spectacular canyon of the Fraser River into the interior of British Columbia. At Hells Gate, about an hour and a half outside the city, you can ride a tram across a narrow gorge and view the river as it thunders through this narrow passage.

So what does make Vancouver special? Not any one tangible thing. It is something far more valuable: a continuing freshness combined with ongoing potential.

A Brief Look at Vancouver's History

The first inhabitants of the area that is now the city of Vancouver were the Coast Salish people, noted for their high culture. Their descendants continue to live near the city, keeping alive an honored heritage through their arts and crafts. Captain James Cook was the first European to sail along here, and a few years later Captain George Vancouver mapped this part of the northwest coast and claimed what he saw for George III, King of England— hence the name Strait of Georgia, the strait on which the city bearing the explorer's name lies.

It was not until the early 1860s, however, that any significant number of people moved in to settle permanently. They were attracted by the prospect of making money in the lumber industry. In those early days Vancouver was a raw, rough, grimy, but booming logging town, inhabited by tough timber and sawmill workers, shrewd entrepreneurs, and those who made big money on the periphery, such as Gassy Jack Deighton, a colorful saloon keeper who has been immortalized in local folklore. Another economic boost came with the completion of the transcontinental railroad, which linked this burgeoning port with the great cities of Eastern Canada, such as Toronto and Montréal. Sir William Cornelius Van Horne, chairman of the Canadian Pacific Railroad, helped accelerate the city's growth as a major port by using it to ship grain from Alberta, Saskatchewan, and Manitoba to foreign buyers.

In the nineteenth century people crazed with "gold fever" sailed for fortune or misery from Vancouver up to major lodes in the Yukon and the Klondike. The opening of the Panama Canal in the early part of this century increased the city's importance as a seaport. Although the early population was mostly of British and American origin, a sizable Chinese community began to develop from among those who had helped to build the transcontinental. During succeeding years the city rapidly expanded as an influential business and population center, attracting new money and ever-increasing numbers of new people.

Unlike Montréal, Toronto, Halifax, and other Eastern Canadian cities, Vancouver has had a relatively peaceful history. It has never experienced destruction from war or the anguish of rebellion and foreign occupation, as have places in Eastern Canada.

The most exciting part of Vancouver's history is happening right now. The extraordinary success of Expo 86 was solid evidence of the city's present and future achievement. Because of its dynamism, location, climate, population, and financial strength, Vancouver is very much Canada's city of the future. Today it ranks second in economic importance, after Toronto. In little more than a hundred years, the progress of Vancouver from a rude logging camp to the bright jewel on the Pacific has been phenomenal. The use of such superlatives in Vancouver's case is not excessive.

The following are key dates and events in Vancouver's history:

1778. Captain James Cook, British explorer, sails into the area, but he keeps on going.

1792. Another Briton, Captain George Vancouver, takes possession of the area for the empire. Vancouver had been a junior officer when Cook first sailed into this part of the world.

1793. Another intrepid explorer, Alexander Mackenzie, treks to the Pacific Coast, becoming the first white person on record to journey across Canada.

1867. What is now downtown Vancouver—the West End—is sold for the minimal sum of 114 pounds, 11 shillings, and 8 pence. Today it is one of the most expensive real estate areas in North America. Also in 1867, Gassy Jack Deighton opens his saloon to satisfy thirsty lumber workers and gold seekers. Today a glitzy section of boutiques and cafes occupies this section, but it continues to be known as Gastown in Jack's honor.

1886. The town of Granville becomes a city and officially takes the name of Vancouver. During this year Vancouver is destroyed by fire in just twenty minutes. The city acquires its first fire engine more than a month later.

1887. The first passenger train arrives from Montréal.

1897. The first Vancouver ship departs for the great gold rush in the Klondike.

1907. Vancouver's stock exchange is incorporated. The Vancouver Stock Exchange merged with the Alberta Stock Exchange and is now known as the Canadian Venture Exchange, the third most important exchange in Canada.

1909. The city gets its first skyscraper. Today's city center is a forest of gleaming skyscrapers.

1915. The Vancouver Millionaires hockey team wins the coveted Stanley Cup.

1944. Vancouver and Odessa, USSR, become sister cities.

1957. Queen Elizabeth II and Prince Philip make their first of several visits to Vancouver.

1976. The University of British Columbia's outstanding Museum of Anthropology opens.

1986. Expo opens and logs twenty-two million visits, making it one of the most successful world's fairs in history. The Dr. Sun Yat-Sen Classical Chinese Gardens open in Chinatown. Vancouver celebrates its one-hundredth birthday as a city.

1987. The Vancouver Convention and Exhibition Centre, one of the largest and best equipped on the North American continent, opens.

1988 to the present. Vancouver becomes "Hollywood North" with a full schedule of major motion picture and television productions.

1990 to the present. The first Vancouver Indy Race takes place on streets around B.C. Place Stadium. It's held on Labour Day weekend.

1991. Rock star Bryan Adams buys and restores the oldest brick building in Vancouver, the Oppenheimer Brothers grocery warehouse at Columbia and Powell Streets.

1993. Vancouver is the venue for a two-day summit meeting between presidents Bill Clinton of the United States and Boris Yeltsin of Russia.

1994. The Grizzlies, Vancouver's NBA entry, opens its first season at GM Place, which play host to both the Grizzlies and the NHL's Vancouver Canucks hockey team.

1995 to the present. The old warehouse district, Yaletown, north of False Creek, is converted into the latest chic and funky "in" place with condos, bistros, and shops carved from old brick buildings.

1996. The new Vancouver International Airport terminal opens, making travel into and out of the region easier. The Open Skies Treaty opens up Canada–U.S. intercity travel.

Vancouver Today: Some Basic Facts

Vancouver is located in the southwest corner of British Columbia, about 48 km/30 mi from the U.S. border.

Vancouver itself is only 114 sq km/44 sq mi, but its metropolitan area, consisting of several municipalities, is 2,787 sq km/ 1,076 sq mi.

Vancouver is Canada's third-largest city in terms of population. The city itself has more than 500,000 residents; the metro area has nearly 1.8 million people.

Vancouver is one of North America's busiest seaports, especially for shipping raw materials produced in Canada (coal, metals, petroleum, potash, grain, timber, and others) to the industrial countries of Asia. It has companies involved in the lumber industries and in fisheries, which are mainstays of the region's economy. It is one of Canada's primary service and financial centers, in sectors such as banking and brokerage companies. Both federal and provincial governments have sizable operations in the metro area. Tourism is another large industry, with attractions and amenities among the finest anywhere.

University and medical facilities are known throughout the world for their excellence. They attract outstanding talent from throughout Canada, the United States, and other countries.

How to Get to Vancouver

A prominent North American city and Canada's door to the Pacific Rim region, Vancouver is served by major transportation companies—domestic and international airlines, transcontinental passenger rail service, buses, and cruise-ship lines from Los Angeles and Seattle (the ship itinerary usually includes the Yukon and Alaska as well). U.S. interstate and Canadian interprovincial highways, such as the Trans-Canada Highway 1, give direct, quick access to the city.

By Car

The main road to Vancouver from Eastern Canada is Trans-Canada Highway 1. The distance on the Trans-Canada, for example, from Calgary, Alberta, to Vancouver is 1,050 km/652 mi. Highway 3 is another route from the Alberta border that takes you through some beautiful country in southern British Columbia, along the border with Montana, Idaho, and Washington. From the Trans-Canada you can pick up Highway 95 a few miles north of Banff; the highway goes by Kootenay National Park and connects with Highway 3 at either Cranbrook or Fort Steele.

If you are traveling north from U.S. west coast cities, I–5 is your best route. The distance from Seattle to Vancouver is 232 km/144 mi. This adds up to a three-hour drive at 100 km/h (55 mi/h), including a stop at Canadian Customs.

A more interesting way to travel to Vancouver from the south is first to tour the magnificent Olympic National Park area of Washington (the Olympic Peninsula), then take the car ferry from Port Angeles on the Strait of Juan de Fuca to the charming capital of British Columbia, Victoria, on Vancouver Island. From Sidney take another car ferry through the Gulf Islands to the city of Vancouver (the ferry docks at Tsawwassen just south of city center, a forty-five- to sixty-minute drive). You might also want to tour Vancouver Island, which is on the open Pacific (see page 168 for more details), and return to Vancouver via car ferries from Nanaimo.

By Boat

A number of cruise-ship lines, such as Holland America, Princess, Crystal, Royal Caribbean, Celebrity, and Norwegian Cruise Lines, include Vancouver as a major port stop on their northwest coast sailings through the Inside Passage and up to Alaska. Contact your local travel agent for details and prices.

As a leading port and sailing center, Vancouver has marina facilities for visiting sailors, but docking space is especially tight during busy seasons.

By Bus

Bus transportation from U.S. and Canadian destinations arrives at and departs from the Greyhound Bus Depot at 1150 Station Street.

By Plane

The following air transportation companies provide service to Vancouver: Air Canada and Canadian Airlines (from major Canadian, U.S., and international departure points); Air B.C. and Time Air (from British Columbia towns and cities, Seattle, and Calgary); also United, Japan, Qantas, British Airways, Lufthansa, Canada 3000, Cathay Pacific, KLM, American, United, Delta, Continental, and Singapore, among others. Contact your local travel agent for schedules and fares.

Vancouver International Airport is located on Sea Island near Richmond, a short ride on Granville Street from Vancouver city center (about 19 km/12 mi; twenty-five minutes). It is one of Canada's busiest and most modern air travel facilities. Shuttle buses and cabs make frequent runs between the airport and city center. All the major car-rental companies have booths in the main terminal, which itself has an array of dining places, lounges, money-changing offices, duty-free and gift shops, and bookstores. Adjacent to the airport are many fine hotels and restaurants. When you arrive at the airport, you must clear Canadian Customs. If you're returning to the States, you can also clear U.S. Customs at the airport.

By Train

Both VIA Rail (the Canadian passenger rail system) and Amtrak (passenger trains serving U.S. destinations) provide service to Vancouver. In the case of VIA Rail, you can count on regularly scheduled service from most points east of Vancouver. You can come into Vancouver through Edmonton and Jasper National Park.

Amtrak will take you via Chicago to Seattle and through to Vancouver. Amtrak trains provide service to Seattle from U.S. West Coast cities, too. Amtrak will help you make reservations for hotels, rental cars, and tours as well.

Vancouver's rail station is located at 1150 Station Street, in the False Creek section of the city, at Main and Terminal.

How to Get Around in Vancouver

Vancouver city center, where most tourist and business activity is focused, is but a tiny part of this large metropolis. It is actually a huge peninsula. Along its north coast is a fjord known as the Burrard Inlet, which splits off into Indian Arm. To its south, the mighty Fraser River forms a delta and flows into the Strait of Georgia. Between Vancouver's Point Grey and the separate municipality of West Vancouver is English Bay, the city's broad front yard of water. Vancouver is surrounded by several municipalities that together compose Metro Vancouver—West Vancouver, North Vancouver, Burnaby, Coquitlam, New Westminster, and Richmond.

Except for side trips to certain attractions, you will probably spend most of your time in the central core of Vancouver, and so it shouldn't be too difficult to get around. Pender, Dunsmuir, Georgia, and Robson Streets, running northwest–southeast, are parallel to one another. Burrard, Hornby, Howe, Granville, Richards, Homer, Hamilton, and Cambie bisect the others at right angles. These are the main streets of Vancouver city center, where you'll find some of the major hotels, shops, office buildings, art museums, and restaurants. The best way to orient yourself is to use the Hotel Vancouver, with its green-copper mansard roof, as your center point (Robson Square here will also do). The hotel faces Georgia Street, which runs northwest toward Stanley Park. A few blocks beyond the back of the hotel is English Bay, and beyond that Vancouver Island. A few blocks past the front of the hotel is the waterfront on Burrard Inlet, the location of the new convention center and the cruise-ship docks. The nearby snow-capped mountains (Coast Mountains) that you see are north of the city. Most of the streets are nicely laid out in an easy-to-comprehend grid pattern.

Most city center attractions, including Stanley Park, can be seen the best and least expensive way on foot. Free maps are available at your hotel or at the **Vancouver Tourism Information Centre,** 200 Burrard Street, (604) 683–2000. The information center will also provide free literature and answer any questions you have about the city. It is an excellent place to start your tour of Vancouver.

Vancouver has superb public transportation to most sections of the city. **Translink** operates the city's bus system, with frequent service from 4:00 A.M. to midnight. Call (604) 521–0400 for fare

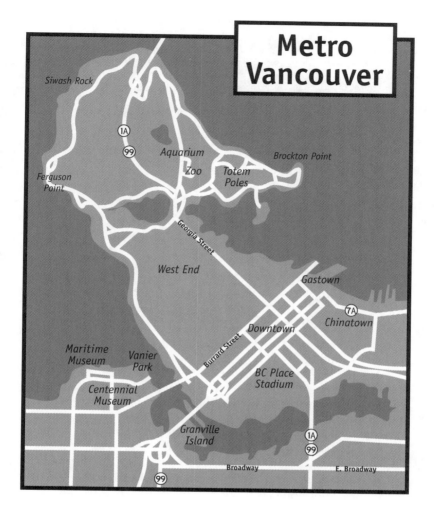

Metro
Vancouver

Siwash Rock

1A

99
Aquarium
Zoo
Totem
Poles
Brockton Point

Ferguson
Point

Georgia Street

West End

Gastown

7A
Chinatown

Downtown

Burrard Street

Maritime
Museum
Vanier
Park

BC Place
Stadium

Centennial
Museum

Granville
Island

1A
99

Broadway
E. Broadway

99

and schedule information. A Seabus—actually two 400-passenger catamarans—connects city center with North Vancouver. The sail across the Burrard Inlet takes fewer than fifteen minutes. You can take aboard a bike on weekends and holidays for a minor additional cost. The Seabus departs from the old CPR (Canadian Pacific Railroad) station near Granville Square in Vancouver city center and from Lonsdale Quay in North Vancouver. For more information call (604) 521–0400. The Seabus, part of Translink, is a great tourist attraction, but avoid weekday rush hours.

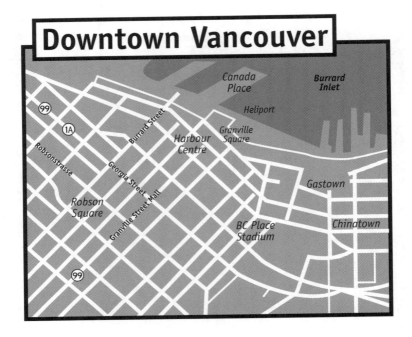

Downtown Vancouver

The public transit ALRT (Advanced Light Rapid Transit) system is run by computers, although a security officer rides along. In city center ALRT is called Skytrain, part of Translink, because it moves on elevated rails. The ALRT system takes commuters and visitors all the way from New Westminster to the waterfront at the new Convention and Exhibition Centre. The return trip takes about an hour. Call (604) 521–0400 for schedules and fares.

Taxicabs are everywhere, but nowhere when you need one the most. Have your hotel get a cab for you, or call Yellow Cab, (604) 681–1111; Black Top; (604) 731–1111, or Maclure's, (604) 731–9211. Yellow Cab, by the way, will give you a tour of the city at the meter rate.

Useful Information

Emergencies: Police, fire, ambulance, dial 911.
Doctor: (604) 733–7758 (College of Physicians and Surgeons will provide referrals to foreign-language-speaking doctors); after 5:00 P.M., 911.

Dentist: College of Dental Surgeons of B.C., (604) 736–3621.

Poison: (604) 682–5050 or 682–2344.

Rape: (604) 872–8212.

Crisis: (604) 872–3311

Veterinarian: (604) 734–7744.

Canadian Coast Guard (search and rescue): (800) 567–5111.

Vancouver General Hospital: 855 West Twelfth Avenue, (604) 875–4111.

Road service (twenty-four-hour service): Must be a member of an auto club; (604) 293–2222 in Vancouver.

Time zone: Pacific (three-hour difference from New York, Toronto, and Montréal).

Telephone area code: 604.

Climate: Sunny but not very hot summers; usually dry, invigorating weather. Rainy in autumn and winter, but very little snow at or near sea level. For the latest report on road conditions, call (604) 299–9000, ext. 7623 (ROAD) from Vancouver (900) 565–4997 from anywhere in British Columbia for a charge of 75 cents per minute. Or visit www.th.gov.bc.ca/bchighways.

Special clothing: Bring a light raincoat, a hat, and an umbrella, plus a warm jacket and sweater for evenings.

Local holiday: B.C. Day, celebrated the first Monday in August.

Mass media: The *Province* (morning newspaper) and the *Vancouver Sun* (morning newspaper); all other major national and international newspapers and magazines are available at newsstands. Both Canadian and American television, including cable programming, and radio are available at the flick of the dial.

Most hotels list the addresses of places of worship and their schedule of services.

Special Tours Outside Vancouver City Center

Royal Hudson Steam Train

Board at B.C. Rail Station, 1311 West First Street in North Vancouver; call (604) 984–5246 for schedule and fares (reservations are advised).

The Royal Hudson, a vintage steam train, takes you along the beautiful coast north of Vancouver. This is a two-hour, 64-km/40-mi trip to the lumber community of Squamish. You pass by

Special Events

January/February
Chinese New Year Celebrations in Chinatown

March
Spring Celebration on Granville Island

April
B.C. Great Outdoors Show
International Wine Festival

May
Vancouver International Marathon
Vancouver International Children's Festival

June
North Vancouver Folkfest

July
Bard on the Beach Shakespeare Festival
Vancouver International Chamber Music Festival
Vancouver Folk Music Festival

August
International Airshow at Abbotsford (biannual)

August/September
Pacific National Exhibition (PNE), a terrific agricultural and industrial fair held annually since 1910. You'll find numerous exhibits and demonstrations, top-line entertainment, a demolition derby, and a midway. The PNE is held at Exhibition Park and operates from mid-August to Labour Day.

September
Vancouver Indy Car Race (Labour Day weekend)
Air Canada Championship (PGA)

October
Vancouver International Film Festival

November
Christmas Fair

December
Christmas Craft Fairs in various parts of the city
Carol Ships, music by school choirs from boats in the harbor

Horseshoe Bay with its many islands (Gambier and Bowen Islands), near tall Douglas firs and the Coast Mountains. The views are spectacular; don't forget to bring your camera. If you let your imagination take wing, you could very well be in the fjord country of Norway. Squamish, the final destination, has restaurants and gift shops.

You can return on the Royal Hudson or take a bus to a dock where you board the MV *Britannia,* a comfortable boat with such amenities as a snack bar offering sandwiches, soft drinks, and beer. The MV *Britannia* sails along the coast back to Vancouver, but the perspectives of the landscapes and seascapes from its decks are entirely different from the views out the windows of the Royal Hudson. Keep a sharp eye out for bald eagles. The round trip consumes the better part of a day, but it's a memorable experience for all ages. To book a rail/boat trip, call Harbor Cruises at (604) 688–7246.

Marine Drives

There are two marine drives: one that goes along the same basic route as the Royal Hudson, and another that goes around Point Grey on the opposite side of English Bay. When you take the **Northern Marine Drive,** you can visit Lighthouse Park; explore many of the small communities along the coast; stop a while and cast a line for fish; take a ferry over to Nanaimo on Vancouver Island; hike trails in thick, primeval woods; and see awesome waterfalls on the way to Squamish via Highway 99. While on this northern route you can also drive—along with taking a couple of extra ferry rides—as far as Powell River on the mainland. The road stops a few miles above Powell River. After that are nothing but wilderness and a few coastal Indian reserves until Prince Rupert, B.C., and Alaska. If you wish to see more of this exceptionally beautiful northern coast, take a cruise-ship voyage or a B.C. ferry from the northern tip of Vancouver Island through the Inside Passage to Prince Rupert. Such a voyage can be one of the great adventures of North America. The town of Squamish, north of Horseshoe Bay, is about as far as most people go in their brief forays from Vancouver. But if you continue inland on Highway 99, you will come to one of British Columbia's prize summer and ski resort areas, Whistler.

The second marine drive is less adventuresome but not without its rewards. This route is officially called **North West Marine Drive** and melds into **South West Marine Drive**. It goes around Point Grey, offering wonderful views of English Bay, the skyline of Vancouver city center, the Strait of Georgia, Vancouver Island, and the Gulf Islands. Along the way you will pass a number of beaches for swimming, sunbathing (including nude sunbathing), windsurfing, and picnicking. You will also circle the campus of the University of British Columbia, with its many museums, including the fabulous Museum of Anthropology; the exquisite Nitobe Memorial Garden (Japanese); and the extensive University Endowment Lands, where you can hike in the midst of botanical splendor. You can reach North West Marine Drive via Burrard and Cornwall. The private homes along the way are extraordinary, and so are their gardens and landscaping. They evoke envy in even the most innocent. There are several golf courses along the South West Marine Drive section; McCleery is open to the public.

Victoria

No visit to Vancouver would be complete without a side trip to Victoria, the tranquil, blossom-festooned capital of British Columbia. Regularly scheduled ferries connect the two cities at Tsawwassen, from Vancouver city center via Highways 99 and 17. (See chapter 6 for a complete description of Victoria.)

Gulf Islands

Reach these islands via ferries from Tsawwassen terminal; call B.C. Ferries at (604) 444–2890 for schedules and fares (reservations required).

In this part of the Strait of Georgia, the Canadian–U.S. international border zigzags to the extent that it's often difficult for a sailor to figure out just which country he or she is in on any given tack. Also here are numerous small islands, some belonging to British Columbia and others to the state of Washington. The Gulf Islands are Canadian, and the San Juan Islands are American, because they are nearest the Strait of Juan de Fuca, which separates the tip of Vancouver Island from the north shore of the Olympic Peninsula. If it all sounds confusing, it is, until you look at a map.

In addition to local fishing families, many professionals and people with artistic bents live on the Gulf Islands, which are small, rural islands tucked away from the frenetic pace of the city but also close enough to it that you can easily go into Vancouver for a

Flight-Seeing by Helijet

A terrific way to see Vancouver, parts of the lower mainland, and the San Juan Islands is to take a flight-seeing excursion by helijet. In a mere thirty minutes, you'll depart from downtown Vancouver and watch major highways turn into winding pieces of string. Lion's Gate Bridge will look like a necklace slung across Burrard Inlet, and you'll see pleasure boats leave white scribbles of wake upon the water.

All too quickly you pass over the farmland patchwork fields of Delta and Ladner, and soon you are over the water. Like friendly sea monsters, small islands thrust upward in a series of dark lumps, and sailboats are small as thorns on the water.

You'll land in Victoria, where a shuttle bus will take you to the Empress Hotel on Victoria's waterfront.

For more information, reservations, and fares, call Helijet Airways at (604) 273–1414.

gourmet meal, a concert, or a stage show. You can visit these lovely islands by car, but a bike or good walking shoes are the best way to explore them. Generally, the people who live on the islands are friendly, and the institution of the general store on some of them continues to be the center of gossip and simple fun. The many beaches, cliffs, and forest parks are good areas to see bald eagles and sea otters. Visit the studios of artisans and buy their elegant wares. The primary islands and their ferry ports are **Galiano Island** (Montague Harbour and Sturdies Bay), **Mayne Island** (Village Bay), **Saturna Island** (Saturna), **North Pender Island** (Otter Bay), and **Salt Spring Island** (Long Harbour, Vesuvius Bay, and Fulford Harbour).

There are good accommodations on the Gulf Islands. For example, the **Cliff Bodega Bed & Breakfast,** on Galiano Island, (250) 539–2260, offers log chalets with fireplaces and stained-glass windows, kitchen facilities, and two trout ponds, all on 10 ha/ 25 acres of meadows and trees overlooking mountains and sea, moderate. Also consider **Surf Lodge** on Gabriola Island, (250) 247–9231, moderate; **Cusheon Lake Resort** on Salt Spring Island, (250) 537–9629, moderate; and **Mallard's Mill Inn** (250) 537–1011 on Salt Spring Island, moderate. Some have dining and lounge facilities and recreational offerings, such as horseback riding, scuba diving, tennis, swimming pools, golf, and trout fishing. For more information on accommodations on the Gulf Islands, call Tourism British Columbia at (604) 450–5622.

Whistler Resort Area

This area, located 121 km/75 mi north of Vancouver via Highway 99, is about a two-hour drive. (Use caution driving, because the road can be hazardous at times.)

The Whistler Resort Area has the best skiing closest to Metro Vancouver. Whistler has become one of the most fashionable four-season resort areas in North America, attracting scores of the rich and famous as well as ordinary folks. It features the highest vertical drop of any mountain in North America—1,609 m/5,208 ft, at Blackcomb Mountain. It has chairlifts, T-bars, and a gondola to take you to the top. There are more than sixty runs, with the longest being 11 km/7 mi, and 50 percent of them are in the intermediate skill range. There are also trails for cross-country skiing and snowshoeing. Equipment rentals are available at Whistler Village Sports and other outlets. The Whistler area gets about 11.4 m/450 in of snow a year, making for a long, satisfying season. Helicopter skiing is also offered here during winter, and helicopter hiking in summer. These nimble whirlybirds take you high up on the Coast Mountains, and you come back down on your own over virgin snow or on foot through magnificent forests, picking a bouquet of wildflowers on the way. For more information and rates, call Whistler Heli-Skiing/Hiking, Ltd., (604) 932–4105.

In the warm-weather months, the Whistler area is a great getaway for fishing, horseback riding, tennis, golf—an eighteen-hole Arnold Palmer–designed course, Furry Creek (604–932–4544); a Robert Trent Jones II course at the Château Whistler (604–938–2095); a Jack Nicklaus Course, Nicklaus North (604–938–9898)—and boating. The Whistler Mountain gondola gives a splendid high-rise ride, with the view from the top being outstanding. Dine at the restaurant on the summit or bring your own picnic.

Both mountains operate mountaintop sight-seeing and dining facilities. Blackcomb utilizes a covered, high-speed quad chair, and Whistler operates a ten-passenger gondola. In its setup and ambience, Whistler is similar in concept to Vail and Aspen in Colorado, attracting the well heeled, the young and beautiful, and just plain folks.

Whistler can be reached from Vancouver by train. For more information call B.C. Rail at (604) 984–5246. Maverick Coach

Whistler-Area Accommodations

Hotels in the Whistler area include:

Château Whistler (604) 938–8000
Blackcomb Lodge (604) 932–4155
Delta Whistler Resort (604) 932–1982
Crystal Lodge (604) 932–2221
Glacier Lodge (604) 932–2882
Holiday Inn Sunspree (604) 938–0878
Le Chamois (604) 932–2882
Listel Whistler Lodge (604) 932–1133
Tantalus Lodge (604) 932–4146

Bed-and-Breakfasts include:

Cedar Springs Lodge (604) 938–8007
Chalet Luise Pension Inn (604) 932–4187
Durlacher Hof Alpine Inn (604) 932–1924
Edelweiss Pension Inn (604) 932–3641
Lorimer Ridge Pension Inn (604) 938–9722

Lines and Greyhound provide bus transportation from downtown Vancouver; call (604) 662–8051.

Recommended places to stay in the Whistler area are numerous, for there is a wide selection of hotels, bed-and-breakfasts, and condos from which to choose. All are within easy reach of Whistler's recreational facilities. All hotels have restaurants or are next to restaurants, and the condos have full living facilities. Condos are spread out throughout the village and valley. Your best bet is to contact Whistler Central Reservations (800–944–7853 or, in Vancouver, 604–664–5625) for information and options.

Recommended nonhotel restaurants include Il Caminetto di Umberto, (604) 932–4442, for exquisite northern Italian cooking (moderate); The Keg, (604) 932–5151 for steaks, (moderate); Ristorante Araxi, (604) 932–4540, for northern Mediterranean cuisine (moderate); Val d'Isere, (604) 932–4666, for continental (moderate to expensive). For swinging nightlife try Crystal's Lounge, (604) 932–2221, in the Crystal Lodge, with live entertainment on weekends; Garfinkle's, (604) 932–2323, for classic rock; the Longhorn Saloon, (604) 932–5999, with live entertainment. One of the best places for shopping is in the Château Whistler, where you'll find many shops in the concourse.

During the warm, dry-weather months, if you want to keep touring this beautiful, mountain- and lake-strewn part of the province, continue heading north on Highway 99 until you reach the town of Lillooet. From here go south on Highway 12 to the community of Lytton, where you pick up Trans-Canada Highway 1. Once you are on the Trans-Canada, you can easily come back to Vancouver or move east toward the great national parks of the Rockies (Banff and Jasper) and the cities of Calgary and Edmonton. Because of dangerous road conditions, this ordinarily pleasant tour beyond Whistler is not recommended in winter or during any prolonged rainy period. The distance from Whistler to Lytton is about 195 km/105 mi.

Touring Services

Vancouver is a delightful and easy city to explore on your own and on foot, but there may be times when you want to let someone else do the driving. The following companies offer sight-seeing tours of Vancouver and nearby attractions:

Gray Line of Vancouver, (604) 879–3363. Free pickup from any downtown hotel. Trips to the Capilano and Grouse Mountain areas, Stanley Park, Victoria and Butchart Gardens; there's also a Royal Hudson/MV *Britannia* trip.

BC Rail Cariboo Prospector, (604) 984–5246. Daily rail trips to Whistler and Lillooet.

SS *Beaver* Cruises, (604) 682–7284, located at Coal Harbour. This replica of B.C.'s first steamship (1835), built in 1966, provides day and evening cruises daily during summer; it is also available for charters.

Pacific Coach Lines, (604) 662–7575, makes pickups at leading hotels. Tours of Metro Vancouver and Victoria, and shuttle service between Vancouver and Victoria.

Harbor Cruises Royal Hudson and MV *Britannia*, (604) 688–7246. Ride the steam train through gorgeous scenery to Howe Sound and Squamish, and cruise back to Vancouver on a ship. One of the best tours in Vancouver.

Harbour Air Seaplanes, (604) 688–1277. See Vancouver and the magnificent surrounding scenery from on high in a seaplane.

Helijet Airways, (604) 273–1414. Shuttle service between Vancouver and Victoria.

Neighborhoods

Four special neighborhoods are among Vancouver's most popular attractions: Chinatown, Granville Island, Gastown, and Robson Square/Robsonstrasse. These are walking places where discoveries are made and pleasures taken at a leisurely pace. To miss visiting them is to dismiss a significant part of the Vancouver experience.

Chinatown

Vancouver has the second largest Chinatown in North America—although the Chinatowns of Los Angeles and Toronto will soon rival Vancouver's in population size (San Francisco's is still the first in size). Vancouver's Chinatown is located just east of city center, a twenty-minute walk from the Hotel Vancouver/Vancouver Art Gallery area. Pender, Keefer, Main, Gore, and Carrall are the principal streets in this section. The architecture of many of the buildings is reminiscent of that of the Orient. Both the Chinese Cultural Centre and Dr. Sun Yat-Sen Classical Chinese Garden are worthwhile places to visit. Chinatown has many restaurants serving the varied cuisine of this most ancient culture—Cantonese, Mandarin, Szechuan, and Vietnamese. There are also plenty of dim sum places. The best part of Chinatown is exploring it on foot, poking in and out of Chinese grocery stores, curio shops, and herbal medicine stores. If you take a car, you should expect difficulty in finding a place to park, particularly on Sunday. Exploring Vancouver's Chinatown is a wonderful experience, and most of the people who live and work here will welcome your presence.

Granville Island

Granville Island is in fact a peninsula in the False Creek area of Vancouver. Only a few minutes from the city center, it is located under Granville Street Bridge. Parking is limited, especially on weekends, because the island is a favorite spot for locals. Take the #51 bus from downtown, or the False Creek Ferries (water taxis).

Until the early 1970s Granville Island was a grubby industrial area. The city fathers, inspired by such markets as Fanueil Hall in Boston, launched a major initiative to transform the area, and a new people-oriented community was the result.

The Granville Island Public Market is one of its major attractions; here you can buy almost every kind of food you like, from fresh basil to freshly caught or smoked salmon. You can rent a boat here, visit the galleries of the Emily Carr College of Art and

Design, play tennis, fish in Alder Bay, see plays at three different theaters, and watch potters, printmakers, glassblowers, and goldsmiths create beautiful things you can purchase. Granville Island has a hotel and several seafood restaurants and cocktail lounges, and many excellent views of the harbor and city. It's a pleasant place within the city but removed from it by a more low-key attitude. The little Aquabus Ferries operating from the foot of Hornby Street and the False Creek Ferries from the Aquatic Centre make frequent runs to and from Granville Island seven days a week year-round.

Gastown

Gassy Jack Deighton, the local saloon proprietor mentioned earlier, bequeathed Gastown its unusual name. Once a rough-and-tumble area frequented by lumberjacks and seafarers, Gastown today is one of the most interesting areas in city center. Water, Cordova, Columbia, Richards, and Cambie are the main streets that run through Gastown. A statue of Gassy Jack in Maple Tree Square depicts him standing on a barrel of liquor near the spot where his saloon was located. At Water and Cambie Streets is a steam clock, the world's first. It blows its whistle on the quarter hour, delighting anyone passing by. Here you can browse in boutiques and unusual shops, take a bite at small restaurants and comfortable cafes, and wander in what was once skid row.

Robson Square and Robsonstrasse

Robson Square is the heart of Vancouver city center. Facing Georgia Street is the Vancouver Art Gallery. Behind it and sandwiched between Hornby and Howe Streets is the 2-block-long Arthur Erickson–designed complex that houses law courts, government offices, restaurants, a food fair, shops, an ice-skating rink, and a theater.

Robsonstrasse, or Robson Street (it crosses the middle of Robson Square), received its Teutonic name from German-speaking people who frequented the many shops that catered to their special tastes in food, fashions, and publications. Along Robsonstrasse you can buy all kinds of sausages and dark breads and the latest magazines published west of the Rhine River. This is also a street of fashionable and expensive boutiques. Strolling down the Robsonstrasse, chomping on wurst-on-rye, and eyeing Paris gowns priced in the thousands is chic and fun to do when bored with all else in attraction- and entertainment-rich Vancouver.

Yaletown

Yaletown, a rehabilitated former warehouse area adjacent to the old Expo 86 fairgrounds along False Creek, is the city's latest "in" place. As you read this, condos are being converted from warehouses and restaurants are being built from merchandise depots.

Located north of Pacific Boulevard and with the main activity on Mainland Street, Hamilton, and Davie, the area's small shops and new high-rise condos are part of the new development of the old Expo grounds along and north of Pacific Boulevard.

Parks and Gardens

Because of its long growing season (as compared with those of other parts of Canada), its relatively mild climate, its high amount of rainfall, and the botanical knack of its citizens, Vancouver has some of the most lavish parks and gardens in North America. This penchant to grow plants and flowers and to manipulate their arrangement stems partly from the British and Japanese gardening influences that are so strongly expressed here. Gardening mania is everywhere, in both public and private places. Lawns surrounding homes appear so uniformly perfect that you'd think there must be an inspector going around measuring the length of grass and comparing its lush color against some official chart. At any rate, however the landscaping is accomplished, one of the great joys of visiting Vancouver is smelling its lovely flowers (even roses in December) and walking among its giant trees.

Stanley Park, north of city center, between Burrard Inlet on the east and English Bay to the west. You haven't completed your visit to Vancouver if you haven't been through Stanley Park (named in honor of Governor-General Lord Stanley). This magnificent park, all 405 ha/1,000 acres of it, lies right next to Vancouver city center and is a few minutes' walk from most of the top hotels. Established for the public's enjoyment in 1888, Stanley Park is one of the largest and most beautiful city parks in North America. You can walk or jog over its forested trails without worrying about cutting through the squads of muggers that frequent many other urban parks. It's on a peninsula that points to West and North Vancouver on the other shore. The city's famous Lion's Gate Bridge connects these communities with city center at Stanley Park.

The attractions within the park are many and varied. Regardless of your age, there's something pleasant for you here. The children's petting zoo, Rainforest Train, and sensational aquarium are well worth visiting. In addition, there are trails through tall Douglas firs and western red cedars. A seawall walk that surrounds the park has a seaside part for walkers and a forestside part for bikers and in-line skaters. It gives access to beaches for swimming and sunbathing and other areas for splendid views. This 9.8-km-/5.8-mi-long seawall was built under the supervision of master stonemason James Cunningham, who worked on it for forty years, from the 1920s to the late 1960s—even after his formal retirement—as an expression of his desire to bring this unique project closer to completion. Also within Stanley Park is a lawn-bowling club that welcomes visitors, a display of First Nations totem poles (carved by Haida Kwakiutl artisans), and a small zoo of mammals. The charming Teahouse Restaurant, a Victorian garden house, is appreciated by Vancouverites and visitors alike. Take your favorite person here; sunset is a perfectly romantic time. You can take a car tour of the park and stop for a picnic. More vigorous souls can rent bikes, including tandems, or in-line skates for enjoying the park; Spokes Bicycle Rentals, 1798 West Georgia provides the wheels.

Perhaps the best experience of Stanley Park can be had by going on a solitary walk among the giant trees and long ferns of the Northwest. You feel as if you are in the Garden of Eden and light-years from a bustling civilization. Every once in a while, you stop and remember that civilization is just beyond the treetops, and then, reluctant to leave, you find your pace slowing.

Queen Elizabeth Park, off Cambie Street, a few miles south of city center; best to take a taxi. From the highest hill at Queen Elizabeth Park you have the second best view of the skyline of Vancouver (the best being from the top of Grouse Mountain). Queen Elizabeth Park, named for the present monarch, contains superior botanical displays, with sunken gardens and creatively designed floral and shrubbery displays everywhere you walk. The floral exhibits within the park are so beautiful that it is hard to imagine this site was once a dismal rock quarry. For the convenience of visitors, the park has a restaurant Seasons in the Park, picnic areas, tennis courts, and the Bloedel Conservatory.

Bloedel Conservatory, in Queen Elizabeth Park. Open daily, except Christmas. Admission is charged. The Bloedel Conservatory sits on the highest hill within the jurisdictional limits of Vancouver. It is from here that you get the dramatic view of the city skyline with its background of snowcapped mountains. On the plaza surrounding the conservatory is a huge sculpture by Henry

Moore. In the morning on a nice day, it is not unusual to see a number of elderly Chinese men and women performing solitary tai chi chuan exercises that are close to ballet in their grace and elegance. The Bloedel building itself is a Buckminster Fuller–style geodesic dome, inside of which are tropical and desert environments. Each one has its indigenous plants and flowers. A wide variety of tropical birds fly around the space at will. Bloedel is the park's pièce de résistance.

Nitobe Memorial Gardens, on the University of British Columbia campus, near the Museum of Anthropology. Open daily during summer and weekdays the rest of the year. Admission is charged. Nitobe is a perfect example of Japanese skill and artistry in botany and landscape architecture. Exceptional balance and harmony are achieved through the arrangement of plantings (Japanese flowering shrubs and trees) within a limited area. There are also classical Japanese accents, such as a teahouse (for display only), a curved bridge, a gazebo overlooking a tranquil pond alive with prize carp, and a stone pagoda memorial in honor of Inazo Nitobe, the garden's benefactor. Inazo Nitobe was one of Japan's representatives to the League of Nations and a major force for linking the best interests of the nations of Asia with those of North America. His remains are interred in Victoria, British Columbia.

VanDusen Botanical Gardens, located at Thirty-seventh Avenue and Oak Street. Open daily. Admission charged. The VanDusen Gardens are famous for walks thickly flanked by pink, purple, red, and white rhododendrons. There is a wide assortment of trees, shrubs, flowers, and other plants, all well labeled. Band concerts are held within the park during summer. There is a restaurant, and **MacMillan Bloedel Place** houses exhibits telling the fascinating story of the Northwest Pacific Coast lumber and paper industries.

Lighthouse Park, via Marine Drive in West Vancouver. Free. Lighthouse Park, a few minutes' drive from city center, offers wonderful woodland and sea-cliff walks. Site of picturesque Point Atkinson Lighthouse, this is a virgin forest of 61-m/200-ft fir trees that are some 2,500 years old. While hiking over the park's 13 km/8 mi of trails, keep a sharp eye out for bald eagles swooping to their nests in the trees. There are great views of the ships in

Vancouver Beaches

The following public beaches for swimming, sunbathing, sailboarding, and picnicking are located in Vancouver:

Point Grey. Kitsilano Beach, Jericho Beach, Locarno Beach, Spanish Banks Beach, and Wreck Beach (nude).

Stanley Park. English Bay Beach, Second Beach (saltwater pool in this area), Third Beach.

Most have facilities for picnics (tables, fireplaces) and can be reached by public transportation. Some have food concessions.

English Bay, Vancouver city center, and Point Grey, where the campus of the University of British Columbia is located. You can climb or sunbathe on the rocks and enjoy a picnic in this exquisite wilderness setting.

Grouse Mountain Recreational Area, in North Vancouver, via Highways 1A and 99, over Lion's Gate Bridge and then to Capilano Road; (604) 984–0661. Admission is charged for the aerial tramway ride to the top.

From the top of Grouse Mountain, 1,200 m/4,000 ft high, you have the best view in this region of the lower mainland and greater Vancouver. You can see all of Metro Vancouver, a good swath of Vancouver Island, surrounding waterways—the Strait of Georgia, Burrard Inlet, English Bay—and on a clear day even south to Mount Baker in the state of Washington. A thrilling aerial tramway ride takes you up and down the mountain, and folks of all ages enjoy the experience. It is not unusual to spot a black bear or a deer on the slopes below. At the summit you'll find the Observatory, a restaurant with superb views, a cafe, and a gift shop. You can hike around Blue Grouse Lake or attend concerts and theatrical productions, which are held from time to time. Brief but spectacular helicopter rides high above the Grouse Mountain area give you views of the surrounding lakes and forest wilderness and make you realize that sophisticated Vancouver is right on the edge of a vast, virtually uninhabited landscape extending to the North Pole.

During the winter Grouse Mountain is the closest skiing area to city center. An adage in Vancouver says, "In the morning we go skiing on Grouse Mountain. In the afternoon we come down to go sailing in English Bay." There are easy runs for beginners, and instruction is available.

North Vancouver Parks, on the way to Grouse Mountain, via Lion's Gate Bridge. The main attraction here is **Capilano Suspension Bridge,** reputed to be the longest of its kind in the world. The great fun of walking across the narrow bridge is that it swings gently from side to side 137 m/450 ft above a raging river. It's an unforgettable experience, to say the least. A restaurant and gift shop are located here; (604) 985–7474. Admission is charged. Also in the area is the **Capilano Regional Park and Salmon Hatchery,** offering tours showing British Columbia's top moneymaking fish in different stages of growth; (604) 666–1790. Free. The park has hiking trails and places for picnics. On the road to Grouse Mountain is **Cleveland Dam,** forming Vancouver's reservoir. There are picnic places and hiking trails in adjacent Capilano Park. This is a fine viewing point of the twin mountain peaks known as the Lions. North Vancouver has another swaying suspension bridge and an interesting ecology center with woodland walks at **Lynn Canyon Park,** best accessed from Second Narrows Bridge and via Lynn Valley Road. Free.

Attractions

Museum of Anthropology, on the campus of the University of British Columbia, (604) 822–3825. Closed on Monday, Christmas Day, and Boxing Day. Admission is charged. The Museum of Anthropology is one of Vancouver's top three attractions (the other two being Stanley Park and the view from Grouse Mountain). If you have but a brief time to spend in the city, this museum should be at the head of your list. If you are staying in the city center, your best bet is to take a cab to the museum, but public transportation is also available.

There are two impressive aspects to the museum: the architecture and the collection. Arthur Erickson's design is based on the Native longhouses once so typical along the Northwest Coast. High windows, framed by a sequence of stark concrete post and lintel portals, look out on a set of fascinating, authentic totem poles. Beyond them are Point Grey Cliffs, English Bay, the towers of the city, and the Coast Mountains. The building is a photographer's delight because it offers so many striking angles. Many consider the Museum of Anthropology one of Erickson's finest buildings.

The museum's collection, the best of its kind in the world, concentrates on artifacts from the northwest coastal tribes. Many anthropological scientists consider these tribes to have developed the most sophisticated and most beautiful visual arts and crafts in North America (the only exception being the advanced cultures of Mexico, Peru, and Ecuador). Artifacts from the cultures of the Pacific region, Asia, and Latin America are exhibited as well. Featured items are dramatically displayed and accessible to viewers; you can actually open the drawers of display cases and see the rare and precious. The museum offers both conducted and self-guided (audio) tours and a full schedule of special presentations.

Vancouver Aquarium, in Stanley Park, (604) 659–3474. Open every day. Admission is charged. In beautiful Stanley Park is Canada's largest aquarium. The thousands of live sea species displayed here include beluga whales, sharks, and tropical fish. An Amazon River display is inhabited by tropical birds, boas, and piranhas. The whale pools have underwater windows through which you can see them look at you. Be sure to see the Pacific Ocean exhibit, as well as the salmon run coming through the aquarium. The aquarium complex itself is one of the best on the continent.

Children's Farmyard, in Stanley Park, is an ideal place for young children to see and pet gentle farm animals. Open daily; admission is charged. There are also pony rides and a miniature railway to ride, for an additional cost.

Vancouver Museum, in the Vanier Park complex near Burrard Street Bridge, (604) 736–4431. Open every day. Admission is charged. The most distinctive architectural feature of the Vanier complex of museums is a circular, funnel-shaped roof symbolizing the ceremonial hats worn by northwest coastal Indians. Within this striking complex is the Vancouver Museum, which has a number of interesting exhibits portraying the city's colorful history—among them Indian artifacts, a car from the first transcontinental passenger train to come into the city, furnishings from the Edwardian age, and a re-creation of an early trading post.

Gordon Southam Observatory, in the Vanier Park complex near Burrard Street Bridge, (604) 738–2855. Call ahead for schedule; open weekends only, and depending on whether volunteers are available. Free. The hands-on astronomy here enables you to learn about the heavens from a scientist and see cosmic wonders for yourself through a telescope.

Maritime Museum, in the Vanier Park complex near Burrard Street Bridge, (604) 257–8300. Open every day. Admission is charged. Vancouver's past, present, and future are inexorably linked to the sea. The city is Canada's door to the Pacific, with all its immense trading possibilities. The Maritime Museum chronicles this rich heritage. Among its exhibits is the *St. Roch,* a two-masted schooner, the first ship to sail through the fabled Northwest Passage in both directions, both west to east and east to west.

City of Vancouver Archives, in the Vanier Park complex near Burrard Street Bridge, (604) 736–8561. Closed Saturday and Sunday. Free. The archives contain books, maps, papers, newspapers, and photographs of historical value. Both scholars and casual visitors are warmly welcomed.

H. R. MacMillan Planetarium, in the Vanier Park complex near Burrard Street Bridge, (604) 736–3656. Closed Monday. Admission is charged. A trip through the galaxy is presented in the afternoon and in the evening. For those already well versed on constellations, planets, and interstellar happenings, there are more theatrical shows. A cafeteria in this part of the complex offers views of the harbor.

Vancouver Art Gallery, 750 Hornby Street in Robson Square; (604) 682–4719. Admission is charged. Housed in what was the city's old courthouse, of solid neoclassical design graced by a brilliantly modern interior, Vancouver Art Gallery has four floors of well-lighted exhibition space. There is a special children's gallery on the ground floor. This art museum is best known for its extensive collection of paintings by Emily Carr, British Columbia's most famous artist. An impressionist of sorts, often considered as important as the Group of Seven (immortal Canadian artists), Carr painted scenes of the Northwest Coast and forests, totem poles, and remote Native villages. There is a mystical quality to her works that sticks in the imagination. The Vancouver Art Gallery is in the heart of city center and should be visited for the Carr collection alone.

University of British Columbia Museums, Point Grey section of Vancouver, a short drive southwest of city center. UBC, as it is called by local folks, is Western Canada's top institution of higher learning. Located on the end of Point Grey, UBC is worth visiting just to stroll its pleasant, attractive campus; there's very much of an "established, elite" feel to it. There are also low-cost dormitory accommodations here; see the "Accommodations" section on pages 125–131. Adjacent to the main campus is **Pacific Spirit Regional Park,** an area of 1,013 ha/2,500 forested acres where you can hike or jog in lovely natural surroundings. The park is inhabited by small mammals, including deer, and it is not unusual to spot bald eagles, which are ubiquitous along British Columbia's coast. Marine Drive, which goes around Point Grey, offers some lovely views, and Wreck (nude bathing here) and Spanish Banks Beaches are in this area. Among other reasons for visiting the UBC campus are its excellent museums:

Museum of Anthropology; detailed earlier in this chapter.

M. Y. Williams Geology Museum; extensive mineral and fossil collection; (604) 822–5586. Closed weekends. Free.

Nitobe Memorial Garden; detailed earlier in this chapter.

Fine Arts Gallery; (604) 822–2759; located in Main Library. Free.

TRIUMF; (604) 222–1047; one of the world's largest cyclotrons for subatomic research.

Granville Island Museums, 1502 Duranleau Street, (604) 683–1939 or www.sportfishingmuseum.bc.ca. This is an unusual trio of museums—the Sportfishing Museum, featuring what may be the world's largest collection of Hardy rods and reels; the Model Ships Museum, with exquisitely detailed large-scale model warships, submarines, and coastal vessels; and the Model Trains Museum, housing the largest collection of model and toy trains on public display in the world. Admission is charged.

Fantasy Garden World, in Richmond, just off Highway 99, between turnoff roads for Vancouver International Airport and the ferry for Victoria; (604) 277–7777. Open daily. Admission is charged. If you are traveling to Vancouver from the state of Washington on B.C. Highway 99 or going south on this same road, visit Fantasy Garden World. This floral theme park features millions of flowers and beautiful landscaping, a farm with many small animals for the kids to pet, a miniature-train ride, a stocked trout lake, a biblical garden with a giant Noah's Ark, a European village where you can sample the foods from several nations, greenhouses, a pretty little chapel where many Vancouverites tie the knot, and a pavilion that serves English tea in the afternoon.

Simon Fraser University (SFU) campus, located on Burnaby Mountain in Burnaby, an approximately forty-minute drive east of city center. Simon Fraser University, designed by architects Arthur Erickson and Geoffrey Massey, has one of the most stunning campuses in the world, in terms of both its contemporary architecture and its setting on Burnaby Mountain with the backdrop of distant snowcapped mountains and great views of the city and sea inlets. Visit SFU's **Art Gallery** and its **Museum of Archaeology and Ethnology,** a fine display of artifacts from northwest coastal

Indian tribes. Open every day; noon to 3:00 P.M. on weekends. Free. Tours of the university; call (604) 291–3397.

Science World, 1455 Quebec Street; (604) 443–7440. Located within a former Expo pavilion. Open every day. Admission is charged. Offers exciting, hands-on science exhibits that are enjoyed by children and adults. An Omnimax theater on the site adds to the excitement with various films.

Burnaby Heritage Village and Carousel Museum, 4900 Deer Lake Avenue in Burnaby; (604) 293–6500. Open daily; closed mid-October to mid-November. Admission is charged. Heritage Village takes visitors back to a simpler time. Here you can visit with a small-town blacksmith, see a sawmill in operation, taste the treats at an ice cream parlor, poke into an early log cabin, general store, and schoolhouse, and marvel at the restored carousel.

Canadian Craft Museum, 639 Hornby Street, (604) 687–8266. Canada's first national cultural facility dedicated to crafts is a showplace for both Canadian and international crafts artists. Located in a beautiful new building, its 900 sq m/10,000 sq ft are on three levels. Small admission fee. Closed Tuesday (except during the summer season).

Accommodations

Vancouver, as the third most important city in Canada and as Western Canada's number one destination, has a large number of hotels, motels, and guest houses. Most are priced in the moderate-to-expensive range, although some decent inexpensive accommodations are available, generally outside city center. During the busy tourist season—from late May to mid-September—rooms at the more desirable hotels are difficult if not impossible to book on short notice. It's smart to make reservations anytime; during busy times, they are essential.

An easy way to make reservations is to contact Super Natural British Columbia at (800) HELLO–BC (in North America) or (250) 387–1642 (outside North America). Or you can visit www.hellobc.com.

Consult with your local travel agent and auto club for their accommodation reservation services, which are usually available at no extra cost. Many places require a cash deposit prior to arrival and/or evidence of credit; both can be accomplished through a major credit card.

Some places of accommodation in this listing are described as "good-value accommodations with many amenities," which means that they are recommended and offer such features as swimming pools, pleasant settings, and/or other conveniences to make your stay comfortable. This designation has been used to increase the number of recommended places to stay during peak seasons.

If you would like to stay at a Vancouver-area bed-and-breakfast, contact this agency for more information and rates: Best Canadian Bed & Breakfast Network, 1090 West King Edward Avenue, Vancouver, British Columbia V6H 1Z4; (604) 738–7207. Old English Bed and Breakfast Registry, P.O. Box 86818, North Vancouver, British Columbia V7L 4L3, (604) 986–5069, is another resource to try.

City Center Accommodations

The following hotels are located in the city center and offer convenient access to major attractions (parks, museums, etc.), business and government offices, shopping areas, entertainment and sporting venues, and restaurants.

Vancouver's Finest

The hotels in this first category are considered by travelers to be the best in Vancouver in terms of customer satisfaction, guest services, facilities, and management. They are also among the most expensive, averaging $200 to $300 per night, per room.

Four Seasons Hotel, 791 West Georgia Street, (604) 689–9333; (800) 268–6282. Certainly one of the premier hotels in the city, with excellent amenities and service. Its main restaurants are Chartwell's (named for Winston Churchill's estate in Kent, England) and the Garden Terrace; lunch is served in the Garden Lounge and, in summer, beside the outdoor pool. There's an indoor/outdoor pool. The Four Seasons is connected to Pacific Centre Mall, which has more than 150 shops. Expensive.

Metropolitan Hotel, 645 Howe Street, (604) 687–1122; (800) 268–1133. This hotel is near the Pacific Centre. The rooms and suites are luxurious, and the service is first-rate. It features a health club, squash and racquetball courts, a billiard room, a swimming pool, and a sauna. Excellent restaurants. Expensive.

Westin Bayshore, 1601 Bay Shore Drive, (604) 682–3377; (800) 228–3000. This excellent hotel in the Westin chain is located near beautiful Stanley Park. You'll find both an indoor and an outdoor pool, as well as a marina with services for your yacht. The Westin offers a family plan and free parking. Its restaurants include Currents and Seawall Bar and Bistro. It has long been a celebrity favorite; Howard Hughes once reserved an entire floor for his lengthy stay.

Westin Grand, 433 Robson Street, (604) 602–1999; (888) 680–9393. This is an exceptional hotel perched on the edge of Yaletown, the city's newest entertainment district. Perhaps the most comfortable hotel in all the city, with its "heavenly beds," deep-soak tubs, and cushy sofas. Some rooms have balconies. The hotel's silhouette of a grand piano adds an interesting note to the city's landscape.

Hotel Vancouver, 900 West Georgia Street, (604) 684–3131; (800) 828–7447. The first Hotel Vancouver was opened in 1887. The present and third Hotel Vancouver, completed in 1939, is the city's landmark place of accommodation, much in the same manner as is the Château Frontenac in Québec City. It would be difficult to imagine Vancouver city center without this venerable hotel. The service here is high class, and the rooms are spacious and pleasant. Dining and dancing are available in the 900 West restaurant (formerly known as the Panorama Roof), or visit Griffins Restaurant for all-day dining. Expensive.

Sutton Place Hotel, 845 Burrard Street, (604) 682–5511; (800) 543–4300. The former Meridien hotel provides luxury in the European manner, with regard to both rooms and service. Its restaurants include Gerard and Café Fleuri. Expensive.

Pan Pacific Vancouver Hotel, 999 Canada Place, (604) 662–8111; (800) 663–1515. A deluxe hotel, the Pan Pacific is part of the dramatic Canada Place complex, located on the waterfront. Its main function is to provide top accommodations to convention delegates, but other travelers are also welcomed. It features a pool, health club, racquetball courts, and twenty-four-hour room service. For dining, there is Misaki, a Japanese restaurant; Five Sails for continental cuisine; and Café Pacifica. Expensive.

Hyatt Regency Vancouver, 655 Burrard Street (in Royal Centre), (604) 683–1234; (800) 228–9000. This Hyatt—more than thirty sparkling floors—offers luxury and all the amenities you need, including a charming lounge and a gourmet restaurant. The Hyatt's situation couldn't be better: It's in the heart of downtown Vancouver and connected to the Royal Centre, an attractive indoor shopping mall. Expensive.

Waterfront Centre Hotel, 900 Canada Place Way, (604) 691–1991; (800) 268–9420. Located directly across from the Pan Pacific Vancouver Hotel. Operated by Canadian Pacific Hotels, it has all of the amenities expected of a first-class hotel. Direct access to the Vancouver Convention and Exhibition Centre. Expensive.

Sheraton Wall Centre Garden Hotel, 1088 Burrard, (604) 331–1000; (800) 331–1001. Expensive.

Other Fine Accommodations

Crown Plaza Hotel Georgia, 801 West Georgia Street, (604) 682–5566; (800) 663–1111. A fine, centrally located hotel with friendly, personal service. An English pub called George V, restaurants, and lounges. A favorite with frequent visitors to the city. Expensive.

Day's Inn Vancouver Downtown, 921 West Pender Street, (604) 681–4335; (800) 325–2525. Located in the financial center. An older hotel with newly refurbished rooms. Restaurants and lounges. A good value in downtown Vancouver. Moderate.

Best Western Chateau Granville, 1100 Granville Street, (604) 669–7070; (800) 663–0575. Offers discounts to seniors. Rooms have balconies or patios, with views of the city, waterfront, or mountains. You'll find a dining room and a place for cocktails and live entertainment. Moderate to expensive.

The Georgian Court, 773 Beatty Street, (604) 682–5555; (800) 663–1144. An intimate, high-class hotel in the European manner. Its William Tell restaurant is one of the best in the city. Near B.C. Place Stadium. Expensive.

Coast Plaza Suites at Stanley Park, 1733 Comox Street, (604) 688–7711; (800) 268–8998. A nice location near Stanley Park and English Bay. Rooms have balconies; most have refrigerators, and some have kitchens. There is an indoor pool and a bar. Moderate to expensive.

Parkhill Hotel, 1160 Davie Street, (604) 685–1311; (800) 663–1525. Rooms have balconies with excellent views of English Bay. Pool and free parking; dining room and lounge. Close to beaches and city center. Expensive.

Residence Inn by Marriott, 1234 Hornby, (604) 688–1234; (800) 426–0670. In midtown, this facility has spacious studio suites with kitchenettes. Moderate.

Century Plaza Hotel, 1015 Burrard Street, (604) 687–0575; (800) 663–1818. An apartment-type accommodation with large rooms; some have balconies and kitchen facilities. Indoor pool and sauna; dining room, coffee shop, and nightclub. Live entertainment in the Rum Runners Lounge. Moderate to expensive.

Holiday Inn Downtown, 1110 Howe Street, (604) 684–2151; (800) HOLIDAY. Downtown location, close to the Pacific Centre. Restaurant, indoor pool. Expensive.

Pacific Palisades Hotel, 1277 Robson Street, (604) 688–0461; (800) 663–1815. Offers full kitchen facilities; Puffin's dining room; a health club and indoor pool; free parking; executive suites. Expensive.

Empire Landmark Hotel, 1400 Robson Street, (604) 687–0511; (800) 325–3535. Rooms with balconies. A revolving restaurant on top, called Cloud Nine, gives superb views of the city, ocean, and mountains. Jazz bar with live entertainment. Family plan. Expensive.

Listel Vancouver Hotel, 1300 Robson Street, (604) 684–8461; (800) 663–5491. Has smoking and nonsmoking floors, twenty-four-hour room service, indoor pool, Jacuzzi, exercise room; also a restaurant, lounge, and sidewalk cafe. Moderate to expensive.

Wedgwood Hotel, 845 Hornby Street, (604) 689–7777; (800) 663–0666. City center location. Balconies, fireplaces, and the Wedgwood Room—one of the best restaurants in the city. Expensive.

Sylvia Hotel, 1154 Gilford Street, (604) 681–9321. This is the hotel that "in-the-know" visitors go to for a terrific view of the water and a comfortable, small-hotel flavor. An older establishment that has character. Decent restaurant. Moderate.

Sunset Inn Apartment Hotel, 1111 Burnaby Street, (604) 684–8763. A former apartment block, this converted facility offers condo suites within walking distance of Stanley Park and English Bay. Moderate to expensive.

Vancouver Vicinity

The following places of accommodation are within a thirty- to forty-five-minute drive of downtown Vancouver and should be considered when hotels in city center are filled. Accommodations in suburban Richmond, located south of city center, are close to the Vancouver International Airport and may be preferable to businesspeople.

Delta Pacific Resort & Conference Centre, 10251 St. Edwards Drive in Richmond, south of Vancouver city center and near the airport; (604) 278–9611. Next to the airport and a twenty-minute drive from downtown. A resort on 5 ha/12 acres, offering three swimming pools, tennis and squash courts, exercise and game rooms. It even has a special fun place for children—the Children's Creative Centre, with games, air hockey, and Nintendo. This resort offers Japanese ambience in its restaurants and lounges. The best accommodation in the airport area. Expensive.

Best Western Coquitlam Inn, 319 North Road in Coquitlam, east of Vancouver city center; (604) 931–9011; (800) 528–1234. Located about 16.1 km/10 mi from city center. Pool, sauna, tropical courtyard, Beef 'n Barrel restaurant, and a lounge with live entertainment. Moderate to expensive.

Best Western Kings Inn and Conference Centre, 5411 Kingsway, Burnaby, east of Vancouver city center; (604) 438–1383; (800) 528–1234. Comfortable accommodations with many amenities. Restaurant. Moderate to expensive.

Best Western Richmond Inn, in downtown Richmond, 7551 Westminster Highway, south of Vancouver city center and near the airport; (604) 273–7878. Nice rooms, heated pool, saunas, health club; restaurants and lounge with entertainment. Moderate.

Radisson Hotel Burnaby, 4331 Dominion Street in Burnaby, east of Vancouver city center; (604) 430–2828; (800) 325–3535. Indoor/outdoor pools, dining facilities, and live entertainment. Family rates. Moderate to expensive.

Best Western Abercorn Inn, 9260 Bridgeport Road in Richmond, south of Vancouver city center and near the airport; (604) 270–7576. In architecture and ambience, a wee bit of rural Scotland in B.C. Restaurant and whirlpool. Moderate to expensive.

Radisson President Hotel and Suites, 8181 Cambie, Richmond; (604) 276–8181; (800) 333–3333. This new hotel has 184 deluxe rooms, including 39 luxury suites. Close to Vancouver International Airport; the focus is business travel. Moderate to expensive.

Best Western Tsawwassen Inn, 1665 Fifty-sixth Street, Delta, about 4.8 km/3 mi from the Victoria ferry terminal and about a forty-minute drive south of Vancouver via Highways 99 and 17; (604) 943–8221; (800) 528–1234. Good-value accommodations with many amenities. Dining room. Moderate to expensive.

Park Royal Hotel, 540 Clyde Avenue, West Vancouver, north via Lion's Gate Bridge on the Capilano River; (604) 926–5511. A Tudor-style country inn set in beautiful surroundings. Minutes from Vancouver city center. Dining room. Moderate to expensive.

Lonsdale Quay Hotel, 123 Carrie Cates Court, North Vancouver, (604) 986–6111. Located above the Lonsdale Quay market, it is one of the most unusual settings in the Vancouver area. On the waterfront and next to the Seabus terminal, it offers wonderful Vancouver skyline views. Moderate.

Inexpensive but Good Places to Stay

University of British Columbia, Student Union Boulevard, southwest of Vancouver city center, (604) 882–1010. Low-cost accommodations for singles, doubles, and families on this attractive campus—a major area attraction in itself—are available from early May until late August. Meals are available at the student union. Downtown is about twenty minutes away. The University of British Columbia offers one of the best accommodation values in this popular travel destination; highly recommended. Inexpensive.

Simon Fraser University, in Burnaby, (604) 291–4503. Fully furnished single and twin rooms; shared bathrooms; lounges on each floor. Guests can use recreational facilities. Inexpensive.

YWCA Hotel, 733 Beatty Street, (604) 895–5830. This is a new, coed accommodation (it welcomes couples and families) located in downtown Vancouver.

Camping Near Vancouver

Contact your camping association and auto club for a complete listing of privately operated campgrounds. Here's one well-established camping spot.

Parks Canada Recreational Vehicle Inn, Highway 17, via Fifty-second Street exit, northeast of the ferry terminal to Victoria; (604) 943–5811. In operation from April through October. Facilities include washrooms, toilets, a heated pool, and a recreation lounge; near a water-slide park, grocery and gift shops, and golf.

Dining

There are hundreds of excellent restaurants in Vancouver, representing the cuisines of about twenty ethnic groups. The deluxe hotels in Vancouver pride themselves on having at least one superb restaurant each, and you probably won't be disappointed in dining at least one evening at yours. Throughout the city there are also the familiar fast-food franchises when you need something fast and cheap. Regardless of your budget, kids seem to prefer fast-food burgers, french fries, and pizza to chateaubriand and flaming pepper steak. Vancouver's best foods are those that come from nearby areas—such as fresh seafood, especially salmon; fresh vegetables; and fruit. Wines are being produced in British Columbia, and you should sample some of them. Vancouver, with the second largest Chinese population of any city in North America, has an abundance of superb Chinese restaurants; it's a bit of an adventure going into Chinatown and discovering the one that may become your favorite. Other ethnic groups have their eateries as well. There are, for example, more than eighty-five Japanese

A Taste of Vancouver:
Barbecued Whole Salmon with Rhubarb and Wild Rice Stuffing

For this recipe, pick any variety of salmon from the Pacific Ocean—sockeye, spring, chinook, chum, or coho. Use only the stalks of the rhubarb, the "lemon of the North," and splurge on some wild rice from the wetlands of the prairies.

1 c wild rice
5 c boiling water
2 tbsp butter
1 c chopped rhubarb
3 green onions, finely chopped
1 celery stalk, finely chopped
1 egg, beaten
1 tbsp brown sugar
½ tsp dried sage
salt and pepper
1 whole 2- to 3-lb salmon, cleaned

Stir the rice into 5 c of boiling water and boil for 5 minutes. Remove from the heat, cover, and let sit for 1 hour. Drain. Melt the butter in a saucepan and saute the rhubarb, onion, and celery until softened. Stir in the wild rice, egg, brown sugar, sage, salt, and pepper and mix well. Stuff the salmon with this mixture, and lace it closed. Bake in a 232°C/450°F oven for 10 to 12 minutes per inch thickness of the fish, plus an extra 10 minutes. Bake any leftover stuffing in a separate dish.

restaurants scattered throughout the greater Vancouver region, with the majority within easy access of downtown. Those serving continental cuisine—meaning French—are among the best of all restaurants. There are also fine Italian, Greek, and Portuguese places. As long as you have money to spend, you won't go hungry for great food to eat in Vancouver. The following recommended places are a small sampling of what's available:

Le Gavroche, 1616 Alberni Street, (604) 685–3924. Le Gavroche is considered one of Canada's finest restaurants. French cuisine is superbly prepared by its chefs and served with style in an elegant environment. An excellent wine list. Make this a special dining treat. Expensive.

The Teahouse Restaurant, in the Ferguson Point area of Stanley Park, (604) 669–3281. The Teahouse in Stanley Park is Vancouver's sentimental favorite place for a light snack or a full-course meal. It is a traditional British greenhouse with a most uplifting decor and splendid views from its windows. The atmosphere is relaxed and civilized in the English manner. Toasting an achievement or a loved one seems to take on special meaning at the Teahouse. Moderate to expensive.

Cloud 9 Revolving Restaurant at the Empire Landmark Hotel, (604) 662–8328. An exceptional restaurant offering continental cuisine and fresh B.C. salmon, as well as panoramic views from your table of the city, mountains, and sea. Famous for its Sunday brunch. Moderate to expensive.

Naniwa-Ya Japanese Seafood Restaurant, 745 Thurlow Street, (604) 681–6177. Traditional Japanese seafood dishes, including sushi and sashimi. Moderate to expensive.

Chartwell's, at the Four Seasons Hotel, 791 West Georgia Street, (604) 689–9333. One of Vancouver's elegant restaurants. Menu selections, wines, ambience, decor, and service are excellent. Continental and nouvelle cuisine prepared with artistry and with strict emphasis on fresh ingredients available in season. Expensive.

Bishop's Restaurant, 2183 West Fourth Avenue, (604) 738–2025. Continental and West Coast cuisine. A mainstay on trendy Fourth Avenue, this intimate restaurant continues to be one of the city's finest year after year. Moderate to expensive.

Five Sails in the Pan Pacific Hotel, 300–999 Canada Place, (604) 662–8111. West Coast cuisine. Moderate to expensive.

Bacchus Restaurant in the Wedgwood Hotel, 845 Hornby Street, (604) 608–5319. Northern Italian. Inexpensive to moderate.

Star Anise, 1485 West Twelfth Avenue, in Vancouver, south of Granville Street Bridge, (604) 737–1485. Progressive Pacific Rim cooking served up by one of the city's finest restaurants. Expensive.

Monk McQueen's Fresh Seafood and Oyster Bar, 601 Stamps Landing on the south shore of False Creek, (604) 877–1351. Casual dining amid the waterfront sea character of sailboat moorings. Great view of the city and mountains. Moderate.

Imperial Chinese Seafood Restaurant, 355 Burrard, downtown, (604) 688–8191. Cantonese cuisine with a view of the mountains and Coal Harbor. Moderate.

The Observatory, atop Grouse Mountain and accessed via the Grouse Mountain Skyride, 6400 Nancy Greene Way in North

Vancouver, (604) 984–0661. Not the finest fare in town, but the greatest view of the city, the Strait of Georgia, and Vancouver Island. Moderate.

Pink Pearl Chinese Seafood Restaurant, in Chinatown, 1132 East Hastings Street, (604) 253–4316. A favorite restaurant with both Chinese and Caucasian patrons. A vast menu of Cantonese specialties will whet your appetite. Peking duck and rainbow lettuce wrap are just two of innumerable delicious dishes. Moderate to expensive.

Salmon House on the Hill, 2229 Folkestone Way, West Vancouver, (604) 926–3212. One of the best places in the Vancouver area for Pacific salmon grilled over alderwood, Amerindian style. Get it served with wild rice and fiddleheads. This is also the place for romantic views of the harbor and distant Vancouver Island. Moderate to expensive.

William Tell, 765 Beatty Street, (604) 688–3504. Seafood and steak dishes are well prepared. Both service and dining comfort get high marks. Expensive.

The Cannery, 2205 Commissioner Street, (604) 254–9606. Get a table with a view of the harbor and order your choice of seafood. The decor is that of an early Northwest Coast fish cannery. Moderate.

Bridges, 1696 Duranleau Street, (604) 687–4400. Meals served alfresco on a spacious deck in the quaint ambience of Granville Island and the marina world of boats, flapping sails, and screeching gulls. Bridges has a formal, enclosed dining room and a wine bar as well. Moderate to expensive.

A Kettle of Fish, 900 Pacific Street, (604) 682–6661. A fine seafood place with a menu that changes according to the availability of fresh finfish and shellfish. Congenial environment in a greenhouse packed with plants, making for an uplifting meal on an overcast day. Moderate.

Wedgwood Room, 845 Hornby Street, in the Wedgwood Hotel, (604) 689–7777. North American, West Coast, and French cuisines. Moderate to expensive.

Shaughnessey Restaurant, 5251 Oak in the VanDusen Botanical Gardens, (604) 261–0011. West Coast continental cuisine, overlooking the peaceful surroundings of the gardens. Moderate.

Caffe de Medici, 1025 Robson, (604) 669–9322. Northern Italian cuisine featuring veal, pasta, and fresh seafood. In the heart of the city. Moderate to expensive.

Il Giardino di Umberto, 1382 Hornby Street, (604) 669–2422. This is a light-splashed restaurant styled after a Tuscany home. Reindeer fillet and pheasant are the house specialties. Moderate to expensive.

Allegro Café, 888 Nelson Street, (604) 684–8485. A favorite spot for lawyers because of its proximity to the courthouse. The fare is Mediterranean inspired, but the noise level is Manhattan. Moderate.

Beach Side Café, 1362 Marine Drive, West Vancouver, (604) 925–1945. A favorite spot for sunset-watching because of its heated deck. A prodigious wine list and local cuisine make it worth the drive over Lion's Gate Bridge. Moderate.

Café de Paris, 751 Denman Street, (604) 687–1418. The place to get your Paris fix. This West End bistro knows its *pommes frites* and *cassoulet.* Moderate to expensive.

Diva at the Met, Metropolitan Hotel, 645 Howe Street, (604) 602–7788. *The* spot in Vancouver for chic, upscale, break-the-budget dining. Find something to celebrate—you won't want to miss this dining experience. Top off dinner with the Stilton cheesecake.

Primo's on 12th, 1509 West Twelfth Avenue, (604) 735–9322. This was Vancouver's first Mexican restaurant, and although over the years it may have aged a bit, it's still intimate and cosy. Giant margaritas and garlic prawns are a must.

White Spot; several locations in the city. This is Vancouver's hamburger joint. The house special burger with its "triple O" sauce, served with generously cut fries and coleslaw punctuated with sunflower seeds, is a longtime Vancouver favorite. The menu is quite varied; you'll find fish-and-chips, macaroni and cheese, and a chicken potpie that are just the thing when you require comfort food.

Internet Cafes

Internet Coffee, 1104 Davie Street, (604) 682–6688. Browse the 'net for $2.50 per fifteen minutes. Fourteen computer stations available.

Kitsilano's Cyber Café, 3514 West Fourth Avenue, (604) 737–0595. Coffee, baked goods, soups, and daily specials combine seamlessly with Internet access, word processing, games, and e-mail.

Wicked Discount Internet, 406–1315 Bute Street, (604) 684–0825. High-speed ADSL connection, six computers, fax, games, copy, scan, and print services.

Entertainment

Vancouver, as is typical of large, important cities, has all forms of entertainment, from the highbrow to the seamy. If you are staying at a major hotel or motel, in addition to dining and lounge facilities, there is a good chance it offers some form of live entertainment—a dance band, pop singers, comedians, dancers, stage revues. There are movie houses throughout the city. Nightclubs and theaters are listed below. You can buy tickets to concerts, plays, sporting events, and special events through **Ticketmaster,** (604) 280–3311 or 280–4444; charge tickets by phone, using major credit cards.

Nightclubs

The following are chic drinking and dancing places, where you can bring a date or come yourself and see the possibilities:

Beatty Street Bar and Grill, 755 Beatty Street at the Georgian Court Hotel, (604) 688–3563.

The Purple Onion, 15 Water Street, Gastown, (604) 602–9442.

Yuk Yuk's Komedy Kabaret, 750 Pacific Boulevard, (604) 687–5323.

Richard's on Richards, 1036 Richards Street, (604) 687–6794.

Babalu's Tapas Lounge, 654 Nelson, (604) 605–4343.

George V Pub and Lounge, Crowne Plaza, 801 West Georgia, (604) 682–5566.

The Palladium Club, 1250 Richards, (604) 688–2648.

The Commodore Ballroom, 868 Granville Street, (604) 739–4550.

Music and Theater

The music and theater scene in Vancouver is active, with enough offerings to satisfy the interests of most visitors. Local talent and performers from other parts of Canada put on splendid shows, and some go on to be stars. Both Michael J. Fox and Arthur Hill, leading actors in films and television, originally came from the area. Vancouver is a main stop on the tours of top international performers; there's a good chance you can see some of your favorites when you visit. In addition to the theaters listed below, both **B.C. Place Stadium** and **Pacific Coliseum** at Exhibition Park are major venues for important concerts and performances.

Orpheum Theatre, on Seymour Street, Ticketmaster (604)

280–3311. Built in 1927 and recently renovated, this highly ornate theater is now the home concert hall for the **Vancouver Symphony Orchestra**, the **Vancouver Chamber Choir**, the **Vancouver Bach Choir**, and other music groups.

Queen Elizabeth Theatre, on Georgia Street, (604) 665–3050. The Queen Elizabeth Theatre seats 2,800 and hosts four major performances a year by the **Vancouver Opera**. The 650-seat Playhouse has its own resident company, which puts on experimental and popular productions from autumn through spring. The **Festival Concert Society** and the **Vancouver Recital Society** have concerts at the Playhouse, which also is the venue for the **Playhouse Theatre Company**.

Bard on the Beach, 1101 West Broadway, (604) 739–0559.

Vancouver TheatreSports League, New Review Stage, Granville Island, (604) 738–7013.

Firehall Arts Centre, 280 East Cordova Street, (604) 689–0926. Various dramatic productions and concerts.

Theatre under the Stars, outdoors in Stanley Park from July through August, (604) 687–0174. Popular Broadway musicals.

Waterfront Theatre, 1412 Cartwright Street, on Granville Island, (604) 685–1731. Performs works by British Columbia writers.

Arts Club Theatre, Granville Island, (604) 687–5315. Lively theater venue with two stages on Granville Island and a third at the newly renovated Stanley Theatre on Granville Street. Full-scale dramas, musicals, and cabaret revues are regularly presented.

Shopping

Vancouver is Western Canada's largest shopping center—it has everything you need. Considering the favorable exchange rate, there are a number of bargains for visitors from the United States. Fashions for women and men are of style and quality as high as those you would find in New York and Toronto. Yet you can also purchase some special products here that would be hard to get elsewhere, such as alderwood-smoked Pacific salmon and northwest coastal Amerindian arts and crafts. Department stores of large national chains—the Bay, Holt Renfrew, and Sears—are here.

Some of Vancouver's most interesting shopping sections include Robson Street (Robsonstrasse), Robson Fashion Centre for Canadian and international designs, Gastown, Chinatown, Granville Island, and the South Granville Street area.

Multistore Malls

Pacific Centre, Georgia at Granville. You'll find 130 shops and services in this two-level mall. Holt Renfrew is the major department store.

The Landing, Water Street, near the Convention Centre. Two levels of exclusive shops and boutiques.

Royal Centre, on Burrard and Georgia.

Harbour Centre, on Hastings Street, between Seymour and Richards.

In West Vancouver, **Park Royal Centre** sprawls for acres on both sides of Marine Drive. As can be expected, it has a large number of shops, several department stores, and supermarkets.

Shops of Special Interest to Visitors

Bushlen-Mowat Fine Arts Ltd., 1445 West Georgia; (604) 682–1234; Canadian contemporary art.

Inuit Gallery, 345 Water Street in Gastown; Inuit and West Coast Indian art and crafts.

Kaya Kaya, 2037 West Fourth Avenue; exquisite Japanese porcelains.

Professional Sports

The **Canucks,** of the National Hockey League, are Vancouver's top professional sports team. The team plays at General Motors Place in downtown Vancouver, opposite B.C. Place Stadium; (604) 899–4625 or 681–2280.

Vancouver Grizzlies, of the National Basketball Association, began play in the 1995–96 season with games at General Motors Place, an arena they share with the Vancouver Canucks; (604) 899–4667 or 681–2280.

The **B.C. Lions,** of the Canadian Football League, play their home games at B.C. Place Stadium, 777 Pacific Boulevard, (604) 299–9000.

Thoroughbred racing takes place at Exhibition Park, at Hastings and Renfrew Streets, (604) 254–1631.

Harness racing is at the Cloverdale Raceway, 6050 176th Street in Cloverdale. Call (604) 579–9141; the season runs from October through April.

The **Vancouver Canadians,** a single-A baseball club, play at a field adjacent to Queen Elizabeth Park, Thirty-third Avenue at Quebec Street, (604) 872–5232.

The **Vancouver '86ers,** a soccer club, are based at the Swangard Stadium, at Boundary and Kingsway, (604) 280–4444.

Recreation

Sports play a big role in this health-conscious city. Most sports activities are organized ad hoc or just enjoyed individually. **Sport British Columbia** is a central source for information regarding most sports activities taking place in the province. The people in this agency will be happy to answer your questions and suggest ways that you can participate in a sport of interest to you; call (604) 737–3000 or visit www.sportsbc.ca.

Bicycling

For information on routes and laws regarding biking, call the Bicycle Hotline at (604) 871–6070. The scenic routes in the city for biking are in Stanley Park (detailed earlier in this chapter) and the Pacific Spirit Regional Park. Rentals are available at **Bayshore Bicycle Rentals,** (604) 688–2453, and **Spokes Bicycle Rentals and Espresso Bar,** (604) 688–5141.

Golf

Contact your own club about playing the private courses in the Vancouver area, or try one of these public courses.

The University Golf Club, 5185 University Boulevard, pro shop, (604) 224–1818.

McCleery Golf Course, 7170 MacDonald Street, pro shop, (604) 257–8191.

Langara Golf Course, 290 West Forty-ninth Avenue, pro shop, (604) 713–1816.

Fraserview Golf Course, 7800 Vivian Street, pro shop, (604) 257–6923.

Burnaby Mountain Golf Course, 7600 Halifax Street, pro shop, (604) 280–7355.

Seymour Golf and Country Club, 3723 Mount Seymour Parkway, North Vancouver, pro shop, (604) 929–5491.

Mayfair Lakes Golf Centre, 5400 North Seventh Road, Richmond, pro shop, (604) 276–0505.

Peace Portal Golf Course, 16900 Fourth Avenue, Surrey, pro shop, (604) 538–4818.

Ice Skating

Lower level of Robson Square in city center.

Indoor Swimming Pools

Most of the major hotels and motels listed in this guide have swimming pools.

University of British Columbia Aquatic Centre, (604) 822–4521.

Vancouver Aquatic Centre, 1050 Beach Avenue, (604) 665–3424.

YMCA Downtown, (604) 681–0221.

Outdoor Saltwater Pools

Kitsilano Beach, (604) 257–8400.
Second Beach at Stanley Park.

Running/Jogging

The best place for running in the city is Stanley Park. Also try the Endowment Lands at the University of British Columbia.

Sailboarding

Windsurfing is a big sport on the waters off Vancouver. Many of the beaches have people giving instruction. For more information on the popular spots and equipment rentals, contact **Windsure Windsurfing, Ltd.**, (604) 224–0615.

Sailing

Seawing Sailing School, 1620 Duranleau, (604) 687–4110, Maritime Mews, Granville Island; rentals of vessels can be bareboat or with captain.

Jericho Sailing Centre Association, 1300 Discovery, (604) 224–4177.

Salmon-Fishing Charters

The following companies, among others, offer salmon-fishing trips from Vancouver:

Westin Bayshore Yacht Charters, (604) 691–6936
Paradise Yacht Charters, (604) 681–8110
Sewell's Landing Marina, (604) 921–3474

These companies supply everything you'll need—food for the fish and you, gear, and even the fishing license.

Scuba Diving

For such a northerly area in the Pacific, the sea life here is fabulous—close to 200 varieties of animals, including whales and octopuses, and more than 325 kinds of fish—making for many fascinating dives. For suggestions on where to dive and equipment to rent, contact the **Diving Locker**, (604) 736-2681.

Skiing

Whistler Resort Area; detailed earlier in this chapter.
Grouse Mountain; detailed earlier in this chapter.
Mount Seymour Provincial Park, 16.1 km/10 mi from city center in North Vancouver; multiple runs, chairlifts, rope tows, snow-tubing, and snowshoeing trails.
Cypress Bowl Ski Area in West Vancouver, downhill and cross country, (604) 922-0825.
Excellent downhill skiing is also available at Mount Baker in the state of Washington.

Small-Boating

You can rent kayaks at **Ocean Kayaking Centre**, (604) 689-7575, and **Deep Cove Canoe and Kayak Rentals**, in North Vancouver, (604) 929-2268.

Tennis

Stanley Park, (604) 257-8400.
Queen Elizabeth Park; detailed earlier in this chapter.

CHAPTER 6

Victoria: England by the Pacific

Victoria • Vancouver Island • The Inside Passage • Prince Rupert to Prince George

Victoria in Brief

No city in Canada is more British in mood and trappings than Victoria. Just as Québec City expresses the essence of *ancien régime* France in North America, Victoria does the same for Canada's other founding nation/culture, Great Britain. And just as Halifax, Nova Scotia, was a major seaport for the Royal Navy on the North Atlantic, so was Victoria on the Pacific. Over several decades British naval officers found the climate and lifestyle of Victoria to their liking. Many retired here, thus permeating a good portion of the city's institutions with their homeland's styles, manners, and attitudes: Afternoon tea with crumpets, scones, and delicate sandwiches served on English bone china is as common as the red double-decker London buses plying Government Street. Downtown stores sell Scottish woolens, Waterford crystal, Doulton china, tweed jackets, Stilton cheeses, and exquisitely wrapped bonbons. You can order a made-to-measure suit from a London tailor. Union Jack flags in all sizes and souvenirs with pictures of members of the royal family are available just about everywhere.

While the British influence is undeniably strong, residents from many other ethnic backgrounds contribute to the high quality of life here—Dutch, Germans, and Chinese, to name but a few.

Although metropolitan Victoria is large in both area and population, the downtown section, where most visitors tend to stay, gives the impression of being smaller and more intimate. You can visit most of the attractions, shops, restaurants, and entertainment spots on foot.

Victoria is an immaculately clean city. Most of the older buildings have been declared heritage places and have been refurbished into boutiques, dining spots, and professional offices. Visually, the city is very attractive—particularly around the Inner Harbour area, which is used primarily for pleasure boats—with its parks and shore walks and flower baskets hanging from lampposts. Victoria has a slower pace than that of Vancouver.

Victoria has the mildest weather in British Columbia. Although there is a great deal of rain in winter, as is the case all along the coast, many colorful flowers bloom in February, and during this otherwise harsh season duffers in tweed knickers are out shooting a round of eighteen holes at the local golf clubs. Spring, summer, and early autumn are truly magnificent, with mostly bright skies and dry air. The grass is lush, and flowers abound. Almost everywhere are views of the sea and distant mountains—those on Vancouver Island and in the state of Washington. Washington's snowcapped volcano, Mount Baker, is a familiar sight, and so are the peaks of the Cascades and those in Olympic National Park.

Victoria is a city of walkers, joggers, bikers, sailors, golfers, and tennis players. All ages participate in exercise and recreation. The Christmas season is a special time in Victoria; both the hotels and the city attempt to create a Dickensian holiday feel, and people come here just to enjoy a Victorian Noel. It takes a little extra effort to get to Victoria, but few visitors come away disappointed.

A Brief Look at Victoria's History

The human history of the Victoria area is many millennia old. First Nations peoples developed an advanced civilization based on fishing and hunting and created art that many connoisseurs consider the finest produced by the indigenous peoples of North America. Their culture went into decline with the coming of the Europeans.

Native Life Before European Settlement

An extensive First Nations population occupied British Columbia's islands, shoreline, and interior rivers for more than 10,000 years prior to the arrival of European explorers. More than thirty groups had developed, each with a distinctive language, culture and territorial identity.

In the northern interior, where resources were scattered, people lived in small and nomadic groups. To the south, along the Fraser and Thompson Rivers, abundant fish and game supported winter villages of sod-roofed pit houses.

The coastal societies were the most highly organized and structured. In many households dozens of people lived under the single roof of a large cedar dwelling. They had their own hunting grounds, fishing sites, and places for gathering berries, roots, and bark. They also devised unique ritual songs, dances, and crests depicting their histories.

Households held "potlaches," elaborate banquets and performances, which sometimes lasted for several days. These occasions celebrated marriages, honored the dead, and repaid debts. A chief's status was measured in the amount of food, tools, and clothing given away.

With little more than stone adzes, chisels, and (later) knives, the coastal societies fashioned bark and wood of cedar trees into clothing, baskets, boxes, totem poles, and dugout canoes. The latter were essential for trade, hunting, and communication with other villages. It was likely that they were also used to row out and meet the newly arriving Europeans.

In 1843 James Douglas, who was the chief factor for the Hudson's Bay Company at Fort Vancouver (on the Columbia River in what is now the state of Washington), chose the tip of this peninsula jutting into the Strait of Juan de Fuca as the site of Fort Victoria. The political reason a trading fort was established here is that the United States and Great Britain were in the process of establishing the forty-ninth parallel as the international boundary between much of British North America (Canada) and the United

States. The tip of Vancouver Island at Fort Victoria extended a considerable distance below the forty-ninth. By maintaining sovereignty over all of Vancouver Island and its valuable resources in this manner, further U.S. territorial claims were blunted. If you look at a map, you'll see that the U.S.–Canada border follows the forty-ninth parallel for thousands of miles until it hits the west coast, where it loops around the southern end of Vancouver Island.

As fur trading faded away in Victoria, the settlement became a major port for the processing and shipment of the island's rich lumber and mineral resources. Gold was also discovered in the Fraser River region in 1858, and Victoria became a boomtown for people en route to seeking wealth there. During the mid-1800s the port was a contrast of bawdy houses and saloons, beautiful mansions and churches, the rough and crude, the gentle and cultivated. It became a city in 1862.

At nearby Esquimalt Harbour, in 1865, the British Admiralty established a naval base. Victoria became first the capital of Vancouver Island and later, in 1871, a part of the province of British Columbia. It remained the major city of British Columbia until the transcontinental railroad linked the vast territory between the Atlantic and Pacific coasts to Vancouver. From then on the economic importance of Victoria diminished while Vancouver's rose. The provincial capital was originally in New Westminster—former name of the city of Vancouver—but protests forced the seat of government to be moved in 1868 to Victoria, where it has remained since.

Victoria Today: Some Basic Facts

Although some light manufacturing (furniture, machinery, food, rubber and plastic products, etc.) takes place in the city, Victoria's main occupation and preoccupation is government, both provincial and federal. Thousands of people are employed in the government bureaucracy. The second most important economic activity is tourism, followed by education, retail sales, and various kinds of personal and professional services. Fishing, ship repair, agriculture, and the shipment, through its seaport, of the island's natural resources (lumber, fish, minerals, and farm products) are other principal ways the people of Victoria make their living.

The population of greater Victoria is about 318,000. The people live in Victoria proper and in the surrounding communities of Sooke, Esquimalt, Oak Bay, and those on the Saanich Peninsula.

Special Events

January
Polar Bear Swim
Victoria Symphony

February
Various musical, theatrical,
   and visual arts events
Flower Count

March
Various musical, theatrical,
   and visual arts events

April
Terrifuice Jazz Party
Victoria International
   Blossom Walks

May
Victoria Day holiday and
   parade
Luxton Pro Rodeo
Victoria Harbor Festival

June
Oak Bay Tea Party
Folkfest International
Jazzfest International

July
Canada Day holiday
Victoria Shakespeare Festival
Rootsfest Music Festival

August
All Day Logger Sports
Classic Boat Festival
Dragon Boat Festival
Symphony Splash
First Peoples Festival

September
Classic Boat Festival
The Saanichton Fall Fair
Vancouver Island Brewery
   Blues Bash
Luxton Fall Fair

October
Royal Victoria Marathon
Goldstream Salmon Run
Ghost Bus Tours

November
Christmas Craft Fair, Crystal
   Gardens
Christmas at Craigdarroch
   Castle

December
Nutcracker, Royal Theatre
Christmas Craft Fair
Victoria Christmas
Christmas at Butchart
   Gardens
Eagle Extravaganza
Festival of Trees, Empress
   Hotel

Victoria is a popular retirement community, attracting hundreds of new inhabitants because of its mild climate, high quality of life, and excellent services for the elderly. There is, however, a good mix of all ages here.

The central city has no excessively tall buildings, except for a few multistory hotels. Almost every structure is on a human scale. There are plenty of nice parks and walking areas, gardens and floral displays, magnificent views of mountains and sea, and top-quality goods in stores. The cultural life—music, stage, and the visual arts—is quite rich and diverse. When discussing Victoria, there are few defects to complain about.

How to Get to Victoria

Although situated on an island, Victoria is easy to reach by private or rented car, by bus, and by air. On Vancouver Island the Trans-Canada Highway itself extends from Nanaimo and ends at "mile 0" in Victoria. The B.C. ferries are modern, large-capacity vessels that link the island with the mainland at several points and also provide trips through the famous Inside Passage (detailed later in this chapter).

By Car

From Vancouver. The quickest way to get here is by Highway 99 South to Highway 17, which leads to the ferry terminal at Tsawwassen. (This is also the best way for those coming up from Washington, Oregon, and California. Highway 99 North, connecting with U.S. I-5, is your best route in B.C.)

Another way—one that allows you to tour more of Vancouver Island—is to take Lion's Gate Bridge to West Vancouver, then follow Highway 99 to the ferry terminal at Horseshoe Bay. The ferry goes to Departure Bay in Nanaimo. Follow Highway 1A for a scenic marine drive or Highway 1 for a more direct route. Both highways will take you to Victoria.

From Seattle, Washington. The ferry terminal is located off Elliott Avenue at Elliott Bay.

From Anacortes, Washington. Take U.S. I-5 North to Highway 20 West to the ferry terminal in Anacortes.

From Olympia, Washington, via the Olympic Peninsula to Port Angeles. Take Highway 101, which circles the peninsula. If you have extra time, tour the west side of the peninsula, which borders on the open Pacific and Olympic National Park, one of the most splendid natural areas in the United States.

By Bus

Frequent, comfortable bus/ferry service is available between Vancouver and Victoria on Pacific Coach Lines. In Victoria call (250) 385–4411; the terminal is at 710 Douglas Street, behind the Empress Hotel. In Vancouver call (604) 662–7575; the terminal is at 1150 Station.

By Ferry

The most pleasant way to get to Victoria/Vancouver Island is on one of the B.C. Ferries. It's amazing how many cars and campers these modern vessels can carry (the average for vehicles is 320). Tractor-trailer trucks go into the bottom hold, while cars are carried on the second level. The enclosed passenger decks have comfortable nonsmoking sections, a coffee bar, a cafeteria, a buffet lounge, and a newsstand. The open decks have benches for relaxation and plenty of space for strolling about. Smoking is not permitted in the interior areas of B.C. Ferries vessels. En route the scenery is gorgeous, with lovely islands and plenty of birds to see, including bald eagles.

From Vancouver to Victoria, using the terminals of Tsawwassen on the mainland and Swartz Bay on the island: During summer (late June to early September) there are sailings every hour from 7:00 A.M. to 10:00 P.M.; the same schedule applies for return trips. The sailing time is approximately ninety minutes.

From Vancouver to Nanaimo, using the terminals at Horseshoe Bay on the mainland and Departure Bay on the island: same schedule and sailing time as above. From Nanaimo you can go farther "up island" to Port Hardy, across the island to Port Alberni and the Pacific Rim National Park, or "down island" to Victoria, which is 112 km/67.2 mi south via the Trans-Canada.

You should be at the ferry terminal at least an hour prior to sailing. Travel is on a first-come, first-served basis. Reservations are available for the Vancouver-Victoria and Vancouver-Nanaimo routes for a $15 fee. You can make reservations by calling (888) BC–FERRY (within B.C.). Complete information and reservation service is available online at www.bcferries.com. Check on length of waiting time during the peak months of July and August. For more information call B.C. Ferries' twenty-four-hour recorded messages—Vancouver, (604) 277–0277; Victoria, (250) 656–0757; and Nanaimo, (250) 753–6626.

Ferry Web Sites

BC Ferries: www.bcferries.com
Washington State Ferries: www.wsdot.wa.gov/ferries
Black Ball Transport: www.northolympic.com/coho
Victoria Clipper: www.victoriaclipper.com

Reservations are available for the Gulf Islands routes on-line as well. Prepayment of the full fare is required in order to confirm reservations.

Ferry service is also available on Washington State Ferries—(206) 464–6400 in Washington; (604) 656–1531 in B.C.—via Anacortes, Washington; there are two sailings daily in summer and one during winter. Sailing time is three hours and twenty minutes. Blackball Transport—(206) 457–4491 in Port Angeles, (260) 457–4491 in Victoria—has four sailings daily (in peak season) between Port Angeles, Washington, on the Olympic Peninsula, and downtown Victoria. Sailing time is one hour and thirty-five minutes. Washington State Ferries offers fares and schedules online at www.wsdot.wa/gov/ferries.

The *Victoria Clipper* ferry provides two-and-a-half-hour service between Victoria and Seattle. Passengers only; no vehicles. Call (250) 382–8100 in Victoria and (206) 448–5000 in Seattle.

By Plane

The following airlines provide regularly scheduled service between the mainland at Vancouver International Airport and Victoria: Air Canada (with connections to major North American and international cities), Air B.C. (this airline provides service throughout the province, even to remote coastal areas), Burrard Air, Canadian Airlines, San Juan Airlines (has several trips daily to and from Seattle), and Skyline Airlines. The Victoria International Airport itself is located in Sidney, off Highway 17, 30 km/18 mi north of Victoria and a few miles south of the Vancouver ferry terminal at Swartz Bay. Rental cars are available at the airport.

By Seaplane

You can also fly from downtown Vancouver to downtown Victoria via Harbor Air (www.harborair.com) seaplane service, or by

Helijet (www.helijet.com). Helijet also flys from Victoria to Seattle (Ogden Point to Boeing Field).

By Train

VIA Rail—(800) 561–8630 from Western Canada—provides Vancouver Island rail service between Victoria and Courtenay, with stops at Nanaimo. From the Victoria area you can get ferries to the United States and to Vancouver via Swartz Bay. From Nanaimo you can take the ferry to the mainland—Horseshoe Bay to the city of Vancouver.

How to Get Around in Victoria

The best way to get around in downtown Victoria is on foot. Most of the major attractions are here—the Royal British Columbia Museum, the boutiques and specialty stores, the wax museum, Inner Harbour, afternoon tea served at the Empress Hotel and other establishments, and so forth.

You can orient yourself on the front steps of the Empress Hotel. Directly across from you is Inner Harbour with its promenade and yacht moorings. The street in front is Government Street. If you go north on Government, you will pass by most of the fine shops selling woolens, china, books, and so on. Government Street will take you to Fisgard Street, which, in this section of the city, is Chinatown.

From the Empress going north, Government bisects Humboldt, Courtney, Broughton, Fort, View, Yates, Johnson, and Pandora; it runs parallel to Gordon, Broad, Douglas, and Blanshard. Within this general area are shops, department stores, boutiques, cafes, restaurants, malls, and theaters.

Going south on Government, you cross Belleville Street, on which are located the Parliament buildings (at a right angle to the Empress on Inner Harbour), Royal London Wax Museum, Undersea Gardens, hotels, the Archives, the Royal British Columbia Museum, Thunderbird Park, the bus station, Crystal Garden, and Victoria's new Conference Centre. Douglas Street, which runs parallel to Government, heading south, goes by Beacon Hill Park and ends at Dallas Road, part of the scenic Marine Drive.

Other areas and their attractions can be easily reached by car, taxi, kabuki cab, horse and buggy, or bus and double-deckers—for example, the campus of the University of Victoria is off High-

Visitor Information Centre

At the junction of Wharf and Government—812 Wharf Street, on the Inner Harbour and across from the Empress Hotel—the Visitor Information Centre is a good source for maps, brochures, directions, and information on accommodations in Victoria. Call (250) 382–2127 for tourism information at any time of the year.

For hotel reservations call this toll-free information number: (800) 663–3883.

way 17, via McKenzie Avenue. Butchart Gardens is off Highway 17 North; follow signs. As a matter of fact, signs leading to attractions are very good in the Victoria area, and you should not get lost.

Public Bus Service

B.C. Transit provides bus service on downtown routes from 6:00 A.M. to midnight every day of the week. The company sells day passes for unlimited rides. Call (250) 382–6161 for information and rates. For online information visit www.bctransit.com.

Taxis, Rental Cars, and Bikes

Ask the concierge or desk clerk at your hotel or motel for assistance in securing a cab, or call the following companies:

Bluebird Taxi, (250) 382–3611.

Budget Rental Car, (250) 953–5300.

Cycle Victoria Rentals, (250) 385–2453, 950 Wharf Street, rents bicycles, motorcycles, and scooters.

Parking

A number of public parking garages are scattered throughout downtown. The P sign will lead you to one in the area you want to visit. There is metered street parking, but pay attention to the time limits and keep the meter honest. Victoria has a reputation for having its tow trucks waiting in the wings to scoop up the vehicles of visitors and residents alike; this situation is one of the few blemishes on an otherwise superb city.

Useful Information

Victoria police: (250) 945–7654 (nonemergency)
Emergency: 911
Medical emergency: 911
Royal Jubilee Hospital: (250) 370–8000 (nonemergency) or (250) 370–8212 (emergency)
Victoria General Hospital: (250) 727–4212
Emergency road services: (250) 383–1155 (twenty-four hours)

Touring Services

The following touring services provide sightseeing in Victoria:
Grayline Tours, (250) 388–5248. Free pickup at major hotels. Sightseeing of local area attractions; trips to Butchart Gardens.
Tally-Ho Sightseeing, (250) 479–1113. Located beside Parliament buildings and opposite Royal London Wax Museum. Provides one-hour, horse-drawn tours of Victoria.
Bird's Eye View Walking Tours, (250) 592–9255. Departs from the Visitor Information Centre for one-hour tours of the Empress Hotel and hour-and-a-quarter historical or theme tours.

Attractions

Butchart Gardens, located 22.5 km/14 mi north of Victoria via Highway 17. Call (250) 652–5256 for recorded information or 652–4422 for questions. Open throughout the year. Because of heavy traffic during the peak months of July and August, admittance into the gardens may be limited. Admission is charged.

If there is a North American paradise for horticulturists and simple lovers of flowers and landscaping, it is Butchart Gardens. Here you will be dazzled by splendid displays of innumerable kinds of flowers, plants, shrubs, and trees, all arranged along a walking tour that takes you through the very heart of Eden itself. Butchart features Italian, English Rose, Japanese, and Sunken Gardens. There are ponds, waterfalls, a dancing fountain, two restaurants, and a coffee bar. Books, seeds, plants, and gardening tools can be purchased at the Seed and Gift Shop. Daily entertainment in the form of stage shows and music is provided from mid-May through September, with the special addition of fireworks on Saturday. Write or phone for a copy of the *Butchart Gardens Enter-*

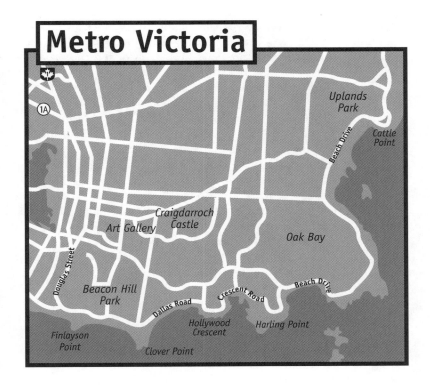

Metro Victoria

Uplands Park

Cattle Point

Beach Drive

Craigdarroch Castle

Art Gallery

Oak Bay

Douglas Street

Beacon Hill Park

Dallas Road

Crescent Road

Beach Drive

Hollywood Crescent

Harling Point

Finlayson Point

Clover Point

tainment Guide. When you're on site, the staff will loan you umbrellas, wheelchairs, and pushcarts for babies. Moorages are also available for visitors in the area on their own yachts. Buses provide frequent transportation to Butchart Gardens from Victoria and from the city of Vancouver. When you walk through the sumptuous gardens, it is hard to imagine that this place was once a drab limestone quarry. The late Jennie Butchart was the main force in transforming gouged-out land into one of the premier horticultural attractions in the world (the work began in 1904). To visit British Columbia and miss experiencing Butchart Gardens is to turn your back on the beauty that the hands of God and human beings have wrought together.

Scenic Marine Drive follows the coastline along Dallas Road and offers spectacular views of the distant Olympic Mountains across the Strait of Juan de Fuca. It passes through parts of the swank Rockland residential area and continues past the lovely Victoria Golf Course, which is in full operation during winter, and through the prestigious Oak Bay community. The drive continues through the high-priced area of Uplands to the Saanich Peninsula and on to Cordova Bay. There are many stopping places along the way where you can enjoy the views and stroll or jog the promenades.

Thunderbird Park, located at the corner of Belleville and Douglas, next to the Royal British Columbia Museum, is a small grass area decorated with tall totem poles and a Kwakiutl dance house. Here's a perfect spot to take pictures of your friends in front of the fantastic carvings of the region's First Nations.

Beacon Hill Park, between Douglas and Cook Streets and bordering Dallas Road (a five-minute walk from the Empress Hotel), is a 62-ha/154-acre enclave of flower beds, ponds, oaks, and cedars. There are communities of royal swans and many different birds, including the giant black raven. At the Dallas Road end of the park is one of the world's tallest totem poles. Also within Beacon Hill Park is a children's farm replete with donkeys, miniature horses, peacocks, goats, and pigs. Children have a place where they can pet the young animals.

Parliament Buildings, Belleville Street, facing Victoria Harbour and at a right angle to the Empress Hotel. Call (250) 387–3046 for tour information. Tours are given in not only English but also French, Japanese, Italian, and German; they're conducted during summer months, but the buildings are open throughout the year. Free. These buildings were designed by Francis Mawson Rattenbury, an Englishman who was also the architect of the Empress Hotel and the Crystal Gardens. The Parliament (provincial legislative) Buildings are impressive enough to grace the capital of a good-size country; they could certainly accommodate Canada's federal Parliament, should it ever decide to move out of Ottawa. Completed in 1898, this complex for enacting legislation and governing the province is a massive building of domes, towers, and arches. The interior is rich with marble. If the legislature is in session while you're passing through, you may observe the proceedings of the lawmakers. During the evening the outline of the complex is illuminated with thousands of bulbs, giving it a Christmasy feel even in midsummer. A large expanse of lawn flows from the center building down toward Victoria's Inner Harbour. Set back a few feet from Belleville Street and in a straight line to the main portal of the complex is a majestic statue of Queen Victoria (one of the best sculptures of her in Canada), from whose patronage this city takes its name.

Royal British Columbia Museum, 675 Belleville Street, near the Parliament Buildings, (250) 387–3014. Open daily, except

Christmas Day and New Year's Day. Admission is charged. This extensive museum is one of Victoria's best attractions. The Royal B.C. Museum concentrates on the peoples, industries, and ecology of the province. The displays of First Nations art are superb. There are mounted animals (the woolly mammoth is awesome), fish, and birds common to B.C. One display re-creates a frontier town, allowing you to walk through as if you've zoomed backward several decades in time. A tearoom and a gift shop are on the main floor.

Helmcken House, 10 Elliot Street, (250) 387–3440. Open daily. Donations are accepted. This historic 1852 residence belonged to Dr. J. S. Helmcken, a man who brought medical science to a needful community in its pioneering days. You can see the original furnishings and medical instruments of that bygone era.

Point Ellice House Museum, 2616 Pleasant Street, (250) 385–4697. Open daily. Admission is charged. A magistrate named Peter O'Reilly built this fine house in 1861. The house itself, its original furnishings, and displays will give you a fair idea of how well the Establishment lived at a rugged and woolly time in the city's early history.

Pacific Undersea Gardens, 490 Belleville Street, (250) 382–5717. Open daily. Admission is charged. This museum of marine life is well worth a visit. In an undersea gallery you see living specimens of thousands of marine animals. The Northwest Coast is an exceptionally rich environment for a wide diversity of marine life, including the world's largest octopuses. A scuba diver puts on a show working with a huge Pacific octopus.

Victoria Heritage Village, 321 Belleville Street. Open daily. Admission is charged to some attractions. Heritage Village is a complex of shops and tourist attractions.

Royal London Wax Museum, 470 Belleville Street, www.wax-world.com. Open every day, with extended hours during summer. Admission is charged. Figures of British royalty, Canadian greats, and famous and infamous figures from throughout history—more than 180 of them, made in London—are here authentically costumed and set in displays portraying their times. The kids love the horror and fantasy displays, and Anglophiles adore the renditions of the queen and members of her family.

Crystal Garden, 713 Douglas Street, (250) 953–8800 or www.bcpcc.com/crystal. Open daily. Admission is charged. The setting is that of a tropical garden containing 150 species of plants and 50 species of exotic birds, monkeys, and reptiles. The attraction has several souvenir boutiques and restaurants as well.

Miniature World, 649 Humboldt Street (at the Empress Hotel), (604) 385–9731 or www.miniatureworld.com. Open daily. Admission is charged. Things miniature have always been popular. At this attraction you'll see what is purported to be the "world's largest doll house," a neighborhood in "ye olde London," and "one of the world's largest rail scenes and the world's smallest operational sawmill."

Anne Hathaway's Cottage, 429 Lampson Street, (250) 388–4353. Admission is charged. Full-size replica of the home of Shakespeare's wife. Fully guided forty-five minute tours explaining Shakespearean life and how many colloquial expressions developed.

Horticulture Centre of the Pacific, 505 Quayle Road, (250) 479–6162. Open dawn to dusk year-round. Admission is charged. A botanical garden with walking paths and benches, this is a living museum. The plant collections on display are those most suitable for the regional climate and soils. The Winter Garden is of special interest from November through March.

Butterfly Gardens, 1461 Benvenuto Avenue, (250) 652–3382 or www.victoriabc.com/attract/butterfly.htm. Open daily; admission is charged. Stroll amid hundreds of dazzling, free-flying butterflies and witness their fascinating life cycle. Birds, fish, and beautiful blooms complete this enchanting indoor tropical garden.

National Geographic IMAX Theatre, 675 Belleville Street, (250) 480–4887. Open daily; admission is charged. Located within the Royal British Columbia Museum building, the National Geographic Theatre shows a variety of films, often in conjunction with the exhibits at the museum.

Victoria Bug Zoo, 1107 Wharf Street, (250) 384–2847 or www.bugzoo.bc.ca. Open daily; admission is charged. This indoor zoo features bizarre and exotic insects, spiders, scorpions, centipedes, millipedes, and more. Entomologists act as interpreters and allow visitors to handle some of the bugs.

Canadian Scottish Regimental Museum, 715 Bay Street, (250) 363–8753 or www.islandnet.com/~csr.muse. Located on the second floor of the Bay Street Armory, a national historic site built in 1914. Artifacts and exhibits depict the history and accomplishments of the citizen-soldiers of Vancouver Island's only Highland Regiment in times of peace and war.

Mineral World and Scratch Patch, 9891 Seaport Place, (250) 655–4367 or www.islandnet.com/~mineral. Open daily; free admission. An outdoor garden patio filled with millions of polished semiprecious stones, tropical shells, a gold-panning pool, museum displays, fossils, gemstone jewelry, and beads.

"Mile 0," where Douglas Street meets Dallas Road. Although "Mile 0" doesn't sound like much of anything, it is the western starting point of the Trans-Canada Highway, the world's longest national highway—7,820 km/4,860 mi. For those of us who have traveled long stretches of the Trans-Canada in all kinds of weather, this is a major attraction indeed.

Bastion Square, entrance off Government Street, between Yates and Fort Streets at the foot of View Street. Here was the original site of Fort Victoria, established by James Douglas of the Hudson's Bay Company in 1843. Several buildings of historic importance are in Bastion Square: the Board of Trade Building (1893); the Court Building (1889), Victoria's first concrete building, which now houses a maritime museum; Law Chambers (turn of the twentieth century), which now has several shops; Burns House (1882), once a brothel; and Strousse Warehouse (1885), which supplied gold miners.

Maritime Museum of British Columbia, 28 Bastion Square, (250) 385–4222 or www.mmbc.bc.ca. Open daily. Admission is charged. The Maritime Museum has a wide assortment of marine artifacts; ship models; exhibits centering on Captain Cook, who sailed hereabouts in the eighteenth century; and displays portraying the history of Britain's Royal Navy and the Canadian Navy as they pertain to British Columbia. The museum houses the *Tilikum* and the *Trekka,* two famous B.C. sailing vessels that circumnavigated the globe.

Art Gallery of Greater Victoria, 1040 Moss Street, (250) 384–4101 or www.aggv.bc.ca. Open daily. Admission is charged. The Art Gallery collection includes European prints and drawings, English decorative art, and Canadian art, both historical and contemporary. Its excellent collection of Japanese art is one of the finest on the continent. The Art Gallery has the only Shinto shrine outside Japan. A cafe and shop are within the Spencer Mansion complex.

Government House, 1401 Rockland Avenue, (250) 387–2080, is the official residence of the lieutenant governor of British Columbia and the place where Elizabeth II, queen of Canada, and other members of the monarchy stay when visiting this part of the province. The beautiful grounds are, however, open to the public—except, of course, when royalty is in residence or during special events. You'll find a sunken rose garden, formal lawns and other gardens, a lily pond, and many exquisite botanical features, both indigenous and specially planted.

Craigdarroch Castle, 1050 Joan Crescent, (250) 592–5323 or www.craigdarrochcastle.com. Open daily. Admission is charged. Scots have a penchant for building grand castles for themselves. This was so with Robert Dunsmuir, who in 1851 left the heather-covered hills of Scotland to settle in Victoria. Dunsmuir, known as the coal king of British Columbia, made a great deal of money and spent $650,000 (a king's ransom in those days) building Craigdarroch Castle. Completed in 1889, Craigdarroch is not a castle in the classic medieval sense. But as an immense, impressive mansion, Craigdarroch can be topped by few other similar places in Canada. There are guides to answer questions and make a visit here memorable.

Craigflower Manor Farmhouse, 110 Island Highway, (250) 356–5137. Phone for hours. Free. The farmhouse and schoolhouse on this site were part of a Hudson's Bay Company farm established in 1853. The farmhouse contains furniture from this mid-nineteenth-century period (most of the pieces are originally from Scotland).

Craigflower School, 2765 Admirals Road, (250) 387–4697. Open daily during summer by appointment only. Free. For those interested in Canada's pioneering heritage, Craigflower School is the oldest standing schoolhouse in Western Canada, built around 1855.

Dominion Astrophysical Observatory, 5071 West Saanich Road (best taken in when going to or from Butchart Gardens), (250) 388–0012. Open daily in summer. Free. You'll find a giant telescope here and interesting exhibits dealing with astronomical phenomena. The public can view the heavens through the telescope on Saturday evening. A fine panoramic view of the countryside can be had from this facility.

Chinatown, on Fisgard Street, is a compact section of small restaurants and stores selling Oriental goods. The food is quite good here. The Chinese community has a number of festivals throughout the year. The entrance to Chinatown is marked by the ornate "Gates of Harmonious Interest," where Fisgard bisects Government Street.

Centennial Square, off Douglas Street, is the location of city hall and the McPherson Theatre, where many entertainments are performed. Shops and restaurants surround a landscaped courtyard.

Fort Rodd Hill National Historic Park and Fisgard Lighthouse, 603 Fort Rodd Hill Road, (250) 478–2816. Open daily, except certain holidays. Free. The Fort Rodd/Fisgard Lighthouse area (designated a national park) offers many acres of lovely, tranquil parkland overlooking Esquimalt Harbour. Explore the nineteenth-century artillery installations. Fisgard is British Columbia's oldest lighthouse, built in 1859.

Maltwood Art Museum and Gallery, at the University of Victoria, (250) 721–8298. Open daily, except Saturday. Free. By visiting this art museum you will also have a chance to stroll the pleasant campus of the University of Victoria. The main gallery, located in the University Centre building, features art exhibits and the Katharine Maltwood collection of decorative arts, paintings, sculptures, graphics, archaeological artifacts, glass, textiles, ceramics, and furniture. Exhibitions by contemporary artists are held at the McPherson Library Gallery.

The Carillon, at the corner of Belleville and Government Streets in Heritage Court. With sixty-two bells, this is the largest carillon in Canada and the seventh largest in the world. It is a gift to the province from Canadians of Dutch ancestry.

All Fun Waterslide Park, north on Trans-Canada Highway 1, 13 km/8 mi from Victoria; (250) 474–4546. Open late May to mid-June on weekends and daily mid-June through Labour Day. Call for hours and fees. The park has fifteen water slides, a whitewater river ride, a car museum, minigolf, and more.

Accommodations

Victoria is one of Canada's most popular tourist cities, and reservations during the summer season and over the Christmas holidays are essential. Call ahead, or have your travel agent do so.

The Empress, 721 Government Street, (250) 384–8111; (800) 442–1414; www.fairmont.com. The Empress is a landmark hotel known to sophisticated travelers throughout the world. It reflects the essence of bygone elegance in its neo-Gothic architecture, ambience, service, and civility. Central to all attractions and within steps of the Parliament buildings, the hotel overlooks Victoria Harbour and the moorings of luxurious yachts. The Empress features fine restaurants, shops, and many amenities. It has become a popular place to stay during the Christmas season, when Victoria takes on a Dickensian feel, and a number of tour companies offer special Christmas holiday trips to Victoria with stays at the Empress; contact your travel agent for details. The most popular tradition at the Empress is afternoon tea, in the English manner. The best of the house is served on bone china with sterling: English honey crumpets, fruit salad, homemade scones with Jersey cream and strawberry jam, assorted tea sandwiches, Empress cakes, and

The Empress Hotel on the yacht harbor in Victoria is one of the world's most famous hotels. Here the tradition of English-style afternoon tea is sacred, ample, and punctual.

Empress blend tea. There are four sittings during summer months and three during winter. Because of its popularity, having afternoon tea at the Empress requires a reservation and proper dress. The Empress has undergone a $45-million renovation. Improvements include the addition of a swimming pool and a health and fitness facility, the total renovation of all guest rooms, a more beautiful and serviceable lobby, and the restoration of the stunning stained-glass ceiling in Palm Court. Expensive.

Clarion Hotel Grand Pacific, 450 Québec Street, (250) 386–0450; (800) 663–7550. A deluxe hotel offering many services and amenities—swimming pool, sauna, whirlpool, health and fitness facilities, restaurant, lounge. Good downtown location. Expensive.

Executive House, 777 Douglas Street, (250) 388–5111; (800) 663–7001. Excellent accommodations, including luxury penthouse suites. Indoor pool, sauna, free parking, and Barkley's Steak and Seafood Restaurant, a fine eatery. This hotel is central to everything—attractions and government and commercial offices. Moderate to expensive.

Ramada Huntington Manor Inn, 330 Québec Street, (250) 381–3456; (800) 663–7557. A top-of-the-line hotel with most amenities. Excellent location. Moderate to expensive.

The Gatsby Mansion, 309 Bellville Street, (250) 388–9191; (800) 563–9656. This is the new name of the Captain's Palace. The mansion is more than one hundred years old and it has lost none of the charm of the former owners. This is one of Victoria's great B&Bs, a return to the 1920s with twenty rooms in a house of crystal chandeliers, stained-glass windows, a martini bar, and hand-frescoed ceilings. A restaurant that specializes in upscale Northwest cuisine overlooks Victoria Harbor. Expensive.

Laurel Point Inn, 680 Montréal Street, (250) 386–8721; (800) 663–7667; www.laurelpoint.com. One of Victoria's best hotels— a superb location; all rooms with balconies and a water view; swimming pools, tennis, dining room, and lounges. Free parking. Expensive.

The Beaconsfield Inn, 998 Humboldt Street, (250) 384–4044 or www.islandnet.com/beaconsfield. Elegant rooms in an English-style mansion located near Inner Harbour. Some rooms have canopy beds. There are fireplaces and down comforters, a guest library, and a sunroom. Moderate to expensive.

Best Western Carlton Plaza, 642 Johnson, (250) 388–5513; (800) 663–7241; www.bestwesterncarlton.com. All amenities, European–style hotel in central downtown. Moderate to expensive.

Queen Victoria Inn, 655 Douglas Street, (250) 386–1312; (800) 663–7007; www.queenvictoriainn.com. A nice location facing Thunderbird Park and other downtown attractions. Offers comfortable rooms, whirlpool and sauna, restaurant, suites with Jacuzzi and marble fireplace. Expensive.

Best Western Inner Harbour, 412 Québec Street, (250) 384–5122; (888) 383–BEST. An excellent hotel in a superb location, facing Inner Harbour and Quadra Park. Amenities include swimming pool, sauna, Jacuzzi, kitchenettes, penthouse suites with fireplaces. Expensive.

Oak Bay Beach Hotel, 1175 Beach Drive, via Marine Drive, (250) 598–4556; (800) 668–7758; www.oakbaybeachhotel.bc.ca. A lovely Tudor-style hotel right on the water's edge, with views of snowcapped mountains in the distance. In addition to the usual hotel amenities, Oak Bay has an English-style pub and a fine dining room overlooking the water and mountains. This is a very friendly place whose staff members are eager to please. Oak Bay also has a yacht for cruising and fishing trips and evening dinner sails. Moderate to expensive.

Harbour Towers, 345 Québec Street, (250) 385–2405; (800) 663–5896; www.harbortowers.com. A full-service hotel near the Inner Harbour, shopping areas, and downtown attractions. Moderate to expensive.

Chateau Victoria, 740 Burdett Avenue, (250) 382–4221; (800) 663–5891; www.chateauvictoria.com. One of Victoria's top hotels, offering an indoor pool, a sauna, satellite TV, free parking, a central location, and the city's only rooftop restaurant, called Vista 18. Expensive.

James Bay Inn, 270 Government Street, (250) 384–7151; (800) 836–2649; www.jamesbayinn.bc.ca. Comfortable accommodations, convenient location, reasonable rates, restaurant. Inexpensive to moderate.

Magnolia Hotel and Suites, 623 Courtney Street, (250) 381–0999; (877) 624–6654. This sixty-six-room European-style hotel is located within Victoria's historic Inner Harbour district and affords guests easy access to all central attractions and shopping. Moderate to expensive.

Embassy Motor Inn, 520 Menzies Street, (250) 382–8161; (800) 268–8161. Located next to the Parliament Buildings and within a few steps of the promenades circling the Inner Harbour; has kitchenettes, a sauna, a pool, parking, and a restaurant. Moderate.

Olde England Inn, 429 Lampson Street, (250) 388–4353. A well-known accommodation that transports you to Elizabethan times. You can sleep in a canopy bed that was previously used by royalty and feast on roast beef and Yorkshire pudding—along with several pints of good stout ale, of course. Part of this complex is Anne Hathaway's Cottage, an authentically furnished sixteenth-century dwelling that seems as though it had been plucked from a street in Stratford-upon-Avon itself. The cottage is filled with furnishings from that period, and the guides are costumed as comely Tudor wenches. Moderate to expensive.

Royal Scot Suite Hotel, 425 Québec Street, (250) 388–5463; (800) 663–7515; www.royalscot.com. The Royal Scot gives you good value by providing a suite for the price of a room. Free local calls, indoor pool, saunas, Jacuzzi, masseur, tearoom, exercise facilities. Moderate to expensive.

Cherry Bank Hotel, 825 Burdett Avenue, (250) 385–5380; (800) 998–6688. Dating from the 1890s, this old building in a quiet residential area has some family suites and kitchens, rooms with canopy beds, plus a lounge and restaurant. No phones or TVs. Three blocks from the downtown area. Inexpensive to moderate.

Crystal Court Motel, 701 Belleville Street, (250) 384–0551. Downtown location, some housekeeping units. Moderate.

University of Victoria Housing Services, P.O. Box 1700, Victoria, British Columbia V8W 2Y2; (250) 721–8395; www.housing.uvic.ca. From May 1 through August 30, comfortable rooms are available at the University of Victoria, located a few minutes' drive north of downtown, as well as on the bus route. Price includes breakfast and free parking. An excellent value for the thrifty. Inexpensive.

Other Good Places to Stay

Best Canadian B&B Network, 1064 Balfour Avenue, Vancouver, British Columbia V6H 1X1; (604) 738–7027.

Vacations West (vacation home rentals), Suite 581, 185–911 Yates Street, Victoria, British Columbia V8V 4Y9; (250) 383–1863; (888) 383–1863; www.vacationswest.com.

Dogwood Manor Hideaway, 1124 Fairfield Road, (250) 361–4441. A 1910 interesting "character" home that offers suites and kitchens and welcomes families. Moderate.

The Henderson House, 522 Quadra Street, (250) 384–3428. Considered one of the most photographed houses in the city; features nicely furnished rooms with antiques. Located near all downtown attractions. Full breakfasts are served in the oak-paneled dining room. Moderate.

Dining

Victoria offers a wide choice of restaurants. Seafood and traditional British dishes are featured. Ethnic fare, such as Chinese, Japanese, Greek, and Italian, is also widely available. French cuisine is excellent. The Bengal Lounge at the Empress serves Indian dishes with chutney and other condiments; its seafood with chutney on Friday is a must. All restaurants in Victoria are nonsmoking.

Blethering Place Tea Room and Restaurant, 2250 Oak Bay Avenue, (250) 598–1413; (888) 598–1413. Located in beautiful Oak Bay, this cozy, friendly tearoom serves breakfast, lunch, and dinner. Moderate.

Camille's Restaurant, 45 Bastion Square, (250) 381–3433. Delicious French cooking, including mouthwatering breads and cakes. Moderate.

Bowman's Rib House, 825 Burdett Street, (250) 385–5380. Here's where you can satisfy your hunger for pork baby back ribs, also steaks and seafood. Inexpensive to moderate.

Chez Daniel, 2522 Estavan Avenue, (250) 592–7424. One of Victoria's old standbys, it is located in Oak Bay. High-calorie cuisine. Expensive.

Don Mee Restaurant, 538 Fisgard Street, (250) 383–1032. A full menu of Chinese delicacies representing the different culinary regions of China. Inexpensive to moderate.

Harbour House, 607 Oswego Street, (250) 386–1244. A top seafood place in a convenient location on Inner Harbour and near the Empress Hotel. Moderate.

Izumi Japanese Restaurant, 739 Pandora, (250) 995–8432. If sushi is your choice of cuisine, you won't do better than this cozy and authentically Japanese eatery. Expensive.

Koto, 510 Fort Street, (250) 382–1514. Private tatami rooms provide an authentic character. There's a wide variety of sushi. Inexpensive to moderate.

Julia's Place Café and Restaurant, 609 Courtney Street, (250) 388–7111. Specializes in Italian food. Moderate.

Restaurant Matisse, 512 Yates Street, (250) 480–0883. French cuisine. The French chef here prepares fresh breads and soups daily. Moderate.

Le Petit Saigon Vietnamese Restaurant, 1010 Langley Street, (250) 386–1412. This restaurant is generally regarded as Victoria's best place for Vietnamese food, with a menu that combines a hint of French with exotic elegance. Expensive.

Ming's Restaurant, 1321 Quadra Street, (250) 385–4405. A gourmet's Chinese restaurant. Inexpensive to moderate.

Pagliacci's, 1011 Broad Street, (250) 386–1662. Italian. Pasta servings are made on site. Chicken in Marsala sauce with fettuccine is one of several house specialties. Moderate.

Periklis, 531 Yates Street, (250) 386–3313. Delicious Greek food—lamb dishes, seafood, and steaks. Guests are treated to Greek dancers and belly dancers. Moderate.

Pablo's Dining Lounge, 225 Quebec Street, (250) 388–4255. You can't beat this for casual fine dining. French continental cuisine that includes seafood, paella, lamb, and poultry. And, like everywhere else in Victoria, you don't have to dress to the gills. Expensive.

Princess Mary, 344 Harbour Road, (250) 386–3456. A fine restaurant in an old ship. Seafood and beef dishes; special children's menu. Moderate.

Rathskeller Schnitzel Haus, 1205 Quadra Street, (250) 386–9348. German and Bavarian cuisine. Inexpensive to moderate.

The Gatsby Mansion, 309 Belleville Street, (250) 388–9191. Breakfast, luncheon, afternoon tea, and dinner elegantly served in a historic Victoria mansion. Good location on Inner Harbour. Bed-and-breakfast accommodation also available here. Moderate.

The Keg, 500 Fort Street, (250) 386–7789. Serves what it considers the ultimate sharing snack—strips of steak or chicken sautéed with green peppers and onions and served hot with relish, cheeses, and a soft tortilla. Also has seven-layer dip, two-way salmon, and Cajun popcorn shrimp. An unpretentious, fun place where the British stiff upper lip is out of place. Inexpensive.

Yokohama Japanese Restaurant, 980 Blanshard Street, (250) 384–5433. If you lust for sushi, this is the place to get your fill. Moderate.

Entertainment

Most of the major hotels have live entertainment (singers, comedians, dance bands, etc.) in their lounges and some in their dining rooms. For current entertainment events ask your concierge or call the organizations listed below. The following groups and theaters feature plays, dance, and musical events, throughout the year or in their formal seasons:

Victoria Symphony Society, 846 Broughton Street, (250) 385–9771

Pacific Opera Association, 1316 Government Street, (250) 385–0222

The Royal Theatre, 805 Broughton Street, (250) 386–6121 (box office)

Phoenix Theatre, at the University of Victoria, (250) 721–8000

McPherson Playhouse, 3 Centennial Square, (250) 386–6121 (box office)

Kaleidoscope Theatre Productions, 556 Herald Street, (250) 383–8124

Shopping

Your best buys are imported goods from Great Britain, locally made candies, Cowichan sweaters, jewelry (B.C. jade and silver) and carvings, books on Canada, and arts and crafts by the province's other artists (weavings, pottery, fashions, paintings, etc.).

Crystal Garden Gift Shops, located across from the Royal British Columbia Museum, offers a fine selection of specialty shops.

Market Square, 201–560 Johnson Street, in the heart of "Old Town"; more than thirty stores and restaurants are set in refurbished heritage buildings, surrounding an old-style covered market. This is an enjoyable place for all ages, whether you buy or just poke around. Special entertainment and recitals are held here throughout the year.

The Bay, 1701 Douglas at Fisgard, Canada's well-known department store, featuring furs; more than 300 patterns of top brands of English china; the Canadiana Shop offering works by local artists and artisans (10 percent off on purchases made in the shop); woolens from England and Scotland; and famous Hudson's Bay point blankets.

Mayfair Shopping Center, 3147 Douglas Street, 1.6 km/1 mi from downtown at Douglas and Finlayson. More than one hundred fashion boutiques. Mayfair is one of the most elegant shopping malls on Vancouver Island. Bus service is available from downtown.

Rogers' Chocolates, 913 Government Street, is the place for connoisseurs of fine chocolate goodies. Rogers' has been in business for more than one hundred years, and its Victoria Creams make taste buds sing heavenly tunes. Dieters beware.

Bolen Books, Hillside Centre, 1644 Hillside Avenue, offers a wide selection of general-interest books and guidebooks.

Copithorne & Rowe, 901 Government Street, featuring fine bone china and giftware such as Waterford and Wedgwood. It also carries a range of specialty products exclusive to the company, including jade and rhodonite jewelry.

Munro's Books, 1108 Government Street, one of the finest bookshops in Western Canada; browsing through the extensive collection is an unhurried pleasure. Housed in one of Victoria's heritage buildings, with high ceilings and colorful wall hangings by Carole Sabiston.

Victoria Limited Editions, 919 Fort Street, has Victoria's largest selection of stemware. Offers low prices on Waterford crystal.

Trounce Alley, off Government Street. A quaint little passage with stores and dining places.

Sports and Recreation

For the visitor, most sports and recreation will involve touring Victoria on foot. It is also a wonderful city for jogging. Almost everywhere, you'll see people of all ages briskly walking, jogging, or cycling. The following additional options are offered.

Fishing Charters
Oak Bay Charters, 2141 Newton, (250) 598–1061
Adam's Fishing Charters, 19 Lotus Street, (250) 370–2326

Golf
Gorge Vale Golf Club, 1005 Craigflower, (250) 683–6451 or www.gorgevalegolf.com. Long and tough.

Cedar Hill Municipal Golf Course, 1400 Derby off Cedar Hill Road, (250) 595–2823. Eighteen holes, par 67.

Henderson Park Golf Course, 2291 Cedar Hill Road (Oak Bay recreational area), (250) 370–2000. Nine holes, par 3.

Olympic View Golf Club, 643 Latoria Road, (250) 474–3673. Great view; 5,805 m/6,450 yd long.

Cordova Bay Golf Course, 5333 Cordova Bay Road, (250) 658–4444. Completed in 1991; 5,902 m/6,558 yd long.

Royal Colwood Golf and Country Club, 629 Goldstream Avenue, (250) 478–8331. Ranked number one in B.C. by many.

Harness Racing

Sandown Harness Raceway, thirty minutes north of downtown via Highway 17; 1810 Glamorgan, Sidney; call (250) 656–1631 for information.

Ice-Skating

Memorial Arena, 1925 Blanshard, (250) 361–0538
Recreation Oak Bay, 1975 Bee, (250) 595–7946

Racquet Sports

Cedar Hill Recreation Centre, 3220 Cedar Hill, (250) 595–7121
YMCA/YWCA, 880 Courtney Street, (250) 386–7511

Sailing Charters

Victoria Sailaway Charters, 1–408 Dallas Road, (250) 216–7245
Explore Charters, 6669 Horne Road, Sooke, (250) 642–6669

Swimming Pools

Crystal Pool, 2275 Quadra, (250) 361–0732
Recreation Oak Bay, 1975 Bee, (250) 595–7946

Tennis

Beacon Hill Park Courts, off Cook Street
Recreation Oak Bay, 1975 Bee, (250) 595–7946

Touring Vancouver Island

Most visitors to the coast of British Columbia concentrate on the cities of Victoria and Vancouver. Both certainly have enough at-

Camping at Provincial Parks

Provincial parks on Vancouver Island that offer camping facilities are listed below. Call Tourism British Columbia, (800) 663–6000, for more information. Camping is on a first-come, first-served basis. There is a small fee for use of camping facilities. Most campgrounds have showers, firewood, and toilets, but the actual range of facilities may vary from park to park.

Bamberton, on the Saanich Peninsula, north of Victoria

Elk Falls, on the Quinsam River, near Campbell River

Englishman River Falls, in the Parksville/Qualicum area

Goldstream, just north of Victoria on the Trans-Canada

Gordon Bay, on Cowichan Lake, north of Victoria

Little Qualicum Falls, off Highway 4 between Parksville and Port Alberni

McDonald, close to Swartz Bay, near the Vancouver ferry terminal

Rathtrevor Beach, south of Parksville

Sproat Lake, near Port Alberni

Buttle Lake Campground and Ralph River Campground, both in Strathcona Park

tractions to keep you busy for an extended period—fishing, golf, touring, whale-watching, crafts shopping, hiking, camping, mountain climbing. Nevertheless, while you are in this area it would be a shame to miss out on experiencing the natural magnificence of Vancouver Island. Here are long stretches of unspoiled beaches, impressive mountains, and forests containing some of the tallest trees in the world. If you've never seen whales or bald eagles, you can do so here; this is their natural habitat. All you need is a sharp eye, binoculars, and a camera. You can fish for salmon and trout and not be disappointed. There are beaches for swimming and slopes for skiing.

Vancouver Island is 405 km/252 mi long and 64 to 128 km/ 40 to 80 mi wide, making it the largest Pacific island off the coast of North America (for comparison's sake, the province of Prince

Edward Island is 5,657 sq m/2,184 sq mi; Vancouver Island is 32,137 sq m/12,408 sq mi. The island extends from just below the fiftieth parallel to about the forty-eighth. About one-fifth of the island—the southwestern tip containing the city of Victoria—extends close to one degree below the forty-ninth parallel, along which almost the entire U.S.–Canadian boundary line runs. In fact, the city of Victoria is far closer to Washington's Olympic National Park than is either Bellingham or Seattle, major cities in that state.

The center spine of the island is a range of high mountains. On the east coast, facing the Strait of Georgia, are most of the communities and broad expanses of agricultural land; the west coast, facing the open Pacific, is very rugged, wind- and rain-swept through much of the year, and relatively uninhabited.

As you tour Vancouver Island, search out West Coast Indian sites and villages that reveal an ancient way of life. There's a mystical aspect to the Native people, a depth of understanding about life and nature, that seems more profound than our own.

The following tour starts in Victoria, rounds the southern tip of Vancouver Island, then backtracks to Victoria to head north-westerly up island.

Sooke

Highway 14 goes around the southern tip of Vancouver Island, from Victoria to Sooke, Jordan River, and Port Renfrew. At Sooke visit the **Sooke Region Museum,** (250) 642–6351, which has a collection of weavings and carvings by the Salish and Nootka peoples and exhibits on early pioneer life; open through the year. Free. Be sure to see **Leechtown Gold Rush Site**—call Sooke Region Museum, above, for details—where gold was discovered in 1864. **Botanical Beach,** between Sooke and **Port Renfrew** at Botany Bay, has natural aquariums, tidal pools, and a great deal of intertidal marine life to see. Be careful of rough seas and winds when exploring in this area. At Port Renfrew you can get over to the west coast hiking trail with some effort, but you would be better off to start the trail at Bamfield, which can be reached from Port Alberni, about a third of the way up island.

Duncan

Return to Victoria then depart from its outskirts on Trans-Canada Highway 1. You will journey over the scenic Malahat section. First cut as a cattle trail in the mid-1880s, this section of the highway climbs from near sea level at Goldstream Park to a summit of

356 m/1,156 ft, with stopping points along the way that offer spectacular, panoramic views of the Saanich Penninsula, the Gulf Islands, and Mount Baker in Washington State.

In Duncan you can purchase thick, exceedingly warm Cowichan sweaters knitted by Native women who live in or around this community. Be sure to visit the following:

British Columbia Demonstration Forest Museum, off Trans-Canada Highway 1, (250) 746–1251. Open from May through September. Admission is charged. Indoor/outdoor exhibits on the forest industry in B.C., woodland walking trails, and steam-train rides.

Cowichan Valley Museum, Duncan Railway Station, (250) 746–6612. Donations are accepted. Small, local historical museum. Pioneer house. Indian art and historic photographs.

The Glass Castle, off the Trans-Canada, (250) 746–6518. Open throughout the year. Admission is charged. An eccentric house made from 180,000 glass bottles.

Whippletree Junction, off the Trans-Canada, (250) 748–1100. Open daily. Admission is charged. Re-creation of turn-of-the-twentieth-century pioneer village; includes an early Chinatown.

Chemainus

In Chemainus see the world-famous outdoor art gallery of murals. Chemainus has won international acclaim for its Festival of Murals, a successful revitalization project that began in 1982 with the unveiling of five huge murals, all professionally painted onto existing downtown buildings. The Festival of Murals has grown; there are now more than thirty. Follow the footsteps around town to see these larger-than-life works of art, vividly depicting the history of the Chemainus Valley.

Ladysmith Area

In Ladysmith stop at the **Black Nugget,** 12 Gatacre Street, (250) 245–4846 (call for hours and admission fee), a local historical museum in an 1881-vintage hotel.

Ladysmith Arboretum, on the Trans-Canada, (250) 245–2218, is open throughout the year. Free. Tree specimens from all over the world; early logging and railroad equipment displays.

Accommodations in Yellowpoint, 13 km/8 mi north of Ladysmith, are available at the **Inn of the Sea,** Yellowpoint Road, (250) 245–2211. A full-facility waterfront resort offering fireside dining, a pool, tennis, and Jacuzzi. Moderate to expensive.

Nanaimo

Nanaimo is the second largest community on Vancouver Island. There are plenty of accommodations, restaurants, and shopping malls. The terminal for ferries to the mainland and the city of Vancouver is here; sailing time is one hour and thirty-five minutes. One of British Columbia's oldest remaining Hudson's Bay Company bastions still guards the harbor. Killer-whale-watching trip services operate out of Nanaimo. Attractions here include the following:

Historic buildings in the downtown area, south of the ferry terminal, include **Nanaimo Courthouse** (1886); the **Palace Hotel** (1889); **Central Drugs,** a 1900-style drugstore that was built in 1985 (in the 1911-vintage Dakin Building); old-fashioned light posts, cobblestone streets, and brick sidewalks.

The Bastion, corner of Bastion and Front Streets, (250) 754–1631 in summer; (250) 754–8474 in winter. Housed in the original Hudson's Bay Fort, the Bastion's collection includes memorabilia from the 1850s to the 1880s. Each day during summer Bastion guardsmen, dressed in colorful naval uniforms of the 1850s, are led to the Bastion by a piper. Under the orders of an officer, the cannon is elaborately cleaned and then fired as a salute to visiting ships—of which there are always many in the harbor.

Nanaimo District Museum, 100 Cameron Street, (250) 753–1821. Open throughout the year. Donations are accepted. Historical and art exhibitions, Chinese art, coal-mine re-creation, local archives.

Make sure to stroll Nanaimo's **Harbourside Walkway,** a 4-km/3-mi promenade between Harbour Park Mall and Departure Bay Ferry Terminal peppered with cafes and galleries.

Nanaimo Annual Events

Empire Days, May

Heritage Days, June

Nanaimo Festival, June and July

Vancouver Island Exhibition, August

Jazz Festival and Vintage Car Challenge, September

Highland Games, September

For dining, try the following restaurants:

The Lighthouse, 50 Anchor Way, (250) 754–3212. An unusual lighthouse restaurant on the water; serves seafood. Moderate.

The Grotto, 1511 Stewart Avenue, (250) 753–3303. Specializes in seafood. Waterfront. Inexpensive.

A Taste of Vancouver Island:
Nanaimo Bars

It's uncertain how such a delicious confection came to be associated with the old coal-mining town of Nanaimo. What is certain is that everyone who tries one loves it!

Bars:
½ c butter
¼ c sugar
5 tbsp cocoa
1 tsp vanilla
1 egg
2 c graham cracker crumbs
½ c chopped walnuts

Topping:
3 tbsp milk
2 tbsp custard powder
5 tbsp butter, divided
2 c confectioner's sugar, sifted
4 oz semisweet chocolate

To make the bars, mix the butter with the sugar, cocoa, vanilla, and eggs in a bowl. Set the bowl in a saucepan of boiling water and stir until the butter has melted and the mixture resembles a thick custard. Mix in the crumbs and nuts and pack into a 9-in-sq pan.

For the topping, mix the milk and custard powder together and cream with ¼ c of the butter. Blend in the confectioner's sugar and spread over the chocolate crumb base. Let stand for 15 minutes to harden slightly. Melt the chocolate and the remaining tbsp of butter in a bowl of standing hot water and drizzle over the top of the custard.

Let stand until set, then cut into squares and watch them disappear.

Accommodations in Nanaimo include:

Coast Bastion Inn, 11 Bastion Street, (250) 753–6601. The best in town. Rooms have water views. Gourmet restaurant, health facility, nightclub, and lounge. Moderate to expensive.

Days Inn Harbourview, on the Trans-Canada South, (250) 754–8171. Moderate.

Four Points Hotel Sheraton, 4900 Rutherford Road, (250) 758–3000. Standard rooms and suites with fireplace and Jacuzzi, situated on a nine-hole, par-3 golf course.

Howard Johnson Harbourside, 1 Terminal Avenue, (800) 663–7372. Adjacent to parks; seasonal heated outdoor pool, buffet-style restaurant.

Best Western Dorchester Hotel, 70 Church Street, (250) 754–6835. Overlooking Inner Harbour; suites have spectacular views. Restaurant, in-room coffeemaker, free parking.

Nanaimo has several large shopping malls where you can find just about any kind of item; it's almost equal to Victoria. Woodgrove Centre, on the North Island Highway, is one of the largest on the island. Harbour Park Mall is in downtown. Rutherford Mall is on the North Island Highway.

The main route heading north out of Nanaimo becomes Highway 19.

Parksville–Qualicum Beach Area

The Parksville–Qualicum Beach area is best known for its long sandy beaches, and during the summer season it is a primary vacation spot for both B.C. residents and visitors. It's also popular with anglers, hikers, and spelunkers. Visit **Craig Heritage Park** in Parksville, (250) 248–6966. Open mid-May to the end of August. Free. Collection features Native and pioneer artifacts. Qualicum Beach is perfect for swimming and sunbathing. Golf, lawn bowling, live theater, and nature hikes are also offered. **Qualicum Falls Provincial Park** has hiking trails and provides areas for overnight camping. The Sand Castle Competition is held in July.

Recommended restaurant:

Maclure House Inn, 1015 East Island Highway, (250) 248–3470. Beautiful oceanfront restaurant and country inn. Continental food. Moderate.

All of the following accommodations have dining rooms and other amenities:

Tigh-Na-Mara Resort Hotel, off the Trans-Canada, (250) 248–2072. Moderate to expensive.

The Best Western Bayside Inn Resort, 240 Dogwood Street,

(250) 248–8333; (800) 663–4232. Best in town. Moderate to expensive.

Gray Crest Seaside Resort, 1115 East Island Highway, (250) 248–6513. On sandy Rathtrevor Beach, these housekeeping condos feature fireplaces and Jacuzzis. Moderate.

Parkesville Beach Hotel, 161 West Island Highway, (250) 248–6759. Kitchenettes, seasonal indoor pool, tennis, and a sandy beach. Moderate.

Qualicum College Inn, Qualicum Beach, (250) 752–9262. Moderate.

Western Vancouver Island

From Parksville you can travel to the western side of the island and the Pacific Rim National Park by taking Highway 4.

Cathedral Grove, on Highway 4 going west to Port Alberni, has splendid stands of tall, 800-year-old Douglas fir and west coast cedar. Cathedral Grove is within **MacMillan Provincial Park,** which also includes Cameron Lake. A small bathing beach is off the road.

Cameron Lake Resort, via Highway 4, (250) 752–6707, has housekeeping cottages, a store, and boat rentals. Moderate.

Port Alberni

Port Alberni, the largest community in the center of the island, has several motels and restaurants. Port Alberni is famous for salmon fishing and has an annual derby offering a cash-rich first prize for a record catch. From here you can take a passenger ferry to Bamfield, where the West Coast Trail begins, or to Ucluelet, a section of the Pacific Rim National Park located at the southern end of Long Beach.

Port Alberni attractions are as follows:

Alberni Valley Museum, 4255 Wallace Street, (250) 723–2181. Open Tuesday through Sunday. Free. Forestry and First Peoples displays.

Martin Mars Water Bombers, via Highway 3, Lakeshore Road, (250) 723–6225; call ahead for visitor information. The world's largest fleet of flying water bombers used to fight forest fires. A must-visit for aviation buffs.

The following accommodations have dining rooms, lounges, and other amenities:

TimberLodge Motor Inn and RV Campground, on Highway 2, (250) 723–9415. Moderate.

Coast Hospitality Motor Inn, 3835 Redford Street, (250) 723–8111. Moderate.

Ucluelet

Ucluelet is a favorite departure point for divers; they can explore shipwrecks around the Broken Group Islands and encounter giant octopuses, king crabs, and other inhabitants below the surface.

Fletchers Cove Bed & Breakfast, 2305 Pacific Rim Highway, (250) 726–7074. A 1990s homestead near Long Beach with queen-size beds and private or shared bath. Full breakfast and in-room coffee. Moderate.

Tauca Lea by the Sea, 1971 Harbour Crescent, (250) 726–4625. Waterfront location with large windows and private balconies. Boardwalk to village stores, restaurants, and galleries. Moderate.

Thorton Motel, (250) 726–7725. Moderate.

Pacific Rim Motel, (250) 726–7728. Housekeeping units. Restaurants nearby. Moderate.

Bamfield

To reach Bamfield, take the ferry from Port Alberni. Bamfield accommodations include the following:

Bamfield Trails Motel, (250) 728–3231. Restaurant nearby. Moderate.

Pinkerton Lodge, Barkley Sound, (250) 683–4187; (800) 501–9611. A small, full-range marine resort that accommodates twenty-eight guests. Moderate.

McKay Bay Lodge, (250) 728–3323. Harbor view. Moderate.

Pacific Rim National Park

Contact Superintendent, Pacific Rim National Park, Box 280, Ucluelet, British Columbia V0R 3A0; (604) 726–7721.

Pacific Rim National Park faces the open Pacific and is comprised of three sections: the West Coast Trail, the Broken Group Islands, and Long Beach. When you stand facing the Pacific here, the entire, immense nation of Canada is at your back. For most visitors to the park, the Long Beach area is the most accessible. You can get to Long Beach by car and easily tour its 34-km/20-mi length. By strolling its hard-packed sand surface, you can catch sight of sea lions, seals, schools of porpoises, and pods of orca whales. Within the woodland areas are black-tailed deer, bald eagles, and many different species of birds. Inasmuch as a great deal of rain falls along this coast, take along "dirty-weather" gear— slickers, warm sweaters, and water-shedding hats. The road that travels the length of Long Beach doesn't always hug the shoreline;

The West Coast Trail

The West Coast Trail, part of the Pacific Rim National Park, runs from Bamfield to Port Renfrew (72 km/44 mi). This challenging trek requires a great deal of preparation and physical stamina and takes several days to complete. There are dangers from wind, rain, and rough seas, as well as on the rugged trail itself. Its rewards are many—opportunities to see surprises in nature, such as the marine, bird, and mammal life of the area; the quickly changing moods of the weather; and the joy of being solitary in a magnificent and dramatic natural environment. In the early part of the century, this trail provided a route for shipwreck victims to find their way to the safety of human civilization, and when the winds are right you can almost hear the voices of those lost at sea off this beautiful but hazardous and mystical coast.

you'll have to look for access roads to get to the beach. Sea Lion Rocks can be seen not far from the main road. To visit the Broken Group Islands, inhabited by many bald eagles, make arrangements in Ucluelet to hire a boat. At Bamfield or Port Alberni, Pacific gray whales pass close to shore starting in late February, as they journey from the Bering Sea to the warm waters of Baja California. Regardless of what season you visit, be sure to bring binoculars and/or cameras with telephoto lenses. Various whale-watching trip services operate out of Tofino and Ucluelet.

The main beach areas from Ucluelet to Tofino are Wya Point, Florencia Bay, Quistis Point, Wickaninnish Bay, Sandhill Creek, Long Beach, Cove Box Island, and Schooner Cove. There are dramatic cliffs at Florencia Bay and Green Point. The Rain Forest Trail will take you into thick stands of cedar and hemlock.

Wickaninnish Centre, (250) 726–7333, in the Ucluelet area, is open daily during summer. Free. Exhibits on the ecology of the park: the sea, land, birds, marine life, mammals, winds, tides, rain. You'll see the Seabird Mural, the Offshore Zone Mural, and *Explorer 10* submersible, as well as exhibits on the local Nuu-Chah-Nulth (Nootka) people. By way of excellent outdoor interpretive programs, guides take you on walks through the different ecological zones and explain what you see. There's an interpretive theater at Green Point.

The two campgrounds in the park are at Green Point, for those with vehicles, and Schooner Walk-In, which has limited facilities (water, wood, toilets, etc.) for those with tents. More basic (frills-free) camping is on the Broken Group Islands, at Benson, Dodd Hand, Clark, Gibraltor, Gilbert, Willis, and Turret Islands. Accommodations and restaurants are available in Tofino and Ucluelet. Access is only by boat. Travelers must make their own arrangements.

Boats can be chartered in Tofino and Ucluelet. You must get a license to fish; licenses are available in Tofino at most marinas and federal fisheries offices and in Ucluelet. Taking shellfish from the beach or waters for eating is usually not advised, because of red tide—potentially lethal dinoflagellates consumed by shellfish. Check with local authorities if red-tide warnings are up. The water around here is too cold for swimming, except for polar bear types, although there's a supervised swimming area at North Long Beach. This is the right place, however, for other water sports—surfing (great waves here), kayaking, and scuba diving (lots of unusual marine life to see). Although the powerful rollers coming off the ocean make canoeing dangerous, there are plenty of inlets, coves, bays, lakes, and streams for you to explore.

Tofino

If you want to get away from civilization but still have a roof over your head, Tofino is the place. In addition to enjoying the beaches and woodlands of Pacific Rim National Park, you can go deep-sea fishing and bathe in natural hot springs. You might also want to curl up beside a log fire and finally read *War and Peace* while a turbulent surf and fierce winds rage outside. Golf, whale-watching trips, and restaurants are here. Since this is a very popular spot for visitors, it is recommended that you reserve accommodations. Call the Tofino Travel InfoCentre, (250) 725–3414, for a list of bed-and-breakfast places.

For accommodations, choose among the following:

The Inn at Tough City, 350 Main Street, (250) 725–2021. Centrally located on the waterfront overlooking Meares Island and Clayoquot Sound. Some rooms have fireplaces and soaker tubs. Moderate.

Himwitsa Lodge, 300 Main Street, (250) 725–3319. Harborview lodge overlooking Clayoquot Sound. Spacious suites have queen-size beds, kitchenettes, cable TV, and hot tubs. Rooms are located on the second floor and accessible only by stairs. Moderate.

Duffin Cove Resort, (250) 725–3448. Moderate to expensive.

The Wickaninnish Inn, Osprey Lane at Chesterman Beach, (250) 725–3100. This spectacularly located inn, set on a rocky promontory at the westernmost point of Chesterman Beach, is one of British Columbia's must-stay facilities. Besides having panoramic ocean views, it has a world-class restaurant, conference rooms, and facilities for storm-watching, whale-viewing, and beachcombing. Rooms have fireplaces, in-room bars, and balconies. Off-season rates. Expensive.

Wilp Gybuu "wolf house," 311 Leighton Way, (250) 725–2330, is a B&B in a contemporary home with a view of Duffin Passage and Clayoquot Sound. Adult oriented, it's near the beach with full breakfast, library, and coffee room. Restaurants are nearby.

Courtenay and Comox

From Tofino you can return on Highway 4 to Highway 19, which runs north–south along the eastern side of the island. Courtenay and Comox are sister communities located along Highway 19. In Courtenay see the exhibits at the District Museum—360 Cliffe Avenue, (250) 334–3611—which include a Coast Salish longhouse, logging equipment, and Chinese and Japanese artifacts. Open daily in summer; closed Sunday. Donations are accepted. Wonderful fishing and bird-watching are in the area, as are cruises to nearby islands. Swimming and hiking can be enjoyed at Comox Lake. In Comox visit the Air Force Museum, at the Canadian Forces Base, (250) 339–8162. Open Tuesday through Sunday, April through October. Donations are accepted. A good collection of vintage aircraft. At Little River you can take the ferry to Powell River, which is on the mainland's Sunshine Coast, just above the city of Vancouver; sailing time is one hour and fifteen minutes.

All of the following hotels have dining rooms and other amenities:

Coast Westerly Hotel, 1590 Cliffe Avenue, Comox, (250) 338–7741. Moderate.

The Washington Inn, 1001 Ryan Road, Courtenay, (250) 338–5441. Moderate.

The Alders Beach Resort, in Comox, (250) 337–5322. Housekeeping cottages with fireplaces; on the beach; salmon fishing. Moderate to expensive.

Port August Inn & Suites, 2082 Comox Avenue, (250) 339–2277. One- and two-bedroom sleeping and housekeeping units, heated pool, near downtown. Moderate.

Campbell River

If there is a mecca for salmon fishing in B.C., it is Campbell River. In August and September Campbell River is "tooth by jowl" with anglers going after the giant king and tyee salmon. There's great fishing throughout the year here—especially for trout in the local lakes—with accommodations ranging from rustic fishing camps to comfortable resorts. Visit the **Campbell River Museum and Archives,** depicting Native cultures, (250) 287–3103. Open year-round. Donation accepted. Take the ferry to Quadra Island to see excellent aboriginal arts and crafts at the **Kwakiutl Museum** at Quathiaski Cove, (250) 285–3733. Open July through August. Donation accepted.

Campbell River also gives access, via Highway 28, to **Elk Falls Provincial Park** and **Strathcona Park,** the largest parks on Vancouver Island. Strathcona offers superb camping, mountain climbing, and canoeing. Highway 28 continues to **Gold River** on Muchalat Inlet—Canada's caving capital, with North America's deepest vertical cave. A cruise boat will take you for a sail down the inlet to the site of an ancient Indian village that Captain Cook visited in 1778. It is said that his first contact with the Native peoples of the coast was made here.

Whale Town

You can take a ferry from Campbell River across a narrow part of the Strait of Georgia to Whale Town, which is on an island adjacent to the B.C. mainland and its Sunshine Coast (see Chapter 4). From Whale Town via ferries and Highway 101 to 99, you can get to the city of Vancouver. This trip is convoluted and time consuming but also truly worthwhile in that you'll experience wonderful scenery and see the interesting ways people live so far from civilization yet so close to it.

Accommodations in the area include the following:
Coast Discovery Inn, 975 Tyee Plaza, (250) 287–7155. Rooms with water views; dining room, lounge, and marina. Moderate to expensive.

Marina Inn Resort, 1430 South Island Highway, (250) 923–7255. Moderate.

The Best Western Austrian Chalet Village, 462 South Island Highway, (604) 923–4231. Moderate.

Anchor Inn Hotel, 261 Island Highway, (250) 286–1131. Oceanfront resort-style hotel with balconies, kitchens, indoor pools and whirlpools, restaurant, and lounge. Moderate.

Heriot Bay Inn & Marina, Heriot Bay, Quadra Island, (250) 285–3322. Cottages overlooking Heriot Bay and bed-and-breakfast units with private baths. There are also RV and tent sites with full hookups, laundry, showers, marina, and moorage. Moderate.

Seascape Waterfront Resort, Gowland Harbor, Quadra Island, (250) 285–3450. Secluded housekeeping chalets with patio decks. Maid service on request. Complimentary canoes and kayaks. Moderate.

Alert Bay

A ferry from Port McNeil will take you to Alert Bay on Cormorant Island, where you will find the tallest totem pole in the world. Visit the Alert Bay **Library and Museum** on Front Street, (250) 974–5721. Open Monday through Saturday, July and August. Donations are accepted. Exhibits of Kwakiutl culture, as well as **St. George's Anglican Chapel.** Also visit **U'Mista Cultural Centre** on Front Street, (250) 974–5213. Open May through September. Admission is charged. This cedar building looks like a Kwakiutl longhouse and has a potlatch collection.

Accommodations are available at **Haida-Way Motor Inn,** in Port McNeil (250–956–3373; moderate), and at **Orca Inn,** in Alert Bay (250–974–5322; moderate).

Port Hardy

Port Hardy—the departure point for the famous Inside Passage journey on B.C. Ferries—was named for Vice Admiral Sir Thomas Masterman Hardy of the British Royal Navy. During the battle of Trafalgar, as captain of the HMS *Victory,* Hardy, according to depictions, held the dying Lord Nelson in his arms. Once a Hudson's Bay Company post, Port Hardy is the last major town of any size or importance on the northern tip of Vancouver Island. Kwakiutl arts and crafts are available for sale in this area. You can take a ferry from here through the Inside Passage (see below) to Prince Rupert on the B.C. mainland and then to southern Alaska. While in Port Hardy, visit the following:

Port Hardy Museum and Archives, 7110 Market Street, (250) 949–8143. Open daily during summer. History of European settlers in the area.

Fort Rupert, Beaver Harbour. Open in summer. Hudson's Bay Company fort and trading post built in 1849.

Whaling Station, Coal Harbour. A place where whales were processed for various markets. There's a 3.7-m/12-ft whale-jawbone arch here.

Vancouver Island Train Adventures

Climb aboard and capture the spirit of Vancouver Island as you ride the rails on the E&N Railiner. From your seat you'll see beautiful scenery—lush greenery, dazzling waterfalls, amazing rock faces, and stunning ocean views. The train takes visitors between Victoria and Parksville. It's a five-hour excursion into a forest hugged by the ocean.

Or try the Pacific Wilderness Railway, which uses locomotives of a bygone era to pull open-window coaches of the 1930s, air-conditioned coaches of the 1950s, and a luxurious 46-seat parlor car. The train pulls out of Victoria and heads north over Malahat Pass. Passengers are met at milepost 20 and chauffeured to the Aerie Resort for a gourmet meal before returning to the train to complete the round trip to Victoria.

All of the following hotels have restaurants:

Thunderbird Inn, 7050 Rupert Street, (250) 949–7767. A large, full-facility motor lodge with dining room, recently renovated. Pub, beer and wine store, entertainment. Moderate.

Pioneer Inn, 4965 Byng Road, (250) 949–7271. In a quiet, parklike setting; complimentary in-room coffee. Free local calls, kitchen units. Moderate.

Seven Hills Golf and Country Club, 2 km/1 mi west on Highway 19. Located on a nine-hole golf course; for self-contained RVs only. Electric and water hookups, central washrooms; $15 per vehicle including electricity and water.

The Inside Passage

A voyage through the magnificent Inside Passage is one of the great trips of the world. It's an adventure that takes you through thickly forested mountains that rise up from the sea and whose walls are almost perpendicular to the surface of the water. The scenery is truly spectacular. As you sail through the passage, you'll see bald eagles, orca and humpback whales, sea lions, loons, porpoises, and many other kinds of wildlife.

B.C. Ferries operates the MV *Queen of the North,* which sails from Port Hardy to Prince Rupert, the province's largest city on the upper coast of its mainland. Prince Rupert is just a few miles south of the B.C.–Alaska border. From the mainland of B.C., you can sail down the Inside Passage on the MV *Queen of the North* from Prince Rupert to Port Hardy. Port Hardy itself is about an eight-hour drive from the city of Victoria. You can also get on Vancouver Island and thence to Port Hardy from the mainland by taking a B.C. Ferry from Horseshoe Bay (Metro Vancouver) or Powell River on the Sunshine Coast (north of Metro Vancouver).

Northbound sailings on the MV *Queen of the North* begin in mid-May. The last sailing is in mid-October. Southbound sailings are also on this schedule. For reservations, write B.C. Ferries, 1112 Fort Street, Victoria, British Columbia V8V 4V2. For information, call (604) 669–1211 (Vancouver) or (250) 386–3431 (Victoria).

The summer cruise between Port Hardy and Prince Rupert takes fifteen hours one way, most of it during daylight; the length of the voyage is 274 nautical miles. The MV *Queen of the North* carries 750 passengers and 157 vehicles. Long-term parking is available only at the Port Hardy terminal. The vessel itself offers overnight cabins, a buffet dining room with a dance floor, a cafeteria, a children's playroom, a video arcade, a bar, a parents' room, an observation lounge, promenade decks, a newsstand, a gift shop, and other amenities.

Sailing north en route to Prince Rupert, you will pass Scarlett Point, site of many shipwrecks in the past; Pine Island, with its lighthouse that marks the entrance to the Inside Passage; Queen Charlotte Sound, where countervailing currents create danger for inexperienced mariners; Egg Island Lighthouse, which marks approaches to Fitz Hugh Sound and to Smith and Rivers Inlets; Addenbroke Island, site of an unsolved murder (Namu whirlwinds blow in the area with great strength, and mountains tower in excess of 1,000 m/3,279 ft); and Pointer Island, where the Codville family operated a lighthouse for forty-two years. At Dean Channel, the great Canadian explorer Alexander Mackenzie ventured into this area. Ocean Falls is a former paper-producing community; Bella Bella, a prosperous fishing and logging town. Dryad Point marks Lama Passage for ships; Ivory Island is the site of an 1898 lighthouse; and Milbanke Sound is an active salmon-fishing area. In the waters off McInnes Island, many marine tragedies took place. Boat Bluff is where one lighthousekeeper requested a transfer because of the many wolves on the island; Swanson Bay is where paper and shingle mills once operated. In Butedale fishing, lumbering, and mining once thrived. Grenville Channel is considered the most spectacular channel in the Inside Passage, surrounded by mountains that rise 450 to 900 m/1,500 to 3,000 ft, densely wooded with pine and cedar. And Ridley Island is a modern bulk-shipping terminal, with goods departing for points around the world.

Prince Rupert to Prince George

Prince Rupert

The end (or beginning) of the Inside Passage voyage for our purpose is Prince Rupert, named for the cousin of King Charles II of England and grand factor of the Hudson's Bay Company. Before the coming of the Europeans, this area was a gathering place for Tshimshian and Haida peoples. Prince Rupert, with a population of some 18,000, is called the City of Rainbows. Its main economic activity is serving as a terminal for natural resources (coal, lumber, and wheat) and finished goods being shipped to all parts of the world. The city also has fish canneries and pulp- and paper-processing factories. During World War II many American military personnel departed from here for service in Alaska and in the Pacific.

Located at the mouth of the Skeena River and set in the midst of fjords, islands, and mountains, Prince Rupert is often also called the Gateway to the North. Fishing, hunting, sailing, diving, and exploring the interior mainland are some of the activities of this area. The city has a mild climate, with very little snow, mostly rain; gardens thrive here. A few miles north of Prince Rupert are Wales and Pearse Islands, which form part of the border between British Columbia and mainland Alaska.

While in Prince Rupert, visit the **Museum of Northern British Columbia,** First Avenue and McBride Street. Open mid-May to the end of August. Local history of the settlement and exhibits on northwest coastal Indian cultures. For more information contact the Prince Rupert Visitors Bureau at its Web site; www.princerupert.com.

The Prince Rupert accommodations listed below have dining rooms and other amenities:

Crest Hotel, 222 First Avenue West, (250) 624–6771. Moderate.

Best Western Highliner Inn, 815 First Avenue West, (250) 624–9060. Moderate.

Coast Prince Rupert Hotel, Second Avenue at Sixth Street, (250) 624–6711. Moderate to expensive.

Side Trip: Queen Charlotte Islands

From Prince Rupert you can take a B.C. Ferry to visit Skidegate and Masset on the **Queen Charlotte Islands.** At Second Beach, Skidegate, Queen Charlotte City, visit the **Queen Charlotte Islands Museum,** (250) 559–4643. Open throughout the year. Exhibits are of Haida totem poles, maritime history, and pioneer settlement. The Queen Charlottes are wonderful for camping, exploring, and fishing. If you're up in the province to fish, stay at **Langara Fishing Lodge,** (250) 873–4228 (call collect), on Langara Island off Graham in the Charlottes. The lodge offers a package that includes fine accommodations, meals, equipment, air transportation from the city of Vancouver, the advice of fishing experts, and catch care. Expensive, but a good value for the dedicated angler.

Inn on the Harbour, 720 First Avenue, (250) 624–9107. Moderate.

From Prince Rupert, you can go to Alaska on the Alaska state ferry system. Between May 1 and September 30, Alaska ferries sail four times a week from Prince Rupert to Skagway (Highway 98 connects Skagway with Whitehorse in the Yukon and the Alaska Highway). Service between Ketchikan, Alaska, and Stewart, B.C., gives you access to the magnificent alpine scenery on Highway 37—the Stewart-Cassiar Highway (37 heading north links up with the Alaska Highway; communities are far apart on this highway, so have supplies and extra gas).

For more information on ferry service between B.C. and Alaska, contact the Alaska Marine Highway System, Box R, Juneau, Alaska 99811; (907) 465–3941, Juneau; (250) 627–1744, Prince Rupert; or (800) 642–0066, other locations.

If you and your vehicle arrive at Prince Rupert by ferry, you have several touring options on the mainland:

You can take the Yellowhead Highway 16 (see Chapter 4) to Prince George (721 km/433 mi) and, on the same route, continue east to the great national parks of the Canadian Rockies and the cities of Edmonton and Calgary in Alberta.

From Prince George you can also head north to Dawson Creek and Fort St. John, which are on the Alaska Highway, and then northwest to the Yukon, the Northwest Territories, and Alaska.

Going south from Prince George via Highway 97 to the Trans-Canada takes you to Vancouver.

When you are traveling between Prince Rupert and Prince George, although it seems as if you are at the northern part of the province, you are only in the middle of the province—north of you stretches a vast wilderness with few communities. The hardy people who live in this region farm, harvest timber, fish, trap fur-bearing animals, work in mining, provide services to the local people and to tourists, and work in government agencies. Pioneering is very much alive in these parts. This is also First Nations country, and you'll have the opportunity to experience something of a culture that predates the arrival of Europeans on this continent.

This is a region of high mountains, thick forests, wild rivers, and sparkling lakes—home to eagles, moose, coyotes, grizzly and black bears (they are dangerous, so don't feed them and don't get out of the car). The many recreational opportunities along the way include camping, fishing, trail riding, and wild-river rafting. Bring your camera and capture the beauty. Use common sense when traveling on remote stretches, plan your stops, and don't be the cause of a forest fire. Otherwise, it's all there for you to enjoy.

Terrace

Terrace is a sizable community about 140 km/84 mi from Prince Rupert. Here you can find accommodations, gas, restaurants, tennis, swimming pools, theaters, and museums. **Terrace Heritage Park,** on Kalum Street, open from mid-May to the end of August, has several old log buildings—a dance hall, a barn, a gold miner's cabin, and others—that represent pioneering life. Snowcapped Sleeping Beauty Mountain is a beautiful local landmark. On Copper River Road is a large bed of marine shell fossils. Highway 37 south from town takes you to **Lakelse Provincial Park** and the community of **Kitimat,** site of one of the largest aluminum-processing plants in the world (which you can tour). There's terrific salmon fishing in the Kitimat area. Visit the **Kitimat Centennial Museum,** 293 City Centre (250–632–7022), open year-round, which depicts the history of Kitimat's growth from a missionary village to an industrial town. Call for hours and fees.

All of the accommodations listed below have restaurants and other amenities:

Coast Inn of the West, 4620 Lakeside Avenue, Terrace, (250) 638–8141. Moderate.

Sandman Inn, 4828 Highway 16 West, Terrace, (250) 635–9151. Moderate.

Kitwanga Area

At Kitwanga you can connect with Highway 37—the Stewart-Cassiar Highway—going north to the Alaska Highway. Kitwanga itself is famous for its number of hundred-year-old totem poles.

'Ksan Village, on the bank of the Skeena River, has one of the province's premier exhibitions of northwest coastal Indian arts and crafts. There's no admission charge to the village itself or to open buildings. Open from late April to mid-October; (250) 842–5544. It features six decorated tribal houses: the treasure, or carving shed, where Native artisans create beautiful objects from their ancient heritage; the studio, where silkscreen prints are produced by 'Ksan artists; the 'Ksan shop, where you can purchase authentic arts and crafts; the firewood house, where you can try your hand at craft making; the wolf, or feast, house, where the potlatch feast is described; and the frog house, portraying the ways of a Stone Age culture. 'Ksan is a few miles north of Hazelton and well worth the diversion from the main route. There is a campground here.

Smithers

Smithers is a regional transportation center. Ranching, mining, lumbering, and services are the main economic activities here. Visit the Smithers Art Gallery, 1425 Main Street, with exhibitions by local artists and traveling shows. Call (250) 847–3898 for hours and fees.

The following accommodations have dining rooms and other amenities:

Hudson Bay Lodge, on Highway 16, East, (250) 847–4581. Moderate.

Aspen Motor Inn, on Highway 16, (250) 847–4551. Moderate.

Forts Fraser and St. James

Fort Fraser is one of B.C.'s oldest communities. Simon Fraser established a post here for the North West Company, which later merged with the Hudson's Bay Company. In addition, in this area the last spike of the Grand Trunk Pacific Railway, Canada's second transcontinental railroad, was driven in, in 1914.

Fort St. James makes an interesting side trip via Highway 27 North off 16. Once capital of New Caledonia (the Scottish dream for a free homeland), it is the second oldest community in B.C. and was founded by Simon Fraser and John Stuart in 1806. At Fort St. James National Historic Park, the old fort has been reconstructed, and summer tours of the grounds, buildings, wharf, and other facilities are offered. In this area, at Necoslie Reserve, is the grave of the famous Chief Kwah. There are also memorials to Father Morice, a missionary who served the Native people of the area. Our Lady of Good Hope, Father Morice's church, still stands and is open to visitors. Near the church is a propeller memorial to Russ Baker, a bush pilot who founded Canadian Pacific Airlines (CP Air merged with Pacific Western in 1987 to create Canadian Airlines). A hike up Mount Pope (1,465 m/4,803 ft) gives great views of the surrounding wild landscape. The annual 25-km Pope Peak Run has a 650-m/2,131-ft uphill section.

Vanderhoof

Vanderhoof is a good place to stop for the night en route to Prince George. In July there's the two-day **Vanderhoof International Airshow**, which is the top one of its kind in Canada. Visit the **Nechako Bird Sanctuary**, with its many different species and thousands of Canada geese. The local museum displays a photograph of Herbert Vanderhoof, an oddball Chicago businessman who gave the town its name.

Grand Trunk Inn, 2351 Church Street (250–567–3188), has a dining room and lounge. Moderate.

Prince George

Prince George, British Columbia's third largest city, is at the junction of the Yellowhead 16 (east–west) and the Alaska 97 (north–south) Highways. This city traces its history back more than 200 years, to when the explorer Alexander Mackenzie came here and noted the location for his employer, the North West Company. Simon Fraser came later, and Fort George was developed on the site. At that time Fort St. James was the capital of this region, and Fort George had a secondary position. Today Prince George is one of the most important communities in B.C. It is a key place for finding accommodations, getting car repairs and extra supplies, and relaxing a bit before heading north on the Alaska Highway, east to the Rockies, or south to the city of Vancouver. The city is enjoying a renaissance of growth. The new University of Northern British Columbia's main campus sits atop Cranbrook Hill, overlooking the city. Opened in 1994, the school's studies emphasize programs of the First Nations, environmental, northern, and women's studies.

The university's presence has spurred other construction, such as the new 1,800-seat Prince George Civic Centre Complex at Seventh and Dominion (which includes one of the finest concert halls in the province), a new domed courthouse, and shopping and recreational facilities. Cappuccino parlors have sprung up around the city.

Prince George Art Gallery, 2820 Fifteenth Avenue, (250) 563–6447, is open daily. Free. Exhibitions by artists from the region and traveling shows.

All of the following accommodations have dining rooms and other amenities:

Ramada Hotel Prince George, 444 George Street, (250) 563–0055; (800) 272–6232. Moderate to expensive.

Connaught Motor Inn, 1550 Victoria Street, (250) 562–4441. Moderate.

Coast Inn of the North, 770 Brunswick Street, (250) 563–0121. Moderate to expensive.

Simon Fraser Inn, 600 Québec Street, (250) 562–3181. Moderate.

Sandman Inn, 1650 Central Street, (250) 563–8131. Moderate.

Esther's Inn, 1151 Commercial Drive, (250) 562–4131. Moderate.

CHAPTER 7

Touring Alberta and the Canadian Rockies

Calgary · Banff · Lake Louise · Jasper · Icefields · Edmonton

Alberta in Brief

You might assume that Alberta was named for Prince Albert, the beloved consort of Queen Victoria. Queen Victoria played such an important role in Canadian history that her name has been liberally applied to cities, mountains, glaciers, and all sorts of things—she was that well loved. It would, then, make sense to name a province for Prince Albert, but in fact the Marquis of Lorne named the province in honor of Princess Louise Caroline Alberta, the fourth daughter of the Great Queen. First, as governor-general of Canada he had the authority to do so. Second, the princess was his wife.

Until the coming of European explorers, trappers, mountain men, fur traders, settlers, ranchers, the Northwest Mounted Police, and the builders of the transcontinental railroad, the people residing on this magnificent land of prairies and mountains were Amerindians. These Native people have lived here in what they call the land of four directions for thousands of years—some say 5,000 years, others close to 8,000; both may be gross underestimates. Today these people are known by the names of Cree, Blackfoot, Blood, Assiniboine, Piegan, Sarcee, and Chipewyan.

The first whites were fur traders and missionaries who came into this region of Canada in the early eighteenth century. By and large, relations between the whites and the aboriginals were amicable. The whites wanted to trade and make money, but they were not interested in developing the land. Appropriating ancestral lands here was not a major issue in the nineteenth century, as it was below the border in the United States. Trouble did, however, come in the form of rough-and-tough whiskey traders who built their own forts in the southern part of the province, exploited the Native people, and created so much tension that in 1873 the Canadian federal government established the Northwest Mounted Police (today's Royal Canadian Mounted Police), under the command of such legendary strongmen as Colonel Macleod, and sent them to this part of the prairies in 1874 to bring law and order by driving out the whiskey traders, protecting the Native peoples, and opening up the area for development and settlement.

Settlement boomed after the tracks of the transcontinental railroad went through in the latter half of the nineteenth century. Villages, towns, and cities sprang up along the railroad as entrepreneurs seeking new ventures and immigrants from many foreign countries, hungry for freedom and opportunity in this promised land, flooded into the area. They turned Alberta into cattle ranches, wheat farms, and mining and forestry operations. Manufacturing, services, education, and culture blossomed, and by 1905 Alberta had grown enough to become a full-fledged province in the Canadian confederation.

Vast reserves of oil and natural gas were discovered here in the early part of the twentieth century, and Alberta found it had more in common with Texas than Ontario or Québec—the oil and cowhand images were essentially the same in both places. The Great Depression of the 1930s hurt, but the post–World War II oil boom made Alberta exceedingly affluent. By the 1970s such cities as Calgary and Edmonton were transformed into urban showplaces, and everyone seemed to be doing all right. But good times don't last forever, and Alberta's economy was dampened by the slide in oil prices during the 1980s. Nevertheless, this is a "can-do" province, and optimism for the future is part of the essence of life here.

Geographically, Alberta is located between sixty degrees latitude north and forty-nine degrees at the Canadian–U.S. border. This is a large province of 661,000 sq km/255,200 sq mi, with

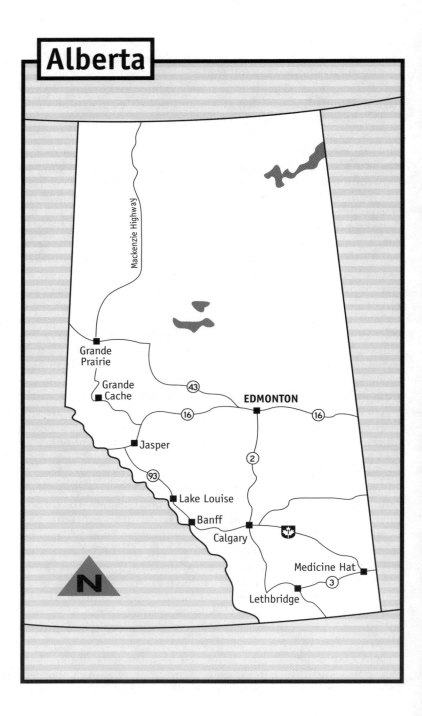

Alberta

Mackenzie Highway

Grande Prairie

Grande Cache

43

EDMONTON

16

16

Jasper

93

2

Lake Louise

Banff

Calgary

Medicine Hat

3

Lethbridge

N

diverse topography, including many rivers, lakes, streams, glaciers, and even sections of badlands (arid stretches of land with little or no vegetation), more suitable for trekking than development. In the southern region some of the most important paleontological finds in the world have been made. On Alberta's western border is British Columbia; on the east, the province of Saskatchewan. To the north are the Northwest Territories, and to the south is the state of Montana. Although the southern and central regions of the province are prairie farms and cattle ranches, the north is mostly forested wilderness and muskeg. Along the western border run the great Rocky Mountains, with their world-famous national parks and resorts—Banff, Lake Louise, and Jasper.

Alberta's winters are long and cold, with low humidity and dry, crisp air; its summers are typically warm and pleasant. A great deal of snow falls in mountain areas—a boon for skiers and winter-sports enthusiasts. During winter chinook winds—warm, dry winds that descend from the eastern slopes of the Rockies and across the prairies—lessen the severity of the cold and make living here, at times, quite enjoyable. Because Alberta doesn't experience the amount of heavy rainfall that the Pacific coast does, travelers are assured, on the one hand, of many sunny days to enjoy their vacations. On the other hand, when in the high mountains, don't be surprised to see brief periods of heavy snow falling in late June—though at that time of year, the snow quickly melts in the bright sun.

The population of Alberta is about 2.5 million, and the people represent many different ethnic and racial backgrounds—British (the majority), as well as German, Ukrainian, French, and First Nations peoples.

Before the building of the transcontinental railroad, the only people who traveled to this region were those in quest of fortune or the salvation of souls; once the railroad was built, however, close to two-thirds of the Canadian continent was opened up for exploration and/or enjoyment by more ordinary folk. With the development of such resort areas as Banff, Lake Louise, and Jasper, tourism here began in grand style. Today tourism is Alberta's third largest economic activity. The diversity of tourism/vacation offerings is vast. You can be joyfully indolent in the midst of some of the most glorious scenery in the world or work your tail off climbing some of the highest mountains in the world. But the bottom line here is neither the scenery nor the attractions. It is the quality of the people of Alberta themselves, who welcome you with open arms and genuinely warm smiles, western style.

Travel Alberta— Tourism Information

Travel Alberta, the provincial government's tourism agency, maintains a year-round toll-free telephone number that can be used throughout the continental United States and throughout Canada. To request information, brochures, or maps, call (800) 661–8888 or visit www.explorealberta.com.

You will find Travel Alberta visitor information centers at these locations:

Walsh, on the Trans-Canada Highway at the Alberta–Saskatchewan border

Milk River, on Highway 4 near the Alberta–Montana border

West Glacier, Montana, junction of U.S. Highway 2 and Going-to-the-Sun Road

Sentinel, on Crowsnest Highway 3 at the Alberta–British Columbia border

Oyen, Highway 9

Jasper, Highway 16

Field, in Field, B.C.

Canmore, near the Trans-Canada Highway in Canmore

Lloydminster, on Yellowhead Highway 16 at the Alberta–Saskatchewan border

Edmonton, third floor, City Centre Building, 10155 102nd Street, open Monday through Friday except holidays, 8:15 A.M. to 4:30 P.M.

Alberta's Extra-Special Attractions

Alberta South

Cardston, via Macleod Trail Highway 2. The **C. O. Card Home and Museum,** 337 Main Street. Open mid-June to the end of August. Admission by donation. A log-cabin home that belonged to

Charles Ora Card, the leader of eleven Mormon families, with whom he emigrated from Utah in 1887. A **Mormon Temple,** 348 Third Street West, (403) 653–3552, offers tours of its visitor center. The **Remington Alberta Carriage Centre,** 623 Main Street, (403) 653–5139, is a 5,850-sq-m/65,000-sq-ft facility housing one of North America's largest collections of horse-drawn vehicles. Open year-round.

Crowsnest Pass, via Crowsnest Highway 3 near British Columbia. Within this municipality are the following points of interest: hundred-million-year-old volcanic rocks; Sulphur Springs, cold waters used for their curative powers by the Native peoples; the Frank Slide Interpretive Centre, (403) 562–7388 (ninety million tons of rock from Turtle Mountain crashed on the town of Frank in 1903 and killed seventy people); Hillcrest, site of one of Canada's worst coal-mining disasters in 1914; and Leitch Collieries, tours of an old coal-mining complex, guided tours in summer, self-guided September through April. Admission by donation.

Cypress Hills Provincial Park, via the Trans-Canada to Highway 41 and then south (located at the Alberta–Saskatchewan border in the southeast corner of the province). This park, situated on a plateau that was untouched by ancient glaciers, not only supports 14 species of orchids but also contains 200 species of nesting birds and is the habitat of deer, elk, moose, and beavers. An archaeological dig found a 7,000-year-old Native encampment. Fishing, boating, camping, and hiking are all possible here. Rent boats at Cypress Hills.

Dinosaur Provincial Park, via the Trans-Canada and Highway 36 North (watch for signs for other access roads). A World Heritage Site (designated as such by UNESCO), this important park (6,075 ha/15,000 acres) protects one of the most extensive dinosaur fields in the world. Bus tours take visitors through the park for a small charge; camping facilities are available.

Drumheller Valley

Northeast of Calgary via the Trans-Canada to Highway 9 North, Drumheller Valley is home to the outstanding **Royal Tyrrell Museum of Paleontology,** (403) 823–7707. Open year-round, this museum is housed in a stunning modern building. The story of millions of years of the Earth's history is told through dinosaur, fossil, and geological exhibits, some of which are interactive. The museum was named in honor of the explorer and geologist Joseph Burr Tyrrell, who found the first dinosaur bones in this area in 1884.

Mountain resort towns offer fine accommodations, dining, entertainment, and shopping. They are also at the doorstep of the best in outdoor sports—skiing, hiking, skating, golf, white-water rafting, horseback riding, and a lot more.

DINO 2000, (403) 823–8100. Drumheller, the Dinosaur Capital of the World, is home to the World's Largest Dinosaur. Standing more than 25m/80 ft tall, this fierce *Tyrannosaurus Rex* features an interactive climb into the dinosaur's mouth, where a viewing platform provides a spectacular panorama of the Drumheller Valley. Open daily, year-round; admission is charged.

Canadian Badlands Passion Play, Drumheller, (403) 823–7750. The thousands of visitors who have seen the Passion Play describe it as "moving" and "world class." It's presented in July; tickets must be reserved for the afternoon and evening performances.

The Hoodoos, via Highway 10 southeast of Drumheller toward East Coulee. The Hoodoos are huge mushroom-shaped rocks formed by wind and water erosion. To walk among them feels like exploring a planet in a science-fiction movie.

Horseshoe Canyon, (403) 823–2000. Canada's mini–Grand Canyon is located on Highway 9 South, 19 km/12 mi west of Drumheller. View the spectacular badlands formations representing seventy million years of history and learn about this area's prehistoric and present-day environments and inhabitants.

The following accommodations feature the most amenities:

Best Western Jurassic Inn, 1103 Highway 9 South, (403) 823–7700 or (888) 823–4366. Moderate.

Drumheller Travelodge, 101 Grove Place, (403) 823–5302 or (877) 464–0646. Moderate.

Super 8 Motel, 600 Second Street S.E., (403) 823–8887 or (888) 823–8882. Moderate.

Fort Macleod

At Crowsnest Highway 3 and Macleod Trail Highway 2, the **Fort Macleod Museum** is a re-creation of the original Northwest Mounted Police fort built in 1874. A mounted police ride is held here daily during the months of July and August. The fort's official season is from mid-May to mid-October. Call (403) 553–4703 or 553–2500. A guided walking tour of Fort Macleod takes you through the streets and thirty buildings, describing the way the police, pioneers, and Native people lived in this area;

these free tours run from May to the end of August. Also within this area, via Highways 2 and 785, is **"Head Smashed In" Buffalo Jump,** a World Heritage Site (designated as such by UNESCO). Here for more than 5,600 years the Natives drove buffalo over the cliff and to their deaths to obtain food and materials for clothing and shelter. Open year-round. Call (403) 553–2731 for more information.

Gleichen

Reach Gleichen via the Trans-Canada Highway east from Calgary to Highway 21. The **Siksika Museum of Human History** is located on the third floor of Old Sun College, 1 km/0.6 mi west of town; (403) 734–3070. Open year-round by appointment only. The historical displays and artifacts of the Siksika (Blackfoot) people interpret four major life transitions of this tribe.

Lethbridge

Lethbridge can be reached via the Crowsnest Highway 3 and Macleod Trail Highway 2 or via Highway 4 from the Alberta–Montana border. This is a thriving city just south of Calgary and north of the international border. In the 1800s it was a well-known coal-mining town, and American whiskey-trading forts were strung out over the landscape in this region. Visit **Fort Whoop-Up,** located in Indian Battle Park; call (403) 329–0444. A great battle took place here in 1870 between the Cree and the Blackfoot peoples. In the park is the **Helen Schuler Coulee Centre,** which has several nature trails. Free. At Seventh Avenue South, in Lethbridge, is the **Nikka Yuko Japanese Gardens,** (403) 328–3511. Open mid-May to the end of September. Admission is charged. The **Sir Alexander Galt Museum,** First Street and Fifth Avenue South, housed in a hospital built in 1891, has displays of local history; (403) 320–3898. Free. The city's crown jewel is the campus of the **University of Lethbridge,** a stunning complex designed by Arthur Erickson. Call (403) 329–2111 for free campus tours.

All of the following accommodations have dining rooms and other amenities:

Lethbridge Lodge Hotel, 320 Scenic Drive, (403) 328–1123 or (800) 661–1232. Moderate to expensive.

Sandman Hotel Lethbridge, 421 Mayor Magrath Drive, (403) 328–1111 or (800) 266–4660. Moderate.

Lethbridge Lodge Motel, 2210 Seventh Avenue South, (403) 329–0100. Moderate.

Best Western Heidelburg Inn, 1303 Mayor Magrath Drive, (403) 329–0555 or (800) 791–8488. Moderate.

Medicine Hat

Medicine Hat is located at the junction of the Trans-Canada and Crowsnest Highway 3. If you are traveling west in the southern part of the province, Medicine Hat is the first large community after the Saskatchewan border. This city boasts the world's largest exhibition of Medalta pottery and Hycroft china, as well as the world's tallest tepee. There are many beautiful parks, hiking trails, and golf courses situated in this oasis in the prairie.

In 1907 Rudyard Kipling said that Medicine Hat was a city "with all hell for a basement"—in reference to the extensive natural gas field discovered here in 1883. Today Medicine Hat—the name evokes images of the Old West—is a center for manufacturing and distribution of agricultural products.

From here you can drive to Calgary on the Trans-Canada Highway or head straight to British Columbia via Crowsnest Highway 3.

Medicine Hat Museum and Art Gallery, 1302 Crescent Street SW, (403) 527–6266. This museum hosts more than twenty top-level exhibitions in its class-A art gallery. In addition to its permanent collection, it has a wide variety of exhibits emphasizing the history of Medicine Hat and its district, the Plains Indians, the Northwest Mounted Police, ranching, farming, the Canadian Pacific Railway, and the early growth of the city.

Downtown Historical Walking Tour, Tourism Centre, (403) 527–4622. This self-guided tour of turn-of-the-twentieth-century architecture includes excellent examples of homes, churches, and businesses.

Rosebud

Rosebud is situated 32 km/20 mi southwest of Drumheller on Highway 9 South. Nestled in the beautiful Rosebud River Valley, Rosebud hosts the Rosebud Dinner Theatre produced by the Rosebud School of the Arts. The dinner theater has three different productions each year, including a Christmas show. The historic Rosebud Hotel and Mercantile look much as they did in their heyday, the 1920s and 1930s.

Most of the following accommodations have dining rooms, as well as other amenities:

Best Western Inn, 722 Redcliff Drive, (403) 537–3700 or (800) 528–1234. Moderate.

Callaghan Inn, 954 Seventh Street SW, (403) 527–8844 or (800) 661–4440.

Comfort Inn & Suites, 2317 Trans-Canada Highway, (403) 504–1700 or (800) 228–5150. Moderate.

Imperial Inn, 3282 Thirteenth Avenue SE, (403) 527–8811 or (800) 661–5322.

Medicine Hat Lodge, 1051 Ross Glen Drive, (403) 592–2222 or (800) 661–8095. Moderate.

Super 8, 1280 Trans-Canadian Way SE, (403) 528–8888 or (800) 800–8000. Moderate.

Travel Lodge Medicine Hat, 1100 Redcliff Drive SW, (403) 527–2275 or (800) 442–8729. Moderate.

Turner Valley Area

Turner Valley, 54 km/34 mi southwest of Calgary via Millarville and Highway 22. Turner Valley was one of Canada's richest oil-producing areas. Visit the Dingman #1 and Royalite #4 wells, Christ Church (Anglican, circa 1910), the Fisher Ranch, the John Ware cairn (John Ware was a famous black cowboy who had his own ranch in the area), and the Black Diamond Mine.

There are also a number of working ranches in Turner Valley, and though they are private operations, you may, as you tour the countryside, see cattle grazing and ranch hands riding or doing chores.

Writing on Stone Provincial Park, via Highway 2 to Milk River and then east on Highway 501. This park has many ancient petroglyphs (carvings and paintings in sandstone cliffs by the Native people who lived here). Naturalists conduct guided tours. There's a camping area among large cottonwood trees.

Central Alberta

In **Camrose,** via Highway 21, south of Edmonton, you can visit the **Centennial Museum,** Fifty-third Street and Forty-sixth Avenue, (403) 672–5456. Open mid-May through September. Donations accepted. The museum has a pioneer church, an early schoolhouse, a log house, a mill, and a fire hall, all from settlement days.

Cochrane Ranch, on Highway 1A at the junction of Highway 22 west of the town of Cochrane, (403) 932–2902. Open mid-May through September. Donations accepted. Alberta's first large-scale cattle ranch was established here in 1881. The present site has 61 ha/150 acres of parkland, lush with wildflowers and nature trails. On a hilltop is a large statue of a cowboy on his horse, the figure sitting frozen in time as a perpetual symbol of Alberta's heritage.

Devon is west of Edmonton on Yellowhead Highway 16. Here in Devon are the excellent University of Alberta **Devonian Botanic Gardens,** (403) 987–3054. Open early May until the end of September. You'll find an herb garden, a Japanese garden, a butterfly house, a Native people's garden, an alpine garden, and indoor floral and plant displays. A nature trail leads past a wide variety of plants, including those that grow in the desert.

Reach **Markerville** via Highway 54. The **Stephansson House Provincial Historic Site,** (403) 932–2902, is located 7 km/4.4 mi north of Markerville, off Highway 592 or 781. In this pleasant house lived Stephan G. Stephansson (1853–1927), Iceland's national poet. Guided tours take you through this furnished literary home in which traditional Icelandic handicrafts are displayed. Open from mid-May through September. Admission charged.

Polar Park, via Highway 14, east of Edmonton, (403) 922–3013. Open year-round. Admission charged. This is a special reserve for cold-climate mammals—fifty species, more than 500 animals from Canada, northern China, Russia, and other countries.

Alberta Heartland

Rocky Mountain House National Historic Park, via Highway 11A, (403) 845–2412. Open May to October. Donations accepted. The interpretive center tells the story of fur trading and the forts serving the traders in this region between 1799 and 1886. There are nature trails and a buffalo paddock.

Siffleur, White Goat, and Ghost River Wilderness Areas, located along the eastern side of Banff and Jasper National Parks, are preserved to protect their natural beauty and character. Visitors on foot are welcome; development, impairment, hunting, fishing, trapping, motor vehicles, horses, and pack animals are prohibited.

Willmore Wilderness Park, located north of Jasper National Park, permits some activities, such as horseback riding, mountain biking, hunting, and fishing. For more information call Alberta Tourism at (800) 661–8888.

In **Wetaskiwin,** Highways 13 and 2A, the **Reynolds Alberta Museum,** (403) 361–1351, opened in fall 1992. This world-class facility interprets the history of ground and air transportation, agriculture, and selected industries in Alberta. It is also home to Canada's Aviation Hall of Fame, located in a hangar amid vintage aircraft. A 1929 Duesenberg Phaeton Royale is also on display.

Alberta Prairie Steam Tours, Stettler, (403) 742–2811. Round-trip day excursions on train powered by a 1920 steam locomotive. The nostalgic 304-km/190-mi journey is a unique way to experience the culture and history of prairie towns. Tours vary from four to eight hours in length, May through October.

Elk Island National Park, via Highway 16, just east of Edmonton. Call (403) 922–6380. A relatively small national park, Elk Island is a tranquil place of meadows, lakes, and forests of aspen and spruce. It is also a preserve for elk and buffalo, which roam free in the park. There are hiking trails throughout the park and an interpretive program.

St. Albert, via Highway 2, north of Edmonton, established in 1861, was one of the first independent communities in Western Canada. It was named for Father Albert Lacombe, a legendary missionary and friend of the Native, Métis, and pioneering peoples of this region. His chapel, restored to look as it did in the 1860s, stands at St. Vital Avenue and welcomes visitors. Visit the museum here, the religious shrine, and Father Lacombe's crypt. The complex is open from mid-May through September, (403) 459–7663. Donations accepted.

Ukrainian Cultural Heritage Village, 50 km/30 mi east of Edmonton on Highway 16. Open mid-May through September, (403) 662–3640. Admission half price after Labour Day. This unique heritage village re-creates an early Ukrainian settlement in Alberta. Canada's famous Giant Ukrainian Easter Egg—7 m (23 ft) long, 5.5 m (18 ft) wide, and weighing 2,270 kg (5,000 lb)—is located at nearby Vegreville. The egg's decorations tell the story of settlement, religious faith, culture, good harvests, and protection received from the Royal Canadian Mounted Police. During the first weekend in July, the annual **Pysanka Festival** features Ukrainian food, song, dance, and crafts.

Northern Alberta

Fort McMurray, via Highway 55 from Athabasca to Highway 63, is in the Athabasca Oil Sands region, a vast area of oil-bearing sand that will eventually become a critical source of energy when other sources of petroleum dry up. This is a vast municipality, home to more than 42,000 people. The wide variety of recreational facilities and state-of-the-art theaters and festivals will make you wonder why you haven't visited before. For more information call the Fort McMurray Visitor's Bureau, (800) 565–3947 or visit www.visitors.fortmcmurray.ab.ca.

Lesser Slave Lake, via Highway 2 north of Edmonton, is called the Nassau of the North. It is Alberta's largest automobile-accessible lake and bordered by no less than three provincial

Roadside Distractions

Paris has its Eiffel Tower, Cairo its pyramids, and South Dakota its Mount Rushmore—all fine monuments and cultural touchstones. Alberta, too, has its monuments; they are just a bit more eclectic.

In the town of St. Paul there's the world's only known genuine UFO Landing Pad, a hopeful symbol of intelligent life in outer space and the town's project for Canada's 1967 Centennial.

Vegreville, east of Edmonton, has a strong Ukrainian heritage and offers a 9-m/30-ft-tall *pysanka,* or Ukrainian Easter egg.

The town of Glendon, also with a strong eastern European connection, has erected a giant pierogi. This humble potato dumpling, a staple of European cuisine, symbolizes the roots of the region's hardy residents as it soars, fork and all, over the town.

To the south, the town of Torrington has created the Gopher Hole, a museum that features thirty-nine dioramas of life on the prairies populated by costumed stuffed gophers.

In Drumheller there's plenty of science and paleontology at the town's famous Royal Tyrell Museum, but you will also find plenty of less scientifically accurate dinosaurs all around the town, ready for photo ops.

And finally, just south of Calgary in the town of Vulcan you will find a large-scale model of the USS *Enterprise—Star Trek* variety.

---

parks. In this region is the northernmost bird observatory, and one of the most ancient sand dune systems in Alberta.

Athabasca, just ninety minutes north of Edmonton via Highway 2, is a region of rolling hills, tranquil lakes, sunny beaches, and wilderness areas. The historic town of Athabasca, gateway to northern Alberta and home of the Magnificent River Rats Festival, has plenty of recreational facilities including golf, cross-country ski trails, and a nationally rated trail system in the Huskey Creek Valley.

Lac La Biche, north of Edmonton via Highway 2 to Highway 55, is the site of **Lakeland Provincial Park,** which offers Alberta's only backcountry canoe circuit. **Lac La Biche Mission,** 11 km/6.6 mi east of town, is a national historic site established by Father

Rene Remas. It is the site of Alberta's first recorded sawmill, printing press, and commercial wheat farm.

Peace River country, Highway 2 North to Slave Lake, then Bicentennial Highway 88. The mighty Peace River sculpts Alberta's landscape for more than 1,000 km/660 mi and then winds its way to the Beaufort Sea and Arctic Ocean. This unspoiled network of clean lakes and rivers is a fishing and canoeing paradise. European settlement in the Peace country dates back to 1706, when the Hudson's Bay Company entered the area. Full settlement began in 1906 when rail lines began to expand northward. The **Dunvegan Provincial Park and Historic Site,** located on the north bank of the Peace River, offers a glimpse into missionary life and fur trading in this remote area.

Wood Buffalo National Park, located in the extreme north of Alberta and overlapping into the Northwest Territories, is accessible by air or by road from Fort Smith, N.W.T. (no road access from Alberta). Wood Buffalo, one of the largest national parks in the world, is very much a wilderness area of great rivers, large lakes, extensive bogs, and thick forests. It's home to moose, wolves, lynx, black bears, and eagles, and a secure nesting ground for the endangered whooping crane as well. The park, which covers an area larger than Switzerland, has areas for camping, boating, and swimming. If you want to get away from it all, literally and figuratively, this is the right place. For more information contact Superintendent, Wood Buffalo National Park, Box 750, Fort Smith, NWT X0E 0P0; (403) 872–2349.

Calgary: A World-Class City and Southern Doorway to the Canadian Rockies

Calgary is a modern, sophisticated city with skyscrapers rising up from the flatlands of the prairies, which end abruptly at the high walls of the Canadian Rockies. The image of the Old West persists in Calgary—it annually holds the largest rodeo in the world, the Calgary Stampede, and authentic cattle ranches with real cowhands are but a short drive from city limits.

Calgary can be best equated with such great Texas cities of Dallas and Fort Worth, for this is one of Canada's major petroleum centers. The oil companies are here, and this is where the deals are cut. The prosperity brought by the petroleum industry is reflected in the affluence of most of the people who live here, the modern city itself, and the recreational and cultural amenities it offers to residents and visitors alike.

In addition to its many attractions, this most modern city is the southern gateway to the great national parks of the Canadian Rockies: Banff and Jasper, with their awesome beauty, famous resorts, and many recreational opportunities.

If you've never been to Calgary, you're in for a few surprises regarding a former Northwest Mounted Police post that in less than a hundred years has become a booming, gleaming, twenty-first-century city, very much in a class by itself.

A Brief Look at Calgary's History

The Native peoples of the Calgary-southern Alberta prairie region can trace their history back 12,000 years. Their civilizations were based on hunting, particularly for buffalo, herds of which were in great abundance. Although explorers and fur traders for the North West Company and Hudson's Bay Company came through this area en route to what is now British Columbia, there were few white habitations as such before the mid-1800s.

Calgary itself was founded in 1875 as a Mountie post called Fort Calgary, located where the Bow and Elbow Rivers come together, and in 1883 became an important center in the development of the transcontinental railroad. Calgary was incorporated as a city in 1893 and continued to grow, serving as a conduit for processing cattle from local ranches into meat and for handling other agricultural products from area farms. For much of its history, until the boom times of petroleum, Calgary was primarily known as Canada's cow town, much the same as Fort Worth, Texas. The first oil find was made nearby in Turner Valley in 1914, and the province's first refinery started operating in Calgary in 1923. The early promoters of Calgary as Canada's oil center were R. A. Brown, W. S. Herron, and A. W. Dingman. In 1947 a major reserve of oil was found at Leduc, and from that post–World War II time to just recently, Calgary has been an oil-boom town, its skyline, affluence, and attractions reflecting the money that has been made here. During its boom years thousands of Canadians from slower-growth areas of the country flooded into Calgary to seek their fortunes, and most of them prospered. When, however, the price of oil sank to distressing lows, the glow faded, and thousands left Calgary for more promising opportunities in other areas, such as coastal British Columbia and southern Ontario. Yet the impressive characteristic about the more than 860,749 people

Extra-Special Event

Whether you are a rodeo buff or have never been to one, the annual **Calgary Exhibition and Stampede** is the biggest and best in the world. But the rodeo is just part of this old-time western extravaganza, which is held for ten days from the beginning of July to mid-month.

A half-million-dollar, three-hour rodeo show held every afternoon features bull riding, steer wrestling, and saddle-bronc, bareback, and wild-horse riding. The Calgary Stampede made championship chuck-wagon racing, held during evening shows, the biggest thrill at rodeos; compared with Calgary-style chuck-wagon racing, the old Romans and their chariots seem tame.

At night singers, dancers, comedians, and acrobats entertain audiences at the Grandstand Spectacular. A Las Vegas–style revue, top-star performers, and a spectacular display of fireworks are among the highlights.

You can visit the agricultural displays and purebred livestock shows, take midway rides, eat everything from fast food to broiled Alberta steaks or ethnic dishes, compete in the annual big-prize-money Blackjack Tournament, tour an Indian prairie village and see people demonstrating skills used in pioneering days, and watch the blows and hammers taking place at the World Championship Blacksmith Competition.

Contact (403) 261–0101, (800) 661–1260, or www.calgary-stampede.com for information. The Calgary Stampede takes place at Exhibition Grounds/Stampede Park, just south of city center via Macleod Trail Highway 2.

of Calgary is their can-do spirit. After several years of economic downturn, Calgary's economy is booming again. The city now has the second highest number of corporate head offices in Canada, having overtaken Montréal, to trail only Toronto.

How to Get to Calgary
By Car

From the east: Trans-Canada Highway 1.

From the west: Trans-Canada Highway 1, or Crowsnest Highway 3 to Macleod Trail Highway 2 North.

From the south: U.S. I–15 to the border at Sweetgrass, Montana, and Coutts, Alberta, which merges with Highway 4 North to Lethbridge and then via Macleod Trail Highway 2 North.

From the north (the city of Edmonton): Calgary Trail Highway 2.

By Bus

Greyhound provides service to and from Calgary. It operates from a terminal at 850 Sixteenth Street NW. Call (403) 265–9111 for schedules and fares. The Red Arrow Express provides luxury bus service four times a day between Calgary and Edmonton. Its terminal is at 205 Ninth Avenue SE, main floor, with pickups at the Quality Inn Airport Hotel, 4804 Edmonton Trail NE; call (403) 531–0350.

By Plane

The following airlines serve Calgary International Airport: Air Canada, Canadian, American, Continental, Horizon, British Airways, Lufthansa, United, and Westjet. The airport is approximately 17 km/10.5 mi—or about thirty minutes—from Calgary city center via Barlow Trail, McKnight Boulevard, and Centre Street. The terminal itself is modern, with full facilities, including restaurants, a duty-free shop, gift shops, a Kidsport area, lounges, magazine and bookshops, and the booths of car-rental agencies. There are taxis, limousines, buses, and shuttle buses. The airport bus picks up on the half hour to and from various downtown hotels.

By Train

VIA Rail bypasses Calgary, linking Alberta to Vancouver through Edmonton. Rocky Mountaineer Railtours, (604) 984–3131 or (800) 665–7245, a private railway operated by the Great Canadian Railtour Company, links Vancouver to Calgary via Banff in luxury style. The two-day trip of 840 km/600 mi is during daylight hours, stopping overnight in Kamloops, British Columbia, so you don't miss a thing along the way. Operates late May to early October.

How to Get Around in Calgary

The city, logically laid out in a grid pattern, is divided into four sections (quadrants), according to points on the compass—NE, NW, SE, and SW. City streets run north and south; avenues go east and west. Numbering of streets and avenues starts from city center, which is at Centre Street and Ninth Avenue, at the base of the Calgary Tower (190.9 m/626 ft), the city's primary landmark.

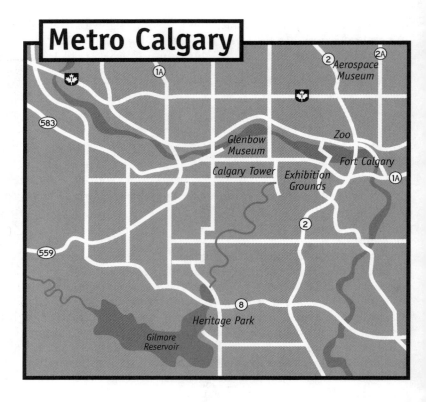

Metro Calgary

Between Fourth and Ninth Avenues in city center is where much of the city's daily hustle and bustle takes place.

The **Calgary Transit System** provides C-Train (light-rail transit) and bus service throughout the city and to outlying shopping malls; call (403) 262–1000 for routes, schedules, and special unlimited-ride passes. The C-Train is free between Tenth Street West and Third Street East; like most of the system's buses, it is accessible for wheelchairs.

City center parking is available at metered street spaces and parking garages. Your best bet is to park in a garage, to avoid fines and towing. Free parking is available during summer at many locations and at meters.

Taxis are readily available. The best locations are in front of downtown hotels.

Useful Information

Local holiday: Heritage Day, first Monday in August.
Time zone: Mountain.

Visitor Information

For current information on accommodations, dining, attractions, sports, tours, and entertainment, call the Calgary Convention and Visitors Bureau, (403) 263–8510, or visit the Visitor Service Centre, Tower Centre, main floor, 101 Ninth Avenue SW. Call (800) 661–1678 toll-free in North America; write the bureau at 200–237 Eighth Avenue SE, Calgary, Alberta T2G 0K8; or visit www.tourismcalgary.com.

Area code: 403.

Emergencies of all kinds: Dial 911.

Entertainment and sports tickets: CCVB at (800) 661–1678 or Ticketmaster at (403) 270–6700.

Religious services: Calgary has most mainline Protestant churches, Roman Catholic churches, and Jewish temples, all of which welcome visitors to their weekly services. Ask the concierge or guest relations person at your hotel for locations and times of services.

Road emergency service: (403) 246–0606 (twenty-four hours).

Road-condition reporting service: (403) 246–5853 (twenty-four hours). Alberta Motor Association.

Touring Service

Brewster/Gray Line Transportation and Tours, Calgary, (403) 221–8242 or (800) 661–1152; Banff, (403) 762–6700; Jasper, (403) 852–3332. Brewster provides tours of the city of Calgary, Banff and Jasper National Parks, Lake Louise, and the Athabasca Glacier, as well as glacier touring on a Snocoach, gondola rides up steep mountains, and boat trips on Maligne Lake and Lake Minnewanka. Reasonable rates.

Attractions

Glenbow Museum, 130 Ninth Avenue, in city center, (403) 268–4100. Open daily. Admission is charged. The Glenbow, housed in modern facilities, is one of the best Western Canadian history museums in North America. Here you can see exceptional exhibitions on the tribes of the Canadian prairies and those of the American plains (actually, for the Native people themselves, theirs was a "land of four directions," without the Europeans' borders

Just over a hundred years ago, Calgary was a small Mountie post on the prairies that was not far from the Rockies. There were few human beings in this southern area of Alberta, except for Indian bands, roaming mountainfolk and whiskey traders, and the Mounties. Today Calgary is Dallas and Houston rolled into one sharply focused city, Western Canadian style.

and topographical designations). There are exhibits telling the stories of the fur trappers, the explorers, the missionaries, the Northwest Mounted Police, Louis Riel and the Métis people, and the building of the transcontinental railroad. If you have time to visit only one attraction in Calgary, see the Glenbow Museum.

Calgary Tower, 101 Ninth Avenue SW, in city center, (403) 266–7171. Open daily. Admission is charged. The Calgary Tower is the city's landmark. At 190.9 m/626 ft high, it offers a spectacular view of the city and surrounding countryside, including the snowcapped Canadian Rockies themselves, from its top observation deck. The tower has a revolving restaurant from which you can see the views while you dine on western or continental cuisines. Call the Panorama Room for reservations, (403) 266–7171.

Calgary Science Centre, 701 Eleventh Street SW, (403) 221–3700. Open daily. Admission is charged. This is an excellent facility for exploring the wonders of the cosmos: You're a space traveler in the Star Chamber visiting destinations throughout the heavens. A Rock and Roll Laser Show entertains. There are displays featuring space-shuttle tiles and the Millarville Meteorite, as well as traveling exhibits. The center is recently renovated and has the finest multimedia theater in Canada.

Fort Calgary, 750 Ninth Avenue SE, (403) 290–1875. Open May 1 through October 9, 9:00 A.M.–5:00 P.M. The Deane House is open year-round. Here is where the original Fort Calgary (1875) stood and where the city began. Exhibits depict the early history of the city and the role the Northwest Mounted Police played in facilitating and securing civilization in this part of the country. Displays show clothing and tools used by Calgary's early pioneers. From the fort—currently being rebuilt—you can walk down to the spot where the Bow and Elbow Rivers converge, a nice area for a picnic or a rest in the sun.

Heritage Park, west of Fourteenth Street and Heritage Drive SW, (403) 259–1900. Open May 13 through September 4, 9:00 A.M.–5:00 P.M.; then weekends only until October 9. Admission

charged. One of Canada's most popular heritage parks, this full-scale prairie town is restored to what it looked like in the early 1900s. There are more than a hundred buildings, most of which have demonstrations and/or guides. There are antique railroad cars and a train trip through 27 ha/66 acres of the park, or visitors can ride aboard a vintage paddle wheeler as it plies Glenmore Lake.

Calgary Zoo, Botanical Gardens, and Prehistoric Park, on St. George's Island, 1300 Zoo Road NE, near city center, (403) 232–9372. Open throughout the year. Admission charged. This park contains life-size exhibits of dinosaurs and other prehistoric animals from the Mesozoic era, an aviary of exotic birds, and beautiful floral displays. The zoo has one of the largest populations of lowland gorillas in North America, as well as some 1,400 other animals, both from foreign lands and from the Western Canadian wilderness. Three sections of the five-part Canadian Wilds exhibit are now complete: the Aspen Woodland, the Northern Forest, and the Rocky Mountains.

Devonian Gardens, on the fourth level of Toronto Dominion Square, (403) 268–3830. Open daily. Free. Calgary has created 1 ha/2.5 acres of exquisite gardens, waterfalls, and reflecting pools—all enclosed within a modern city center office complex. Escape winter winds or broiling summer sun in climate-controlled Devonian Gardens, a special world of beauty, tranquility, and comfort. On a miniscale these enclosed gardens, which are connected by enclosed passageways that lead to all parts of city center, demonstrate that it is possible to create a pleasant year-round environment in climates far more rugged than Calgary's. Perhaps the future of northern Canada has its roots here.

Spruce Meadows Equestrian Centre, via Macleod Trail Highway 2 to Highway 22X West, (403) 254–3200. Open daily. Free. Spruce Meadows is Western Canada's premier equestrian facility, not to be missed if you love any aspect of this multifaceted sport. You can see riders practicing their jumps on magnificent Hanoverians, which are bred at this ranch, or attend a competition.

Every year a series of major equestrian competitions takes place at Spruce Meadows. For example, the Spruce Meadows National, one of North America's top jumping competitions, was held here; the Texaco Invitational attracted leading Canadian and U.S. riders; and the Spruce Meadows Masters drew the finest riders from around the world.

Calaway Park, 9.6 km/6 mi west of Calgary on the Trans-Canada, (403) 240–3824. Open from mid-May to mid-October.

Admission is charged. Calaway is Western Canada's largest theme park. Twenty exciting rides, attractions, live entertainment, food and gift shops, games, and a nice park environment provide fun and relaxation.

Aero Space Museum of Calgary, Hangar 10, 64 McTavish Place North, (403) 250–3752. Open daily except Saturday. Admission is charged. Here you can see aircraft being restored and displays of engines and aviation memorabilia.

Museum of the Regiments (Lord Strathcona's House), 4520 Crowchild Trail SW, (403) 975–2853. Open daily; donations accepted. Artifacts from cavalry and armored history of the regiment, including full-size dioramas, models, and miniatures.

Nickle Arts Museum, on the University of Calgary campus; main entrance is from Thirty-second Avenue NW, (403) 220–7234. Open throughout the year; closed Monday. Free on Tuesday. This museum has a fine collection of ancient coins and exhibitions of contemporary and historical art.

Naval Museum of Alberta, 1820 Twenty-fourth Street SW, (403) 242–0002. Royal Canadian Navy memorabilia including the only collection of three fighter craft (Seafire, Sea Fury, and Banshee jet) used by the navy. Open year-round. Admission is charged.

Tsuu T'ina Culture Museum, 3700 Anderson Road SW, (403) 238–2677. Open Monday through Friday. Free. Displays on the life and culture of the Tsuu T'ina nation include artifacts, a model tepee, and clothing.

Canada Olympic Park/Olympic Hall of Fame, Highway 1 west of the city, (403) 247–5452. Open daily. Admission is charged for tours. Exhibits relating to the fifteenth international Olympic Games held in February 1988 in the Calgary area. In summer "Road Rocket" rides are available; in winter try the Bobsleigh Bullet, if you are very brave, at $45 per person. The Bobsleigh Bullet whizzes down the Olympic track at 95 km/60 mi per hour.

Accommodations
Top Hotels and Motels
The following hotels and motels are recommended choices when staying overnight in Calgary:

Palliser Hotel, 133 Ninth Avenue SW, (403) 262–1234; (800) 441–1414. Superior accommodations, considered by many travelers to be Calgary's finest. Restored to a new grandeur. Central to businesses and attractions in city center; a Calgary landmark in itself. Some rooms with minibars, a nonsmokers' floor, exercise facilities. Rimrock Dining Room with large fireplace; Oak Room Lounge with entertainment; a deli and boulevard cafe. Expensive.

Westin Hotel, 320 Fourth Avenue SW, (403) 266–1611; (800) 937–8461. Superior accommodations. Top notch in most respects; many travelers return to the Westin repeatedly. Suites, swimming pool, and numerous services and amenities. Expensive.

Delta Calgary Airport, within the Calgary International Airport complex, 2001 Airport Road NE, (403) 291–2600; (800) 441–1414. Excellent accommodations with top-quality amenities Expensive.

Delta Bow Valley, 209 Fourth Avenue SE, (403) 266–1980; (800) 268–1133 (Canada); (800) 268–1133 (U.S.). City center location. Conservatory Dining Room, two lounges, indoor pool, whirlpool, saunas, and exercise room. Expensive.

Marriott, 110 Ninth Avenue SE, (403) 266–7331; (800) 228–9290. Excellent accommodations; twenty-four-hour room service, sundeck, nonsmoking floors, swimming pool. Centrally located; limousine service; dining at the Trader's Room and at the Wheatsheaf Café. Expensive.

International Hotel, 220 Fourth Avenue SW, (403) 265–9600. An executive-suite hotel (two rooms); swimming pool and other amenities. Moderate to expensive.

Sandman Hotel, 888 Seventh Avenue SW, (403) 237–8626; (800) 736–3626. Excellent accommodations; nightclub, swimming pool, many other amenities. Moderate.

Other Fine Places to Stay

All the places listed below offer fine accommodations and many amenities (such as swimming pools, dining rooms, and lounges), and some have nightclubs.

Best Western Hospitality Inn, 135 Southland Drive SE, (403) 278–5050; (800) 528–1234. Moderate.

Best Western Village Park Inn, 1804 Crowchild Trail NW, (403) 289–0241; (800) 528–1234. Moderate.

Blackfoot Inn, 5940 Blackfoot Trail SE, (403) 252–2253; (800) 661–1151. Moderate.

Sheraton Cavalier, 2620 Thirty-second Avenue NE, (403) 291–0107; (800) 325–3535. Moderate.

University of Calgary, 2500 University Drive NW, (403) 220–3202. Open during summer months when the resident population is on vacation. Pleasant accommodations in a campus setting. An excellent value for families, couples, or the single traveler. Inexpensive.

Other inexpensive places to stay in summer include **Mount Royal College,** (403) 249–7224, and **Southern Alberta Institute of Technology (SAIT),** (403) 284–8013. To find inexpensive accomodations year-round, call the Bed and Breakfast Association, (403) 531–0065.

Calgary International Hostel, 520 Seventh Avenue SE, (403) 269–8239.

Dining

Calgary has a wide assortment of restaurants serving all kinds of foods in every price category. Below are some of the city's worthy eateries:

Hy's, 316 Fourth Avenue SW, (403) 263–2222. Well known in Western Canada for excellent beef dishes served in an elegant setting. A fine selection of wines. Moderate to expensive.

Traders, at the Radisson Plaza, Ninth Avenue and Centre Street, (403) 266–7331. One of the better restaurants in the city; noted for its excellent cuisine, service, and atmosphere. Expensive.

La Chaumière, 139 Seventeenth Avenue SW, (403) 228–5690. French cuisine at its best served in an elegant environment. Moderate to expensive.

Teatro, 200 Eighth Avenue SE, (403) 290–1012. Italian market cuisine served in a renovated old bank building. Moderate to expensive.

Grand Isle Seafood, 200–128 Second Avenue SE, (403) 269–7783. Excellent Chinese restaurant with buffet and dim sum plus regular menu. View of the Bow River. Moderate.

River Café, Prince's Island Park, (403) 261–7670. Delightful island location, open from February through December. Fusion cuisine. Moderate.

Owl's Nest, at the Westin Hotel, 320 Fourth Avenue SW, (403) 266–1611. Beautiful interior. High-class, Old World service. Continental cuisine and dishes made with Western Canadian prime ingredients—salmon and Alberta beef. Moderate to expensive.

Panorama Room, Calgary Tower, Ninth Avenue and Centre Street SW, (403) 266–7171. Revolving restaurant on top of the tower, offering great views and Alberta beef dishes. Moderate to expensive.

Japanese Village, 302 Fourth Avenue SW, (403) 262–2738. Traditional Japanese favorites. The food is sliced, diced, and grilled at your table. Moderate.

Cannery Row Restaurant, 317 Tenth Avenue SW, (403)

A Taste of Alberta:
Chuck-Wagon Buttermilk Pancakes

Every year at the Calgary Stampede, chuck-wagon breakfasts are featured. Pancakes are flipped, eggs are fried, and platters are piled high with sausages and rashers of bacon. Try these at your own "chuck wagon."

1 c flour
1 tsp baking powder
pinch of salt
1¼ c buttermilk
1 egg
2 tbsp melted butter

Stir the flour, baking powder, and salt together in a bowl. In a separate bowl, mix the buttermilk, egg, and butter together, then pour into the flour mixture. Beat just until smooth. Lightly grease a skillet and pour one-fourth of the batter into the pan. Cook until lightly brown on the bottom and bubbly all over the top. Turn and cook the other side. Continue with remaining batter. Serve with hot butter and Canadian maple syrup.

269–8889. Fresh seafood and Creole restaurant. Live New Orleans jazz. Moderate.

Cross House Garden Cafe, 1240 Eighth Avenue SE, (403) 531–2767. Set in a historic home in the Inglewood district with a grand lawn and garden. Alberta beef, salmon, Arctic char specialties.

McQueen's Upstairs, 317 Tenth Avenue SW, (403) 269–4722. Chicago speakeasy-style atmosphere. Same building as Cannery Row Restaurant. Seafood and Alberta beef. Moderate.

Deane House Historic Site & Tea Room, 806 Ninth Avenue SE, (403) 269–7747. Elegant 1906 Edwardian home, a must-visit. Lunch or afternoon tea in glass-enclosed veranda. View of Elbow River. Inexpensive to moderate.

Entertainment

The focus of the city's cultural life is the **Calgary Centre for Performing Arts,** in city center. It is home for the Calgary Philharmonic Orchestra, Theatre Calgary, Alberta Theatre Project, and One Yellow Rabbit Theatre Company. This complex consists of the Jack Singer Concert Hall, the Max Bell Theatre, and the Martha Cohen Theatre. For information on events and tickets, call (403) 266–8888, or Ticketmaster, (403) 270–6700.

The following clubs offer entertainment, food, and drink:

King Edward Hotel, 438 Ninth Avenue SW, (403) 262–1680. Home of the blues in Calgary; live music and dancing.

Ranchman's, 9615 Macleod Trail South, (403) 253–1100; country-and-western music and dancing.

McQueen's, 317 Tenth Avenue SW, (403) 269–4722; blues, jazz, seafood, and drinks.

Stage West, 727 Forty-second Avenue SE, (403) 243–6642; dinner theater.

Garry Theatre, 1229 Ninth Avenue SE, (403) 233–9100; drama productions.

Jesters Comedy Club, 239 Tenth Avenue SE, (403) 269–6669; amateur and professional comics.

Cowboy's Dance Hall, 826 Fifth Street SW, (403) 265–0699. Dancing, live entertainment.

Dusty's Saloon, 1088 Olympic Way SE, (403) 263–5343. Dancing, country-and-western music.

Kaos Jazz & Blues Bistro, 718 Seventeenth Avenue SW, (403) 228–9997. Live jazz.

Shopping

Calgary city center, between Ninth and Fourth Avenues, is the main shopping district. The C-Train or bus will also take you to other large shopping malls where you will find large department stores and a wide assortment of shops, from those selling local arts and crafts to high-fashion boutiques.

Calgary has several other interesting shopping districts:

Kensington, the area between Tenth and Fourteenth Streets along Kensington Road and Tenth Street; small shops, casual dining, coffee bars.

Mount Royal Village, along Seventeenth Avenue SW between Fourteenth Street and Fourth Street SW; shops and restaurants.

Atlantic Avenue, along Ninth Avenue SE between Twelfth Street and Fort Calgary; antiques and coffee bars.

Eau Claire Market, along the Bow River next to Prince Island Park; a new market full of shops and restaurants.

The following are some interesting shops worth your time and credit cards:

Lammle's Western Wear, nine locations, (403) 269–6450; cowboy hats, boots, and other gear.

Cottage Craft Gifts, 6503 Elbow Drive SW, (403) 252–3797; a wide variety of high-quality gifts to bring home.

Chase Cattle Company, TD Square, third floor, (403) 269–6450; Old West and native clothing, jewelry, sculpture.

Professional Sports

Calgary Flames, of the NHL, are former Stanley Cup Champions; call Ticketmaster, (403) 777–0000, for ticket information and the home schedule. The Flames play at the Canadian Airlines Saddledome in Stampede Park.

Calgary Stampeders, of the Canadian Football League; call Ticketmaster, (403) 777–0000, for ticket and schedule information. The Stampeders play at McMahon Stadium, adjacent to the University of Calgary.

Calgary Cannons Professional Baseball Club; call (403) 284–1111 for ticket and schedule information. The Cannons are members of the Pacific Coast League and play at Foothills Stadium.

Thoroughbred and harness racing take place at Stampede Park. Call (403) 261–0214 for schedules.

Recreation

The people of Calgary have created four-season indoor environments that simulate summertime at the beach. The many leisure centers throughout the city provide warm indoor beaches, swimming, water slides, and even bodysurfing, which is possible because of machine-made waves that rival those on a real ocean beach. In addition, these centers contain indoor rinks, weight-lifting areas, racquet courts, restaurants, and many other facilities. Most of the major hotels have swimming pools and health and fitness facilities. Golf, jogging, biking, tennis, and horseback riding are also in the area. For details on recreation during your stay,

your hotel concierge or guest relations person is your best source for information and for making arrangements for your enjoyment.

Calgary has a unique pathway system joining all areas of the city. It is used by cyclists, joggers, walkers, and in-line skaters. Pathway maps detailing the 420 km/260 mi of trails are available at many locations. The visitor centers operated by the Calgary Convention and Visitors Bureau are at the airport and at the base of the Calgary Tower.

Waterton Lakes National Park

Located at the extreme southwestern corner of the province on the Alberta–Montana border, Waterton Lakes National Park and Glacier National Park (to the south into Montana) were joined to form Waterton-Glacier International Peace Park, the first of its kind in the world. Waterton itself has been described as the place "where the mountains meet the prairies." The transition between these two topographical zones is abrupt here, because there are no foothills as such (the same can be said for much of the western length of the Rockies in Alberta). Ancient glaciers, however, did carve out lakes and valleys, leaving moraines, eskers, and kames (different kinds of rock and dirt formations). Upper Waterton Lake, the park's deepest (148 m/485 ft), juts from Alberta into Montana, crossing the international border. Some unique aquatic species live here—deep-water sculpins, pygmy whitefish, and opossum shrimps. The park also has zones of short-grass prairie, aspen groves, and alpine meadows lush with wildflowers. There are many species of birds and waterfowl, elk, mule deer, bighorn sheep, black bears, and grizzly bears. The Waterton-Glacier area supports many grizzlies. If you are hiking or camping, please heed the park's warnings and precautions—people have been severely mauled and killed by these animals.

For your hiking enjoyment, the park has 183 km/113 mi of trails that lead to lakes, canyons, waterfalls, forested valleys, and alpine meadows. Scenic auto drives, such as the Promenade Akamina Parkway, wind throughout the park. Cruise boats on Upper Waterton Lake provide tours. You can also tour the park on bus or horseback. The park offers an interpretive program and camping facilities at Crandell Mountain and Belly River. There are boat rentals and fishing (get a permit at Cameron Lake). An eighteen-hole public golf course, surrounded by magnificent scenery, is near the park.

Waterton Lakes National Park can be reached via Highways 2 and 6 South from Calgary, Highway 5 West from Lethbridge, or U.S. Highway 17 from Great Falls, Montana, to Alberta Highway 5. For more information contact Superintendent, Waterton Lakes National Park, Waterton Lakes, Alberta T0K 2M0; (403) 859–2445.

Accommodations

Prince of Wales Hotel, (403) 226–5551; reservations are a must. Whenever pictures of Waterton Lakes National Park are published, the baronial structure of the Prince of Wales Hotel is in the foreground, sitting on a bluff overlooking a sparkling lake and surrounded by snowcapped mountains. The building and the setting are superior, although the hotel lacks some of the amenities typical of other equally expensive places. Moderate to expensive.

Aspen Village Inn, (403) 859–2255. Excellent accommodations with many amenities. Moderate.

Bayshore Inn, (403) 859–2211. Excellent accommodations with many amenities. Moderate to expensive.

Kilmorey Lodge, (403) 859–2334. Year-round accommodations. Moderate.

Banff–Lake Louise Area

Banff is Canada's most popular national park, not just for its natural beauty but also for its many recreational and cultural offerings throughout the four seasons. The Banff and Lake Louise region was originally developed as a prime resort and recreational area by the Canadian Pacific Railroad, which built the transcontinental railroad in the 1800s. The great resorts of Banff Springs Hotel and Chateau Lake Louise, among the world's most famous, have attracted the rich, the celebrated, and the ordinary for generations. The park itself is in the heart of the Canadian Rockies, with awesome, snowcapped mountains in every direction. The mountain scenery is accented by the ultramarine waters of lakes, the greenish tan rush of streams and rivers, and the dark blue-green shades of deep evergreen forests—habitats for grizzlies, elk, bighorn sheep, and coyotes. Because the mountains often pierce through fast-moving clouds and the temperature varies so greatly at different levels of elevation, the weather is very changeable. This is a place where you need a loaded camera close at hand at all times. Perhaps one of the most inspiring experiences of the

Special Event

The Banff Festival of the Arts, from June through August, is one of Western Canada's premier arts festivals. It brings together the finest professional talent and the best of young Canadian talent at the Banff Centre School of Fine Arts. During summer the public can partake of more than a hundred events in classical music, jazz, ballet, opera, musical theater, drama, and literary readings. These superior performances are held at Margaret Greenham Theatre, Eric Harvie Theatre, Roubakine Auditorium, Max Bell Auditorium, and Donald Cameron Hall. There are workshops in musical theater, dance, and opera. Art exhibitions are held at the Walter Phillips Gallery. The Banff Festival of the Arts makes summer here splendid, and it all happens right in town. Tickets are scarce close to performance dates and must be obtained in advance. This festival is as much a part of the Banff experience as the Rockies themselves. For schedule and ticket information, call (403) 762–6300; (800) 413–8368.

park is to go off by yourself—even if it's off the road a bit—and listen to the wind and view the mountains and clouds. Whether you're just plain folks or a big shot, you'll be humbled and elevated in spirit at the same time.

One of the most photographed scenes in the park is Mount Rundle with the Vermilion Lakes in the foreground, at the town of Banff; the best view is from the Trans-Canada. The town of Banff is the major tourism center in the park, offering accommodations, dining, shopping, and entertainment.

Northwest of the town, via the Trans-Canada (west), is **Lake Louise,** named in honor of Princess Louise Caroline Alberta, fourth daughter of Queen Victoria and wife of the Marquis of Lorne, governor-general of Canada. (The province of Alberta was named in her honor also.) Watch for the side road off the Trans-Canada that takes you through the village into higher country and then to the lake itself. What has made Lake Louise famous for generations is the ethereal atmosphere here: the clear waters, the high surrounding mountains, the Victoria Glacier and Mount Victoria at the western end of the lake, and the hotel Chateau Lake Louise. The best way to describe Lake Louise is that it is at the bottom of a deep bowl with steep, beautifully decorated, fluted sides. A trip to the Canadian Rockies would not be complete without a visit to Lake Louise; for some it is a pilgrimage of sorts.

Banff National Park's 1,600 km/980 mi of trails encourage you to get into the beautiful countryside on foot or horseback or by rock climbing or cross-country skiing. A number of interpretive programs are given by professional naturalists and guides. The park has thirteen campgrounds (2,799 campsites for those with vehicles).

Banff National Park can be reached from the west (Vancouver) and from the east (Banff is 130 km/78 mi west of Calgary) via Trans-Canada Highway 1; also via Highway 93 from southern B.C. and through the Kootenay region; and from Edmonton via Yellowhead Highway 16 West and then on Highway 93 South; also from Edmonton via Highway 2 South to 11 West to 93. For more information contact Superintendent, Banff National Park, Box 900, Banff, Alberta T0L 0C0, (403) 762–1500; or Banff/Lake Louise Tourism Bureau, Box 1298, Banff, Alberta T0L 0C0, (403) 762–8421.

The Bow Valley Parkway (a secondary highway that parallels the Trans-Canada Highway) gives access to all attractions and to Lake Louise and the town of Banff. Just north of Lake Louise, as the Trans-Canada turns west toward Vancouver, Icefield Parkway (Highway 93) continues north to Columbia Icefields, Jasper National Park, and the resort town of Jasper.

Sports and Recreation
Bicycle Rentals
Bactrax Bike Rentals, (403) 762–8177
Banff Adventures Unlimited, (403) 762–4554
Clock Tower Sports, (403) 762–8177
Inns of Banff Rental Shop, (403) 760–3525
Mountain Magic, (403) 762–2591
Wilson Mountain Sports Ltd., Lake Louise, (403) 522–3636

Boat Cruises
Minnewanka Tours, located at Lake Minnewanka, just east of downtown Banff; (403) 762–3473, fax (403) 762–2800. Cruises around this beautiful lake to Devil's Gap and various scenic points. The organization also provides fishing trips.

Downhill Skiing
Banff Mount Norquay, the area's oldest resort, has been totally redesigned and expanded to world-class standards. Long

famous for its beginner and expert terrain, it has now expanded its intermediate skiing area on Mystic Ridge by a full 28 ha/70 acres. Ten minutes from downtown Banff, its season is from early December to mid-April. Lift capacity is 6,300 people an hour; snowmaking covers 90 percent of the terrain. The runs are split between 11 percent novice, 45 percent intermediate, 28 percent advanced, and 16 percent expert. Lessons and ski equipment, night skiing on Friday, mountain tours, and day care are all available. For more information contact Banff Mount Norquay, Box 219, Suite 7000, Banff, Alberta T0L 0C0; (403) 762–4421, or Calgary snow phone, (403) 221–8259, available twenty-four hours.

Just an hour from Banff is Kananaskis, known as one of the best ski regions in North America. **Nakiska,** in the Kananaskis area, was the site of alpine events during the 1988 Winter Olympic Games. This new ski area is world class in every way. At nearby Kananaskis Village are deluxe hotels, fine restaurants and shops, and some of the best après-ski fun anywhere. The highest elevation is 2,250 m/7,381 ft; vertical rise is 918 m/3,012 ft. The longest run is 3,196 m/10,486 ft. Skiing terrain is 16 percent novice, 70 percent intermediate, and 14 percent expert. There are one double chairlift, one triple chairlift, and two detachable high-speed quad lifts; lift capacity is 8,000 people per hour. Nakiska offers a ski school, day care, downhill and cross-country equipment rentals, and many other recreational opportunities. For more information contact Nakiska, P.O. Box 1988, Kananaskis Village, Alberta, T0L 2HO, (403) 591–7777.

Sunshine Village, located 16 km/10 mi from the town of Banff and at the tree line in a high alpine bowl, is noted for an abun-

Kananaskis Village Accommodations

Hotel Kananaskis, (403) 591–7711; (800) 268–9411. Top place in this recreational area. Expensive.

Kananaskis Inn, (403) 591–7500. Suites with fireplaces. Steam room and hot tub. Expensive.

The Lodge at Kananaskis, (403) 591–7711; (800) 268–9411. Excellent accommodations. Expensive.

dance of 100 percent natural powder and the longest ski season in the region—from early November to late May. Highest elevation, 2,806 m/9,200 ft; vertical rise, 1,070 m/3,514 ft; longest run, 8 km/5 mi; skiing terrain, 20 percent novice, 50 percent intermediate, 20 percent advanced, and 10 percent expert; lift capacity is 17,000 people per hour; annual snowfall, 1,000 cm/400 in. A ski school, cross-country skiing, mountain tours, equipment rentals, day care, and restaurants and accommodations are all here. For more information contact Sunshine Village, Box 1510, Banff, Alberta T0L 0C0; (403) 762–6500 or a twenty-four-hour snow phone, (403) 762–6543.

Lake Louise (see page 221), via the Trans-Canada Highway, is famous for its beauty, and many travelers have said that it is the most beautiful part of the Canadian Rockies. The ski area has facilities on two mountains—Mount Whitehorn and Mount Lapalian. There are open slopes, bowls, mogul fields, gladed timberline, and a great deal of delightful powder. The season runs from November to mid-May. Highest elevation, 2,636 m/8,650 ft; vertical rise, 1,010 m/3,365 ft; longest run, 8 km/5 mi; skiing terrain, 25 percent novice, 45 percent intermediate, and 30 percent expert; lift capacity, 16,400 people per hour; annual snowfall, 360 cm/140 in. You'll find a ski school for various levels of expertise and specialties, equipment rentals, mountain tours, cross-country skiing, ice skating, day care, torchlight dinners, and sleigh rides. For more information, contact Skiing Louise, Box 5, Lake Louise, Alberta T0L 1E0; (403) 522–3555 or snow phone (403) 244–6665.

Fishing

Banff Fishing Unlimited, (403) 762–4936, fax (403) 678–8895. Provides licensed guides, tackle, foul-weather gear, lunch. Staff members clean and pack your catch. Also offers ice fishing in winter.

Monod Sports, (403) 762–4571.
Mountain Fly Fishers, (403) 678–9522.
Alpine Anglers, (403) 762–8222
Hangwild Fly Fishing Guides, (403) 760–2446
Rocky Mountain Fly Fishing Ltd., (403) 678–7870
Upper Bow Fly Fishing, (403) 760–7668

Golf

Banff Springs Hotel Golf Course, twenty-seven hole par 71. This course is smack in the middle of some of the most inspiring scenery in the world. It's not unusual to see elk race across the fairways. The facility has a driving range, practice green, equipment and cart rentals, restaurant, lounges, a pro shop, and a clubhouse. Book your game well in advance by calling (403) 762–6801; lessons at (403) 762–6833.

The Golf Course at Silver Tip is located in Canmore, twenty minutes east of Banff townsite. The world-class course, designed by golf architect Les Furber, is a par-72 championship course with some breathtaking scenery.

Gondola Sight-Seeing

Sulphur Mountain Gondola Lift; (403) 762–2523, fax (403) 762–7493. Admission is charged. Takes you to the summit (2,285 m/7,500 ft high) where on a clear day you can virtually see forever. The ride up is exciting and fun, and there's a restaurant in the observation complex. You can hike up and down for free.

Lake Louise Sightseeing Lift and Gondola, (403) 522–3555. In operation from June through September. Admission is charged.

Helicopter Hiking/Skiing

Helicopter hiking/skiing has become a popular sport in the Canadian Rockies. A helicopter takes you to the top of a mountain and drops you off with a top-notch guide and supplies; you then hike or ski down through a pristine wilderness that seems to belong to you alone. The following companies provide helicopter skiing in the Canadian Rockies, both in the mountains of Alberta and those nearby in British Columbia (also consult your travel agent; several package-tour operators do provide helicopter skiing/hiking vacations in the Canadian Rockies):

Canadian Mountain Holidays, (403) 762–7100
R.K. Heli-Skiing, (403) 762–3771
Assiniboine Heli Tours, (403) 678–5459
Alpine Helicopters, (403) 678–4802

Hostelling

Southern Alberta Hostelling Association, headquarters in Calgary, (403) 283–5551, has facilities at Calgary, Ribbon Creek, Spray River, Banff International, Castle Mountain, Mosquito Creek, Ramparts Creek, and Hilda Creek.

Hot-Spring Bathing

Upper Hot Springs Pool, Mountain Avenue, near the Banff Springs Hotel, (403) 762–1515. Open throughout the year.

Bathing-suit and towel rentals. Upper Hot Springs Pool has attracted bathers from all over the world to its therapeutic waters of natural hot springs. In this pool the ordinary have bathed along with the rich and famous, seeking relaxation and/or cures to their aches and pains. The Banff experience would not be complete without a good hot soaking here.

Mountaineering

Yamnuska, Inc., 200, 50–103 Bow Valley Trail, Canmore, (403) 678–4164. Canada's leading mountain school and guide service offers the usual training plus wilderness treks and hikes to some of the most spectacular points in the national parks. Ideal for those who want the adventure but not the climb.

Trail Rides

Holiday on Horseback, Box 2280, Banff, Alberta T0L 0C0; (403) 762–4551, (800) 661–8352, fax (403) 762–8130. From weekend-long to six-day trips into remote areas of the Canadian Rockies.

Timberline Tours, Box 14, Lake Louise, Alberta T0L 1E0; (403) 522–3743. Outdoor packages.

Lake Louise Stables, Box 964, Banff; (403) 762–5454

Wild-River Rafting

Rocky Mountain Raft Tours, Box 1771, Banff, Alberta; (403) 762–3632. One- and three-hour tours on the scenic Bow River. June 1 to mid-September.

Attractions

Banff Park Museum National Historic Site, 93 Banff Avenue, (403) 762–1558. Open daily. Built in 1903, this is the oldest history museum in Canada and features displays on the diverse natural history of the area. It also has prints of Robert Bateman, a Canadian artist who has become world famous for his wildlife studies.

Buffalo Nations Luxton Museum, One Birch Avenue, (403) 762–2388. Open daily. Closed Monday and Tuesday in winter. Admission is charged. An excellent collection of Plains Indian artifacts.

Cave and Basin National Historic Site, Cave Avenue, (403) 762–1557. Open daily. Admission is charged. The center has historical and geological exhibits, including a replica bathhouse

(1887) and the Discovery Trail, a natural history walk. Interpretive center and restaurant that is open only in summer.

Whyte Museum of the Canadian Rockies, 111 Bear Street, (403) 762–2291. Open daily. Call for hours and fees. Has exhibition galleries that show the works of Canadian artists and those from other countries. The **Archives of the Canadian Rockies** is also here.

Walter J. Phillips Gallery, Banff Centre Complex, St. Julien Road, (403) 762–6281. Open daily. Free. Named in honor of W. J. Phillips, a prominent Canadian landscape artist, this gallery shows works by leading artists as well as students and faculty of the Centre of Fine Arts.

Canada Place, Banff National Park, (403) 762–1500. A visitor center where folks of all ages can discover interactive displays that explore Canada's natural heritage, as well as the history of the events and people who helped shape them. Admission is free; open year-round.

The Town of Banff

Banff, Alberta, has only one reason for being—tourism. When the transcontinental railroad was being built, Banff (named for a county in Scotland), because of its surrounding beauty and natural hot mineral springs, was selected as a spa for the wealthy to relax and regain their zest for pursuing their various social, political, and commercial interests. The huge, sprawling Banff Springs Hotel was built just to serve such clients. When the late Duke of Windsor was a young Prince of Wales, he vacationed at Banff Springs Hotel, and his presence served as a magnet that drew more of the "carriage set" to the Canadian Rockies. As time went on many others came here to vacation, and a thriving, lovely community grew on the valley flats. For much of the town's history, the only way to get here from distant points was by the Canadian Pacific Railroad. Today the Rocky Mountaineer Railtour carries on the tradition of visiting Banff and Lake Louise by train. In the post–World War II period, the Trans-Canada Highway was built, and today Banff and Lake Louise are easily accessible to all.

The main street of Banff, running north–south, is Banff Avenue, where you will find many shops, restaurants, and services. Going northeast on Banff Avenue will take you to Tunnel Mountain Campground. The Trans-Canada, the train station, and Mount Norquay are all directly north of downtown; west of downtown are the Vermilion Lakes. Banff Avenue will also take you across the Bow River, past the national park administrative building and its lovely floral displays to Spray Avenue, which leads to the Banff Springs Hotel. Even if you are not staying in the hotel, you should go in and see the beautifully decorated public rooms and the fantastic view from the terrace overlooking the golf course (elk come out on the fairways at dusk to feed), Bow Valley, and the surrounding mountains. Once you see this view, you'll instantly know why Banff became such a popular vacation paradise and has continued as such for so long. The dining and lounge facilities of the hotel are open for use by nonresidential guests.

Tourist Information

Banff/Lake Louise Tourism Bureau Information Centre, 224 Banff Avenue, Banff, Alberta T0L 0C0; (403) 762–8421, fax (403) 762–8163.

Touring Services

Brewster Independent Travel, (403) 762–6700 or (800) 661–1152.

Mountain Park Tours, (403) 762–5652.

The Trail Rider, 132 Banff Avenue, (403) 762–4551; provides horse-drawn carriage rides to Banff Springs Hotel and other attractions and horseback trail rides of two to six days.

Discover Banff Tours, (403) 760–1299 or (877) 565–9372.

Accommodations

Banff has many places to stay; the ones listed here are the best in town. If you require lower-priced accommodations, contact the Banff/Lake Louise Tourism Bureau, (403) 762–8421. Since Banff is one of Canada's most popular resort towns during the peak season of summer, reservations for accommodations are essential. For camping information call the Parks Information Centre, (403) 762–1550.

Banff Springs Hotel, Spray Avenue, (403) 762–2211; in Canada, (800) 441–1414. One of Canada's best-known hotels, this huge baronial castle surrounded by the splendor of the Rockies has undergone extensive renovations that have greatly helped in sprucing up the rooms (those with views of Bow Valley are superior). The hotel has three dining rooms serving excellent cuisine, and the main dining room is one of the most elegant in Western Canada. There are lounges, a world-class spa, a great twenty-seven-hole golf course, several tennis courts, hot springs, shops, live entertainment, and many other services and amenities. Expensive.

Rimrock Resort Hotel, at Mountain Avenue, (403) 762–3356; (800) 661–1587. A four-diamond hotel with grand views of Bow Valley and surrounding mountains. Classico Ristorante, Primrose

Dining Room, and the Larkspur Lounge. Indoor pool, sauna, hot tub, exercise room, and new spa facilities. Expensive.

Banff Park Lodge, Lynx Street, (403) 762–4433; (800) 661–9266. Excellent accommodations, Terrace and Chinook Dining Rooms, Glacier Lounge with nightly entertainment, indoor pool. Close to ski areas, cross-country trails, boating, fishing, and other sports. Expensive.

Banff Rocky Mountain Resort, 1029 Banff Avenue (403) 762–5531; (800) 661–9563. Chalet units with fireplaces and various kitchen conveniences. Restaurant, lounge, squash and tennis courts, indoor pool. Expensive.

Inns of Banff, 600 Banff Avenue, (403) 762–4581; (800) 661–1272. Deluxe rooms, Reflections Dining Room, Belvedere Lounge with entertainment, indoor pool, squash court. Expensive.

Lake Louise Accommodations

Chateau Lake Louise, on the shore of Lake Louise, (403) 522–3511; (800) 441–1414. Lake Louise is not all that large a body of water. What makes it mystical and beautiful are the high, steep, snowcapped mountains surrounding it; the high Victoria Glacier at the opposite end of the lake from the hotel; the dark green forests all around; and the sky often made moody by fast-moving clouds. All these facets reflect off the lake and give it a pantheism that other lakes lack. It's a memorable experience to be here just for a few moments, and so much better if you can stay for a few days. This hotel's Victoria Dining Room offers excellent cuisine and service. You'll find an indoor pool, steam room, exercise room, and tanning room, as well as canoeing on the lake, ice-skating, hiking, horseback riding, and other activities, one of the best of which is simply walking lakeside, and meditating on the glories of nature before you. Expensive.

Lake Louise Inn, in Lake Louise Village, (403) 522–3791; (800) 661–9237. Excellent accommodations and facilities in a superb natural area; restaurant, swimming pool, health club, and lounge. The best all-around choice in Lake Louise, except that it does not front the lake itself as Chateau Lake Louise does. Moderate to expensive.

Deer Lodge, near the lake, (403) 522–3991; (800) 661–1595. A pleasant inn that has a fine restaurant. Moderate.

Dining

For a small resort town, Banff has a broad choice of fine restaurants. The high quality of restaurant offerings makes sense when you consider the large number of sophisticated travelers who come here every year and are not afraid to take local chefs to task for any slip below standards. For the average traveler this extra attention to detail is a bonus, for in Banff you know you can dine very well. The following is but a sampling of fine Banff eateries.

Banff Springs Hotel, Spray Avenue, (403) 762–2211. The Bow Valley Grill for contemporary cuisine. The fine-dining restaurant, the Rob Roy Room, is currently being renovated.

Guido's Ristorante, 116 Banff Avenue, (403) 762–4002. Tender veal dishes, linguine, smoked fillet of trout. Inexpensive to moderate.

Balkan Restaurant, 120 Banff Avenue, (403) 762–3454. Greek fare—shrimp and herbs baked with feta, broiled marinated lamb chops, moussaka, and baklava for dessert. Moderate.

Le Beaujolais, corner of Buffalo Street and Banff Avenue, (403) 762–2712. Excellent French restaurant, perhaps the best in the Canadian Rockies. Chateaubriand, lobster soup, filet mignon, and other haute cuisine dishes. Very nice decor and a good wine list. Expensive.

The Pines Restaurant, Rundlestone Lodge, (403) 760-6690, uses only products and ingredients of Canada. The innovative menu is a dining delight. Moderate.

Joe BTFSPLK's Diner, 221 Banff Avenue, (403) 762–5529. This is 1950s Canada, complete with jukebox, red vinyl booths, and great, affordable food. Save room for made-from-scratch apple pie.

Entertainment

The larger hotels and motels in both Banff and Lake Louise have lounges with live entertainment, and a number of independent lounges in town offer bands, singers, dancers, and comedians.

Banff Springs Hotel has both sedate ballroom dancing and a frenetic disco.

The Rose and Crown, at 202 Banff Avenue, is a British-style pub that offers live entertainment and darts.

Wild Bill's Legendary Saloon, 210 Banff Avenue, second floor, (403) 762–0333. Liveliest spot in town. Call for group bookings.

Aurora Nightclub, Clock Tower Village Mall, (403) 769–5300.

Shopping

What would a resort town be without lots of shops to keep tourists busy and happy? Banff has its share.

Art of Man Gallery, Chateau Lake Louise; Inuit sculptures.

Mountain Magic Sportswear, 224 Bear Street; outdoor sports equipment.

Monod Sports, 111 Banff Avenue (also at Chateau Lake Louise); climbing and camping gear, clothing for the outdoors, swimsuits.

Jasper National Park

Jasper National Park is one of North America's largest natural areas preserved for present and future generations. Within the boundaries of this magnificent park are high mountains, many lakes—including Maligne Lake—forests, alpine meadows, Columbia Icefield, Athabasca Glacier, and Sunwapta Falls. This is the terrain of grizzly bears, elk, bighorn sheep, and elusive mountain goats. Native peoples, trappers, botanists, geologists, prospectors, and mountain people have been through here. Explorers such as David Thompson, Captain John Palliser, Sir Sanford Fleming, and Philadelphian Mary Schaffer trekked through this inspiring country; their records of and enthusiasm for Jasper (named for the fur trader Jasper Hawes) have attracted countless numbers of people since.

The park has 1,000 km/600 mi of trails for hiking; campgrounds (Whistler's, Wapiti, Pocahontas, Snaring River, Wabasso, Mount Kerkeslin, Honeymoon Lake, Jonas Creek, Columbia Icefield, and Wilcox Creek); and places for fishing, boating, trail riding, scuba diving, downhill and cross-country skiing, and body soaking at Miette Hot Springs. The resort town of Jasper offers fine accommodations, dining, entertainment, and shopping.

Jasper National Park can be reached from the south (Banff) via Highway 93 and from Edmonton or Vancouver via Yellowhead Highway 16. For more information contact Superintendent, Jasper National Park, Box 10, Jasper, Alberta T0E 1E0, (403) 852–6176; or Jasper Tourism and Commerce, Box 98, Jasper, Alberta T0E 1E0, (403) 852–3858.

Sports and Recreation
Bike Rentals

Bicycle rentals and touring information:

Beyond Bikes, 4 Cedar Street, (780) 852–5922.

Freewheel Cycle, 611 Patricia Street, (780) 852–3898.

On-Line Sport & Tackle, 600 Patricia Street, (780) 852–3630.

Beauvert Boat & Cycle, at Jasper Park Lodge, (780) 852–5708.

Maligne Lake Boat Tours

Maligne Lake, intensely explored by Mary Schaffer, an affluent Quaker from Philadelphia, is, in terms of its beauty and mystical qualities, close to the natural splendor of Lake Louise. Maligne Tours takes you out in its boats for two hours, and you can experience a bit of what Mary Schaffer did. These boat tours operate from June through September. Call (403) 852–3370 for information.

Boat Rentals

Canoes, sailboarding equipment, and fishing boats are all available for rent:

Beauvert Boat & Cycle, at Jasper Park Lodge, (780) 852–5708.

Pyramid Lake Boat Rentals, at Pyramid Lake, (780) 852–3536.

Downhill Skiing

Marmot Basin, located 365 km/225 mi west of Edmonton on Yellowhead Highway 16 and 19 km/12 mi southwest of the town of Jasper on Highway 93A, has a season that lasts from early December to early May. Highest elevation, 2,423 m/7,950 ft; vertical rise, 701 m/2,300 ft; longest run, 5.5 km/3.5 mi; skiing terrain, 30 percent expert, 35 percent intermediate, and 35 percent novice; lift capacity, 8,684 people per hour. Marmot Basin offers ski instruction, equipment rentals, and dining facilities. For more information, contact Marmot Basin, Box 1300, Jasper, Alberta T0E 1E0; (780) 852–3816.

Fishing

Curries's Guiding, 622 Connaught Drive in Jasper, (780) 852–5650.

On-Line Sport & Tackle, 600 Patricia Street, (780) 852–3630.

Golf

Jasper Park Lodge, call (780) 852–6090 for tee-off reservations. A superior eighteen-hole golf course in the middle of fantastic scenery. Watch out for such hazards as deer and coyotes darting across the fairways.

Gondola Sight-Seeing

Jasper Tramway, (780) 852–3093. The tramway is in operation from mid-April to Canadian Thanksgiving. It takes you to the top of Whistler's Mountain. During both the ride up and the ride down, the views are spectacular.

Hot-Spring Bathing

Miette Hot Springs, 61 km/37.8 mi east of Jasper on Highway 16, then right at Pocahontas Junction. Open during summer. This large outdoor pool has some of the hottest water coming up from the bowels of the Canadian Rockies.

Other Winter Sports

In addition to downhill skiing, Jasper National Park offers Nordic skiing, canyon crawling, helicopter skiing, ice climbing, ice fishing, ice skating, sleigh rides, and snowshoeing.

Scuba Diving

Spring-fed lakes near Jasper town offer excellent visibility (down to 20 m/65 ft) for viewing rock gardens, aquatic vegetation, and the wreck of a World War II–era barge. No gear rentals are available in the park; you must bring your own or rent from Calgary or Edmonton.

Trail Riding

Skyline Trail Rides, Jasper Park Lodge; (780) 852–4215.

Wild-River Rafting

Rocky Mountain River Guides, 600 Patricia Street, (780) 852–3777.

Maligne River Adventure, 626 Connaught Drive, (780) 852–3370.

Whitewater Rafting, 702 Connaught Drive, (780) 852–7238. Trips down the mighty Athabasca River.

Jasper Raft Tours, 314 Connaught Drive, (780) 852–3613. River-rafting packages.

The Town of Jasper

Jasper is the second most important resort town in the Canadian Rockies. It's the human oasis within Jasper National Park. Because Jasper is neither as large nor as bustling as Banff, its pace and intimacy make it an excellent choice for travelers staying for a time in the Canadian Rockies. The Jasper Park Lodge, a superior resort, is as well known as its sister hotels in the south, Banff Springs and Chateau Lake Louise. VIA Rail provides service to Jasper from points east and west in Canada. Greyhound has daily trips to and from the city of Edmonton. Jasper is easy to reach by car via Yellowhead Highway 16 (East or West) or Highway 93 from the south. Connaught Drive, which parallels the tracks of the railroad and the Yellowhead Highway, is Jasper's main street; Patricia Street also has a number of services for tourists. Most places to stay (except Jasper Park Lodge), restaurants, and shops are within a few steps of one another. There are many lakes, such as Patricia and Pyramid, and the Athabasca River is the major waterway. For more information, including accommodation options, contact Jasper Tourism and Commerce at Box 98, 632 Connaught Drive, Jasper, Alberta T0E 1E0, (403) 852–3858.

Accommodations

Reservations are essential during peak summer and winter months. The following places are the best that Jasper has to offer. There are also budget places and campgrounds.

Jasper Park Lodge, via Lodge Road, (780) 852–3301; (800) 441–1414. The popular image of Jasper Park Lodge that comes to mind is that of waiters riding bikes around the resort while carrying trays of cocktails. The facilities here are superior, possibly among the best in the Canadian Rockies. The list of offerings includes an eighteen-hole golf course, a swimming pool, tennis, horseback riding, fishing and touring trips, a health club, sailboats, bikes, and excellent restaurants. Book well in advance. Expensive.

Alpine Village, junction of Highways 93 and 93A, (780) 852–3285. Moderate.

Chateau Jasper, corner of Juniper and Geikie Streets, (780) 852–5644; (800) 661–9323. Fine accommodations and dining room. Moderate to expensive.

Jasper Inn, at Bonhomme and Geikie Streets, (780) 852–4461; (800) 661–1933. Moderate to expensive.

Lobstick Lodge, at Juniper and Geikie Streets, (780) 852–4431; (800) 661–9317. Moderate.

Marmot Lodge, on Connaught Drive, (780) 852–4471. Moderate.

Sawridge Hotel Jasper, on Connaught Drive, (780) 852–5111; (800) 661–6427. Moderate to expensive.

Dining

Jasper Park Lodge; for reservations, call (780) 852–3301.

Sightseeing Diversions

The Icefields Parkway, which stretches 229 km/142 mi from Banff National Park to Jasper and straddles the massive icefields of the Continental Divide, is an extraordinary sight-seeing experience. Allow at least half a day to drive this route and take time to see its many points of interest.

Hector Lake, 16 km/10 mi north of Lake Louise, is forest enclosed at its southern end, while the northern part is set hard against rugged mountains.

Bow Lake, 93 km/58 mi north of Banff, is the source of the Bow River. A large icefield covers an extensive area of the Great Divide, and the Bow Glacier extends from this field over the cliff.

Peyto Lake, 40 km/25mi north of Lake Louise, is the highest point on the Icefields Parkway—2,088 m/6,852 ft above sea level. A short trail takes you to the Peyto Lake lookout.

Weeping Wall Viewpoint, 125 km/78mi south of Jasper. Water from melting snow high on Cirrus Mountain finds its way through cracks in the seemingly impenetrable cliff of the Weeping Wall, cascading downward as a series of graceful waterfalls.

Columbia Icefields, 105 km/65 mi south of Jasper. This area of glacial ice covers 389 sq km/150 sq mi. From the highway you can see the Athabasca, Stutfield, and Dome Glaciers. For an up-close and personal view, try the Snocoach tours on the Athabasca Glacier. Tours operate daily from May 1 through October 15; for information call (403) 762–6735 or visit www.brewster.ca/columbiaice.

Tangle Falls, 96 km/60 mi south of Jasper, is a beautiful waterfall that tumbles down the Tangle Ridge. Bighorn sheep are frequently seen in this area.

Stutfield Glacier, 95 km/59 mi south of Jasper, features a pair of icefalls that spill down the face of Mount Stutfield.

Sunwapta Falls, 55 km/34 mi south of Jasper, is where the Sunwapta River abruptly changes course from northwest to southwest and plunges into a deep canyon. Take the access road 1 km/0.6 mi from the Icefields Parkway to Sunwapta Falls and Canyon.

The Icefields Parkway is best traveled during the summer months. It has its own spectacular, snow-covered grandeur in winter, but motorists should be well prepared with chains and emergency supplies because the traffic is very sparse.

Beauvert Dining Room, overlooking Lac Beauvert, serves continental cuisine; expensive. Edith Cavell offers four-star dining; expensive. Meadows Café has light and casual fare; moderate. Tonquin Dining Room has gourmet food; expensive. Moose's Nook for dining and dancing; moderate to expensive.

Beauvallon Dining Room at the Chateau Jasper, (780) 852–5644. Superb French cuisine, great steaks, freshly made desserts. Moderate to expensive.

Amethyst Dining Room at the Andrew Motor Lodge, 200 Connaught Drive, (403) 852–3394. Fresh pasta dishes, Alberta steaks, veal piccata Milanaise, apple strudel. Moderate to expensive.

Tonquin Prime Rib Village, Juniper Street, (780) 852–4966. Excellent place for prime rib of beef, fresh salmon, Arctic char, and West Coast oysters. Moderate.

Becker's Gourmet Restaurant, Jasper/Banff Highway, (780) 852–3535. Beautiful views of the Athabasca River from the dining room. Menu features fine continental cuisine. Moderate to expensive.

Entertainment

The lounges at many of the better places of accommodation feature live entertainment and/or dancing. Check with the desk person at the place you are staying to find out what's happening at night when you're there.

Shopping

Malowney's British Woolens, 606 Patricia Street. Imported woolens and cashmeres.

Sherriff's of Jasper, 610 Connaught Drive. English china, Italian silver, Ammolite jewelry.

Edmonton: Canada's Festival City

To lovers of malls and theme parks, the West Edmonton Mall and Galaxyland make Edmonton special. To business wheeler-dealers working the rich oil and natural gas fields near the city, Edmonton is prime playing field. To those who want to experience the magnificence of the great national parks of the Canadian Rockies, with their resorts and many recreational opportunities, Edmonton's proximity to Jasper and Banff makes it special. And to those who want to kick up their heels at a rip-roaring festival, there are dozens to choose from in Edmonton.

Before the European explorers and fur traders, First Nations cultures had inhabited this region of Alberta for more than 5,000 years. Their descendants still live here, both in the city and in rural reserves. In 1795 the North West Company built Fort Augustus near what is now the town of Fort Saskatchewan. That same year William Tomison set up a competing fur-trading post for Hudson's Bay Company, an enterprise he called Fort Edmonton, in honor of the birthplace in England of Sir James Winter Lake, deputy governor of Hudson's Bay Company. By 1821 Fort Edmonton had become the dominant post. In 1830 it was moved to where the Legislature Building now stands; the fort was demolished in 1915.

In 1897 Edmonton became the gateway for the gold rush to the Yukon. There was no clear route as such, and some who had gold fever perished en route; others turned back and went home with empty pockets; and still others stayed in Edmonton and helped expand the city's population. Edmonton, with 9,000 residents, was incorporated as a city in 1904, and when Alberta itself became a province in 1905 Edmonton was designated its capital. Alexander Cameron Rutherford was Alberta's first premier.

When, in 1942, construction began on the Alaska Highway—thereby making the country north of Edmonton accessible by car—the city clearly became the gateway to the North. Perhaps the most important date in its history was February 13, 1947, when the Leduc #1 well spouted black gold. This discovery made Edmonton the Oil Capital of Canada. Thousands of oil and gas wells were found within a 160-km/96-mi radius of the city, and today Edmonton is a supply center to the vast oil-sand plants to the north.

Today Edmonton is, in land area, one of Canada's largest metropolitan centers. Its present metropolitan population exceeds 919,000. Close to half the people here are of British background, and other large ethnic groups are German, Ukrainian, French, Scandinavian, Polish, Chinese, and Hungarian.

The thriving economy of the city is based on manufacturing, tourism, food processing, petroleum refining, agriculture, government and professional services, transportation/distribution, retailing, medicine, and education. Edmonton is a city of grace, vitality, culture, and vision.

Special Events

Edmonton's appellation of Festival City is well deserved. Following is a list of some of the major events that take place. For additional information visit Edmonton's Web site, www.tourism.ede.org.

Edmonton Comedy Arts Festival, late January

The Resound Festival of Contemporary Music and Canadian Birkebeiner Skin Festival, February

Local Heroes International Film Festival, March

Northern Alberta International Children's Festival, late May

Edmonton International Street Performers Festival, mid-July

Jazz City International Music Festival, late June

River City Shakespeare Festival, June through July

Jazz City International Festival, late June through early July

Klondike Days, mid- to late July. Celebrating the heritage of Edmonton and its role as the gateway to the gold fields of the Yukon. There are parades, pancake breakfasts, gambling casinos, gold panning, a Taste of Edmonton, the World Championship Sourdough Raft Race, and the Sunday Promenade.

Heritage Festival, early August. Ethnic food, dance, culture, and fun.

Folk Music Festival, early to mid-August. The city comes alive with music—folk, country, bluegrass, string band—and dancing.

Fringe Theatre Event, mid- to late August. Old, new, and experimental plays in the city's Old Strathcona district; more than 650 performances; Canada's largest alternative-theater festival.

Edmonton Caribbean Arts Festival and Dragon Boat Festival, late August

Symphony Under the Sky Festival, Labour Day weekend

Canadian Finals Rodeo, November

First Night Festival, New Year's Eve

How to Get to Edmonton
By Car
Edmonton is 294 km/184 mi north of Calgary via Calgary Trail Highway 2, and 362 km/226 mi east of Jasper via Yellowhead Highway 16. If you are coming from the east, take the Trans-Canada Yellowhead west from Saskatoon, Saskatchewan.

By Bus
The Edmonton bus station is located at 103rd Avenue and 103rd Street. Service to Jasper and Calgary is provided by Greyhound, (780) 413–8747. Red Arrow provides service to Calgary and Fort McMurray, (780) 424–3399.

By Plane
Edmonton International Airport is located 29 km/18 mi south of city center. This facility has restaurants, lounges, newsstands, and a duty-free shop; nearby are accommodations. Sky Shuttle provides shuttle-bus service to and from city center. There are also taxis and limousines. Several major rental-car firms have booths at the airport and offices in city center. The following airlines are among those that serve Edmonton: AirBC, Air Canada, Air Transat, Canada 3000, Canadian, Canadian Regional, Horizon Airlines, LOT Polish Airlines, Martinair, Northwest Airlines, NWT/First Air, Royal Airlines, and Westjet.

By Train
VIA Rail provides service to Jasper and Vancouver in the west and to Saskatoon, Winnipeg, and major eastern cities. The VIA Rail station is located at 12360 121st Street, (780) 422–6032. VIA Rail's toll-free number in Alberta is (800) 561–8630.

How to Get Around in Edmonton
Edmonton is spread out in an easy-to-comprehend grid pattern. The city center is where 101st Street bisects Jasper Avenue. The Telus Tower, at One Hundreth Street and One Hundreth Avenue, is a landmark you can use in finding your way around. Another landmark is Edmonton Centre—with its three black towers—at 101st Street and 102nd Avenue. The city's LRT (light-rail transit) and bus systems will take you to most places you want to see, including the West Edmonton Mall.

Useful Information
Local holiday: Heritage Day, first Monday in August
Time zone: Mountain

Metro Edmonton

Yellowhead Trail

(2)

(16)

Space Science
Center

Saskatchewan River

West Edmonton
Mall

(14)

Area code: 780

Emergencies of all kinds: Dial 911

Tourist information: Edmonton Tourism, 9797 Jasper Avenue,
(780) 496–8400; (800) 463–4667

Touring services: Out and About Tours (780) 909–TOUR or
www.outandabouttours.com; Brewster Bus Lines, (780)
762–6700 or www.brewster.ca; Magic Times Tour & Convention Services, (780) 940–7479.

Attractions

The West Edmonton Mall, 170th Street and Eighty-seventh Avenue, (780) 444–5200; (800) 661–8890. Open every day. Admission is charged for nonshopping attractions. Shuttle-bus service is
provided to and from the mall from some Edmonton hotels. The
mall has become one of Western Canada's prime attractions. A
visit here is like nothing else you've experienced and should not be
missed.

There is no doubt about this fantastic place—it is the world's largest and most pleasurable shopping mall, with more than 800 stores and services, as well as numerous other attractions. Actually, it is a major theme park that has been merged with a mall. Within this sprawling complex are the world's largest indoor amusement park, with more than twenty rides, including a triple-loop roller coaster and a thirteen-story free-fall ride; World Waterpark, a 2-ha/ 5-acre indoor lake with twenty-two water slides, surfing on 2-m/ 6-ft waves and a wild-river ride; Deep Sea Adventure, an indoor lake 122 m/400 ft long and 10 m/30 ft deep that offers rides and four submarines, a marine theater with trained dolphins, and a replica of the 24-m/80-ft *Santa Maria* galleon; Professor Wem's Adventure Golf, Europa Golf, an eighteen-hole minigolf course; Ice Palace Skating, an NHL-size skating rink with equipment rentals; Sea Life Caverns with saltwater aquariums, shark tanks, alligators, and penguins. There are thirteen Italian marble fountains throughout the mall. The Europa Boulevard features boutiques with Parisian storefronts. Bourbon Street has nightclubs, jazz, and restaurants. Motorized carts are available for those who want to ride to shops and attractions. The mall cost more than $1 billion to build and employs more than 15,000 people.

The mall incorporates the Fantasyland Hotel, which has 355 rooms, 127 themed to depict different cultures and periods in history, such as the Polynesian Room (with a waterfall), the Roman Room (with marble sculptures and an authentic Roman bath), the Truck Room, the Coach Room, the Hollywood Room, igloo- and African-themed rooms, and the Arabian Room. Excellent restaurants and lounges are in the hotel; kosher food is served on request. This is also a convention hotel, one that would delight delegates. Call (780) 444–3000 or (800) 661–6454. With accommodations like these, the price is expensive.

Alberta Legislature Building, 107th Street and Ninety-seventh Avenue, (780) 427–7362. Open daily. Free. Tours commence in the Interpretive Centre and Gift Shop. This provincial capitol is noted for being constructed out of terra-cotta blocks. The terracotta and steel-reinforced dome has never shown a crack. Beautiful gardens, as well as a reflecting pool and water displays, surround the building. Carillon bells sing every day at noon. The cornerstone was laid in 1909 by Earl Grey, governor-general of Canada, and the building was officially opened in 1912 by another governor-general, the Duke of Connaught.

Alberta Railway Museum, 24215 Thirty-fourth Street, (780) 472–6229. Open daily May through September. Admission is charged. Displays of early railroading equipment used in the development of Western Canada—steam and diesel engines, rolling stock, vintage 1877 to 1950.

Edmonton Art Gallery, 2 Sir Winston Churchill Square, (780) 422–6223. Open throughout the year. Admission is charged. Exhibitions of classical and contemporary art.

Edmonton Police Museum, 9620 103A Avenue, (780) 421–2274. Open Monday through Saturday. Free. Displays portraying the history of law enforcement in Alberta.

Fort Edmonton Park, via Whitemud and Fox Drive, (780) 496–8787. Open mid-May through September. Admission is charged. On the banks of the North Saskatchewan River and south of city center, Fort Edmonton is a re-creation of a noteworthy early Hudson's Bay trading post (circa 1846). Within this park are several of Edmonton's historic homes and replicas of early street scenes; the Reverend George McDougall Shrine, honoring a pioneering missionary; and rides on an old-time streetcar and a steam train. Visit Kelly's Saloon for soda and ice cream, the Jasper House for good meals, and the Masonic Hall, where you can relax and sip sarsaparilla. This large historic park is divided into two main sections: (a) the Fort Complex and (b) the settlement, consisting of streets that capture their eras—1885 Street, 1905 Street, and 1920 Street. Fort Edmonton Park is an interesting, enjoyable attraction for all ages.

John Janzen Nature Centre, located next to Fort Edmonton Park, (780) 496–2939. Open throughout the year. Free. Exhibits of Edmonton flora and fauna, including bees, ants, snakes, and salamanders. Nature walks.

Edmonton Space and Science Centre, 111th Avenue and 142nd Street, (780) 493–9000 or 452–9100. Open throughout the year. Admission is charged. This is Canada's largest planetarium, featuring the Star Theatre; the IMAX theater, which uses special effects; and science exhibits.

John Walter Museum, 10627 Ninety-third Avenue; open Sunday; (403) 496–7275. Four historic homes (circa 1875 through 1915) owned by John Walter, one of the city's first settlers. Displays portray the early development of the province.

Muttart Conservatory, Ninety-sixth Avenue and 96A Street, (780) 496–8755. Open daily. Admission is charged. Four pyramid-shaped glass buildings containing plantings of the arid, tropical, and temperate climatic zones; the fourth structure has changing exhibits.

The Provincial Museum of Alberta, 12845 102nd Avenue,

(780) 453–9100 or www.pma.edmonton.ab.ca. Experience Alberta's fascinating natural and human history at one of Canada's most popular museums. Exhibits center on aboriginal peoples, wildlife, geology, live insects, dinosaurs, and ice age mammals.

Rutherford House, 11153 Saskatchewan Drive on the University of Alberta campus, (780) 427–3995. Open year-round. Admission is charged. Home of Alexander Cameron Rutherford, the first premier of Alberta. Restored and furnished to its early-1900s appearance. Costumed interpretive guides. This is an impressive mansion for a "man of means and considerable influence"—which Rutherford clearly was.

Great Divide Waterfall, located on the High Level Bridge, 109th Street, (403) 496–8400. Niagara Falls in miniature during the summer holiday weekends.

Alberta Aviation Museum & Learning Centre, 11410 Kingsway Avenue, (780) 453–1078. Vintage planes dating from the 1920s, restored aircraft, archives, library, and a gift shop on site.

Ukrainian Canadian Archives and Museum of Alberta, 9543 110th Avenue, (780) 424–7580. Open year-round. Donations are accepted. The largest Ukrainian museum in Alberta.

Ukrainian Museum of Canada (Alberta Branch), 10611 110th Avenue, (780) 483–5932. Open May through August. Free. Displays of beautiful, embroidered tablecloths; wood carvings; hand-painted Easter eggs; ceramics; sculptures; and paintings.

Valley Zoo, 13315 Buena Vista Road, (780) 496–9611 or www.gov.edmonton.ab.ca/valleyzoo/. The zoo is home to more than a hundred exotic, endangered, and native species. Take a camel ride, travel on the miniature train, or head to the Little Children's Zoo.

Accommodations
Top Hotels
Edmonton has accommodations ranging from deluxe to budget. There are places to stay along all major routes leading to the city. The deluxe hotels at city center are among Canada's finest. For additional suggestions, contact your travel agent or auto club, or call Edmonton Tourism, (780) 496–8400; (800) 463–4667.

Hotel MacDonald, 10065 One Hundredth Street, (780) 424–5181; (800) 441–1414; www.hotelmacdonald.com. The familiar chateau-styled Canadian Pacific Hotels add a note of character to Edmonton's modern skyline. This charming and gracious hotel features an indoor swimming pool, a fine restaurant, a lounge, and meeting rooms. Expensive.

Sheraton Grande Edmonton Hotel, 10235 101st Street, (780) 428–7111; (800) 263–9030. One of Edmonton's top hotels. Located in city center and adjoining the Edmonton Centre Mall, this hotel offers fine service and many luxurious amenities, elegant dining, an indoor pool, and saunas. Expensive.

Westin Hotel, 10135 One Hundredth Street, (780) 426–3636; (800) 228–3000. City center location. Fine service and amenities, gourmet dining, indoor pool, and exercise facilities. Expensive.

Crown Plaza/Château Lacombe, 101st Street at Bellamy Hill, (780) 428–6611; (800) 227–6963. A modern, circular tower structure in city center. Dining at La Ronde, a revolving restaurant. Expensive.

Edmonton House Suite Hotel, 10205 One Hundredth Avenue, (780) 420–4000; (800) 661–6562; www.maclabhotels.com. All the space and comfort of a mini-apartment. Restaurant, lounge, pool, exercise room, indoor pool, shuttle to West Edmonton Mall. Moderate.

Fantasyland Hotel, at West Edmonton Mall, (780) 444–3000; (800) 661–6454. Moderate to expensive.

Mayfield Inn, 16615 109th Avenue, (780) 484–0821; (800) 661–9804. Excellent accommodations and service. Indoor pool, health club, trade center, four racquetball courts. Dining room, lounge, and live entertainment. Moderate.

Other Fine Places to Stay

All the places listed below offer fine accommodations and many amenities, such as swimming pools, dining rooms, and lounges; some have nightclubs.

The Coast Edmonton Plaza Hotel, 10155 105th Street, (780) 423–4811; (800) 423–4811. Expensive.

Econolodge, 10209 One Hundredth Avenue, (780) 428–6442. Inexpensive to moderate.

Mayfair Hotel, 10815 Jasper Avenue, (780) 423–1650. Moderate.

Executive Royal Inn West Edmonton, 10010 178th Street, (780) 484–6000; (800) 661–4879. Five blocks from the West Edmonton Mall. Full service. Moderate.

Dining

In Edmonton cuisine the emphasis is on Alberta beef, which may be the best in North America. Fancy continental and hearty ethnic cuisines are also the pride of Edmonton's chefs.

Japanese Village, 10126 One Hundredth Street, (780)

422–6083. Traditional Japanese dishes prepared at your table; also has a sushi bar. Moderate to expensive.

La Ronde Revolving Restaurant, at the Crowne Plaza/Château Lacombe, (780) 428–6611. This restaurant gives you views of the city from the top, while you dine on prime roast beef, steak, or a fancy continental dish. Moderate to expensive.

Hy's Steak House, 10013 101st Avenue, (780) 424–4444. A Canadian classic chain serving up steaks in a manly, clubby atmosphere. Expensive.

The King and I, 8208 107th Street, (780) 433–2222. Voted the city's best Thai restaurant. Inexpensive to moderate.

Syrtaki Greek Island Restaurant, 16313 111th Avenue, (780) 484–2473. Bright, Greek island setting. Inexpensive to moderate.

Mirabelle Restaurant, 9929 109th Street, (780) 429–3055. Continental cuisine. Moderate to expensive.

La Boheme, 6427 112th Avenue, (780) 474–5693. French cuisine in a historical setting. Moderate to expensive.

Ginger, Etc., 11003 124th Street, (780) 452–2282. Authentic northern- and southern-style Chinese. Casual. Inexpensive to moderate.

Packrat Louie Kitchen & Bar, 10335 Eighty-third Avenue, (780) 433–0123. Next to the Old Strathcona Farmer's Market, this restaurant serves up spinach-and-feta pizza, goat-cheese crêpes, and grilled ostrich among its entrees. Moderate to expensive.

Sorrentino's, 10612 Eighty-second Avenue, (780) 434–7607. This award-winning restaurant offers an array of Italian specialties including gnocchi with wild game ragout, goat-cheese-crusted rack of lamb, and medallion spinach pasta. Expensive.

That's Aroma, 11010 101st Street, (780) 425–6708. A new restaurant whose menu is devoted to garlic dishes.

Entertainment

The Citadel Theatre, 9828 101A Avenue; for ticket and schedule information, call (780) 426–1820. This is a beautiful, modern complex of several theaters. Plays are performed in the Shoctor, Rice, and Maclab Theatres. The Tucker Amphitheatre in the Lee Pavilion is set amid indoor gardens that have 4,000 tropical plants, a reflecting pool, and a 9-m/30-ft waterfall.

Jubilee Auditorium, Eighty-seventh Avenue and 114th Street, is the home of the Edmonton Opera; for performance dates and ticket information, call (780) 427–2760.

The **Francis Winspear Centre for Music** is a $35-million, 1,900-seat concert hall located adjacent to the Citadel Theatre and

Churchhill Square, the cultural hub of downtown Edmonton. Home of the Edmonton Symphony Orchestra, (780) 429–1992.

Shopping

If you want to spend hours of enjoyable shopping, go to the West Edmonton Mall, which not only is the largest in the world but also combines amusements and theme parks—enough diversions to keep you busy for several days. It's one of the city's great attractions. In city center the Edmonton Centre Mall has a large number of shops from glitzy to budget-busting boutiques.

The following are interesting shops for gifts:

Bearclaw Gallery, 10780 124th Street. Canadian Indian and Inuit arts and crafts.

Alberta Crafts Council Gallery, 10106 124th Street, (780) 488–6611. A collection of local and provincial crafts.

Northern Images Gallery, West Edmonton Mall, Inuit and Native art and clothing.

Professional Sports

Edmonton Oilers, five-time Stanley Cup champions (1984, 1985, 1987, 1988, and 1990), play at Skyreach Centre, 118th Avenue and Seventy-fourth Street. For game dates and tickets, call (780) 451–8000.

Edmonton Eskimos, of the Canadian Football League, play at Commonwealth Stadium, 11100 Stadium Road. For game dates and tickets, call (780) 448–3757.

Edmonton Drillers Soccer Club, 10233 Ninety-sixth Avenue, (780) 471–5425. Indoor professional soccer from November through March at the Skyreach Centre.

Thoroughbred and harness racing, at Northlands Park, 115th Avenue and Seventy-ninth Street. Call (780) 471–7379 for racing dates.

Canadian Finals Rodeo, at Skyreach Centre, 118th Avenue and Seventy-fourth Street. Call (780) 471–7210 for dates.

Edmonton Trappers, of the triple-A baseball Pacific Coast League, play at the new Telus Field, 10233 Ninety-sixth Avenue, (780) 429–2934.

Recreation

Edmonton offers visitors a wide assortment of recreational activities and venues—golf, tennis, swimming pools, family recreation centers, health clubs, ice skating, and so on. Your hotel concierge or guest relations person will be happy to offer suggestions and make arrangements.

Traveling from Edmonton to Alaska or Yellowknife

If you are traveling from Edmonton to the Yukon, the Northwest Territories, and/or Alaska, take Highway 43, which begins just west of the city, via Yellowhead Highway 16. Continue on Highway 43 until you reach the town of Valleyview (a more scenic but longer route is Highway 2 from Edmonton via Lesser Slave Lake to Valleyview or Grande Prairie). At Valleyview turn west on Highway 34, which will take you to Grande Prairie. From here take Highway 2 to Dawson Creek, British Columbia; it is at Dawson Creek that the Alaska Highway officially begins. From Dawson Creek follow Alaska Highway 97 North to Highway 4 and/or 2, via Whitehorse in the Yukon, and thence to the state of Alaska.

To reach Yellowknife, the capital of the Northwest Territories, from Edmonton, take Highway 43 North to Valleyview, then Highway 35 North, which connects with Northwest Territories Highway 1. Highway 1 West will take you to Highway 3 North (around the southwest shore of Great Slave Lake) and then on to Yellowknife via Highway 4 East.

CHAPTER 8

Touring Saskatchewan

Regina · Saskatoon

Saskatchewan in Brief

Saskatchewan will surprise you. The combination of prairies, highlands, deserts, and evergreen forests presents a variety of faces to its visitors. In a province that stretches 1,288 km/800 mi from top to bottom, you have a choice of landscapes, from sun-drenched grasslands to rugged Precambrian wilderness. Just as the Atlantic and Pacific are awesome and inspiring in their particular ways, so, too, is the vast ocean of Saskatchewan's wheat-laden prairie land. Most familiar to visitors is the vista of rolling, sun-kissed prairie, where brightly colored grain elevators give towns their distinctive (and only) skyline. To see what this part of the province looked like before the plow, explore Grasslands National Park, a place of subtle beauty and pervasive solitude.

In Saskatchewan there are two brilliant cities, national parks and historic sites, rodeos and Indian powwows, lakes and rivers for swimming and fishing, and more varied cultural offerings than you would have time to sample.

The human history of the province is one of noble men and women from many different backgrounds who shaped and made productive a land that was not easy to tame. The first inhabitants of Saskatchewan were the Native peoples—Chipewyan, Cree, and Assiniboine. In the north their culture developed around hunting

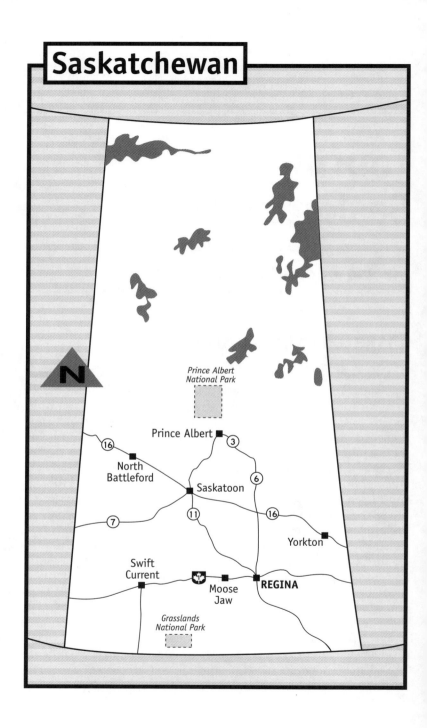

Saskatchewan

Prince Albert National Park

Prince Albert

North Battleford

Saskatoon

Yorkton

Swift Current

Moose Jaw

REGINA

Grasslands National Park

such animals as the moose and the caribou; in the south they hunted buffalo.

One of the first Europeans to come into this region was Henry Kelsey. Kelsey, an employee of the Hudson's Bay Company, explored the Saskatchewan River in 1690. In the decades that followed, other explorers left their footprints on Saskatchewan soil, and their visions motivated others—Pierre Gaultier de Varennes La Vérendrye, Peter Pond, David Thompson, Peter Fidler, Sir John Franklin, Dr. John Richardson, John Palliser, and Henry Hind.

Several key events in the nineteenth century radically changed the development of Saskatchewan: the Canadian Confederation in 1867; the relinquishing by the Hudson's Bay Company of lands in Saskatchewan to the federal government of Canada in 1869; the founding of the Northwest Mounted Police in 1873 to establish and maintain law and order in the Canadian West; through treaties, the confinement of the Native peoples into reserves; the final defeat in 1885 of the Métis; the building of the transcontinental railroad connecting Saskatchewan to the rest of Canada; and the Dominion Lands Act, which opened up the land to homesteading and immigration. And the immigrants came in droves: Doukhobors, Ukrainians, Germans, Hutterites, Mennonites, Scandinavians, French, Americans, Chinese, and many others. They came to this fertile part of Canada fleeing religious and/or political persecution or simply because they saw better opportunities here than those available from where they came. With a great deal of hard work and sacrifice, they put plows to the tough prairie soil and made it bloom with an overflowing cornucopia of nutritious food.

On September 1, 1905, Saskatchewan entered the Canadian Confederation (the alliance of provinces that created a self-governing Dominion of Canada) and has been a province of significance ever since. Among the many outstanding men and women Saskatchewan has contributed to the national life of Canada was John George Diefenbaker. Although born in Ontario in 1895 and having lived some of his early years in the Northwest Territories, Diefenbaker (called Dief by his friends and foes) was more closely associated with Saskatchewan than with any other province. After distinguishing himself in local and provincial politics, he was elected in 1940 to the federal Parliament in Ottawa. As leader of the Progressive Conservative party from 1956 to 1967, Dief was constantly a thorn in the side of the ruling Liberals, but he had a high-minded vision for Canada, based on the values of democracy and self-reliance he had learned on the prairies and rough country of Saskatchewan. In 1957 he became prime minister of Canada, giving the nation its first Tory government since R. B. Bennett's (1930–35).

Another noteworthy Canadian from Saskatchewan, Jeanne-Methilde Sauvé (née Benoit), born at Prud'homme, was the first woman in the nation's history to be appointed (in May 1984) governor-general. In this capacity, Madame Sauvé, previously a journalist and politician, represented the queen (Elizabeth II) in Canada and as such held the highest government position in the country, although without the considerable executive powers of the prime minister, who is elected by House of Commons members of the majority party.

Tourism Saskatchewan

To get the best out of traveling in Saskatchewan, use the province's information and travel-planning assistance services, both of which are available free of charge. The folks at Tourism Saskatchewan will answer your questions, make suggestions, and send you free maps and brochures. If you are interested in destination attractions, accommodations, fishing, hunting, canoeing, white-water rafting, mountain biking or bike touring, houseboat charters, hiking, nature tours, outfitting organizations, or wilderness lodges, ask for the booklet *Saskatchewan Vacation Guide* or the *Saskatchewan Fishing and Hunting Guide,* which have everything you need to know (plus maps).

Other free guides from Tourism Saskatchewan that you may find useful are *Saskatchewan Accommodation, Resort, and Campground Guide* (including camping, hotels/motels, and farm vacations), *Events Guide, The Angler's Guide,* and *The Hunting and Trapping Guide.*

Tourism Saskatchewan can be reached throughout the year at (800) 667-7191; Regina area, (306) 787-2300; or visit the Web site www.sasktourism.com.

Saskatchewan Special Events

Saskatchewan has a great variety of festivals and special events. Some, such as rodeos, are familiar. Others, such as bee beard competitions, snowmobile grass drags, and world bannock championships (a Russian game played with horse-ankle bones), are just plain strange but are terrific fun. Here's a sampling of some of the best special events taking place in the province during the summer vacation season:

May
Strathcona Mounted Troop & Musical Ride, Regina
Northern Saskatchewan International Children's Festival, Saskatoon
Quill Plains Children's Festival, Humboldt

June
Shakespeare on the Saskatchewan, Saskatoon
Bazaart, Regina
Western Canada Farm Progress Show, Regina

July
Ranch Rodeo, Maple Creek
Yorkton Exhibition Summer Fair, Yorkton
Souris Valley Theatre, Estevan
Saskatchewan Air Show, Moose Jaw
Colonial Days, Lloydminster
Trial of Louis Riel, Regina; one of the longest running stage shows in
    Canada, this reenactment features dialogue taken directly from
    court transcripts
Saskatchewan Handcraft Festival, Battlefords
Taste of Saskatchewan, Saskatoon
Canadian National Horseshoe Championships, Manitou Beach

Saskatchewan is a province of many natural wonders. Its Cree name is Kisiskatchewan, "the river that flows swiftly," namely the Saskatchewan River. The province—651,900 sq km/251,700 sq mi—is wide open and almost the size of Texas. To the north Saskatchewan borders the Northwest Territories; to the south, the states of Montana and North Dakota; to the west, Alberta; and to

August
Buffalo Days, the Provincial Exhibition, Regina
Saskatoon International Fringe Festival, Saskatoon
Mozart at Mission Ridge, Fort Qu'Appelle
La Fete Fransaskoise, Zenon Park
The Ex, Saskatoon
Weyburn Wheat Festival, Weyburn
Canada Remembers International Air Show, Saskatoon

September
Canadian National Dressage Championships (Western Division),
    Regina
Cowboy Poetry Gathering and Western Art Show, Maple Creek
Harvest Hoe Down, Humboldt

October
Humboldt Oktoberfest Week, Humboldt
Canadian Cowboys Association Rodeo Finals, Saskatoon
Stockade Roundup, Lloydminster

November
Yorkton Harvest Showdown, Yorkton
Victorian Market, Regina
Canadian Western Agribition, Regina
Wintergreen, Regina
Sundog Handcraft Faire, Saskatoon

the east, Manitoba. Prairies dominate much of the landscape in
the south; parklands, in the center—a transitional zone of farms
and rolling terrain with forests; and thousands of square miles of
Precambrian wilderness, with more lakes and streams than an angler could enjoy in several lifetimes, in the northern portion. Winters, even in the southern portion, can be very cold. Summers,

however, are typically warm, dry, and pleasant. During June, July, and August the weather is perfect for all kinds of outdoor recreation. Moreover, during summer just about every town and city has festivals, rodeos, ethnic events, heritage days, or cultural happenings.

The North and South Saskatchewan, the Assiniboine, and the Churchill are the province's major river systems, and they all flow in a northeasterly direction and empty into Hudson Bay. The largest lakes in northern Saskatchewan are Athabasca, Lac la Ronge, Cree, Wollaston, Reindeer, Churchill, and Peter Pond. There are more than 100,000 throughout the province, and the many beaches, such as Waskesiu in Prince Albert National Park, are good places to cool off. Cypress Hills in southeast Saskatchewan (1,392 m/4,564 ft) is the highest point of land between Labrador and the Rockies.

The province has approximately one million inhabitants. Regina is the capital and second largest city; Saskatoon is slightly larger. Canada's only training academy for the Royal Canadian Mounted Police is located in Regina.

The economy is based on agriculture, mining, manufacturing, construction, oil and petroleum, and tourism. The province produces 60 percent of all wheat grown in Canada, and more than half of the world's known recoverable potash reserves (used in making fertilizer) are located here.

Useful Information

Time zone: Central
Area code: 306

National Parks

Grasslands National Park

Grasslands National Park, located in the south-central part of the province, provides an opportunity to explore one of the last frontiers of the Canadian West. Geologically and culturally rich, this vast open landscape represents some of the last of the original mixed-grass prairie. It is also home to some unique and endangered flora and fauna.

Paleontological history is evident in the dinosaur remains of the Killdeer Badlands and the plateaus and coulees in the French-

Saskatchewan Is for the Birds!

Where the South Saskatchewan River meets the west end of Lake Diefenbaker, just north of the town of Cabri, two little-known bays play host to hundreds of thousands of migratory birds each fall. Geese, ducks, and cranes temporarily populate Galloway and Miry Bays to the half-million mark, or more in dry years.

The shallow bays lie in a wide river valley that offers sandbars and temporary islands as resting spots for the birds as they pass through.

A visit here may also include sightings of bald and golden eagles, peregrine and prairie falcons, American white pelicans, and piping plovers.

The Canadian Wildlife Service in Saskatoon, (306) 975–5595, has information on all sightings in the province.

man River Valley. Remnants of tepee rings and buffalo rubbing stones, weathered rails patrolled by the Northwest Mounted Police, and the seasoned homesteads of ranches show the diverse history of the region. It was here that Sitting Bull took refuge after the battle of Little Big Horn.

Divided into two blocks, the East Block contains the Killdeer Badlands and the Wood Mountain Uplands. The West Block presents the Frenchman River Valley, dissected plateaus, and famous 70 Mile Butte.

Grasslands National Park was established in 1981 to protect a special ecosystem of rolling terrain covered with spear grass and other vegetation and inhabited by pronghorn antelope, prairie rattlesnakes, sage grouse, prairie dogs, and a variety of birds, including the threatened ferruginous hawk and burrowing owl. This is the only preserve of its kind in North America.

The area surrounding the park boundaries is the former site of the Wood Mountain Northwest Mounted Police Post, the Jean-Louis Legaré Trading Post; the Fort Walsh–Wood Mountain Trail runs through the area, some sections within park boundaries. Today farming and ranching operations surround the park.

Grasslands National Park is located in southwestern Saskatchewan, near the Montana border, accessible by Highways

4 and 18, about 120 km/80 mi south of Swift Current. For more information contact Superintendent, Grasslands National Park, Val Marie, Saskatchewan, S0N 2T0; (306) 298–2257.

Prince Albert National Park

Prince Albert National Park, located due north of Saskatoon, can be reached via Highway 2 North from the city of Prince Albert. Highways 263 and 264 lead to the entrance of the park, as well as to some of the key areas within it. For more information on facilities and services, contact Superintendent, Prince Albert National Park, Box 100, Waskesiu Lake, Saskatchewan S0J 2Y0; (306) 663–5322.

Located in the center of the province, Prince Albert National Park, named in honor of Queen Victoria's beloved consort, is a vast, oblong-shaped ecological bridge between the aspen parkland of central Saskatchewan and its vast northern forest. Prince Albert has many lakes, streams, and bog areas and supports abundant wildlife—badgers, coyotes, black bears, otters, elk, deer, moose, loons, bison, pelicans, foxes, wolves, lynx, caribou, ospreys, and eagles.

The three largest lakes are Waskesiu, Crean, and Kingsmere, which along with the many other lakes are favorites with anglers; perch, walleye, whitefish, trout, and northern pike are among the species waiting to be caught. The town of Waskesiu Lake, on the shores of the lake bearing the same name, is a resort community catering to anglers, boaters, campers, swimmers, and those seeking the solitude and beauty of the park.

One early naturalist, author, and orator who lived in this wilderness was Archibald Stansfield Belaney. Taking the name of Grey Owl and believing himself to be the son of a Scottish father and an Apache mother, this eccentric Englishman became immortal for his work in the cause of conservation and as author of *The Men of the Last Frontier, Pilgrims of the Wild, The Adventures of Sajo and Her Beaver People,* and *Tales of an Empty Cabin.* Grey Owl's writings on the beavers he raised—Jellyroll and Rawhide—became almost as famous as he. To those of us urban and suburban dwellers, Grey Owl said, "You are tired with years of civilization and I come to offer you, what? . . . a single green leaf." Grey Owl's cabin, at Lake Ajawaan (a 19.5-km/12-mi hike from the end of. Highway 264), is preserved. You can visit it and hear his voice in a gentle breeze: "I offer you . . . a single green leaf."

Prince Albert National Park's offerings include interpretive programs; campgrounds at Beaver Glen, Narrows, Trapper's

Lake, Namekus, Sandy Lake, and Kingsmere Lake; swimming from the park's main beach at Lake Waskesiu, as well as at all other lakes except Lavalle; an eighteen-hole golf course in town plus another eighteen-hole course outside the park limits via Highway 264; bike rentals; hiking trails; canoe rentals and canoe routes; horseback riding; and fishing with a park permit.

Waskesiu Lake
Take advantage of the following:
Paddlewheeler Tours, (306) 663–5253
Nature Centre, open June through August, (306) 663–4522
Country Crafts, (306) 764–7575
Accommodations include the following:
Lakeview Hotel, (306) 663–5311. Open May 1 to October 1. Dining room. Moderate.

Haywood Inn, (306) 663–5911. Year-round, luxury rooms, self-contained suites, licensed dining room. Moderate to expensive.

Chateau Park Chalets, (306) 663–5556. Year-round self-contained chalets. Moderate to expensive.

Kapasiwin Bungalows, (306) 663–5225, May 1 to October 15. Modern cabin accommodations. Moderate to expensive.

Prince Albert
The city of Prince Albert, the gateway to the national park, is a vibrant city on the banks of the North Saskatchewan River, its scenery a blend of grain fields to the south and forests to the north. Some of its attractions include:

Prince Albert Historical Museum, located in the Old Fire Hall, River Street and Central Avenue, (306) 764–2992. Open May through September. The histories of Prince Albert and of this area are told through photographs, documents, and artifacts.

Diefenbaker House, 246 Nineteenth Street West, (306) 764–2992 or 953–4863. Open mid-May through September. Free.

Grace Campbell Art Gallery, in the John M. Cuelenaere Library, 125 Twelfth Street East, (306) 763–8496. Open throughout the year. Free.

Northern Lights Casino, 44 Marquis Road (adjacent to the Prince Albert Inn), (306) 764–4777; (888) 604–7711. Open year-round. A full-service casino with restaurant, lounge, and weekly entertainment.

Also visit the **Nisbet Church, Prince Albert Forest Nursery,** and historic **La Colle Dam.**

Accommodations are listed below:

Marquis Inn, Sixth Avenue, (306) 922–9595. Moderate.

Imperial 400 Motel, Highways 2 and 3, (306) 764–6881. Moderate.

Comfort Inn, Second Avenue and Marquis Road, (306) 763–4466; (800) 228–5150; www.hotelchoice.com. Moderate.

Marlboro Inn, 67 Thirteenth Street, (306) 763–2643. Moderate.

Prince Albert Inn, 3680 Second Avenue, (306) 922–5000. Moderate.

National Historic Parks

Fort Walsh National Historic Site, (306) 662–3590, open mid-May to mid-October, near the Alberta–Saskatchewan border, can be reached via the Trans-Canada, then south on Highway 271 from Maple Creek (adjacent to Cypress Hills Provincial Park, an important attraction and recreational area in itself). For more information contact Superintendent, Fort Walsh National Historic Park, P.O. Box 278, Maple Creek, Saskatchewan S0N IN0.

In 1873 the Cypress Hills Massacre took place in this region, known as Whoop-Up Country because of the frenetic trading and whiskey drinking that went on here. A group of white wolf-hunters got into a drunken brawl with Assiniboine Indians, and twenty of the Natives, as well as one of the wolf-hunters, were killed. With the territory on the verge of anarchy, the Northwest Mounted Police established a base of operations here at Fort Walsh (named for the first superintendent, James Walsh, a flamboyant but popular commander). From Fort Walsh the Mounties chased out the American whiskey traders operating in this region, secured the international border, and protected the Indians. Superintendent Walsh offered Chief Sitting Bull and his people refuge after the battle of Little Big Horn.

Today Fort Walsh has been re-created and looks as it did in the late 1800s. A high wooden wall encircles and thus protects several buildings. Nearby are Solomon's and Farewell's Trading Posts. If you let your imagination go, you can almost hear bugles, the voices of troops, and the sounds of horses preparing to venture forth and tame a wild land.

There are camping and recreational opportunities at the 18,225-ha/45,000-acre **Cypress Hills Inter-Provincial Park,** (306) 662–4411. Open throughout the year. A park entry fee is charged.

Supplies and various tourist services can be obtained in the town of Maple Creek.

Fort Battleford National Historic Site Area, (306) 937–2621, is located near the town of Battleford, 153 km/92 mi northeast of Saskatoon. The best access is off Yellowhead Highway 16. For more information contact Superintendent, Fort Battleford National Historic Site, Box 70, Battleford, Saskatchewan S0M 0E0.

A great tragedy took place here in 1885—one of the battles of the North West Rebellion, conducted by one of the proudest and noblest leaders of the Native peoples of the Plains, Cree Chief Poundmaker, adopted son of a great Blackfoot leader, Chief Crowfoot. According to one version, this uprising occurred because by the late 1880s the native Cree and Blackfoot peoples felt hemmed in by the white settlements, whose inhabitants believed that the land was for the taking, and by the building of the transcontinental railroad. The Indians could no longer move freely across this limitless landscape; their primary food source—the buffalo—was disappearing; and their liberty was increasingly controlled by white people's laws. According to another version, the battle took place because of the traditional, long-standing antagonism between the Cree and the Blackfoot.

At any rate, the Mounties built Fort Battleford to serve as a buffer between the two tribes. From the fort the police could serve the Indians by distributing annuity payments, enforcing the laws, and settling them on reserves. In 1885 Chief Poundmaker and his Cree warriors laid siege to the fort, where 112 men were stationed—the largest mounted police division then in Western Canada. The Mountie superintendent, Colonel William Otter, pursued Cree warriors from the fort and engaged them in battle at Cut Knife Hill. Eight warriors were found guilty of murder by the Mounties and were hanged within the stockade. Although pleading innocent to treason and felony charges, Chief Poundmaker was sentenced to three years in prison but was released after one year. He died shortly thereafter, on July 4, 1886, and is buried on a hill where the battle of Cut Knife was fought. Visit Chief Poundmaker Historical Centre and Teepee Village, where Poundmaker's grave is on site. The museum features historical displays, artifacts, and videos interpreting the history of Poundmaker's Cree Nation.

The residence of the commanding officer, General Frederick Middleton, still stands within the stockade; it is furnished with decorations and items from the late nineteenth century. Government House, a two-story building constructed in 1877, was the seat of the territorial capital. In the late 1870s Battleford was

Saskatchewan's Ukrainian Connection

Ever since the lands of Saskatchewan were opened for settlement in the late nineteenth century, people from all over the world have come to the province to start new lives. One ethnic group that has contributed much to the development of Saskatchewan, particularly in agriculture, is the Ukrainians, who for the most part came to this part of Canada from the Bukovyna and Halychyna regions of western Ukraine. In many ways the terrain and climate of the prairies were not unlike those on the fertile steppes of Ukraine. Just as Ukraine was the breadbasket of the old Soviet Union, so, too, is Ukrainian Canada the breadbasket here.

Along with their commitment to the land, the Ukrainians have contributed aspects of their rich culture to Canada. You can experience this influence in their beautiful onion-dome churches, Byzantine or Latin rituals, and elaborate decorations or icons; in their festivals; and most particularly in their exuberant dancing groups, which have thrilled audiences throughout the world. You can visit Ukrainian places of interest (museums, churches, schools) located along or near Yellowhead Highway 16 from Lloydminster at the Alberta border to North Battleford, Radisson, Saskatoon, Wynyard, Foam Lake, Sheho, Insinger, Theodore, Yorkton, and Rokeby near the Manitoba border (admission charges, if any, and hours are individually posted). Even in some small communities, don't be surprised to see two Ukrainian churches, one aligned with the Orthodox hierarchy and the other with the Roman Catholic Church. In Saskatoon visit the **Musée Ukraina Museum,** 202 Avenue M South, (306) 244–4212. Open throughout the year. Donations are accepted. This museum has 2,000 artifacts describing the Ukrainian culture in Europe and in Canada.

---

the capital of the North West Territories, as much of Western Canada was then known. In 1882 the capital was moved to Regina, which was right on the line of the transcontinental railroad and thus linked to primary urban centers throughout Canada.

Batoche National Historic Site, located 88 km/53 mi northeast of Saskatoon on the east bank of the South Saskatchewan River, can be reached from Saskatoon via Highway 11 North to

Highway 312. For more information contact Site Coordinator, Batoche National Historic Site, Box 999, Rosthern, Saskatchewan S0K 3R0; (306) 423–6227.

Batoche was the site of the epic battle in 1885 between the Métis and the established authority of Canada. The Riel Rebellion was the closest Canada ever came to civil war, although there were other rebellions in the nineteenth century. The Métis considered themselves a distinct people, neither French nor Indian but a merging of cultures and genes from both. They were the sons and daughters of men who were French or Scottish voyageurs (trappers and/or haulers of furs) and women who were Cree, Saulteaux, or Ojibwa.

Batoche, located on the Carlton Trail, a trade route between Fort Garry, Manitoba, and Fort Edmonton, Alberta, was part of a larger district known as the Saint-Laurent Settlement. In the mid-1880s this territory was embroiled in conflict. There were battles between the Indians and the Northwest Mounted Police, and the Métis expressed grievances against encroachments by the Canadian federal government. Some took up arms against the Mounties, who moved in on the Métis at Batoche. General Frederick Middleton's force of 800 attacked 100 Métis and Indians. His first attack failed, but the Mounties bombarded the Métis with their artillery for about three days. On May 12, 1885, General Middleton and 130 of his men drew the Métis to an area where a Mountie Gatling gun was firing (a Gatling gun is on display at the park), and then a Mountie force rushed down on the Métis, who by this time were firing nails and stones from their rifles. Within a few minutes the battle was finished, and so was the Métis cause—at least from a military perspective.

Both Louis Riel, the charismatic political leader of the Métis cause, and General Gabriel Dumont, its military chief, escaped. Riel surrendered later and was eventually tried and convicted of treason in Regina. He was hanged in that city on November 16, 1885.

The trial and the sentence have been controversial in Canada ever since, especially among those French Canadians who believe that the severity of Riel's sentence was due as much to his ethnic background and religion as to the severity of his crime. Gabriel Dumont escaped to the United States, where he joined Buffalo Bill Cody's Wild West Show as a trick rifle shooter. General Middleton was found to have illegally confiscated furs from a Métis prisoner; he returned to England, where Queen Victoria made him Keeper of the Crown Jewels in the Tower of London.

The Batoche Park has become a kind of shrine in Canada, expressing the struggle of a people both to retain their liberty and to preserve their culture. The park contains the church and rectory of Saint-Antoine-de-Padoue, the East Village, the battlefield itself, and General Middleton's encampment. An interpretive center features a presentation, dioramas, and displays.

Other locations associated with the North West Rebellion in Saskatchewan are Steele Narrows, Fort Pitt, Frog Lake, Frenchman Butte, Prince Albert, and Fort Carlton.

Seager Wheeler Farm National Historic Site, located on Highway 312 near Batoche National Historic Site. Established in 1898 by Seager Wheeler, Maple Grove Farm illustrates the realities of prairie farming and its evolution. Persevering through the "Dirty Thirties" (the depression years), Seager Wheeler successfully demonstrated that by using selective breeding and soil conservation techniques, agriculture could work on the prairies.

Walk around the farmstead and explore an orchard, extensive flower gardens, shelter beds, remnants of Wheeler's seed plots, and many original buildings. The site is operated by the Wheeler Historical Society. For more information contact Seager Wheeler Farm Historical Society, Box 476, Rothern, Saskatchewan S0K 3R0, (306) 232–5959.

Claybank Brick Plant National Historic Site, located on Highway 339, about an hour's drive from Regina. Nestled in the Dirt Hills, Claybank Brick Plant used the natural resources of the region to manufacture clay into brick for three-quarters of a century. The plant produced the unique T-P Moka face brick that was used in structures all across the prairies and in landmarks such as the Château Frontenac in Québec City. Firebrick, which lined the fireboxes of Canadian National and Canadian Pacific Rail locomotives and Corvette warships in World War II was also produced here. For more information contact the Claybank Brick Plant Historical Society, Box 4, Briercrest, Saskatchewan S0H 0K0, (306) 768–4774.

Motherwell Homestead National Historic Site is reached via the Trans-Canada east from Regina to Highway 10 at Balgonie, and then 9 km/15.5 mi south of Highway 10 on Highway 22. For more information, contact Area Superintendent, Motherwell Homestead National Historic Park, Box 247, Abernethy, Saskatchewan S0A 0A0; (306) 333–4801 or 333–2202.

William Richard Motherwell, one of many settlers from Ontario who contributed considerably to the development of Saskatchewan, created an oasis of refined civilization on his prairie lands. He named his estate Lanark Place, after Lanark County in Ontario. The Italianate-style mansion he built in 1897 was of cut fieldstone with a double-pitched gambrel roof; this became one of the most popular architectural styles for the nouveaux riches on the prairies. Motherwell had a distinguished career as cofounder and president of the Territorial Grain Grower's Association at Indian Head. He was the province's first minister of agriculture and, as a member of the House of Commons in Ottawa, served as federal minister of agriculture. The mansion, buildings, and grounds ("the homestead") have been restored to reflect the peak period of Motherwell's career.

Saskatchewan's Special Attractions

The treasure chest that is Saskatchewan requires exploring and discovery. You won't be disappointed with the new experiences and perceptions you'll find. The following is just a sampling of what a few Saskatchewan communities have to offer.

Wanuskewin Heritage Park, 3 km/2 mi north of Saskatoon, just off Highway 11, (306) 931–6767. Open year-round. (The park is detailed later in this chapter.)

Manitou Springs Mineral Spa, 6 km/4 mi north of Watrous, located at Manitou Beach in south-central Saskatchewan. One of the oldest and best-known resorts in Western Canada. Manitou Beach has long been a popular destination because of the supposed curing properties of briny Little Manitou Lake, known as the lake of "healing waters" by early Plains Indians. The spa is connected to a resort hotel. Call (306) 946–2233 or (800) 667–7672. Open daily.

In Gravelbourg (reached via the Trans-Canada and Highway 58), a French-Canadian cultural center on the prairies, visit **Our Lady of Assumption Cathedral,** Main Street, (306) 648–3322. Open throughout the year. Beautiful interior with paintings by Charles Maillard. Built in 1918, it has been declared a Provincial Historic Site.

Stop in Maple Creek, on the Trans-Canada near the Saskatchewan–Alberta border, to see the **Old Timer's Museum,** 218 Jasper Street, (306) 662–2474. Open year-round. Admission is charged. This is the oldest museum in the province, with a fine collection of pictures and artifacts of the Native people and early settlement.

Moose Jaw is located on the Trans-Canada. Legend says that during the 1800s, a Red River cart (a wagon mounted on two large wheels that was better able to traverse the rough and soggy ground than other vehicles of the times) broke down in this area and was fixed by an Englishman using a moose's jawbone. Impressed Indians named the place Moose Jaw, and the name has stuck ever since. The most popular and believable theory notes the warm, prevailing winds and concludes that Moose Jaw is derived from *moosegaw*, a Cree word meaning "warm breezes." Today Moose Jaw, on the line of the transcontinental railroad and the Trans-Canada Highway, is one of the province's largest cities, with an economy based on agriculture and industry. Moose Jaw is home to the **Saskatchewan Air Show** in mid-July, featuring the Snowbirds, a precision-flying team. Visit the **Temple Gardens Mineral Spa Hotel and Resort,** 24 Fairford Street E, (306) 694–5055; (800) 718–7727. Open year-round, this geothermal mineral spa features indoor and outdoor pools fed by naturally heated therapeutic mineral water, a spa salon with massage therapy, and a spa shop.

In St. Victor (reached via Highway 2), visit **St. Victor Petroglyphs Historic Park,** (306) 694–3659, which features a series of rock carvings showing expressive human faces, hands and feet, grizzly bear and other animal tracks, turtles, and various symbolic images. The meaning of these petroglyphs has been lost in time, but it's thought they may have played a role in ancient rituals, including shamans' attempts to control buffalo herds. Open throughout the year. Free.

Wood Mountain Post Historic Park, in Wood Mountain on Highway 18, (306) 694–3659. Open from the end of May through September. Reconstructed buildings have displays on the lives of the Lakota Indians and the Northwest Mounted Police in this area of the province.

Wood Mountain Stampede, held in early July, is the oldest continual rodeo in Canada.

Worth a visit is Eastend, a small town nestled in the Frenchman River Valley on Highway 13. Tour the **Eastend Fossil Research Station,** which features a world-renowned *Tyrannosaurus rex*

skeleton excavated in 1994–95—one of only a dozen or so such skeletons in the world. Open year-round. Admission is charged. (306) 295–4144.

In Esterhazy (reached via Highways 16, 80, and 22), stop at the **Kaposvar Historic Site Museum,** (306) 745–2692. Open mid-May to mid-October. Free. Here is the site of the first Hungarian colony in the province, settled more than a hundred years ago. The museum complex contains a pioneer homestead, a barn, a smokehouse, a school, and various artifacts.

Fort Qu'Appelle can be reached via Highway 10 east of Regina. Located in the beautiful Qu'Appelle Valley is **Fort Qu'Appelle Museum,** Bay Avenue and Third Street, (306) 332–6443. Open July through September. The museum is joined to an original 1864 Hudson's Bay Company post and displays Indian artifacts, Hudson's Bay Company articles, pioneer photos, and more.

The lovely Qu'Appelle Valley runs almost across the central/ southern part of the province. The name Qu'Appelle has been adopted by the Cree and means "who calls?" This is a wonderful touring area of productive farms, meandering rivers and streams, many lakes, and fine parks for the recreational pleasure of visitors. If you have extra time, a sojourn through Qu'Appelle would be most worthwhile. In a very real sense, it does call the traveler and answers the Cree legend.

Visit the **National Doukhobor Heritage Village** in Veregin on Highway 5. Early homes reveal the lifestyles and habits of pioneer Doukhobors. Included are a bathhouse and prayer room, a museum, barns, a blacksmith shop, and agricultural equipment. Open year-round. Admission is charged. (306) 542–4441.

Duck Lake Regional Interpretive Centre is in Duck Lake (reached via Highway 11), (306) 467–2057. Open throughout the year. Admission is charged. The museum features thousands of items related to the North West Rebellion and to pioneer life in this region. Also visit nearby **Fort Carlton Provincial Historic Park,** reached via Highway 212; (306) 467–4512. Open mid-May through September. This reconstructed stockade has buildings of a fur-trading post with furnishings from the 1800s. There are interpretive programs and walking trails. Stop, too, at **St. Laurent Shrine,** (306) 467–2212. Open June through September. Free. This structure was inspired by the shrine at Lourdes; pilgrimages are held once in July and once in August.

Fort Pitt Provincial Historic Park is south of Frenchman Butte (reached via Highway 3), (306) 787–9573. Open throughout the year. Free. Interpretive panels tell the story of the fur trade.

Nearby is **Frenchman Butte Historic Site,** where you can see gun pits used in the 1885 skirmish.

In Loon Lake (reached via Highways 55 and 26), visit **Steel Narrows Provincial Historic Park,** (306) 837–2092 or 787–2854. Open throughout the year. Free. The skirmish between the Cree and the Mounties, which was the last military engagement of the North West Rebellion, took place at this site.

The Battlefords

The city of North Battleford and its neighbor, the town of Battleford, form the Battlefords, a popular vacation spot in the historic heart of Saskatchewan. The two communities are linked by the largest bridge in the province, spanning the fast-flowing North Saskatchewan River. While in the Battlefords, be sure to stop at the following:

Allen Sapp Gallery, 1091 One Hundredth Street (306) 445–1760, in the old Carnegie Library. Open year-round, this public gallery will open you to the sensitive and powerful images of the Northern Plains Cree through the art of renowned Cree artist Allen Sapp.

Golden Eagle Casino, north side of Highway 16, (306) 446–3833. Video lottery terminals, eight blackjack tables, roulette wheels, poker tables, and coin-in, coin-out slot machines.

Western Development Museum, at Highways 16 and 40, (306) 445–8033. Open April through September. Admission is charged. Exhibits tell the story of settlement and agricultural development, including demonstrations of farming techniques (summer only). Also here you can walk through the re-creation of a small town in the early twentieth century. **Northwest Territorial Days,** held in late July at North Battleford Exhibition Grounds near the museum, features exhibits, entertainment, chuck-wagon races, chariot races, a fiddlers' hoedown, fiddlers' contest, parade, and demolition derby.

Regina: Queen City of the Prairies

In 1882 it was a tent settlement. Today Regina is a vibrant modern city, Saskatchewan's capital, and the home of the Royal Canadian Mounted Police. Regina, Canada's Queen City, has rich artistic and multicultural traditions that incorporate its aboriginal history and immigrant influences.

The Cree name for Regina was Oskana, meaning "pile of bones." On the bank of Wascana Creek, near the present-day Legislative Building, the early Indians created a huge pile of buffalo bones as a religious landmark and oblation to the deity for successful hunts. The buffalo, or bison, was essential to their way of life and supplied them with nourishing food and with materials for clothing, shelter, and weapons.

Fur traders came through the Wascana area and settled for a time, only to move on when the prospect of riches beckoned elsewhere. The development of a permanent settlement at "Pile O' Bones" (the name of the first settlement) was made possible by the Northwest Mounted Police, who provided protection to the Indians from American whiskey traders and security for immigrants developing the region's agriculture. In 1857 the name was misunderstood and recorded as Wascana, by which name the creek has since been known. With the Canadian Pacific Railway's decision to build its main line across the southern prairies, the actual town site of Regina was established. Anxious to find a suitable territorial capital to replace Battleford, which was too far north of the proposed railway line, Sir John A. Macdonald—Canada's prime minister at the time—left the decision of the town location in the hands of the CPR. The Mounties provided the security needed for expansion of the Canadian Confederation across the prairies. Today, although the RCMP headquarters is in Ottawa, the only training academy for this elite force is in Regina.

In 1882 the city became the capital of the province of the Northwest Territories, which at that time encompassed much of Western Canada (later the prairie provinces and the Yukon Territory evolved out of this vast land area and entered the confederation). The name "Leopold" had been proposed for the town, but when Princess Louise, wife of the governor-general, suggested Regina in honor of her mother, Queen Victoria, her suggestion was accepted.

In 1905 Regina became the official capital of the province of Saskatchewan. Today it is a modern city of 180,000 people, a center for agriculture, manufacturing, government, finance, medicine, tourism, education, transportation, and food processing. Although the dominant ethnic groups are British and German, Regina is a cosmopolitan city in which many different cultures merge and contribute their own unique flavors and perspectives. The bottom line here, regardless of your heritage, is good old-fashioned prairie friendliness.

How to Get to Regina
By Car
Regina is located on Trans-Canada Highway 1 in the southern part of the province. U.S. Highway 16 from Sidney, Montana, and U.S. Highway 52 from Minot, North Dakota, provide direct access to Regina. U.S. Highway 16 connects with Saskatchewan Highway 6 North, and U.S. Highway 52 connects with Saskatchewan Highway 39 to 6. If you are traveling Yellowhead Highway 16 from Alberta, take Highway 11 south in Saskatoon, which will bring you directly into Regina.

By Bus
Regina Bus Depot, 2041 Hamilton Street. Greyhound has daily service to Regina from many destinations in Western Canada. For information on fares and schedules, call (306) 787–3340.

Saskatchewan Transportation and Moose Mountain Lines connect Saskatchewan communities.

By Plane
The following major airlines provide daily service to Regina: Northwest Airlines, Air Canada, and Canadian Airlines. The Regina Airport is located in the southwestern part of the city. Its terminal has full facilities, including rental cars. Travelers from the United States can reach Regina via connecting flights.

How to Get Around in Regina
Regina is laid out in a logical grid pattern. Its two main streets, which bisect each other in city center, are Albert Street and Victoria Avenue. The heart of the city is Wascana Centre, which is comprised of the Legislative Building, the Royal Saskatchewan Museum, and other attractions; it's located at Albert and College. Many of the biggest hotels are on or near Victoria.

Regina Transit provides bus service throughout the city; call (306) 777–7433. There are a number of taxi services in the city.

For information on the city, contact Tourism Regina, Highway 1 East, (306) 789–5099; or Tourism Saskatchewan, 1900 Albert Street, (306) 787–2300, www.sasktourism.com.

Touring Services
Ferry Boat Tours offers thirty-minute cruises on Wascana Lake; (306) 522–3661.

Attractions

Royal Canadian Mounted Police Centennial Museum, Depot Division, Dewdney Avenue West, (306) 780–5838. Open throughout the year. Free. The RCMP museum is one of Regina's finest attractions. Here thousands of men and—more recently—women have been trained to be members of Canada's elite police force, highly respected throughout the country and the world. The standards to get in are high, and the training is comparable to that of the U.S. and Royal Marines. Mounties serve on highway patrols, as law officers in remote communities and areas, as security for political leaders, and as the nation's intelligence service.

The RCMP museum, officially opened by Queen Elizabeth in 1973, contains uniforms, weapons, flags, documents, and many other artifacts relating to the history and heritage of the Mounties. It has the uniform belonging to Superintendent Walsh, who gave refuge to Chief Sitting Bull and his people after the battle of Little Big Horn; exhibits on the mad trapper of Rat River; and the crucifixes that Louis Riel carried to his hanging here in Regina. Also within the complex is the chapel—the spiritual heart for the RCMP, originally built as a mess hall in 1883. It is decorated with stained-glass windows depicting noble moments in the Mountie heritage and with flags from past campaigns, such as the North West and Indian Rebellions; its baptismal font honors a comrade who fell at the battle of Cut Knife Hill. Outside, in Parade Square, is a monument to the *St. Roch,* an RCMP boat that was the first to sail through the Northwest Passage. The *St. Roch* is now permanently on exhibit in Vancouver at the Maritime Museum. There are other memorials as well. An old cemetery is nearby.

Be sure to attend the stirring Sergeant Major's drill parade, 12:45 P.M. weekdays, and the Sunset Retreat ceremonies, Tuesday evening in midsummer.

Wascana Centre, bounded by Twenty-third Avenue, Albert Street, and College Avenue, (306) 522–3661, is the most beautiful part of Regina. It covers 1,000 ha/2,500 acres, through which flows Wascana Creek, forming man-made Wascana Lake. Within the park are located some of Regina's most important attractions: the Legislative Building; a band shell and marina; Wascana Place, which features films and exhibits and provides tourist information; Wascana Waterfowl Park; the Royal Saskatchewan Museum; the Saskatchewan Centre; and the University of Regina. During summer live entertainment and boat cruises are offered. Picnic areas are provided, and walks through the beautifully landscaped park lead you past colorful flower beds. You can take a brief ferry ride to Willow Island, where there are picnic areas. Of all of Canada's provincial capitols, Saskatchewan's in Wascana Centre is the most beautifully sited in terms of the surrounding landscaping, extensive lawns, flower beds, and promenades and of its axis on Wascana Lake. The modern campus of the University of Regina is also within Wascana Centre, and you are welcome to stroll the grounds.

Legislative Building, in Wascana Centre, (306) 787–5357. Open throughout the year; tours (free). This fine, domed structure, in cruciform shape, imitates the architecture of eighteenth-century England and France, but it is also solidly North American. The rotunda area, jewel of the building, is faced with marble and decorated with a mural painted by Edward Morris. An art gallery here (open daily; free) displays portraits, photographs, and other objects relating to Saskatchewan history.

Saskatchewan Science Centre, Winnipeg Street and Wascana Drive in Wascana Centre, (306) 791–7914 or 352–5811 (recorded twenty-four-hour message), is Saskatchewan's number one year-round family tourist attraction, with eighty hands-on exhibits, demonstrations, and world-class visiting exhibits. Experience the Kramer IMAX Theatre.

Saskatchewan Centre of the Arts, Lakeshore Drive in Wascana Centre, (306) 565–4500. This modern facility is the home of the Regina Symphony Orchestra. Other groups also present performances here—ballet, opera, top star talent, and so on.

Diefenbaker Homestead, Wascana Centre, west of Broad Street, on Lakeshore Drive, (306) 522–3661. This landmark was the boyhood home of the late prime minister John G. Diefenbaker. The house was moved from Borden to Regina in 1967. The three rooms contain items given by the Diefenbaker family, and many donated by other pioneer families from Saskatchewan. Open daily, 10:00 A.M.–7:00 P.M., May through September.

Royal Saskatchewan Museum, in Wascana Centre on the corner of College Avenue and Albert Street, (306) 787–2815. Open throughout the year. Free. The First Nations Gallery traces 10,000 years of aboriginal culture. The Earth Sciences Gallery depicts two billion years of geological evolution. A must-see attraction.

Regina Plains Museum, 1801 Scarth Street, fourth floor of the historic Old Post Office downtown, (306) 780–9435. Admission is charged. Here are displays on the history of the Indians, Métis, and pioneers who lived in the Regina area. There are pioneer artifacts and period rooms, including a sod hut, schoolroom, kitchen, and parlor.

Government House, Dewdney Avenue at Connaught Street, west of Lewvan Drive, (306) 787–5726. Open throughout the year. Free. This was the official residence of Saskatchewan's lieutenant governors from 1891 to 1945. You are allowed to tour the rooms, whose period furnishings are elegant.

Saskatchewan Archives, 3303 Hillsdale near Saskatchewan Center of the Arts, (306) 787–4068. Open Monday through Friday. Free. Open to those seeking historical and genealogical information.

Saskatchewan Sports Hall of Fame & Museum, 2205 Victoria Avenue, (306) 780–9232. Dedicated to preserving the history of sports in the province. Displays include portraits and citations of inductees, memorabilia, and artifacts.

Art Galleries

Given its size and distance from art centers like Montréal, Toronto, and New York, Regina has a large number of galleries that feature outstanding art and craft works by artists from the province as well as other areas of Canada and the world. Many of these works are for sale—perfect souvenirs that tend to appreciate in value with time.

MacKenzie Art Gallery, 3475 Albert Street, southwest corner of Wascana Centre, (306) 522–4242. Open year–round. Excellent collection of historical and contemporary works by Canadian, American, and international artists. Gallery shop, cafeteria, 175-seat theater that stages *The Trial of Louis Riel* during the month of August.

Rosemont Art Gallery, Neil Balkwill Civic Arts Centre, 2420 Elphinstone Street, (306) 522–5940. This small museum houses contemporary works by some of the province's finest painters, sculptors, and new-media artists.

Accommodations
Top Hotels

Hotel Saskatchewan Radisson Plaza, 2125 Victoria Avenue, (306) 522–7691; (800) 667–5828. After a $20 million renovation, this classic hotel has been restored to its original Georgian character. All 215 rooms, 26 suites, and amenity rooms and parlors are as fresh as when the hotel was first constructed in 1927. Expensive.

Delta Regina, 1818 Victoria Avenue, (306) 569–1666; (800) 665–1666. The Delta Regina, one of Regina's top hotels, has a beautiful lobby, nice rooms, fine restaurants, and many amenities, plus a swimming pool and whirlpool. Moderate to expensive.

Regina Inn, 1975 Victoria Avenue, (306) 525–6767; (800) 667–8162. A good-value hotel, offering fine accommodations, dining, and a health club. Its restaurants and lounges include the Courtyard, Reflections, Splendidos, and Lauderdale's. Moderate to expensive.

Ramada Plaza Hotel, 19191 Saskatchewan Drive, (306) 535–5255; (800) 667–0400. A deluxe hotel located near the Convention Centre and downtown attractions. Excellent accommodations, restaurants, lounges, nightclub, three-story water slide, swimming pool, and other amenities. Moderate to expensive.

Regina Travelodge Hotel, 4177 Albert Street, (306) 586–3443; (800) 578–7878. Award-winning hotel, indoor waterslide, Oscar's Restaurant, Blarney Stone Irish Pub. Moderate.

Days Inn—Regina, 3875 Eastgate Drive East, (306) 522–3297; (800) DAYS–INN. Minutes from downtown and close to the RCMP training academy and museum. Color TV, dataports, nonsmoking rooms, indoor pool, and free continental breakfast. Moderate.

Country Inn & Suites, 3321 Eastgate Bay, (306) 789–9117; (800) 456–4000. Located at the east side of the city and easily accessible from Highway 1. Standard rooms or two-room suites are available. Complimentary continental breakfast, free movies, and videocassette players. Moderate.

Other Good Places to Stay

Chelton Inn, 1907 Eleventh Avenue, (306) 569–4600; (800) 667–9922. Moderate.

Imperial 400 Motel, 4255 Albert Street, (306) 584–8800. Moderate.

Comfort Inn, 3221 East Eastgate Bay, (306) 789–9964; (800) 228–5150. Moderate.

Travel Inn, 1735 Prince of Wales Drive, (306) 789–2223; (800) 465–2223. Moderate.

West Harvest Inn, 4025 Albert Street, (306) 586–6725. Moderate.

Seven Oaks Best Western, 777 Albert Street, (306) 757–0121; (800) 667–8063. Moderate.

Turgeon International Hostel, 2310 McIntyre Street, (306) 791–8165. Inexpensive.

Bed-and-Breakfasts

Aunt Bea's Bed & Breakfast, 8302 Struthers Crescent, (306) 545–3937. A modern home in the West Hill Park district on the northwestern limits of the city. Private bedroom with bath and double bed. Adults only, nonsmoking. Inexpensive.

Creekside Terrace Bed & Breakfast, 2724 Angus Boulevard, www.creeksideterrace.sk.ca. Charming home on the banks of Wascana Creek. Built with material originally intended for the Grand Trunk Hotel, Creekside is one of the homes on the city's Heritage Walking Tour. Moderate.

Creek Crossing Bed & Breakfast, 2738 Cameron Street, (306) 584–0900 or swiebe@cableregina.com. Situated in a tranquil cul-de-sac next to Wascana Creek. Organic, vegetarian breakfast is served; nonsmoking. Inexpensive to moderate.

Dining

Diplomat House, 2032 Broad Street, (306) 359–3366. Elegant restaurant with steak at its best. Expensive.

Memories, 1711 Victoria Avenue, next to the Howard Johnson's, (306) 522–1999. Continental cuisine. Expensive.

Victoria's Regina Inn, Victoria Avenue and Broad Street, (306) 525–6767. Good food from an extensive menu; good service, ambience, and entertainment. Expensive.

Neo Japonica Japanese Restaurant, 2176 Hamilton Street, (306) 359–7669. Convenient downtown location; offers irresistible tempura, sushi, teriyaki, and sukiyaki. Moderate to expensive.

Alfredo's Fresh Pasta, Old City Hall, Scarth Street Mall, (306) 522–3366. Best of Italian cuisine. Contemporary dining in a relaxed heritage setting. Moderate.

Chimney Restaurant, 2710 Montague Street, (306) 584–7777. Dine around the fireplace in Regina's only log-cabin setting. Greek, ribs, and seafood. Moderate.

Park Place, next to the marina in Wascana Place, (306) 522–9999. Regina's only restaurant on the lake. Casual dining, picnic baskets, outdoor patio. Inexpensive.

Melrose Place, 4030 Albert Street, (306) 347–9999. Family restaurant, ribs, pizza, souvlaki, pasta, seafood. Inexpensive to moderate.

Bartleby's, 1920 Broad Street, (306) 565–0040. This "dining emporium and gathering place" is a veritable museum of western memorabilia. Big sandwiches and beef, especially prime rib. Reservations recommended. Moderate.

Brewsters, 1832 Victoria Avenue, (306) 761–1500. Saskatchewan's first brew pub sports copper kettles and shiny fermentation tanks as an integral part of its decor. Try one of the

A Taste of Saskatchewan:
Moose Jaw Snow Muffins

Winters in Moose Jaw can be long and hard, with the temperature dropping to –40° (Celsius *or* Fahrenheit). This is the time to stay indoors and bake. For this recipe you need only open your door about an inch, scoop up some fresh snow, and hurry back to the kitchen.

2 c flour
1 tbsp baking powder
½ c brown sugar
pinch of salt
¾ c milk
½ c orange juice
grated zest of ½ orange
3 tbsp melted butter
½ c raisins
1½ c dry snow or clean frost scraped from your freezer
    or substitute 2 eggs

Preheat the oven to 204°C/400°F. Sift the flour, baking powder, sugar, and salt into a bowl. Stir in the milk, orange juice, orange zest, and butter and mix well. Fold in the raisins and snow and pour into greased muffin tins. Bake for 15 to 20 minutes.

eleven in-house concoctions on tap. Pub snacks and full meals available. Inexpensive.

Bushwakker, 2206 Dewdney Avenue, (306) 359–7276. Another of the city's brew pubs, Bushwakker has developed a reputation for high-quality brews. Lively and fun atmosphere. Inexpensive.

"Joey's Only" Seafood Restaurant, 360 Albert Street North, (306) 775–3474. Fish-and-chips are the house specialty. Tuesday features an all-you-can-eat menu. Inexpensive.

Simply Delicious, 826 Victoria Street, (306) 352–4929. Everything is homemade in this unassuming, country-style cafe. Cinnamon buns, fresh pies, chicken noodle and vegetable soup. Inexpensive.

Entertainment

Call the following performing arts organizations for their schedules and ticket information (for information on current "hot" nightspots and meeting places, ask your hotel concierge or guest relations person for recommendations):

The Saskatchewan Centre of the Arts, Lakeshore Drive in Wascana Centre, (306) 565–4500, is the home of the Regina Symphony Orchestra, which plays in the 2,000-seat Centennial Theatre. Within this complex is Jubilee Theatre, used for recitals and dramatic productions.

The Globe Theatre, in Old City Hall, on Scarth Street, (306) 525–9553, is Regina's main stage for plays professionally produced.

Regina Little Theatre, 1077 Angus, (306) 352–5535.

Regina Summer Stage, 1077 Angus, (306) 522–9078.

Applause Feast and Folly Dinner Theatre, in the Regina Inn, (306) 525–6767.

Casino Regina, 1880 Saskatchewan Drive, (800) 555–3189 or www.casinoregina.com. Open seven days a week, 9:00 A.M. to 4:00 P.M. You must be nineteen years of age or older.

Shopping

Regina has major shopping centers. Downtown, visit the **Cornwall Centre,** which has a hundred stores, including two large department stores, Sears and Eaton's; the **Golden Mile Centre,** at Albert and Twenty-fifth; and the **Scarth Street Mall.** The **Galleria at Scotia Centre** has more than seventy stores and services. It is located at Hamilton and Eleventh. The city's two other large shopping centers, located on either end of Albert Street, are the **Northgate Mall** and **Southland Mall.**

Book and Brier Patch, 4065 Albert Street. The largest independently owned bookstore in Saskatchewan. The largest selection of books in Regina.

The **Children's Corner Bookstore,** 2335 Eleventh Avenue. Fun and educational books, toys, videos, games, and records for children.

Derek Olson Goldsmith, 2333 Albert Street. Custom-designed and handcrafted jewelry.

Professional Sports

The Saskatchewan Roughriders, a professional football team in the Canadian Football League, play at Taylor Field, (306) 525–2181.

The Regina Pats play amateur hockey at the Agridome in Exhibition Park, (306) 527–0688.

Standardbred and harness racing, at Queensbury Downs in Regina Exhibition Park, (306) 757–2674.

The Regina Cyclones play in the Prairie League of professional baseball, (306) 949–2255.

Recreation

Regina has many recreational opportunities for visitors—tennis, golf, swimming, jogging, horseback riding, water parks, and lots more. Your hotel concierge or guest relations person will be happy to offer suggestions and make arrangements for you.

Saskatoon: Hub City of Saskatchewan

Located in the heart of the Great Plains, Saskatoon, the City of Bridges, is a community with that rare combination of big-city amenities and small-town spirit. Established in the summer of 1883 by a group of settlers looking for Utopia, the name Saskatoon comes from the Cree Indian name *mis-sask-quah-toomina* for what we know today as saskatoon berries.

Originally a gathering place for settlers, the city is now an education center, a base for mining and manufacturing, a leader in agriculture biotechnology, and the home of the Canadian Light Source Synchroton Project.

Saskatoon enjoys more hours of sunshine than any other major Canadian city. It's easy to understand why there are so many golf courses (more per capita than any other city in Canada), parks, jogging trails, and natural areas to play.

A cultural oasis, the city has several live theater companies, a symphony, a jazz society, and museums.

How to Get to Saskatoon
By Car

Saskatoon is located south of the geographic center of the province, on trans-Canadian Yellowhead Highway 16. From Regina the city can best be reached by taking Highway 11 North; from Prince Albert, Highway 11 South.

By Bus

Greyhound provides bus service to and from Saskatoon and many other Western Canada destinations; Saskatoon Bus Depot, 50 Twenty-third Street East, (306) 933–8000.

By Plane

Air Canada, Canadian, Westjet, Transwest, and Royal Airlines provide service to Saskatoon. The Saskatoon Airport is located northeast of city center, via Circle Drive. Its terminal has full facilities, including rental cars.

The Western Aero Centre, (306) 652–9121, is a new facility for private, corporate, and business planes.

By Train

VIA Rail provides service to and from Saskatoon. Call (800) 561–8630 in Canada or (800) 561–3949 in the United States.

How to Get Around in Saskatoon

Saskatoon is located on the South Saskatchewan River. The main streets of city center are Spadina Crescent, Queen Street, First through Fifth Avenues, and Twentieth to Twenty-fifth Streets. Saskatoon Transit provides bus service throughout the city, and there are taxi services. For information on the city, call Tourism Saskatoon, (306) 242–1206.

Touring Services

Shearwater Boat Cruises/Day Tours, aboard the *Saskatoon Lady* along the South Saskatchewan River, (306) 549–2400. Tours depart from the Mendel Art Gallery Wharf.

Saskatoon Cycling Club Tours, (306) 244–7332. Start from Mendel Art Gallery.

Attractions

Mendel Art Gallery, 950 Spadina Crescent, (306) 975–7610. Open throughout the year. Free. The Mendel is one of Western Canada's most important public art galleries. It was given to Saskatoon by Frederick Mendel, a German immigrant who made his fortune from meatpacking. The permanent collection has works by Emily Carr, David Milne, Feininger, Utrillo, Chagall, and Pissarro. There are also significant traveling exhibitions throughout the year. The Mendel has a conservatory of rare plants and flowers as well as a gift shop.

Little Stone School House, on the University of Saskatchewan campus, (306) 966–8382. Free. This is Saskatoon's first school and the city's oldest public building. It was called the Old Victoria School.

Musée Ukraina Museum, 202 Avenue M South, (306) 244–4212. Open throughout the year. Donations are accepted. A superior collection of Ukrainian artifacts and arts and crafts.

Wanuskewin Heritage Park, 5 km/3 mi north of Saskatoon, just off Highway 11, (306) 931–6767 or www.wasnuskewin.com. This National Historic Site, open year-round, interprets 6,000 years of history. There are nineteen archaeological sites in a serene valley, many twice as old as King Tut's tomb. The center offers cultural demonstrations, overnight tepee programs, art exhibits, an amphitheater, and restaurants. Yes, you can even try a bison burger at the restaurant. Most impressive is the visual re-creation of a bison hunt.

Gordon Snelgrove Art Gallery, in the Murray Memorial Building at the university, (306) 966–4208. Features work by students and faculty from the art department and local artists. Open weekdays, 9:00 A.M. to 4:30 P.M.

Kenderdine Gallery, in the Agriculture Building at the university, (306) 966–6816. Exhibits historical and contemporary art from the university's permanent collection. Open weekdays, 11:30 A.M. to 4:30 P.M.

Saskatoon Western Development Museum, 2610 Lorne Avenue South, on the Exhibition Grounds, (306) 931–1910. Open throughout the year. Within this museum is a re-creation of a street, circa 1910, containing an early bank, stores, Chinese laundry, church, school, hotel, railroad station, pool hall, and theater. Walking down this street you really feel as if you're in boomtown Saskatchewan. There's also a gallery of Saskatchewan arts and crafts and a gift shop.

St. Thomas More Art Gallery, on the University of Saskatchewan campus, (306) 966–8953. Open from mid-September to mid-April. Free. Exhibitions of paintings by provincial and regional artists. Be sure to see the stunning Kurelek mural in the St. Thomas More Chapel. The late William Kurelek was one of Canada's most distinguished contemporary artists. His paintings of ordinary life were highly realistic and also highly mystical in a religious sense.

The Diefenbaker Canada Centre, on the campus of the University of Saskatchewan, (306) 966–8384. Open throughout the year. Free. Diefenbaker museum and archives. Dief's grave is next to the building.

Ukrainian Museum of Canada, 910 Spadina Crescent East, (306) 244–3800 or www.saskstar.sk.ca/umc. Open year-round; admission is charged. Displays on Ukrainian culture in Canada, decorative textiles, and immigration history. The gift shop features reasonably priced Ukrainian cookbooks, Easter eggs, art, and handicrafts.

Saskatchewan Railway Historical Museum, 4 km/2.5 mi southwest of Saskatoon via Highways 7 and 60 en route to Pike Lake Provincial Park, (306) 382–9855. Open from May through September. Saskatchewan's railway history is displayed over 2.5 ha/ 6 acres with a diesel engine, streetcar, cabooses, restored railway buildings, and other artifacts. You'll also find an interpretive center, gift shop, and motor-car and model-train rides.

Accommodations
Top Hotels

Delta Bessborough, 601 Spadina Crescent East, (306) 244–5521; (800) 268–1133. This "castle" on the South Saskatchewan River has graced Saskatoon's skyline for decades. Originally built in 1929 and completely renovated in 1990, this remains *the* place to stay in the city. If you have a special occasion to celebrate, book the suite with its own Jacuzzi. The hotel has a comprehensive fitness center, indoor pool, and two restaurants: the Garden Bistro and Samurai, a Japanese steak house. Expensive.

Sheraton Cavalier, 612 Spadina Crescent East, (306) 652–6770; (800) 325–3535. This Sheraton has a wonderful complex of swimming pools, water slides, hot tubs, and other recreational facilities. It offers excellent accommodations and fine dining. Moderate to expensive.

Radisson Hotel, 405 Twentieth Street East, (306) 665–3322; (800) 333–3333. This bright, modern hotel offers excellent accommodations and services. It has a swimming pool with a great water slide, a restaurant, and a health club. Moderate to expensive.

Ramada Hotel, 90 Twenty-second Street, (306) 244–2311; (800) RAMADA. This hotel, located downtown, across from the Centennial Auditorium, has a special executive section called the Commonwealth Club. Its top restaurant is R. J. Willoughby's; you'll also find a swimming pool and other facilities. Moderate to expensive.

Sandman Hotel Saskatoon, 310 Circle Drive West, (306) 477–4844; (800) 726–3626; www.sandman.ca. New hotel with exercise facilities, efficiency rooms with fridge and microwave, plus a Denny's restaurant on site. Moderate.

Hotel Senator, 243 Twenty-first Street East, (306) 244–6141. Victorian settings and personalized service. Coffee shop and hair salon on site. Inexpensive.

Other Good Places to Stay

Best Western Inn, 1715 Idylwyld Drive North, (306) 244–5552; (800) 528–1234. Moderate.

Country Inn & Suites, 617 Cynthia Street, (306) 934–3900. Moderate.

Imperial 400 Motel, 610 Idylwyld Drive North, (306) 244–2901. Moderate.

ParkTown Hotel, 924 Spadina Crescent East, (306) 244–5564; (800) 667–3999. Moderate.

Saskatoon Inn, corner of Circle Drive and Airport Drive, (306) 242–1440; (800) 667–8789. Moderate to expensive.

Travelodge Hotel, 106 Circle Drive West, (306) 242–8881; (800) 578–7878. Moderate.

Heritage Inn, 102 Cardinal Crescent (Airport Drive and Circle Drive), (306) 665–8121; (888) 888–4374; www.heritageinn.com.

Campgrounds

Gordon Howe Campsite, Avenue P South, (306) 975–3328 or www.city.saskatoon.sk.ca. There are 135 serviced sites here, some pull-through, along with free showers, laundry facilities, play areas, and barbecues. Open April through September.

Saskatoon 16 West R.V. Park, 1.6 km/1 mi northwest of Saskatoon on Highway 16, (306) 931–8905; (800) 478–7833. You'll find 100 serviced sites, 70 pull-through sites, full hookups, free showers, propane, a playground, barbecues, and trout fishing. Open April through October.

Parkland Campground, 3.2 km/2 mi south on Highway 11, (306) 373–6806. Look for 90 serviced pull-through sites, a heated outdoor pool, laundry, showers, and a children's playground.

Dining

The Granary, 2806 Eighth Street East, (306) 373–6655. Prime rib is the house specialty, and the setting is prairie memorabilia. Expensive.

Jamieson Street Restaurant, #3 305 Idylwyld Drive North, (306) 664–9555. Fine dining in a Victorian atmosphere. Located in the historic CPR station. Moderate to expensive.

Samurai Japanese Steak House, at the Delta Bessborough, (306) 244–5521. Here you can feast on hibachi steak or scallops—a shogun special that includes steak, chicken, and lobster—or a vegetarian platter of onions, green peppers, Japanese mushrooms, and other vegetables. Moderate.

Saskatoon Station Place, Idylwyld Drive and Twenty-third Street, (306) 244–7777. Located in an old railroad station, this is Saskatoon's most colorful restaurant. It features an extensive menu of goodies: ribs, shrimp, stuffed mushrooms, Greek salad, French onion soup, pork chops, lobster tails, halibut steak, stuffed sole, omelets, burgers, pasta, souvlaki, prime roast rib of beef, steaks, lamb, and more. Moderate.

Cheers Brew Pub, 2105 Eighth Street East, (306) 955–7500. An in-house brewery featuring southern Cajun specialties, Italian food, and smoked prime rib. Moderate.

Boomtown Cafe, Western Development Museum, 2610 Lorne Avenue South, (306) 931–1910. Home-cooked specialties that include saskatoon-berry baking—all in a 1910 setting. Inexpensive.

St. Tropez Bistro, 243 Third Avenue, (306) 652–1250. A touch of Europe here, featuring homemade soups, bakery, pasta, and salads; specials every day. Very popular place in town. Inexpensive.

Blue Diamonds, 1428 Twenty-second Street West, (306) 652–6464. A tasty place for ribs, pizza, scampi, steaks, barbecued chicken. Inexpensive.

Taverna, 219 Twenty-first Street East, (306) 652–6366. Located in the heart of downtown and serving huge portions of Italian goodies—pasta, meats, and seafood. Inexpensive to moderate.

Berry Barn Eatery and Gift Shop, 830 Valley Road, (306) 384–6964 or www.sk.sympatico.ca/derdge. Saskatoon-berry preserves, chocolates, candles, unique gift items, and an eatery tucked inside a traditional prairie barn. Inexpensive.

Elephant & Castle, Midtown Plaza, (306) 652–5535. Part of a chain, but the shepherd's pie and fish-and-chips are worth a visit. A good selection of brews rounds out the menu. Moderate.

The Keg, 301 Ontario Avenue North, (306) 653–3633. The steaks, prime rib, and salad bar are always dependable. Moderate to expensive.

Entertainment

For suggestions on the currently popular nightspots, dramatic offerings, and music events, ask your hotel concierge or guest relations person for recommendations.

Saskatoon Centennial Auditorium, 35 Twenty-second Street East, (306) 975–7777. A major venue for the city's performing arts groups and for visiting talent. Box office is 938–7800.

Saskatoon Symphony, Centennial Auditorium, (306) 665–6414 or www.saskatoonsymphony.org. The season runs from September through May; the classics, pops, and family concerts.

Saskatoon Jazz Society, downstairs at 245 Third Avenue South, (306) 682–2277 or jazzsociety@sk.sympatico.ca. The society operates the Basement, a licensed jazz club with live jazz on weekends.

Persephone Theatre, 2802 Rusholme Road, (306) 384–7727. Live professional theater showcasing classical and contemporary dramas, musicals, and comedies.

25th Street Theatre, St. John's Cathedral Hall, (306) 664–2239 or www.interspin.com/25thstreet. Professional theater company devoted to the development and production of original Canadian works.

Off Broadway Dinner Theatre, 639 Main Street, (306) 653–2145. Full buffet dinner and full-length feature comedy plays in a cozy atmosphere. Nonsmoking; fully licensed.

Shakespeare on the Saskatchewan Festival, June to mid-August, on the banks of the South Saskatchewan River downtown, (306) 652–9100 or www.zu.com/shakespeare. This award-winning festival has earned acclaim for its innovative interpretations in contemporary as well as traditional styles.

Shopping

Midtown Plaza, located in city center at First Avenue and between Twentieth and Twenty-second Streets, has many shops and services. The Bay is nearby on Twenty-second and First.

Other shopping centers include the Confederation Mall, Grosvenor Park Centre, the Mall at Lawson Heights, Market Mall, and the Scotia Centre.

The Trading Post, 226 Second Avenue South (306) 653–1769. Unique Canadian crafts, including Inuit carvings and Indian jewelry.

Homespun Craft Emporium, 250A Second Avenue South, (306) 652–3585. Quilts, quilting supplies.

Antique Cellar, 38 Twenty-third Street, (306) 244–0488. More than 335 sq m/3,600 sq ft of quality antique glass, china, and collectibles from throughout Canada.

The Antique Mall, 126 Twentieth Street West, (306) 653–5595 or www.antiqueviking.com. Saskatoon's largest antiques mall and consignment store.

Bronco's Western Outfitters, 305 Confederation Drive, (306) 382–2744. You'll fit right into the western landscape after a shopping expedition here. Hats, boots, shirts, and accessories.

Meewasin Valley Centre Gift Shop, 402 Third Avenue South, (306) 665–6888 or www.lights.com/meewasin. Unique items relating to Saskatoon's history and the environment.

Sports and Recreation

Consult with your hotel concierge or guest relations person about recreational opportunities in the city—golf, tennis, jogging, family and water parks, and so forth.

Golf

Saskatoon has more golf courses per capita than any other city in Canada. Here's a sample of what you will find:

Elk Ridge Golf, Waskesiu Lake, (306) 663–4653 or www.golfcanada.com. An eighteen-hole championship golf course, bent-grass tees, greens and driving range, restaurant, lounge, and pro shop.

Greenbryre Country Club, (306) 373–7600. An eighteen-hole regulation (par-70) course in a rolling, well-treed natural setting. Driving range, two putting greens, power carts, equipment rentals, and pro shop.

The Willows Golf and Country Club, 382 Cartwright Street, (306) 965–4653 or www.willowsgolf.com. A world-class thirty-six-hole public golf course offering challenge to both novice and accomplished golfers.

Hockey

Junior hockey at Saskatchewan Place, (306) 975–3155.

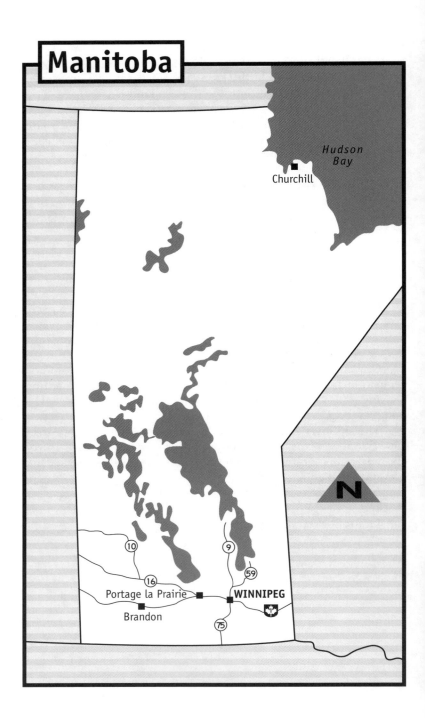

Manitoba

Hudson Bay

Churchill

N

10

9

59

16

Portage la Prairie

WINNIPEG

Brandon

75

CHAPTER 9

Touring Manitoba

Winnipeg · Churchill on Hudson Bay

Manitoba in Brief

When you look at the map of Canada—that line of huge provinces from the Atlantic to the Pacific—you'll see that Manitoba is smack in the middle. It is like a keystone that cements the different blocks of an arch into a strong, symmetrical whole. The province is considered the gateway to Western Canada when traveling from the East. Here is where Western Canada began for settlers, entrepreneurs, and developers from Ontario, Québec, and Atlantic Canada and for the thousands of immigrants seeking a new life in the New World.

Manitoba is a very large province—403,772 sq km/250,946 sq mi—and the only one in Western Canada (excluding Nunavut) that has extensive shoreline on Hudson Bay. In the province you can travel from southern wheat fields to northern wilderness areas where polar bears roam in large numbers. Manitoba has the largest lake—Lake Winnipeg—within its interior of any province in Canada. (The Great Lakes are not within the interior of any province but share shoreline and territorial waters with various American states.) Specifically, Manitoba has both the Hudson Bay and the province of Ontario at its eastern border; the states of Minnesota and North Dakota on its southern edge (the forty-ninth parallel, the straight-line international border between Canada and the United States); Saskatchewan on its western border; and Nunavut to the north.

In the southern portion of the province, where most of the one

Travel Manitoba

Travel Manitoba, the provincial government's tourism agency, provides this toll-free number for your use: (800) 665–0040, ext. SD1 (operative throughout the continental United States and Canada). Or you can write to Travel Manitoba, Dept. SD1, Seventh Floor, 155 Carlton Street, Winnipeg, Manitoba R3C 3H8; or visit www.travelmanitoba.com.

Travel Manitoba will provide free maps, brochures, and personal counseling on how you and your party can get the most out of your travels and vacation time in the province. Travel Manitoba has information centers at the following locations, open mid-May through early September:

Manitoba–U.S. border, at Highways 75 and 10.

Manitoba–Ontario boundary, at Trans-Canada Highway 1.

Manitoba–Saskatchewan boundary, at Trans-Canada Highway 1.

Manitoba–Saskatchewan boundary at Highway 16.

Downtown Winnipeg at the Explore Manitoba Centre at The Forks and the Manitoba–U.S. border at Highway 75 are open year-round.

Many local communities also maintain their own tourism information bureaus.

million Manitobans live, the climate is similar to that of the other prairie provinces—cold, invigorating winters and warm, pleasant summers. The climate in the south is so congenial, in fact, that agriculture flourishes: Wheat and other grains, vegetables, and fruits grow here. In the south, where Winnipeg, the province's capital, is situated, spring tends to come sooner than in other places. Topographically, Manitoba is a relatively flat landmass, patterned over by many lakes and rivers. The land in the south has been extensively developed for agriculture; in the midsection it is thick with forests; and in the north it is subarctic with boreal forests and tundra. The climate in the north during summer, particularly near Hudson Bay, tends to be cooler than northern sections of Alberta and Saskatchewan, but it is a very attractive area to those interested in experiencing the ecology created by this climatic zone.

Humans have inhabited Manitoba for thousands of years. The first Europeans to arrive and put down stakes were the fur trappers and traders of the Hudson's Bay Company, which established a post and fort at York Factory in 1682. Furs brought into York Factory from countless inland points of origin were placed on ships that sailed up Hudson Bay, through Hudson Strait, into the Atlantic, and on to markets in England (during summer months Churchill had a direct link with Liverpool, England, 4,698 km/ 2,936 mi away).

For close to 200 years, Manitoba, known as Rupert's Land (an appellation given to most of Western Canada in honor of Prince Rupert, one of the founders of the Hudson's Bay Company), was virtually a "factory" that produced furs for English merchants and European fashions. In 1812, however, the first Selkirk settlers, under the leadership of Thomas Douglas, fifth earl of Selkirk, arrived and, along with fur trading, began a serious effort at expanding agriculture, transforming the rich potential of the grass prairies. With burgeoning agriculture, stable communities were built and grew as more people, seeing potential for themselves in Manitoba, arrived and settled. Lord Selkirk formed a habitation of new hope called the Red River Settlement, composed mainly of dispossessed Scottish sharecropping farmers. Rupert's Land was sold by the Hudson's Bay Company to Canada in 1870, and in 1871 the first legislature of Manitoba met, consisting of twelve English-Canadian and twelve French-Canadian members. A year earlier, in 1870, Manitoba actually became the fifth province in the Canadian Confederation as a result of the Manitoba Act, which received assent from Queen Victoria.

Although the majority of Manitobans are of British extraction (Scots, English, Irish, Welsh), there are also sizable French, German, Polish, Icelandic, and Ukrainian groups. The Mennonites, a German-speaking religious sect, are another large group.

Many of the early French fur trappers and a smaller number of Scottish trappers married Native women. Their progeny became the Métis, who formed a colony at Red River, from which Louis Riel and his people launched a rebellion in 1869 and 1870 when the land was transferred from Hudson's Bay Company to the Canadian government. Métis settlements were in the Red River Valley, in and around Winnipeg, and the Métis influence continues to be strong in a number of communities in southern and central Manitoba.

Today Manitoba's economy is based on agriculture, mining (nickel and precious metals), hydroelectric energy, forestry, food

Special Events

International Music Camp and Athletic Camp, Peace Gardens, all summer

Festival du Voyageur, St. Boniface, mid-February

Winnipeg International Airshow, Winnipeg, early June

Winnipeg International Children's Festival, Winnipeg, June

Manitoba Summer Fair, Brandon, mid-June

Red River Exhibition, Winnipeg, late June

La Fête de la Saint-Jean Baptiste, La Broquerie, late June

Trout Festival, Flin Flon, late June to July 1

Winnipeg Folk Festival, Winnipeg, early July

Highland Gathering, Selkirk, early July

Canadian Turtle Derby, Boissevain, mid-July, features international turtle-racing championships.

Manitoba Stampede and Exhibition, Morris, mid-July

Threshermen's Reunion and Stampede, Austin, late July

Sunflower Festival, Altona, late July

Northwest Round-Up, Swan River, late July

National Ukrainian Festival, Dauphin, first week in August; features stirring, beautiful, and wild Ukrainian dancing and singing; old-country food; and traditional arts and crafts. One of the most impressive moments in the festival is Obzhynky, the Ukrainian

processing, manufacturing, transportation, and tourism. Winnipeg, because of its central location, is a major transportation hub for all of Canada. The city is also well known throughout the world for its cultural life, particularly its Royal Winnipeg Ballet.

For the vacation traveler, Manitoba has it all: a sophisticated city, significant history, beautiful scenery, many attractions and recreational opportunities, adventure north to the polar bears and Hudson Bay, and friendly people who say "Welcome!" in many different languages.

harvest ritual in which an honored guest is presented with bread and salt, an ancient custom symbolizing warmth and hospitality. Another highlight is the enactment of a traditional four-phase Ukrainian wedding—the matchmaking, the engagement, the marriage, and the wedding feast—which in past times went on for several days.

Steinbach Pioneer Days, Steinbach, early August; celebrates the Mennonite heritage in Manitoba with traditional foods, arts and crafts, demonstrations of pioneer life, and entertainment.

Frog Follies, Canadian national frog-jumping championships, St. Pierre-Jolys, early August

Islendingadagurrin, the Icelandic Festival of Manitoba, Gimli, early August

Folklorama, Canada's cultural celebration, Winnipeg, two weeks in early August. International pavilions located throughout the city showcase cultural stories through food, art, and performance. For fourteen evenings you can sit down to opulent feasts, wander through displays of folklore, or watch artisans whose carefully honed skills are family legacies.

Opasqwayak Indian Days, The Pas, late August

Oktoberfest, Winnipeg, early to mid-September

Manitoba Fall Fair, Brandon, early November

Touring Services

The following is a partial listing of companies that provide tours to the major attractions in Manitoba. For a complete listing contact Travel Manitoba and ask for the *Manitoba Explorer's Guide*.

Churchill Wilderness Encounter, (204) 675–2248; bchartier@compuserve.com. Birding, beluga whale, history, and natural history tours from June through November in Churchill.

Great Canadian Travel Company, (204) 949–0199; sales@gtc-mst.com. Sight-seeing tour packages customized for groups and individuals.

North Star Tours, (204) 675–2629; nortours@cancom.net. Trips to Churchill attractions and to Eskimo Point in Nunavut.

Riding Mountain Nature Tours, (204) 636–2968; mail@ churchillnaturetours.com. Hiking, trail riding, mountain biking, bird-watching, and wildlife safaris in Riding Mountain National Park.

Fehr-Way Tours, (204) 989–7011. Escorted motor-coach tours of Manitoba.

Frontiers North, (204) 949–2050; info@frontiersnorth.com. Specializing in Arctic tundra, polar bear, and beluga whale destinations.

Sea North Tours, (204) 675–2195; seanorth@cancom.net. Boat trips to Fort Prince of Wales on Hudson Bay and beluga-whale-watching.

Tundra Buggy Tours, (204) 949–4790; info@tundra-buggy-tours.com. Guided polar bear, bird, and naturalist tours all aboard the tundra buggy.

Paddlewheel River Rouge Tours, (204) 942–4500; paddle wh@escape.ca.

Aurora Canada Tours, (204) 942–8104. Specializing in northern lights and birding packages.

Riding Mountain Guest Ranch, (204) 848–2265. Ecotourism, wildlife photo safaris, and horseback riding and nature tours.

Useful Information

Emergencies: Throughout the province, dial 911
Time zone: Central
Area code: 204

Winnipeg:
Where Western Canada Begins

Winnipeg, located where the Assiniboine and Red Rivers converge, is almost the center of the continent—both north–south and east–west. Ever since the mid-1800s Winnipeg has been known as the Gateway City to Western Canada, much in the same manner as St. Louis, Missouri, and the American West.

La Vérendrye, the French explorer and entrepreneur, set up a trading post called Fort Rouge here at The Forks in 1738. Thomas Douglas, fifth earl of Selkirk, a Scot with big ideas for his beleaguered Highlanders, created the Red River Settlement in 1812. St.-Boniface, one of the French settlements in this area, is now a part of greater Winnipeg and considered the largest center of French culture in Western Canada. In 1816 the Seven Oaks Massacre took the lives of twenty pioneers in the Red River Settlement. Under Lord Selkirk's leadership, the colony again took hold, expanded, and became prosperous. The Red River (along with trails using the famous Red River carts, made distinctive by their two huge wheels) became the main highway of commerce between Winnipeg and St. Paul, Minnesota. Today Winnipeg and St. Paul share a sisterly relationship based on a common pioneering heritage.

In 1873 Winnipeg was incorporated as a city. Its growth boomed when the transcontinental railroad came in 1881, making Winnipeg the distribution center for almost all of Western Canada. (It still plays that role for the heartland of the country. If you take a VIA Rail trip across Canada—one of the great rail adventures of the world—Winnipeg will be the midpoint in your journey.)

The city became the grain-market center for the prairies with the establishment of the Winnipeg Grain Exchange in 1887. What oil is to Calgary and cod is to St. John's, grain is to Winnipeg; it's the main commodity of economic prosperity for thousands of people.

In 1919 the city went through the Winnipeg General Strike, a huge historical watershed for the Labour movement in Canada. Most of the strikers and first to strike were women telephone operators. The strike divided the city along social, economic, and geographic lines. Then, just as the wounds from the strike were being healed, Winnipeg became one of the many North American casualties of the Great Depression of the 1930s. The supply and human resource demands of World War II helped boost Winnipeg's economy, and it has been on an upswing ever since because of the optimism, hard work, and intelligence of its citizens.

In the sphere of international culture, most people outside Canada may never have heard of Manitoba, but they surely know of the Royal Winnipeg Ballet, one of the foremost classical dance companies in the world. In addition to dance, there's excellence in visual arts and in dramatic art.

Although the first people of Winnipeg were aboriginal peoples, French, Scots, Irish, and English, succeeding waves of immigrants seeking their fortune were Germans, Ukrainians, Poles,

Dutch, Italians, Scandinavians, Hungarians, Jews, and Asians. As a result, Winnipeg, although English on the surface, is a merging of many nationalities into one people working together for the common good, yet distinct within their own noble heritages.

Today Winnipeg is a modern city that has been able to blend its historical heritage nicely with gleaming skyscrapers. Its population now numbers 667,209 people, who are employed in various industries and services: manufacturing, tourism, food processing, transportation, aerospace, electronics, government, medicine, and education. The standard of living is quite high here, with abundant cultural, educational, shopping, and recreational opportunities for residents and visitors.

In Winnipeg, art isn't contained within gallery walls; it's all over the city, thanks to the hundreds of murals that now cover the sides of buildings and bridges in character neighborhoods such as Selkirk Avenue, West Broadway, and Osborne Village. One of the major forces behind this continuing mural project is Take Pride Winnipeg, a nonprofit community beautification program.

When you arrive in Winnipeg, you are where Western Canada begins or ends. This is a significant geographical point, one also rich in human history, particularly as concerns the development of Canada as an independent nation-state. To stay a while in Winnipeg is not only to absorb this significance but also to enjoy the treasures of a cultural oasis in a vast prairie land.

How to Get to Winnipeg
By Car
Traveling from Calgary and Regina, continue on Trans-Canada Highway 1; from Edmonton and Saskatoon, stay on Yellowhead Highway 16. Traveling from Ontario and Eastern Canada, take the Trans-Canada to Winnipeg. Coming north from Minnesota and North Dakota, use I–29 to the border and then Manitoba Highway 75, which will take you straight into Winnipeg.

By Bus
Greyhound provides bus service throughout much of Western Canada. The terminal is located at 487 Portage Avenue; (204) 775–8857 or (800) 661–8747.

By Plane
Winnipeg International Airport is located a few miles west of Winnipeg city center. The terminal has full facilities: restaurant,

lounge, gift and duty-free shops, and so on. Rental-car booths are also here. The following major airlines serve Winnipeg: Air Canada, Canadian Airlines, American Airlines, and Northwest, plus several regional carriers.

By Train
VIA Rail provides train service to and from Winnipeg. The terminal is located on Main Street near the Upper Fort Garry Gate. Call (800) 561–8630 for the toll-free VIA Rail number serving your area code. In Winnipeg call (204) 944–8780 for schedule information and for fares and reservations.

How to Get Around in Winnipeg
Winnipeg is a very easy city to get around in. To the south of city center is the Assiniboine River, and to the east are the Red River and the French-speaking community of St.-Boniface. Portage Avenue and Main Street are among the primary streets. The provincial Legislative Building is located at Osborne and Broadway. If you require additional information regarding your stay in the city, call Tourism Winnipeg at (204) 943–1970 or (800) 665–0204; visit www.tourism.winnipeg.mb.ca; or visit its facilities at 279 Portage Avenue or at the airport.

Winnipeg Transit operates bus service throughout most of the city; call (204) 986–5700 for information.

The following companies provide taxi service: Duffy's, (204) 775–0101; Yellow, (204) 942–7555; Preston Limousine, (204) 633–6715; Grosvenor, (204) 947–6611; and Unicity, (204) 947–6611.

Attractions
The Forks, located at the junction of the Red and Assiniboine Rivers, (204) 98–FORKS (983–6757); www.forksnhs_info@ pch.gc.ca. This historic site has been a meeting place for more than 6,000 years and has witnessed many of the key events in the history of the Canadian West. Aboriginal peoples, fur-trading rivals, settlers, merchants, railway and riverboat workers, politicians, province makers, and immigrants have all come to this special place.

The rivers were shipping routes for furs, trade goods, and pemmican. Two rival fur-trading companies, the Hudson's Bay Company and the North West Company, both built forts here. This settlement thrived as the Red River Settlement and gradually evolved into the city of Winnipeg, the Chicago of the North.

A six-story glass tower and observation deck stand sentinel over The Forks, Winnipeg's most popular tourist attraction. The $20 million complex includes shops and restaurants built from eighty-year-old railway stalls.

Today The Forks combines unique restaurants and shops with a riverside promenade, landscaped prairie gardens, a theater, an adventure playground, and a Parks Canada kiosk with comprehensive travel information.

Manitoba Museum of Man and Nature, opposite city hall, north of Portage and Main, (204) 956–1360 or www.manitoba-museum.mb.ca, encompasses seven interpretive galleries exploring the history and environment of Manitoba from the Arctic coast to the southern grasslands. The museum, the Planetarium and Science Centre, and the Centennial Concert Hall are all located in the Centennial Centre.

The Exchange District, a several-block area in city center. This visually and architecturally rich district has a fine collection of turn-of-the-twentieth-century commercial buildings that have been preserved and restored: Massey-Harris Building (1885), Bate Building (1883), Traveller's Block (1907), Imperial Dry Goods Block (1899), Confederation Life Building (1912), Pantages Playhouse Theatre (1913), J. H. Ashdown Warehouse (1895), Donald H. Bain Building (1899), Telegram Building (1882), and Canadian Imperial Bank of Commerce (1910). Also in this historic district are many fine shops, restaurants, clubs, and theaters.

Also in this area are the Centennial Concert Hall, Warehouse Theatre, Manitoba Theatre Centre, and Pantages Playhouse Theatre. Guided walking tours of the district start from the information booth in Market Square.

Chinatown in the area of King and Princess Streets may not bustle like a neighborhood in Hong Kong, but this picturesque postage-stamp district supports a sizable residential and commercial Asian community with restaurants, grocery stores, and import shops. Thanks to a redevelopment initiative, Chinese gardens and an ornate gate now markedly define this district.

Fort Whyte Centre, 1961 McCreary Road, (204) 989–8355 or www.fortwhyte.org. Explore 81 ha/200 acres of forest, lakes, and self-guiding trails with floating boardwalks that wind through marshland. You'll encounter white-tailed deer, myriad songbirds, and twenty-three species of ducks and geese. The 930-sq-m/ 10,000-sq-ft interpretive center features the Torch Museum and

the Aquarium of the Prairies. In winter you can rent snowshoes or bring your own skates, toboggan, or ice-fishing gear.

Aquatic Hall of Fame, Pan-Am Pool Building, 25 Poseidon Road, (204) 284–4031. Open throughout the year. Free. This hall of fame honors Canadians who have distinguished themselves in aquatic sports.

Legislative Building, at Broadway and Osborne; call (204) 945–5813 to arrange a guided tour. Open daily. Free. The architect of Manitoba's Legislative Building was Frank Worthington Symington from Liverpool, England. Gracing the dome of the building is a 73-m/240-ft-high heroic statue known as the *Golden Boy,* who holds a sheaf of wheat; it's one of the best-known symbols of the prairie spirit in Manitoba. The building, constructed of Manitoba's Tyndall stone and Italian marble, is considered one of the finest examples of neoclassical architecture in Canada. It stands on the bank of the Assiniboine River. On the beautiful grounds surrounding the provincial capitol are statues of Queen Victoria, Louis Riel, and the great Ukrainian poet Taras Shevchenko. The mansion of the lieutenant governor is also on the grounds, and nearby is Memorial Park, a tranquil place during summer.

Riel House National Historic Site, 330 River Road, (204) 257–1783; forksnhs_info@pch.gc.ca. Open mid-May to the end of September. Free. Louis Riel, although tried and hanged for treason, is considered the father of the province of Manitoba (technically, from 1869 to 1870 he was known as the leader of the Provisional Government of Assiniboia and the North West). This house, which belonged to his family, has been restored and furnished to reflect the lives of the Riel and Lagimodiére families, who lived here in the late 1880s. Riel's grave can be found in the churchyard of St.-Boniface Basilica.

Oseredok (the Ukrainian Cultural and Educational Centre), 184 Alexander Avenue East, (204) 942–0218. Open Tuesday through Sunday. Free. This ethnic museum has a fine collection of Ukrainian folk costumes, embroidery, weaving, decorated Easter eggs *(pysanky),* wood carving, and ceramics; also coins, stamps, and documents from the Ukrainian National Republic of 1918–21. You'll also find a library of 40,000 volumes, an art gallery, and archives.

Centre Culturel Franco-Manitobain, 340 Boulevard Provencher, (204) 233–8972. Call for performance dates and prices. Home of these performing groups: Cercle Molière (Canada's oldest continual French theater company); Les Danseurs

Golden Boy

Towering above the city, sheaf of wheat and torch in hand, this statue is Winnipeg's most recognizable landmark. It was designed to top the new provincial Legislative Building, which was started in 1911. World War I almost halted the building's construction, and in France—where *Golden Boy* was sculpted by Georges Cardet—the foundry was bombed as Cardet prepared it for shipping. Luckily, both artist and statue escaped unscathed. In 1918 *Golden Boy* was finally lifted onto a French cargo ship bound for the United States. Before the ship could leave the harbor, it was commandeered for war purposes. The statue spent the remainder of the war on the ship as it crisscrossed the Atlantic. It finally arrived in Winnipeg a year after it had begun its journey.

Golden Boy, now covered in 23.5-k gold leaf, was equipped with a permanently lighted torch in 1967 to mark Canada's centennial and to commemorate Manitoba's entry into the confederation in 1870.

de la Rivière Rouge (folk-dance troupe); Le Cent Nons (young singers and musicians); and L'Alliance Chorale Manitoba, Les Blés au Vent, and Les Intrépides (choral groups).

Royal Canadian Mint, 520 Lagimodiére Boulevard, (204) 257–3359. Open May through September. Tours are offered, and you can see coins being produced for use as Canadian and foreign currency.

Assiniboine Park, Corydon Avenue West at Shaftsbury, (204) 888–3634. Open all year. Explore more than 153 ha/378 acres along the Assiniboine River. The zoo, English garden, Leo Moi Sculpture Garden, French formal garden, and a Tudor-style pavilion are a few of the features within the park. Picnic areas and cycling and walking trails are popular with visitors. In winter enjoy cross-country skiing, tobogganing, and skating on the duck pond.

Leo Moi Sculpture Garden, Assiniboine Park, (204) 986–6531. Visit the only garden in North America dedicated to the works of a single artist. Bronze sculptures, porcelains, paintings, and sketches by the celebrated local artist are on display. Open year-round.

Did You Know . . .

that Winnie the Pooh was named for Winnipeg? There's a statue commemorating Winnie the bear and her owner, Captain Harry Colebourne, at the Assiniboine Park Zoo.

Assiniboine Park Zoo, Assiniboine Park, (204) 986–6921. View exhibits displaying 1,200 animals of 275 different species, including native polar bears, cougars, elk, and bald eagles. There are also animals from around the world, such as the red panda, tigers, leopards and monkeys. Open daily, year-round.

Lyric Theatre, Assiniboine Park, (204) 885–5466. This outdoor theater showcases performances by the Winnipeg Symphony and Royal Winnipeg Ballet, as well as jazz, folk, and drama festivals. Bring a lawn chair and a picnic for a summer evening.

Dalnavert National Historic Site, 61 Carlton Street, (204) 043–2835 or www.mhs.mb.ca/museums/dalnavhp.htm. Explore a typical Victorian home with lovely stained-glass windows, rich wood paneling, and cherished objects from the 1890s. Once the home of Hugh John Macdonald, son of Sir John A. Macdonald, prime minister of Canada, Dalnavert is a prime example of Queen Anne Revival architecture and has been designated a National Historic Site. Open Tuesday through Thursday and Saturday and Sunday. Admission is charged.

The Tin Lizzie Car Barn, ten minutes west of Winnipeg on Highway 26, (204) 864–CARS. A two-level barn filled with vintage and classic cars, related memorabilia, a car buff's shop, candy shop, and diner. Operates year-round.

Western Canadian Aviation Museum, located in Hangar T2 at the airport, 958 Ferry Road, (204) 786–5503; www.wcam.mb.ca. Open throughout the year. Admission is charged. Here is an excellent collection of aircraft: Avro 504K, Vickers Vedette, Canada's first helicopter, Bellanca Aircruiser, Fokker Super Universal, North American Harvard, Vickers Viscount, DeHavilland Tiger Moth, and many others.

St.-Boniface Museum, 494 Tache Avenue, (204) 237–4500 or stbmus1@mb.sympatico.ca. The Grey Nuns Convent, Winnipeg's oldest building, houses the St.-Boniface Museum. Originally built for the Grey Nuns, who arrived at the Red River Settlement in

1844, this is an example of early Red River frame construction. The museum presents an impressive collection of artifacts that reveal the lives and culture of the Francophone and Métis populations of Manitoba. During the building's time it has also served as a hospital, girl's school, orphanage, and seniors' home.

Winnipeg Art Gallery, 300 Memorial Boulevard, (204) 786–6641; www.wag.mb.ca. Open daily throughout the year. Call for hours and fees. An excellent example of contemporary architecture and the pride of the city; the gallery has more than 20,000 works of art in its permanent collection, including the largest display of Inuit (Eskimo) sculpture in the world with 9,000 pieces. It also has a fine restaurant and a gift shop. The gallery was officially opened in 1971 by Princess Margaret.

University of Manitoba, off Pembina Highway on University Crescent; call the information center, (204) 474–8346. Visitors are welcome to tour the campus of the oldest university in Western Canada. Bookstores, lectures, and exhibitions are open to the public.

Manitoba Children's Museum, at The Forks, (204) 956–1888. Admission is charged. Canada's top children's museum, this facility allows children to create their own television broadcast, put on puppet shows, or make their own video images.

Spirit Island, at the junction of the Assiniboine and Red Rivers, (204) 925–2029. This center for learning, sharing, celebration, and respect is the product of a longtime dream of cultural understanding and community healing. Spirit Island hopes to be a meeting place for all people and a monument to First Nations, Métis, and Inuit cultures. The island features an amphitheater, rock and herbal gardens, a perpetual flame, a healing and mediation facility, a tepee village, and a Métis settlement.

Historic Churches

St.-Boniface Basilica, 190 avenue de la Cathedrale in St.-Boniface. The oldest Roman Catholic cathedral in Western Canada; the original structure was built in 1818. Here is one of the centers for French-Canadian life and culture in Western Canada. In the churchyard is the grave of Louis Riel, a hero of Western Canadian history.

St. James Church, Portage Avenue and Tylehurst Street. The oldest log church in Western Canada (1853).

St. John's Cathedral, 135 Anderson Avenue. The oldest Anglican church in Western Canada; the original church structure on this site was built in 1820.

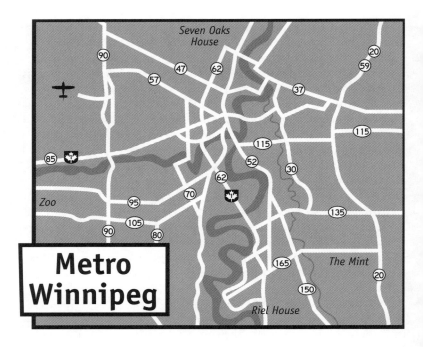

Metro Winnipeg

St. Nicholas Ukrainian Catholic Church, Main Street and St. John's Avenue. Byzantine architecture and interior decoration.

St. Paul's Anglican Church, Balderstone Road off Main Street. Built in 1825.

St. Vladimir and Olga Cathedral, 115 McGregor Street. Domed towers and an ornate interior are noteworthy aspects of this Ukrainian house of worship.

Ukrainian Greek Orthodox Cathedral, 1175 Main Street. Byzantine domes are a dominant shape on the city's skyline.

St. Andrews, via Highway 9 North to St. Andrews Road. The oldest continuously used Protestant church in Western Canada.

Kildonan Presbyterian Church, Black Avenue and Main Street. The first Presbyterian church in Western Canada, built in 1853, still stands.

Knox United Church, 400 Edmonton Street. An attractive church, built in 1917 of Manitoba stone.

Parks

Assiniboine Forest, Shaftsbury Boulevard and Chalfont Avenue. Trails give you access to view wildflowers, deer, and waterfowl.

Kildonan Park, 2021 Main Street, on the Red River. Contains some of the largest trees still standing in the province; also has a public swimming pool, an outdoor theater, and a restaurant.

Fun Mountain Waterslide Park, on Murdock Road, east of the city, via the Trans-Canada or the Perimeter Highway, (204) 255–3910. Admission is charged. Features several exciting water slides, an inner-tube slide, a giant hot tub holding 150 people, and much more. A fun place for a young family.

Winnipeg:
The Christmas Capital of Canada

Frosted with snowflakes and sparkling with lights, Winnipeg truly shines in the holiday season. If you've been yearning for an old-fashioned Christmas destination for the family, this is the place. Winnipeg guarantees you snow at Christmas! (It's one of only three Canadian cities that can make this claim.)

Start with a visit to Donner, Blitzen, and the rest of Santa's high-flying team at the Assiniboine Park Zoo. You'll find them standing antler to antler next to polar bears, Siberian tigers, and snow leopards. When the sun sets the zoo comes to life with Lights of the Wild: Animal sculptures, some more than 6m/20 ft high, are created in lights.

Take a step back in time to Christmas of the 1920s. The Manitoba Museum of Man and Nature transforms its "urban" gallery into a nostalgic experience with authentic decorations and costumes. Stroll the wooden sidewalks and peek into homes dressed in their holiday finest—glass beads, tinsel garlands, and tissue-paper honeycomb bells.

Join the throng of holiday revelers at The Forks to shop, have a meal, or glide down the river (or the rink) on your skates.

Ready to dash through the snow? Winnipeg has fourteen toboggan slide locations throughout the city, from Assiniboine Park to St. Vital, Omand Park, and Kildonan Park.

"Elves" in Winnipeg help Santa answer 85,000 letters addressed to the North Pole. The letters come from twenty-three different countries around the world and are answered in the language in which they are written.

Provincial Parks and Forests Near Winnipeg

The countryside surrounding Winnipeg is a delightful cornucopia of sandy beaches, hiking trails, lakes for fishing, and forests and open spaces for wildlife viewing—all under the Provincial Parks umbrella. For information and directions, call (800) 214–6497 or in Winnipeg, 945–6784; or visit www.gov.mb.ca/natres/parks.

Whiteshell Provincial Park, on the Manitoba–Ontario border, via Highways 312 and 44 off the Trans-Canada. Manitoba's first and largest provincial park features a number of hiking and natural history trails, camping facilities, and areas for canoeing, fishing (northern pike, perch, smallmouth bass, walleye, and trout), and hunting. At the Canada goose sanctuary in the park, during May and June, you can get close enough to see hundreds of goslings.

Agassiz Provincial Forest, on the north side of the Trans-Canada, east of Winnipeg. This is mainly a natural preserve, although there are areas where you can picnic.

Sandilands Provincial Forest, on the south side of the Trans-Canada, east of Winnipeg, directly opposite Agassiz Forest. Another forest preserve with picnic sites.

Spruce Woods Provincial Heritage Park and Forest, south of Carberry on the Trans-Canada, west of Winnipeg, has camping and hiking. Spirit Sands is a desertlike island surrounded by a cool stand of spruce trees. It also has lizards and cacti.

Birds Hill Provincial Park, northeast of Winnipeg via Highway 59. You'll find an aspen fitness trail, several natural history trails, a bike trail, camping facilities, horseback riding, and hiking.

Accommodations
Top Hotels

The Lombard, 2 Lombard Place, (204) 957–1350; (800) 441–1414; www.cp.ca. The Lombard is a faithful standby for business and leisure travelers. The only four-diamond hotel in the city, it features a pool, fitness center, whirlpool, and sauna. The Velvet Glove, the hotel's main dining room, is a quiet delight. Moderate to expensive.

Radisson, 288 Portage Avenue, (204) 956–0410; (800) 268–1133; www.radissonhotel.ca. Located in city center and connected by a walkway to the city's largest downtown shopping complex, this hotel offers excellent accommodations with many amenities, as well as dining, entertainment, and an indoor swimming pool with a sun deck and view of the city. Its Signature's Dining Room offers good food. Moderate.

Delta, 350 St. Mary Avenue, close to the convention center, (204) 942–0551; (800) 465–4329. Excellent guest rooms with all amenities; fine dining rooms (the Market Grill is superb) and lounges; indoor and outdoor pools; exercise facility; many other features. Expensive.

Sheraton Winnipeg, 161 Donald Street, (204) 942–5300; (800) 325–3535; www.sheraton.com. This newly renovated hotel offers attractively furnished guest rooms. In-room amenities include Starbuck's coffee, on-command video, and Nintendo. The hotel also has twenty-four-hour room service, a restaurant, and a sports bar. Expensive.

Hotel Fort Garry, 222 Broadway, (204) 942–8251; (800) 665–8088; www.fortgarryhotel.com. Located in the heart of downtown, minutes from The Forks, this national landmark hotel has all the usual amenities and a ghost (so they say). Moderate to expensive.

Charter House Hotel, 330 York Avenue, (204) 942–0101; (800) 782–0175. Located across from the Winnipeg Convention Centre, within walking distance of The Forks, museums, concert hall, and shopping. Moderate.

Place Louis Riel All Suite Hotel, 190 Smith Street, (204) 947–6961; (800) 665–0569; www.placelouisriel.com. Downtown Winnipeg's all-suite hotel has studio, one-bedroom, and two-bedroom accommodations. Kitchen facilities are available in all suites. Moderate to expensive.

Greenwood Inn, 1715 Wellington Avenue, (204) 775–9889; (888) 233–6730; www.greenwoodinn.ca. The newest full-service hotel in Winnipeg is mere minutes from the airport. All the comforts of home, including coffeemakers, fridges, hair dryers, dataports and high-speed Internet access, an indoor pool, a fitness facility, and a whirlpool tub. Moderate to expensive.

Canad Inn Fort Garry, 1824 Pembina Highway, (204) 261–7450; (888) 332–2623; www.canadinns.com. A few minutes from downtown, this reasonably priced hotel is a favorite with both families and business travelers. Maybe it's because of the indoor water slide. Moderate.

Bed-and-Breakfast and Country Farm Vacations

A cozy and peaceful approach to vacation travel is to get out of the city and relax in a bed-and-breakfast or country farmhouse.

Cowan's Castle, 39 Eastgate, (204) 786–4848 or www.cowanscastle@yahoo.com. This 1907 home on the Assiniboine River is only about a twenty-minute walk from The Forks, downtown, and the art gallery. The house includes a fireplace by Frank Lloyd Wright, antiques, and a screened sunporch. A full breakfast with homemade bread and jam is served. Moderate.

Villa in the Woods Bed & Breakfast, 6 Oakgrove Bay, (204) 897–1177; (897) 897–1177. January through October only. An elegant and comfortable bungalow in a secluded neighborhood with a river view. Two bedrooms each have a private Jacuzzi bath and deck. Full or continental breakfasts are available. Moderate.

Six Pines Ranch Bed & Breakfast, Box 27B, Rural Route 2, Winnipeg, (204) 633–3326 or www.sixpines.mb.ca. Country living just minutes from Winnipeg is featured in this turn-of-the-twentieth-century home situated on 1.8 ha/4.5 acres of farmyard. Moderate.

Manitoba Country Vacation Association, Box 93, Minto, Manitoba R0K 1M0; (204) 776–2176 or www.countryvacations.mb.ca. Feel the urge to spend time on some green acres? Country Vacations provides old-fashioned hospitality in a rural setting. Join the family and try your hand at a few chores, or just relax. Moderate.

Dining

Winnipeg has an eclectic array of restaurants—from the elegant continental with a high-priced tab to match, to casual ethnic eateries. Here's a sampling of what's in town:

Amici, 326 Broadway, (204) 943–4997. An elegant restaurant specializing in Tuscan cuisine. Very innovative. Lunch and dinner. Expensive.

Le Beaujolais, 131 Provencher Boulevard, (204) 237–6276. Local foods prepared with a French flair in a warm, intimate setting. The dessert selection is positively decadent. Expensive.

Green Gates, 6945 Roblin Boulevard, (204) 897–0990. Located just outside the city, this is the place to go for great country cooking. Local ingredients, fresh herbs from the garden, and a new menu every three months. Moderate to expensive.

Tavern in the Park, 2799 Roblin Boulevard, Assiniboine Park, Shaftesbury entrance, (204) 896–7275. Located in the historic Pavilion Building in Assiniboine Park, this elegant dining room serves some very contemporary creations, such as lamb chops with tequila, herbs, and goat cheese. Sunday brunch is really quite special. Expensive.

Old Swiss Inn, 207 Edmonton, near the convention center, (204) 942–7725. Excellent cheese fondues and chocolate fondue; also fondue bourguignonne and *bunderfleisch*. Moderate.

A Taste of Manitoba:
Preparing Goldeye

Manitoba, Land of 10,000 Lakes, is home to Canada's goldeye, a freshwater fish named for the golden color it turns after being smoked. An early settler's recipe called for the cook to "clean fish, rub well with salt, wrap in clean leaves, cover with mud and bury in hot ashes." Another recommended salting the skin of the fish, letting it stand for twenty minutes, and then broiling. The following method of wrapping in husks or leaves keeps the fish deliciously moist.

> 4 half-goldeye fillets (or substitute rainbow trout)
> 2 tsp salt
> 2 tsp pepper
> 2 tbsp butter
> 1 lemon, sliced
> grated zest of 1 lemon
> 4 ears corn on the cob, or 8 large romaine lettuce leaves

Pat each fish dry and rub inside and out with salt and pepper. Place a knob of butter and one-fourth of the lemon zest inside each, with a slice of lemon on top. Soak the ears of corn in cold water for 15 minutes. Remove the cob and the silk from the ears and wrap a goldeye or trout in each husk, tying at the open end. (If you're using lettuce leaves, place each fish on a leaf, place another leaf on top, and tie with string, making sure the lettuce is wrapped tightly around the fish.) Either barbecue over medium heat for 15 minutes, turning once, or bake in a preheated 191°C/375°F oven for 10 to 15 minutes.

Tiffani's, seventeenth floor, rooftop, at 133 Niakwa, (204) 256–7324. An elegant restaurant serving fine gourmet food, with great views of the city. Expensive.

Merteen's, fourteenth floor, 210 Oakland Avenue, (204) 334–2106. Another top restaurant, with panoramic views of the city. Flambé dishes are a specialty. Expensive.

Alycia's, 559 Cathedral Avenue, (204) 582–8789. Here you can dine like a Cossack on great Ukrainian cuisine for a song. Inexpensive.

La Vieille Gare, 630 rue des Meurons in St.-Boniface, (204) 237–5015. This is one of Winnipeg's best French restaurants—veal dishes in various preparations, rack of lamb, steak with savory sauces, and coquilles Saint-Jacques are but a few menu selections for a memorable feast. Expensive.

Velvet Glove, at the Lombard hotel, (204) 957–1350. An elegant dining room serving gourmet food. One of the best in the city. Expensive.

The Rib Room/Charter House, 330 York Avenue, (204) 942–0101. One of the city's favorite beef eateries—steaks, prime rib, and ribs are great here. Moderate.

Entertainment

As the cultural center of the prairies, Winnipeg has entertainment galore, from highbrow to wacky fun. Here are some possibilities:

Royal Winnipeg Ballet is the oldest ballet company in Canada and one of the most prestigious dance companies in the world. It's also certainly one of the most traveled, having performed in more than 535 cities in forty-one countries. Some dancers, such as Evelyn Hart, have achieved international stardom. For information on performance dates and tickets, call (204) 956–0183 or (800) 667–4292. Performances are at the Centennial Concert Hall or, during summer, at Assiniboine Park.

Winnipeg Symphony Orchestra, Centennial Concert Hall, 555 Main Street, (204) 949–3999. A fully professional orchestra presenting a wide variety of concerts for all musical tastes.

Manitoba Opera, (204) 780–3333; www. manitobaopera.mb.ca. Local singers and international artists are supported by the Winnipeg Symphony and a variety of conductors. Recent productions have included Puccini's *Tosca,* Humperdink's *Hansel and Gretel,* and Verdi's *Macbeth.*

Le Cercle Molière, 340 boulevard Provencher, St.-Boniface, (204) 233–8053 or www.netcom.ca/~moliere. Canada's oldest continuously operating French theater company has celebrated more than seventy-five years of operation. Enjoy an intimate theater experience, in French, at the Theatre de la Chappelle, 825 rue St.-Joseph, from October through April. The cafe-theater setting is unique to Winnipeg and very Gallic in flavor. English synopsis is provided for all plays.

Manitoba Theatre Centre, 174 Market Avenue, (204)

Winnipeg Festivals

Centara Corporation New Music Festival, late January; (204) 949-3999. The Winnipeg Symphony Orchestra presents new works, many in their world-premiere performances.

Le Festival du Voyageur, February; (204) 237-7692 or www.festivalvoyageur.mb.ca. This is Western Canada's largest winter festival: Live entertainment, traditional French-Canadian cuisine, international dogsled races, ice sculptures, and live performances.

Winnipeg International Airshow, early June; (204) 257-8400. The skies come alive with Canadian and American military aircraft.

Jazz Winnipeg Festival, mid-June; (204) 989-4656 or www.jazzwinnipeg.com. "It don't mean a thing if it ain't got that swing" and this Winnipeg festival has been swinging for almost a dozen years.

Winnipeg Folk Festival, early July; (204) 231-0096 or www.wpgfolkfest.mb.ca. Internationally acclaimed, this is a major event with seven daytime stages, an evening main-stage, and food and handicrafts from around the world.

Winnipeg Fringe Theatre Festival, late July; (204) 956-1340 or www.mtc.mb.ca. This festival features more than a hundred theater troups from around the world for eleven days of noon-to-midnight entertainment.

Folklorama, early August. This is Manitoba's biggest festival. Forty cultures display their food, crafts, and entertainment in venues scattered around the city. This is a fourteen-night cultural blitz that demonstrates the unique multi-ethnic mix that is Winnipeg.

942-6537 or www.mtc.mb.ca. A regional theater producing plays in two state-of-the-art theaters, and the Winnipeg Fringe Festival.

Prairie Theatre Exchange, 393 Portage Avenue, (204) 942-5483. An intimate theater located on the third floor of Portage Place Shopping Centre.

Shakespeare in the Ruins, ruins of St. Norbert Trappist Monastery, (204) 957–1753. A most unusual setting provides the venue for plays by Shakespeare and other classics. Professional actors lead the audience through the ruins of the monastery and surrounding grounds as the plays unfold.

Celebrations Dinner Theatre, 1824 Pembina Highway, (204) 982–8282. A four-course themed menu combined with a three-act musical comedy makes for an evening of high-energy, high-calorie entertainment. All shows are original, and the audience is invited to participate.

Contemporary Dancers, 109 Pulford Street, (204) 452–0229.

Westend Cultural Centre, 586 Ellice Avenue, (204) 775–1055; new theater for popular- and folk-music events.

Rainbow Stage, (204) 942–2091; outdoor theater in Kildonan Park during July and August.

Dine-and-dance cruises: Paddlewheel River Rouge Boat Cruises, (204) 942–4500.

Shopping

Academy Road, (204) 487–7300. High-end shopping with original designer fashions, gourmet food and wine stores, a chocolatier, coffeehouses, bakeries, restaurants, and an old-fashioned general store.

Corydon Avenue, (204) 284–3700. Manitoba's largest outdoor shopping center, Corydon is a magical street that transforms itself to suit your mood. An eclectic mix of fashion boutiques, curio and antiques shops, upscale secondhand stores, and restaurants.

Osborne Village, on the south side of Osborne Street Bridge, near the Legislative Building. Sixty shops, restaurants, galleries, and services are housed in restored buildings.

Portage Place Shopping Centre, 3 blocks on North Portage Avenue, (204) 925–4636. More than 140 shops, restaurants, and services spread over two levels. Portage Place is home to the Prairie Theatre Exchange, an IMAX theater, and a movie multiplex.

St. Vital Centre, (204) 257–5646. This is a traditional mall with a twist—two magnificent 15-m/50-ft-high fireplaces dominate the food court. For shopping you'll find the Bay, Sears, Chapters, and more than one hundred other stores and services.

Professional Sports

Thoroughbred and harness racing: Assiniboia Downs, twenty minutes east of city center, via Portage Avenue and Highway 101 (Selkirk exit); call (204) 885–3330 for racing schedules.

Winnipeg Blue Bombers of the Canadian Football League. Call (204) 780–7328 for schedule and ticket information; games played at Winnipeg Stadium, 1430 Maroons Road.

Manitoba Moose of the International Hockey League play at the Arena: call (204) 987–PUCK for schedule and ticket information.

Winnipeg Cyclone of the International Basketball Association. Winnipeg Convention Centre, (204) 925–HOOP.

Winnipeg Goldeyes, (204) 982–2273, play double-A baseball at Canwest Global Park.

Recreation

The greater Winnipeg area offers horseback riding, golf, tennis, swimming, and many other recreational opportunities. Your hotel concierge or guest relations person will be happy to offer suggestions and make arrangements.

Manitoba's Special Attractions

Churchill on Hudson Bay

Although a prairie province, Manitoba has extensive shoreline on Hudson Bay, that immense inland sea that also touches the borders of Ontario, Québec, and Nunavut. During summer, when the ice is out, you can sail from Manitoba to Greenland, Iceland, Ireland, and the British Isles. This is just the way the fur-trading entrepreneurs of the Hudson's Bay Company traveled more than 300 years ago. Prince of Wales Fort was built here in the eighteenth century to enforce the territorial sovereignty of the Hudson's Bay Company, and it still stands for the benefit of interested travelers. A plaque at the fort commemorates Samuel Hearne, who reached the Arctic Ocean via the Coppermine River in 1771.

In 1769 Churchill, named for the first duke of Marlborough, was where the first astronomical observations were made in Canada. The displays of aurora borealis (northern lights) here are magnificent—some say the most intense illumination in the world.

A railroad was completed in 1931 to connect Churchill with southern cities so that grain could be shipped more economically to international markets via Hudson Bay–Atlantic Ocean routes. This railroad is now also used by VIA Rail to transport tourists to Churchill.

In the 1940s the U.S. military had a base at Fort Churchill that was used first for air operations during World War II and later as a joint Canadian-American training and experimental facility. The base was closed in 1980.

In and around Churchill you will discover a thriving arctic animal kingdom, including some species that are seen nowhere else on earth. Best known are the polar bears, which in autumn wander onto the ice floes in the bay to hunt seals. Tourists come here to ride the "tundra buggies"—giant wheeled vehicles—to the places where the bears gather.

As cute and cuddly as the polar bears may appear, they have nasty tempers, very sharp teeth and claws, and absolutely no hesitation about attacking human beings who venture too close to their space. Make sure to heed all the safety warnings. In addition to the polar bears, you can see caribou, beluga whales, four species of seals, Canada and snow geese, and close to 200 other species of birds. Wildlife photo opportunities are everywhere; telephoto lenses are recommended.

Every July and August up to 3,000 white beluga whales gather along the shore of Hudson Bay and in the river estuary to feed and calve. The whales are playful and highly intelligent. Tour boats take visitors out to watch these peaceful mammals face to face and listen to them talk to each other in high-pitched chatter language that has earned them the nickname sea canaries.

Some of the points of interest are Bird Cove for bird-watching; Inuit Museum, with its excellent collection of carvings and artifacts; the Churchill Northern Studies Centre, conducting ecological studies; Cape Merry National Historic Site, a good place from which to see beluga whales; tundra tours on specially designed tracked or rubber-tired vehicles at the junction of three ecological zones—boreal forest, tundra, and taiga; a polar bear denning area, where cubs are born; and Prince of Wales Fort, a star-shaped stone bastion built in 1731 with walls 12 m/40 ft thick.

York Factory is a huge fur-trading depot incongruously set in the remote wilderness of Hudson Bay. For more than 250 years, it was an important trading post and the gateway to the interior for traders, settlers, and soldiers. At its peak this little-known part of Manitoba's heritage had more than fifty buildings and hundreds of residents.

Wapusk National Park is a vast, remote subarctic wilderness that protects the world's largest known denning area for polar bears and the nesting grounds of 45,000 pairs of snow geese. The park is also a sanctuary for arctic foxes, wolves, caribou and wolverines. The name of the park, Wapusk, is Cree for "white bear."

The best way to get to Churchill and experience everything is to use the services of the appropriate tour companies listed on pages 293–94. There is no highway to Churchill (the highway stops at Thompson), and the only way to get here is by air or VIA Rail. The area is also known for sport fishing and for waterfowl and ptarmigan hunting; there are outfitters here who will take good care of anglers and hunters. In Churchill itself you'll find a curling rink, a public swimming pool, and a bowling alley; shops where you can purchase Native prints and carvings; restaurants; liquor stores; and churches. While in town, orient yourself to the attractions of the area by visiting Parks Canada at Bayport Plaza, (204) 675–8863.

For more information about Churchill, contact Travel Manitoba, (800) 665–0040, or the Churchill Chamber of Commerce, (204) 675–2022.

Accommodations

Accommodations are all in the moderate price range.

The Aurora Inn, Box 1030, Churchill, Manitoba R0B 0E0, (204) 675–2071; (888) 840–1344; www.cancom.net/~aurora. Apartment suites accommodating four to six people, kitchens, cable TV, VCRs, and e-mail. Within a short distance of restaurants, bars, shopping, and the train station.

Bear Country Inn, Box 788, Churchill, Manitoba R0B 0E0, (204) 675–2899 or www.cancom.net/~awt/bcinn.html. Free shuttle service, complimentary morning tea and coffee, nonsmoking rooms, cable TV and private baths.

Churchill Motel Ltd., Box 218, Churchill, Manitoba R0E 0E0, (204) 675–5833. Twenty-six rooms with private bath, TV, fridge, and telephone. Free airport and train shuttle.

Northern Lights Travel Lodge, Box 70, Churchill, Manitoba R0E 0E0, (204) 675–2043 or nnlaktie@cancom.net. Cocktail lounge, hot tub, and sauna.

Polar Inn, Box 1031, Churchill, Manitoba R0E 0E0, (204) 678–8878. One-bedroom apartments; kitchen studio and kitchenette suites; standard rooms with coffee machine and fridge.

Seaport Hotel, Box 339, Churchill, Manitoba R0E 0E0, (204) 675–8807. Cocktail lounge, pub with video lottery terminals, cable TV, fridge, and telephone. Airport shuttle.

The Tundra Inn, Box 999, Churchill, Manitoba R0E 0E0, (204) 675–8831; (800) 265–8563; tundra@cancom.net. A modern hotel with double or queen-size beds, private bath, cable TV, fridge, and coffeepot in each room.

Western Manitoba

Riding Mountain National Park is located north of the Trans-Canada and the Yellowhead Highways, via Highway 10 North, and approximately halfway between the border of Saskatchewan and Lake Manitoba. For more information on the park itself, contact Superintendent, Riding Mountain National Park, Wasagaming, Manitoba R0J 2H0; (204) 848–7275.

Riding Mountain National Park (3,000 sq km/1,150 sq mi) has the distinction of being near the geographical center of Canada. The park has three distinct ecological zones: a deciduous forest; aspen and grasslands; and a boreal forest with spruce and fir. Each zone has self-guiding nature trails. Within the park are the Lake Katherine, Whirlpool, and Moon Lake Campgrounds. A visitor center conducting various interpretive programs is located in the town of **Wasagaming**. A campground and resorts, as well as supplies and services, can be found here. Enjoy golfing, horseback riding, canoeing, swimming, overnight backpacking, fishing, and tennis. Visit the bison herd numbering about thirty animals maintained on a range at Lake Audy.

Experience the rich traditions of the Anishinabe people with Anishinabe Camp at Lake Katherine. Camp in traditional tepees and dine on traditional Anishinabe foods.

One of Canada's most celebrated conservationists lived and worked in Riding Mountain National Park in 1931. His name was Grey Owl, and he was said to be the son of a Scottish father and an Apache mother. He was, in fact, an Englishman living out a boyhood dream. Despite his fictional heritage, Grey Owl's passion for the environment was genuine. His ability to inspire public support for conservation made him a popular speaker on European lecture tours in the 1930s. Grey Owl left Riding Mountain to continue his work in Saskatchewan's Prince Albert National Park.

For more information on the park itself, contact Superintendent, Riding Mountain National Park, Wasagaming, Manitoba R0J 2H0, (204) 848–7275.

If you continue through the park on Highway 10, you will come to the town of Dauphin, where the famous National Ukrainian Festival is held each summer.

Selkirk

Lower Fort Garry National Historic Park is twenty minutes north of the city of Winnipeg on Highway 9, (204) 785–6050 or (877) 534–5678 (in Manitoba). Open from mid-May to Labour Day. Lower Fort Garry was built in the 1830s as a Hudson's Bay Company post. It has been restored to reflect its role in the early days of fur trading and in the development of Manitoba. During your visit, you will see people in period costumes moving about and doing chores—baking scones and oatmeal cookies in outdoor ovens, loading carts with grain and produce, making tallow candles, and shoeing horses. You can poke around the restored buildings, view the historical exhibits, have a satisfying meal at the restaurant, and buy a gift from the prairies for the folks back home. A trip to this fort is a worthwhile excursion back into the early history of the province.

Visit the **Marine Museum of Manitoba,** in Selkirk Park at Eveline and Queen Streets, (204) 482–7761. Open from mid-May to September 30. Admission is charged. This museum is dedicated to Manitoba's marine history and the preservation of vessels used on its waterways, such as the SS *Keenora,* a beloved passenger steamship; the CGS *Bradbury,* an icebreaker; and *Peguis II,* a dredge tender. Also in the park is a replica of a Red River ox cart, which helped develop this part of Canada because it could more easily travel through mud. The replica is 6.6 m/22 ft high and 13.5 m/45 ft long.

Lake Winnipeg Area

From Selkirk you might want to explore some of the lower shoreline of Lake Winnipeg, via Highways 8 and 9 on the west side or 59 on the east.

Traveling along the west side of the lake, you will come to **Gimli,** the largest Icelandic community outside the homeland. In Gimli (the name means "the great hall of heaven," from Norse legend) you'll find an Icelandic heritage museum, a giant statue of a Viking, and the annual Islendingadagurrin (Icelandic Festival of Manitoba), which is held during the first weekend in August.

Gimli has a waterfront area in which its fascinating maritime heritage has been preserved with period lighting, walkways, and signs. In **Arnes,** just above Gimli, there's a plaque honoring Vilhjalmur Stefansson, the famous Arctic explorer, who was born here in 1879.

Continuing along Highway 8 will take you to **Hecla Provincial Park** (145 km/90 mi north of Winnipeg), whose islands stretch nearly across the narrows of Lake Winnipeg. This beautiful park features facilities for camping, hiking, tennis, fishing, and sailing. There's a large moose population; thick flocks of waterfowl, bald eagles, great blue herons, and western grebes mass here. The Icelandic influence is expressed in the Gull Harbour Resort and

Conference Centre, a luxury accommodation within the park that is open throughout the year. For reservations and more information, call (800) 267–6700. Moderate. Also available are camping, B&Bs, and cabins.

A drive up the eastern shore of Lake Winnipeg, via Highway 59, will bring you to **Grand Beach Provincial Park.** This park has some of the finest sand beaches in North America. Shifting sand dunes here rise close to 9 m/30 ft in height. A lagoon behind them is a perfect habitat for pelicans, cranes, orioles, and finches. The park features camping, tennis, windsurfing, fishing, lake swimming, and an amphitheater program. Inexpensive accommodations are available in the nearby town of Grand Marais.

Southern Manitoba

In Steinbach see the **Mennonite Heritage Village (Canada),** which can be reached via the Trans-Canada, east of Winnipeg, and then south on Highway 12, (204) 326–9661. Open from May to the end of September. Admission is charged. This village museum is an excellent tribute to the heritage and accomplishments of Mennonite pioneers who settled in the Steinbach area in 1874. The village consists of early Mennonite farm buildings; farming machinery; a pristine, unadorned church for meditation and prayer; an obelisk monument to the early settlers; simple homes with period furnishings; and perhaps the most magnificent shingled windmill in all of Canada. There are demonstrations of farming activities, wagon rides, a barn restaurant that serves traditional Mennonite cooking, and a shop where you can buy souvenirs. A visit here is highly recommended.

South of Steinbach, near the Minnesota border, is Gardenton (reached via Highways 59 and 209, south of Winnipeg). Here is **St. Michael's Ukrainian Orthodox Church,** the first Ukrainian Orthodox church built in North America in 1896. There are also a museum and a heritage village in town. Admission charged.

International Peace Garden, a U.S.–Canadian Masonic project near Boissevain, is located along the east boundary of Turtle Mountain Provincial Park (reached via Highway 10 south of Brandon on the Trans-Canada). Open mid-May to mid-September. Admission is charged. The International Peace Garden spans the border between Manitoba and North Dakota in the southwestern region. It honors the longest unfortified border in the world and is a symbol of the strong, warm, and enduring friendship that exists between the peoples of Canada and the United States. Within the park are beautiful flower gardens and extensive landscaped areas; a flower clock (at the entrance); the Peace Chapel; a fountain encircled by stone walls engraved with the writings of famous people on the theme of peace; the Peace Tower, symbolizing the coming together of people from all parts of the world to form two great nations; and the Errick F. Willis Memorial Centre, which has arts and crafts exhibitions. During summer the park is the site of the International Music Camp and the Royal Legion Athletic Camp.

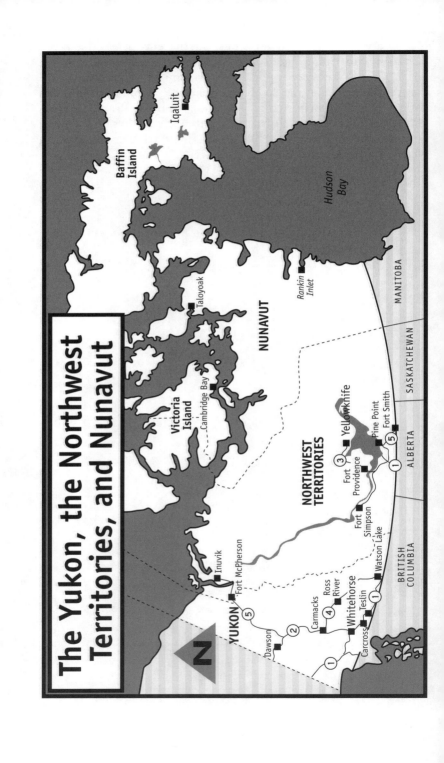

The Yukon, the Northwest Territories, and Nunavut

CHAPTER 10

Exploring the Yukon, the Northwest Territories, and Nunavut

The Yukon: Land of Dreamers

The first people of the Yukon settled here more than 50,000 years ago, perhaps considerably more. The majority of Yukon First Nations peoples belong to one of the Athapaskan- or Tlingit-language families. It is said that the first white person to penetrate the interiors of the Yukon was Robert Campbell, a Hudson's Bay Company fur trader.

In the Yukon Territory are five places that have become ingrained in North American mythology—the Klondike, Chilkoot Pass, White Pass (both passes are partly in Alaska), Dawson City, and Whitehorse. In the late 1800s the Yukon was the site of the famous gold strikes, and "gold fever" drew thousands of people here from North America and other parts of the world. George Carmack, Skookum Jim, and Dawson Charlie struck gold at Rabbit "Bonanza" Creek, a tributary of the Klondike River, in 1896. And the dreamers came here in great numbers, about 50,000 of them by 1899, all seeking a fortune that would turn their lives

Tourism Yukon

For touring and camping information (brochures—especially helpful if you are driving along any of the routes mentioned earlier—and maps), write or call Tourism Yukon, Box 2703, Whitehorse, Yukon Y1A 2C6, (403) 667-5340.

Visitor Reception Centres, open from mid-May to mid-September, are located in Watson Lake, Carcross, Whitehorse, Beaver Creek, Haines Junction, and Dawson City.

around and make them as rich as J. P. Morgan. Enough did strike it rich to keep passionate fires burning in the minds of many others who would, after much struggle and hardship, fail. And along with the seekers of wild dreams came the merchants, the bankers, the dance-hall women, and the preachers. Some stole the dreamers' purses, while others tried to save their souls. To survive in this country you had to be handy with your fists—to make your way through an often cruel wilderness and to knock the other guy down before he could do it to you. To say that the heritage of the Yukon was wild, rough, and woolly is about as precise as you can get. This was, after all, where Jack London got his inspiration for novels of life and death in the North. But it was also much more. The Yukon meant exerting personal courage and vision against all odds and sometimes winning. It was stranger helping stranger to keep going to survive. The traditions of fellowship are so strong here that you can't do better than have Yukon people as friends. It was a pioneering spirit that, when the gold fever finally cooled down, produced stable communities of hardy, creative people who took the long view of things, generation after generation. And so it is right now in the Yukon. Gold is still plucked from here, but heavy earthmoving equipment and sluice boxes have replaced the gold pan of yesteryear. The Yukon's true future lies with dreamers of a different sort, ones better educated and seeing more productive possibilities.

The Yukon, 482,500 sq km/186,000 sq mi, is essentially a magnificent wilderness with gorgeous mountains, lakes, rivers, forests, and tundra. There is an abundance of wildlife here: bears, mountain goats and sheep, moose, caribou, many species of birds and waterfowl, wolves, and salmon. Sport hunters and anglers from all over the world come to the Yukon for prize trophies and for adventure. For such a vast area, though, there are only 31,000 people residing in the Yukon, mostly in the communities of Whitehorse (the capital), Dawson City, Beaver Creek, Faro, Ross River, Mayo, Watson Lake, Haines Junction, Teslin, and Carcross. They also live in tiny pioneering towns and, in the case of the Gwich'in, in the remote village of Old Crow.

The Yukon borders Alaska to the west and south, the Northwest Territories to the east, and British Columbia to the south along the sixtieth parallel. The Yukon extends north beyond the Arctic Circle and has well over 200 km/120 mi of shoreline on the Beaufort Sea. Herschel Island in the Beaufort Sea is near the territory's most northerly point. Among the Yukon's many river systems, the Yukon River and the Porcupine River are two of the largest. Mount Logan (5,959 m/19,550 ft)—part of the St. Elias Range and located in Kluane National Park in the southwest corner of the Yukon, close to the Alaskan border—is Canada's highest mountain and second in height only to Alaska's Mount McKinley, North America's highest peak.

Turn the Lights On!

Visitors to the Yukon in winter (there's too much light during summer months) will marvel at the stunning displays of the northern lights, or aurora borealis. They light up the winter sky like cosmic ribbons of light, dancing and undulating across the sky. They appear in different forms, almost always in wavering motion, and they radiate colors from pale yellow to lime green and an awe-inspiring red.

The northern lights are caused by a huge explosion on the surface of the sun known as a solar flare. These explosions send a wave of high-energy particles—a solar wind—into space. The solar wind is drawn toward the earth's magnetic fields and concentrated on the North and South Poles. Upper-atmosphere gases are "excited" by the solar wind and light up when bombarded by the energy waves. Different gases glow different colors.

The lights occur 96 to 128 km/60 to 80 mi above the earth's surface, so it doesn't make any sense that they can be heard. Yet many people perceive a sensation of crackling or rustling noise when they see the lights.

Special Events

January
Robbie Burns Night, Whitehorse

February
Trek Over the Top Adventure Tour, Dawson City
Gold Rush Centennial Ball, Dawson City
TAGS 200 Snowmobile Race, Watson Lake
Yukon Quest Sled Dog Race, Whitehorse
Frostbite Music Festival, Whitehorse
Yukon Sourdough Rendezvous, Whitehorse
Cabane A Sucre, Whitehorse

March
Thaw-Di-Gras Spring Carnival, Dawson City
Percy De Wolfe Memorial Mail Race, Dawson City
Haines Junction Snow Mobile Rodeo, Haines Junction

April
Celebration of Swans, Whitehorse

May
Dawson City International Gold Show, Dawson City

The main highway access into the Yukon is through the town of Watson Lake on the Alaska Highway. Another route is the Inside Passage, delivering passengers to Skagway, Alaska, then on to Carcross, Yukon, and Whitehorse, along the Klondike Highway. Coming south from Fairbanks, Alaska, the town of Beaver Creek, Yukon, is a gateway at the western border. The Alaska and the Klondike are the Yukon's two main highways. Other roads, mostly gravel and with limited services, provide touring into various regions; the Dempster Highway will take you all the way to Fort McPherson in the Northwest Territories and beyond to Arctic Red River and Inuvik, all of which are on the Mackenzie Delta (where the Mackenzie, one of Canada's great rivers, empties into the Beaufort Sea). The Yukon has a sophisticated highway system

June
Commissioners Grand Ball, Dawson City
Alsek Music Festival, Haines Junction
Kluane-Chilkat International Bike Relay, Haines Junction
Mayo Midnight Marathon, Mayo
Yukon River Quest Canoe Race, Whitehorse
Yukon International Storytelling Festival, Whitehorse
Gathering of Clans and Celtic Festival, Whitehorse

July
Yukon Gold Panning Championships, Dawson City
Kluane Lake Fishing Derby, Dawson City
The Commissioner's Potlach, Whitehorse

August
Discovery Days, Dawson City
Yukon River Bathtub Race, Dawson City
Klondyke Harvest Fair, Dawson City

September
Great Klondike International Outhouse Race, Dawson City
Klondike Trail of 98 Relay Race, Whitehorse

that makes driving easier than it is in Alaska or the Northwest Territories.

Summer days, especially during July, can be quite warm—up to 30°C/86°F (the average is between 10° and 20°C). Among the bonuses of visiting the Yukon during summer—and for that matter Alaska and the Northwest Territories—are the long days. Dawson City has almost twenty-four hours of sunlight each day in June and twenty hours in July; Whitehorse has twenty hours of light during June and eighteen hours in July. Unfortunately, the reverse is true during the winter: minimal daylight and temperatures that fall to −40°C. The very low humidity, though, makes the winter temperatures more tolerable. If you want a wilderness adventure along with your cross-country skiing, snowmobiling,

There aren't many boundaries in the Yukon.

dogsledding, or ice fishing, the Yukon is the perfect place for you to test your skills and resolve and have some fun in the process. Rock hounds will find prizes in the Yukon: hematite (from which the Alaska black diamond is made) in Hunker, Dominion, and Haggart Creeks; agate (in its various forms) in the Carmack area; azurite, malachite, and chrysocolla (lapidary materials) in the Whitehorse Copper Belt area; garnet in the Von Wilzon Lake region; jasper along the Alaska Highway; and rhyolite in the Wheaton River Valley.

The Yukon: Some Basic Facts

The Yukon River begins near the Pacific Ocean and flows for 3,218 km/2,000 mi to the Bering Sea.

In the Yukon above the Arctic Circle, the sun never sets on June 21; it never rises on December 21.

The Yukon is 15 percent larger than the state of California, but it has only one person per 11 sq km/7 sq mi.

Southwest Yukon has the largest concentration of grizzly bears in North America and the largest number of Dall sheep in the world.

More than a billion Canadian dollars' worth of gold has been taken out of the Klondike over the years. (No wonder people got the itch to get there as fast as possible.)

How to Get to the Yukon
By Car

The southern border of the Yukon is 2,200 km/1,367 mi from Vancouver, British Columbia, via Trans-Canada Highway 1 east to Cache Creek, then Highway 97 to the Alaska Highway. From Edmonton, Alberta, take Yellowhead Highway 16 west to Highway 43 to Valleyview and Highway 34 to Dawson Creek and then the Alaska Highway—to the Yukon border, a distance of 1,600 km/994 mi. See Chapter 2 for safety and driving tips when taking the Alaska Highway. Much of the highway is paved with asphalt, although there are gravel sections. Other routes of entry into the Yukon are Highway 2 from Skagway, Alaska; Highway 3 from Haines, Alaska; Highway 2 from Fairbanks, Alaska; and Stewart-

Cassiar Highway 37 from southwestern British Columbia (a very scenic route but with few services; see Chapter 6). The highways in this region are well maintained through all seasons, not just for visitors but for the very survival of the people who live here. A number of communities offer full services (fuel, supplies, accommodations) en route to the Yukon and through to Alaska—Siberia it's not. For reports on highway conditions, call Yukon Highways, (867) 667–8215 (twenty-four hours), and British Columbia Highways, (250) 663–4997.

By Boat

The following regional ferries provide access to the Yukon via Prince Rupert, British Columbia: British Columbia Ferries, (604) 669–1211; and the Alaska Marine Highway, operating out of Juneau, (907) 465–3941. The Alaska Marine Highway ferries stop at Haines, Skagway, and other Alaska ports, and travelers may then continue on to Whitehorse by private vehicle or bus. Costa, Cunard, Exploration, Holland America, Princess, Regency, and Royal Viking are all cruise lines that bring visitors to the Yukon. Check with your travel agent about the itineraries these cruise lines use for the Inside Passage of coastal British Columbia and Alaska.

By Plane

Daily jet service is provided to Whitehorse from Vancouver by Air Canada; regional airlines also provide service in the Yukon and from Alaska. Several European charter airlines, such as Condor Air and Balair, provide summer service to the Yukon.

By Train

The White Pass and Yukon Route provides scenic rail trips from Skagway, Alaska, to Fraser, British Columbia, and on to Carcross, Yukon, through the historic White Pass. Motorcoach connections are available from Fraser on to Whitehorse. For more information call (800) 343–7373 or (907) 983–2217.

Useful Information

Climate: Generally, summers in the Yukon are dry, pleasant, and comfortable.
Area code: 867
Time zone: Pacific

Package Tours and Touring Services: Adventures, Fishing, and Hunting

Package Tours

Beringia Tours, 4103 Fourth Avenue, Whitehorse, (867) 688–7391 or beringia@ynet.yk.ca. Custom-designed tours, First Nations tours, boat tours, and lodges.

Cardinal Travel, 732 Forty-first Avenue NE, Calgary, Alberta (403) 230–9304 or www.cardinaltraveltours.ab.ca. Fully escorted inclusive tours of the Yukon and Alaska from Whitehorse.

Gray Line Yukon, Box 4157, Whitehorse, (867) 688–3225 or www.yukon.net/westours. Package tours to Atlin, Dawson City, Eagle, and Alaska destinations.

Premier Pacific Tours, 5851 No. 3 Road, Richmond, British Columbia, (604) 278–3772 or www.premierpacific.com. Driver-guided and escorted packaged tours to the Yukon and Alaska.

Adventure Travel

Ancient Voices Wilderness Camp, Box 5323, Whitehorse, (867) 993–5605 or www.yukon.net/avwcamp. First Nations traditional way of life experiences. Rustic cabins, walled tents, and meals.

Dalton Trail Lodge, Box 5331, Haines Junction, (867) 634–2099 or www.daltontrail.com. Canoeing, hiking, mountain biking, wilderness cabins, river rafting, gold panning, and fishing.

Frontier Spirit Cycling Tours, Box 5390, Whitehorse, (867) 393–3802 or www.frontierspirit.com. Road cycling tours throughout the Yukon and Alaska. Tours include the Dempster Highway, Kluane Park, and the Klondike-Dawson area.

Kluane Ecotours, Box 5334, Haines Junction, (867) 634–2626 or http://users.internorth.com/~thecabin/kluaneecotours. Certified guides and interpreters, two- to ten-day packages, all-inclusive.

Tatshenshini Expediting, 1602 Alder Street, Whitehorse, (867) 633–2742 or www.tatshenshiniyukon.com. Guided one-day trips on the Tatshenshini River. Also raft-, canoe-, and kayak-rental packages.

Fishing

2-Fly Fishing Adventures, Box 5971, Whitehorse, (867) 667–2359 or www.tiayukon.@yknet.yk.ca. Guided fly fishing with certified instructors, for all game fish.

Dalton Trail Lodge, Box 5331 Haines Junction, (867) 634–2029 or www.daltontrail.com. Trophy fishing for lake trout, arctic grayling, pike, salmon, and rainbow trout.

Frances Lake Wilderness Lodge, Box 4543, Whitehorse, (867) 667–2028 or www.naturetoursyukon.com. Lodge accessed by boat and plane only. Fish for lake trout, pike, and Dolly Varden.

Peacock's Yukon Camps, Box 5980, Station N, Whitehorse, (867) 667–6076 or www.fishingyukon.com. Fly-in fishing for lake trout, northern pike, and arctic grayling with housekeeping camps on eight lakes north of Whitehorse.

Registered Hunting Outfitters

Dickson Outfitters Ltd., Box 9130, 29 Wann Road, Whitehorse, (867) 633–5456 (phone and fax).

Ruby Range Outfitters, Box 5449, Whitehorse, (867) 821–4055 or frontier@yknet.yk.ca. Hunt for Dall sheep and grizzly and black bears in the Ruby Mountains bordering Kluane National Park.

Safari Adventures Yukon Ltd., Box 3995, Whitehorse, (867) 633–4470 or safari@hypertech.yk.ca. First-class hunting expeditions from fully equipped camps.

Government Campgrounds

On the Alaska Highway from Watson Lake to the Alaska border, there are numerous campgrounds. Their location is indicated by the kilometer mark location on the highway heading north from Watson Lake. Most campsites have drinking water, and some have special features, such as beaches and fishing.

Watson Lake, 1,024.9 km (637 mi)
Rancheria, 1,143.4 km (710 mi)
Teslin Lake, 1,309 km (813.1 mi)
Squanga Lake, 1,366 km (850.5 mi)
Marsh Lake, 1,429.6 km (888.4 mi)
Wolf Creek, 1,458.6 km (907 mi)
Takhini River, 1,542.6 km (958.6 mi)
Kusawa Lake, 1,542.6 km (958.6 mi)
Otter Falls, 1,602.2 km (995.6 mi)
Aishihik Lake, 1,602.2 km (995.6 mi)
Pine Lake, 1,628 km (1,013 mi)
Congdon Creek, 1,722.7 km (1,071 mi)
Lake Creek, 1,853.7 km (1,152.1 mi)
Snag Junction, 1,912.8 (1,188.8 mi)

There are also campsites on the Haines Road, Atlin Road 7, Tagish Road 8, the Klondike Highway, Silver Trail 11, South Canol Road, the Robert Campbell Highway, and the Dempster Highway (contact Tourism Yukon, Box 2703, Whitehorse, Yukon Y1A 2C6, for details).

The Yukon's Special Attractions
Hiking the Chilkoot Trail
If you are the hardy type and are trekking the Yukon, hike the Chilkoot Trail, which is actually a slender slice of British Columbia between Alaska and the Yukon. The trail begins a few miles from Dyea, north of Skagway, a major port of call for Inside Passage ships. If any single place embodies the struggle of hundreds of men trying to reach the gold fields of the Yukon, it is Chilkoot Pass. In old documentary films and photos, you can see hundreds of men trying to push themselves and their supplies up what seems like a wall. Many were injured and some killed in the attempt to cross over. At the summit, the Northwest Mounted Police set up a post where they weighed the supplies of each man. By police decree, each man had to have enough provisions to last one full year (about 400 kg/2,000 lb) in order to continue on. Those who were shy of the requirement were sent back down—to go home or start again. Some of these dreamers were so insistent on reaching the Yukon that they tried going over Chilkoot Pass in the dead of winter, with often disastrous results. Today you can hike this trek in a leisurely manner to enjoy the magnificent scenery and to reflect upon the lives of the dreamers who came this way hungry for gold many decades ago. The trail itself will take you through rain forest, through alpine meadow, over talus rock up the pass, and then to the summit, the scene of so many victories and defeats. Reservations to climb the trail must be made with Heritage Parks Canada, (800) 661–0486. There is a $35 (Canadian) registration fee.

Kluane National Park
Kluane National Park is located at the junction of Highway 3 and the Alaska Highway 1, in the southwest corner of the territory, bordering British Columbia and Alaska. The key town for the park is Haines Junction, at Highways 1 and 3, 158 km/98 mi (a two-hour drive) west of Whitehorse. For more information contact Superintendent, Kluane National Park, Haines Junction, Yukon Y0B 1L0, (867) 634–2251.

Kluane National Park is an immense wilderness. It has the highest mountains in Canada; Mount Logan, at 5,959 m/19,550 ft in the St. Elias Range, is the nation's highest—and the second highest on the North American continent. Mount St. Elias was the first to be climbed—in 1897 by the duke of Abruzzi. Mount Logan was climbed in 1925. Scientists from different disciplines and top climbers have been attracted for decades by the park's rugged and splendid ecology, and many come here every year to study and experience its natural wonders. The mountains within the park are among North America's youngest and most attractive, with faults averaging a thousand a year. You can see how the earth shifts in this area by watching the seismograph at the visitor center in Haines Junction. This is also a landscape of many glaciers, perhaps as many as 4,000. The snows laid down over thousands of years along the St. Elias Range have made these the most extensive icefields outside the polar regions. The Kaskawulsh Glacier can be reached by a tough two-day hike. Along the Alaska Highway, from which most people see the park, the Front Range Mountains form a 2,400-m/8,000-ft wall that shields the St. Elias Range and Mount Logan from view. To get into the park and near Mount Logan by trekking takes excellent physical conditioning, much planning, and the right gear (contact the Sierra Club or similar organizations for information on how to take on this adventure so that it's safe and memorable). Another way to see Mount Logan is to fly over it with an air-tour service; some of these services are listed in this chapter.

Kluane National Park has large populations of grizzly bears, Dall sheep, and other wildlife. If you are camping in the park, keep the grizzlies away from your site by using proper procedures in storing food and garbage (see Chapter 2). An Indian village on Klukshu Creek is thought to be the oldest settlement in this part of the territory. Several hiking trails lead off the Alaska Highway: the Rock Glacier Trail, the St. Elias Trail, the Auriol Range Trail, and the Sheep Mountain Trail. Silver City on Kluane Lake is a classic western ghost town that you should visit. Shells of original buildings remain, as does a sense of the people who long ago put their hearts and souls into ventures that have drifted away with the winds. South of Haines Junction is Kathleen Lake, the park's major campground, open from mid-June to mid-September, with a maximum stay of two weeks. There are a number of other campgrounds along this eastern edge of the park. Motorboating and fishing are allowed on Kathleen Lake; canoeing is discouraged because of the rough water. Mountaineering parties who wish to climb the St. Elias and Icefield Ranges must obtain a permit three months in advance from the Warden Service (write to Kluane

National Park). The Warden Service will want to know the health, physical condition, and skill of each member of your party; you must provide doctors' certificates and information on supplies and communication support. All these precautions are essential, because Kluane is the very essence of the Yukon wilderness. North of Haines Junction on the Alaska Highway at Destruction Bay and Burwash Landing is Kluane Lake, the largest lake in the Yukon.

Accommodations in the Haines Junction area (all have dining rooms) are **Mountain View Motor Inn,** (867) 634–2646 (moderate); **Cozy Corner Motel & Restaurant,** (867) 634–2511 (moderate); **Kluane Park Inn,** (867) 634–2261 (moderate); and **MacKintosh Lodge,** (867) 634–2301 (moderate).

All of the following accommodations in Destruction Bay and Burwash Landing have dining rooms:

Talbot Arm Motel, in Destruction Bay, (867) 841–4804. Moderate.

Burwash Landing Resort, (867) 841–4441. Moderate.

Kluane Wilderness Village, near Burwash Landing, (867) 841–4141. Moderate.

Pine Valley Motel, 87 km/54 mi north of Burwash Landing, (867) 862–7407. Moderate.

Koidern River Fishing Lodge, 114 km/71 mi north of Burwash Landing, (867) 862–7402. Moderate.

White River Motor Inn, 122 km/76 mi north of Burwash Landing, (867) 862–7408. Moderate.

Scenic Highways

See Chapter 2 for safety and driving tips on driving the gravel roads of the Yukon.

Taking **Alaska Highway 1** from the southern provinces and states to the Yukon and Alaska is one of North America's great road adventures. Driving across the southwest corner of the Yukon from British Columbia to Alaska (Watson Lake to Beaver Creek) is a distance of 912 km/567 mi, a journey that can take several days if you don't rush but rather take the time to enjoy the natural beauty and heritage of the Yukon. There are plenty of services, accommodations, gas stations, and restaurants along the way. Be sure to visit Kluane National Park and to tour the city of Whitehorse.

Klondike Highway 2 from Whitehorse will take you to historic Dawson City, a boomtown in gold rush days. Both Jack London and the poet Robert Service had cabins here. Carcross is the important town on this scenic highway. Its attractions include the

Museum of Yukon Natural History, Frontierland Heritage Park, Carcross Desert, Matthew Watson General Store, and the Visitor Reception Center located in the Old Train Depot.

From Dawson City you can drive **Top of the World Highway 9** into Alaska. This road is open only during summer; it connects with Alaska Highway 1 and continues to Fairbanks.

Haines Road Highway 3 goes from Haines, Alaska, the terminus of the Alaskan Marine Highway System, along the eastern edge of Kluane National Park to Haines Junction in the Yukon. From here you can travel the Alaska Highway north or south.

Robert Campbell Highway 4 moves in a northwesterly course from Watson Lake on the British Columbia border to the communities of Ross River, Faro, and Carmacks, which are in the south-central part of the territory. When you reach Carmacks, you can take Klondike Highway 2 north to Dawson City or south to Whitehorse.

Dempster Highway 5 is a true explorer's road, but you should take it only in summer. If you follow the Dempster from Dawson City to the literal end of the road, you will have crossed the Arctic Circle, entered the Northwest Territories, passed through Fort McPherson (the largest community in this part of the world) and over the mighty Mackenzie River, and made it to Inuvik, an Inuit (Eskimo) community where the road does indeed end. From Inuvik you can take a flight to visit the remote Inuit village of Tuktoyaktuk. Between Dawson City and Fort McPherson, you'll find only one gas station and hotel, so plan accordingly. Check at the visitor center in Dawson City for suggestions for the trip, or consult your local auto club or environmental society (e.g., Audubon Society or Sierra Club). Finally, the road all the way is gravel, and a reliable, sturdy RV is your best transportation, although any vehicle will do for the trip as long as it is mechanically sound and equipped with at least two spare tires. There are government campgrounds at strategic points. The only commercial lodge facility is at Eagle Plains.

Watson Lake

Watson Lake is the gateway to the Yukon from the provinces and the States. Its major attraction is a signpost forest with many signs pointing to cities throughout the world and giving the distance to each. This tradition was started by a lonely American GI working on the construction of the Alaska Highway (25,000 Americans and Canadians worked on the highway). On the one hand, standing at this signage display, you would think that Watson Lake is the navel of the earth. On the other hand, if you are here, it surely is. Don't leave without having someone take a photo of you by the sign.

Alaska Highway Interpretive Centre, (867) 536–7469. If you are traveling all the way to Fairbanks or on long sections of the highway through the Yukon, this is a good place to get oriented to what's ahead and to learn the history of this tremendous engineering and construction effort.

The new **Northern Lights Center,** (867) 536–7522, is the only planetarium in North America featuring the myth and science of the northern lights.

The following accommodations have dining rooms:
Belvedere Motor Hotel, (867) 536–7712. Moderate.
Gateway Motor Inn, (867) 536–7744. Moderate.
Watson Lake Hotel, (867) 536–7781. Moderate.

Whitehorse

Whitehorse, capital of the Yukon Territory, is located on the Alaska Highway and on the Yukon River, which meanders for 3,185 km/1,980 mi north to the Arctic Ocean. This city owes its birth and initial development to the Klondike gold rush of the late 1800s. Both the river, on which plied steamboats, and a railroad, built from Skagway, made Whitehorse a vital transportation and supply center for the rapidly growing population attracted to the region by visions of getting rich quick. When gold mania subsided, enough people remained to make Whitehorse a permanent settlement, although by 1941 the population fell to fewer than 800 people. Today the city's population is about 23,000. For a short while copper mining pumped new life into the local economy, but that also ended. During World War II Whitehorse became part of the Northwest Staging Route, a chain of airfields that briefly brought in thousands of Canadian and U.S. construction workers. The Alaska Highway, the major land route that links this region with the provinces and states to the south, made Whitehorse a primary transportation center. Whitehorse has fine hotels and restaurants for travelers and a number of interesting attractions. When you're in town the folks at the new **Yukon Visitor Reception Center,** 1,475.7 km/917 mi Alaska Highway, (867) 667–2915, will answer your questions and assist you in whatever way they can.

The official season for most Whitehorse attractions listed below is from mid-May to about mid-September:
Yukon Permanent Art Collection, Yukon Government Administration Building. Northern landscapes and lifestyles from

Whitehorse Travel Services

Car Rentals
Budget, 4178 Fourth Avenue, (867) 667–6200, 667–6220
Norcan Leasing, mi 917.4 Alaska Highway, (867) 668–2137
Avis, 306 Ray Street, (867) 946–3680

Camper Rentals
Klondike Recreational Rentals, 108 Industrial Road, (867)
   668–2200
Ambassador Motorhome & Recreational Services, (867) 667–4130
Norcan Leasing, mi 917.4, Whitehorse, (867) 668–2137
Whitehorse Motors U-Drive, 4178 Fourth Avenue, (867) 667–7866
CanaDream Campers, 110 Copper Road, (867) 668–3610

Air Charter Services
This is a good way to experience the territory—Kluane National
Park and northern Inuit settlements near the Beaufort Sea—if
you're short on time.
Air North, (867) 668–2228
Alkan Air, (867) 668–2107
Peacock Air, (867) 667–2846
Kluane Airways, (867) 667–4070

promising Canadian artists. Open weekdays 8:30 A.M. to 5:00 P.M.

Whitehorse Heritage Walks, (867) 667–4704. A walking tour will show you many of the historic homes and buildings of the city.

Frantic Follies Vaudeville, (867) 668–2042, in the Westmark Whitehorse Hotel. A Gay Nineties revue with high-kicking cancan dancers, magic shows, Robert Service humor, and wacky skits. This is the best show in town.

MacBride Museum, First Avenue and Wood Street, (867) 667–2709. There are artifacts and photos from the gold rush period, including Sam McGee's cabin (McGee was a local character, celebrated in Robert Service's poem "The Cremation of Sam McGee"), as well as a display of stuffed and mounted Yukon animals.

Old Log Church Museum, Third Avenue and Elliott Street, (867) 668–2555. Opened in 1900, this Anglican church served

Whitehorse for sixty years. It now contains artifacts, photos, and documents telling the story of missionary work in the territory and its development.

SS *Klondike* **Sternwheeler National Historic Site,** downtown, (867) 667–4511. Launched in 1929, this restored sternwheeler was the largest used on the Yukon River. It has been fully fitted and furnished, and it is open for your inspection.

Takhini Hot Springs, located 27.4 km/17 mi from the city on Klondike Highway 2, (867) 633–2706. This is the place to soothe your aching body in warm mineral waters. Bathing suits can be rented. If you want more aches along with some pleasure, you can go on guided trail rides from Takhini and then come back for a soaking.

Guided Nature Walks, 302 Hawkins Street, (867) 668–5678. The Conservation Society takes visitors on nature hikes in the Whitehorse area.

The new **Yukon Beringia Interpretive Center,** on the Alaska Highway, just south of Whitehorse Airport, is a multimedia exposition that features life-size exhibits of animals of the last ice age. Interactive CD-ROM kiosks and dioramas depict the unique landscape, flora, and fauna of Beringia. Highlights include a full-size cast of the largest mammoth ever recovered and a reconstruction of the 24,000-year-old Cluefish Caves archaeological site.

All of the following accommodations have dining rooms and other amenities:

Edgewater Hotel, 101 Main Street, (867) 667–2572. Moderate.

Gold Rush Inn, 411 Main Street, (867) 668–4500. Expensive.

River View Hotel, 102 Wood Street, (867) 667–7801. Moderate.

Westmark Klondike Inn, 2288 Second Avenue, (867) 668–4747. Expensive.

Westmark Whitehorse Hotel, Second Avenue and Wood Street, (867) 668–4700. Expensive.

Yukon Inn Hotel, 4220 Fourth Avenue, (867) 667–2527. Moderate to expensive.

Dining possibilities in Whitehorse are varied:

Cellar Restaurant, at the Edgewater Hotel, 101 Main Street, (867) 667–2572. A gracious dining room in which are served excellent beef, steaks, lobster, and the regional specialty—king crab. Moderate to expensive.

Pandas Fine Dining, 212 Main Street, (867) 667–2632. European cuisine and seafood dishes. Moderate to expensive.

Talisman Café, 2112 Second Avenue, (867) 667–2736. European and North American cuisines. Moderate.

Dawson City

Dawson City was called the City of Gold, the end of the rainbow for thousands of dreamers who flooded here seeking their fortune in the gold fields near the city. In its heyday, when it was a gold rush boomtown, people who knew the place called Dawson the Paris of North America, meaning that it offered many pleasures (albeit without the beauty and civilization of the real Paris). It was certainly one of the liveliest cities in North America. Among the colorful characters who made Dawson famous were Robert Service, Jack London, Diamond Tooth Gertie, Klondike Kate, and the Northwest Mounted Police. The stereotypical tales of Mounties chasing mad trappers and gold seekers came from here, as did (probably) the slogan "the Mounties always get their man." This was Dawson's exciting, frenetic, crazy, fascinating period. While some dreamers found gold along Bonanza Creek and other gold-rich streams, a large number went bust—but that's the risk dreamers always take, whether in search of gold or Shangri-la.

Today Dawson City is a civilized, proper place of commerce, but with enough gold rush charm to make it a must-see destination for visitors to the Yukon.

For information on things to see and do in Dawson City and on places to stay and dine, stop in at the **Visitor Reception Centre,** Front Street at King, (867) 993–5566.

Midnight Dome, located 8 km/5 mi from town via King Street, is an 884-m/2,900-ft mountain that overlooks Dawson City, the Yukon and Klondike Rivers, Bonanza Creek, and many mountain ranges, such as the Ogilvies. This mountain is called Midnight Dome because at midnight every June 21 the sun shines at the top. (Actually, it does so everywhere in this region, but the thrill is to be at the top of the mountain on June 21 at midnight and still be able to see the surrounding scenery because of the daylight.) The road up Midnight Dome is very steep, and extreme caution should be taken in driving. Your best bet is to use the services of a Yukon tour company.

Dawson City Museum, Fifth Avenue, (867) 993–5291, is the city's heritage museum, featuring exhibits telling the story of the gold mania that took place in this area, the city as a boomtown during this exciting period, and its development thereafter. Call for hours and fees. The museum also has a genealogy service for you to track down dreamers in your family tree—perhaps one who became wealthy beyond dreams.

Diamond Tooth Gertie's Gambling Hall is where you make a quick buck or lose a bundle while being entertained by wildly

The Sourtoe Cocktail

Strange things are done 'neath the Midnight Sun . . . and one of the strangest is the Sourtoe Cocktail.

You might expect a Dawson City bar to create a Sourdough Cocktail. It fits with the gold rush imagery. But a Sourtoe?

If you walk into the Sourdough Saloon in the Downtown Hotel almost any day during happy hour, you'll meet "Captain" Bill Holmes initiating the brave into the Sourtoe Cocktail Club.

Captain Holmes relates the story of the original appendage connoisseur, Captain Dick Stevenson, as he gently plops the pickled toe into the drink of your choice. (Sorry, water is not allowed.)

If you swallow your fear (and *not* the toe—Captain Bill is very strict about his rule that any lost toe must be replaced) and slam back the toe-filled drink, you are officially among the nearly 15,000 worldwide members of the Sourtoe Cocktail Club.

Captain Dick began the Sourtoe saga in 1973. The idea sprang from a human toe found in Dick Stevenson's new cabin, and a conversation about an Ice Worm drink in a famous Robert Service poem.

As we said, "Strange things are done 'neath the Midnight Sun."

kicking cancan dancers and honky-tonk music. Open May through September. Call the Klondike Visitors Association, (867) 993–5575, for information. Gertie's is the best show in town and sufficient reason to visit Dawson. Gertie herself was a colorful and now-legendary "woman of the flesh" who was also a savvy business entrepreneur catering to the dreamers' needs for female company, strong drink, and games of chance.

Gaslight Follies, (867) 993–5575, provides an evening of good entertainment. Arizona Charlie Meadows built the Palace Grand Theatre at the turn of the twentieth century to provide high-class entertainment to the dreamers and wheeler-dealers of the Yukon. "Olde Tyme" shows are presented nightly, except Tuesday.

Bonanza Creek is located 22 km/14 mi away via the Klondike Highway and Bonanza Creek Road. Along here some prospectors found gold. Claims were based on this measurement: 10 BD, meaning "10 claims Below the initial Discovery"; 25 AD was "25 claims Above Discovery." In this area is dredge #4, purported to be the largest gold-recovery dredge in the world.

Visit the **Jack London Cabin,** (867) 993–5575. Call the Klondike Visitors Association for hours. Free. North America's immortal author Jack London had a cabin in the bush on Henderson Creek. It was later relocated to Dawson City, with half of the original structure going to Jack London Square in Oakland, California. London's books told of life in the Yukon and Alaska as a mystical struggle of individual men and women against an unyielding environment and against their own limitations. Readings of London's works—*Call of the Wild* and others—are presented at the cabin.

Robert Service Cabin, (867) 993–5462, is also open to visitors. Call for hours. The poet Robert Service (1874–1958) is called the "bard of the Yukon." He wrote most of his poetry— "Songs of a Sourdough"—in his cabin, and there are daily recitals of his poetry. As you travel through the Yukon, the images Robert Service wrote about will be seen everywhere you go.

Harrington's Store, Third Avenue and Princess Street, has a photo exhibit showing early boomtown days in Dawson City.

Stamps can be purchased at the historic **1901 Post Office.** It is a favorite stop for stamp collectors.

Claim #33 Below Discovery is 10 km/6.2 mi up the Bonanza Road, (867) 993–5804. Call for hours and cost. Here you can pan for gold; pans and other gear are supplied, with some gold in every pan.

At **Guggieville,** (867) 993–5008, located 2 km/1.2 mi outside town on Bonanza Creek Road, you can pan for gold at what was Guggenheim's mining camp, which operated in the early 1900s.

Gold City Tours, (867) 993–5175, offers tours of Dawson, Bonanza Creek, and Midnight Dome.

All of the accommodations listed below have dining rooms and other amenities:

Dawson City Bunkhouse, Princess Street, (867) 993–6164. Newly built, reasonable prices, 1 block from downtown. All amenities. Moderate.

Downtown Hotel, Second Avenue and Queen Street, (867) 993–5346. Expensive.

Eldorado Hotel, Third and Princess Street, (867) 993–5451. Expensive.

Klondike Kate's, (867) 993–6527. Moderate.

Midnight Sun Hotel, Third and Queen Street, (867) 993–5495. Moderate.

Westmark Inn, (867) 993–5542. Expensive.

Here's a restaurant that you may want to sample:

Nancy's, (867) 993–5633. Homemade soups, sandwiches, pastries, ice cream. Also herbal teas and flavored coffees; sour-dough-pancake breakfasts. Inexpensive.

Beaver Creek

Beaver Creek is the last town of any size on the Alaska Highway at the Yukon–Alaska border. The **Westmark Inn,** (867) 862–7501, has good rooms, a restaurant, dinner theater, RV park, minigolf, store, and lounge. Expensive.

The Northwest Territories

As of April 1, 1999, the Northwest Territories divided to create two territories, the Inuit self-governing territory of the Eastern Arctic called Nunavut, and the Northwest Territories.

The landmass and water areas comprising the Northwest Territories are so vast that you could place much of Europe inside with plenty of room left over. On the southern border, along the sixtieth parallel, are the provinces of British Columbia, Alberta, and Saskatchewan. Within the Northwest Territories are Great Slave Lake, Great Bear Lake, the Mackenzie River, Banks Island, and the Parry Islands. About half of the region is above the Arctic Circle. The area is the site of the fabled Northwest Passage, from Europe to the Orient. This is the land of the Inuit (Eskimo), Déné, and Métis, a place where countless explorers, from Franklin to Byrd, have sought fame. The Northwest Territories is one of the harshest yet most magnificent regions on earth. Thanks to aviation, many exceptional natural areas and remote communities are accessible within a few hours of such cities as Edmonton, Winnipeg, Calgary, and Vancouver.

The western portion of the Northwest Territories borders the Yukon to the west; British Columbia, Alberta, and Saskatchewan to the south; the Beaufort Sea and the Amundsen Gulf to the north; and the Coppermine River and eastern shores of Great Slave Lake to the east. The high Mackenzie Mountains and the Franklin Mountains rise up in the west; a boreal forest makes a swath across the southern zone; the Mackenzie River, including Great Bear and Great Slave Lakes, are among the earth's great water systems; and the Beaufort Sea, part of the Arctic Ocean, provides many miles of shoreline.

Northwest Territories Tourism

For travel information, contact the Northwest Territories Tourism, Box 1320, Yellowknife, Northwest Territory X1A 2L9; (800) 661–0788, (867) 873–7200, fax (867) 873–0163; arctic@nwttravel.nt.ca or www.nwttravel.nt.ca

In Yellowknife you can rent cars from Avis, Budget, Hertz, and Tilden. Call your local rental-car agency for rates and reservations.

Here is an arctic climate with long, extremely cold winters. Nonetheless, midsummer days can have temperatures up to 30°C/89°F. Summers tend to be warmer in the Mackenzie River Valley. A tundra environment, during warm weather, does produce mosquitoes. If you are trekking and camping, it is a good idea to wear bug jackets to cover exposed skin areas and use repellent lotions and sprays. Once you overcome this annoyance, you'll love every moment of your stay. June, July, and August are the best months for visiting the Northwest Territories. Mid-August through September is prime time for viewing the northern lights. If you want a real adventure, come here in winter, go dogsledding or snowmobiling, view the spectacular northern lights, or sleep in an igloo you made yourself. When traveling here during summer, comfortable casual clothes are best, including a sweater or two, a windbreaker, and good hiking or walking shoes with cushioning socks. Cameras with telephoto lenses and binoculars are also important bring-alongs.

There are 41,807 people living in the Northwest Territories, giving the region one of the lowest population densities per square mile on earth. The capital of the Northwest Territories is Yellowknife, located on the north shore of Great Slave Lake, with highway access to British Columbia and Alberta (and thence to all major North American centers). Yellowknife became the capital of the Northwest Territories when the office of federal commissioner was transferred from Ottawa to this city. Its population is now 18,000. Fort Smith, Hay River, Fort Simpson, and Inuvik are Northwest Territories communities with populations between 2,000 and 3,000 people. There are only thirty-three communities in all of the Northwest Territories. People make their living here from mining gold and diamonds, fishing, tourism, arts and crafts, hunting, and trapping. The Native people of this part of the Northwest Territories are famous for such arts and crafts as moose-hair tufting, porcupine-quill work, traditional embroidery and beadwork, fine leathercraft, and fur-garment making.

The Northwest Territories: Some Basic Facts

The Northwest Territories was split into two northern territories in 1999. Stretching from the Manitoba border to the northern tip of Ellesmere Island, the newly named portion, Nunavut, is larger than any other province or territory. The land-claim settlement from which the split results gives the Inuit outright ownership of about 18 percent of the land, while the remaining 82 percent remains Crown lands. It is the largest and richest Native land claim ever in Canada—and, notably, the friendliest and most peaceful division in history.

Fort Smith had the highest recorded temperature in the Northwest Territories: 35.4°C/95.7°F; it also had the lowest recorded temperature: −53.9°C/−65°F.

The Mackenzie River is 1,800 km/1,118 mi long. When considered as including Slave, Peace, and Finlay Rivers, it is about 4,216 km/2,635 mi long, the second longest river in North America.

Great Bear Lake is the ninth largest lake in the world.

Great Slave Lake is the sixth deepest lake in the world.

The Northwest Territories entered the Canadian Confederation on July 15, 1870.

The first white explorers were the Vikings, in about A.D. 1000. In 1576 Martin Frobisher was the first of a long stream of explorers who came here searching for the Northwest Passage. Samuel Hearne and Alexander Mackenzie both trekked over much of the uncharted land during the eighteenth century. John Franklin and his expedition in the mid-1800s tried to find the Northwest Passage, but the party disappeared in the Arctic and the search for them was a major cause célèbre for many years. Other nineteenth-century explorers included M'Clure, Amundsen, Sverdrup, and Stefansson.

Useful Information

Area code: 867
Time zone: Mountain

Nahanni National Park

There is no access by land vehicle into Nahanni National Park, as it is essentially a wilderness park, but you can experience some of the park's natural wonders, such as Virginia Falls, by using the services of an air charter or an adventure tour organization providing canoe or wild-river rafting trips. Wild-river tours on the South Nahanni are considered among the top adventure experiences in North America; some of the companies providing Nahanni trips are listed at the beginning of this chapter. Fort Simpson is the base of operations for air and many other expeditions into the park, and the town can be reached via Highways 7 or 1. Floatplane tours can also be booked at Watson Lake in the Yukon and Fort Nelson in British Columbia. July and August are the best months in which to visit the park. If you are not an experienced wilderness traveler, it is advisable to explore the Nahanni with a guided tour group. The tour and outfitting services are well versed and supply commentary on the park, its features, and history. For more information on the park, contact Superintendent, Nahanni National Park, Box 300, Fort Simpson, Northwest Territories X0E 0N0, (867) 695–3151.

An exceptional North American wilderness park, Nahanni was the first such area in the world to be designated by UNESCO in 1979 as a natural site of universal importance. One of the wildest waterways in the park is the South Nahanni River, which charges more than 322 km/193 mi before plunging down Virginia Falls, twice the height of Niagara Falls. Downriver from the falls are 8 km/4.9 mi of turbulent rapids and waves. It is not unusual to see wild orchids blooming next to patches of snow near Virginia Falls. The park also has four great canyons, which are as deep as 1,200 m/3,935 ft. Rabbitkettle Hotsprings and Wildmint Hotsprings are other natural features. The waters gushing up from Rabbitkettle are 20°C/68°F and form a terraced mount of tufa rock that is more than 27 m/88.5 ft high. The park has 13 species of fish, such as Arctic grayling and Dolly Varden trout; more than 120 species of birds, including the golden eagle and trumpeter swan; and more than 40 species of animals—wolves, grizzly and black bears, caribou, and beaver. Although now a wilderness park, Nahanni during the gold rush days was combed over by dreamers in search of fortune, mostly to no avail. Their travails gave names to places in the park, such as Deadmen Valley and Headless Creek.

Yellowknife

On the north shore of Great Slave Lake, with a population of close to 17,700, Yellowknife is the capital of the Northwest Territories. It was founded in 1934 as a result of a minor gold rush. In

Special Events in Yellowknife

Caribou Carnival, winter celebration and coming of spring, late March

Canadian Championship Dog Derby Race, World Cup-sanctioned event of dogsled racing, late March

Midnight Sun Golf Tournament, mid-June

Raven Mad Daze, celebrating the solstice, mid-June

Under the Midnight Sun Festival, series of one-act plays, early July

Festival of the Midnight Sun, second week in July

Folks on the Rocks, Déné and Inuit folksingers and performers, mid-July

Commissioner's Cup Race, a sailboat race on Great Slave Lake, September

the area is one operating gold mine. Yellowknife is a good base from which to explore remote areas of the Northwest Territories. There are adequate accommodations, restaurants, shops, and services in town. Also visit the **Bush Pilot's Monument,** a memorial to the pilots who, in the early days, explored and assisted in the development of the Northwest Territories. For further information, contact the NWT Arctic Tourism Office at (800) 661–0788; or for Yellowknife information contact the Northern Frontier Visitors Centre, (877) 881–4262 or www.northernfrontier.com.

How to Get to Yellowknife
By Car or Recreational Vehicle

Yellowknife is the hub city for visiting the Northwest Territories. Most roads and air routes lead to and radiate from Yellowknife. If you are interested in driving to the northwest corner of the region (Fort McPherson, Arctic Red River, and Inuvik), use the Dempster Highway from Dawson City, Yukon (see the description of this route in the Yukon section).

If you are traveling the Alaska Highway and reach Fort Nelson in British Columbia, you can take Highway 7 North past Nahanni National Park to Mackenzie Highway 1 East, which leads to Highway 3 and then 4 to Yellowknife. If Yellowknife is your

How Far Is It?

Road distances to the Northwest Territories border using the Mackenzie Highway:

Edmonton: 990 km/615 mi
Calgary: 1,276 km/793 mi
Vancouver: 2,330 km/1,448 mi
Winnipeg: 2,357 km/1,465 mi
Toronto: 4,582 km/2,848 mi
Montreal: 4,734 km/2,942 mi
Los Angeles: 3,960 km/2,461 mi
Alberta border: 528 km/316 mi

primary destination in the north and you are traveling from the east, your best route is Mackenzie Highway 35 North from Edmonton, Alberta, which connects with Northwest Territories Highways 1, 3, and 4 to the city (see the safe driving tips in Chapter 2). Mackenzie Highway is paved to Rae with ongoing construction and paving upgrades during summer months between Yellowknife and Rae.

By Plane

Daily air service to Yellowknife from Edmonton and Calgary is provided by Canadian North and First Air. Air service within the Northwest Territories is provided by charter and scheduled airlines, such as Calm Air, Air Providence, First Air, Air Tindi, Buffalo Airways, Northwestern Air Lease, Arctic Excursions, and Wolverine Air. For details, call NWT Tourism's toll-free number, (800) 661–0788, or your travel agent.

In addition to jet planes, commonly used aircraft in the region are the twin-engine Otter, the workhorse of the North; Piper T 1040; F-28; Gulfstream 1; DC-3; Metro II; Navajo Chieftain; Aztec; Cheyenne III; De Havilland Turbo; and Cessna 185. Many of these planes are equipped with floats so that they can land in water in remote areas where there are no airfields. In winter skis can be used. Flying in the Northwest Territories can be an adventure in itself, and the pilots here are among the finest in the world.

Attractions in Yellowknife

Prince of Wales Northern Heritage Centre, named in honor of HRH Prince Charles, (867) 873–7551. Open throughout the year.

The collection in this museum includes artifacts from Inuit, Déné, and Métis cultures, early mining and aviation history, and other aspects of the ecology and human heritage of the Northwest Territories.

Bush Pilot's Monument. Atop a solid mass of Precambrian Shield. Follow Ingraham Drive up to the top and then climb the stairs for a spectacular view of Great Slave Lake and the Yellowknife skyline, including Nerco Con Mine, Giant Mine, and Old Town. The monument honors bush pilots who opened the north to industry and exploration.

Wildcat Café. Opened in 1937 and operated as a cafe into the 1960s, it then reopened briefly when bush pilots returned to Yellowknife for the dedication of the Bush Pilot's Monument in 1967. Today the cafe is open only during summer months.

Northern Frontier Visitors Centre. Across the causeway from the Prince of Wales Northern Heritage Centre, this visitor center is full of information on local adventure tours, lodges, and things to do in the city. The building itself has a stylish spiral gallery in which to view photos and read information.

Yellowknife Courthouse. Just a block away from the visitor center is the courthouse where, on the second floor, you can view the Sissons-Morrow collection of Inuit carvings depicting cases heard by the NWT's first resident supreme court judge. The collection was given to the people of the North after Judge J. H. Sisson died in 1969.

NWT Legislative Assembly Building. Officially opened in November 1993, the permanent home of the Legislative Assembly is in a natural setting on the shore of Frame Lake, a short walk from the center of Yellowknife. Tours are available at no charge.

Birchwood Gallery, Yellowknife Center Mall, Franklin Avenue, (867) 873–4050, displays original paintings and prints from northern artists.

Yellowknife Book Cellar, Panda II center, (867) 920–2220, specializes in books about the North.

Northern Images, 4801 Franklin Avenue, (867) 873–5944, sells soapstone sculptures, Inuit prints, parkas, and wall hangings.

Gallery of the Midnight Sun, located in Old Town, (867) 873–8064, offers a selection of Inuit sculptures, arts, and crafts.

Nor-Art, Centre Square Mall, (867) 920–7002, sells original paintings, silks, carvings, and pottery.

Accommodations in Yellowknife

Discovery Inn, 4701 Franklin Avenue, (867) 873–4151. Moderate to expensive.

Executive Hotel, 4920 Fifty-fourth Avenue, (867) 920–3999. Completely furnished suites. Moderate to expensive.
Explorer Hotel, Forty-first Street at Forty-ninth Avenue, (867) 873–3531. Moderate to expensive.
Northern Lites Motel, 5115 Fiftieth Street, (867) 873–6023. Moderate to expensive.
Igloo Inn, Franklin Street, (867) 873–8511. Moderate to expensive.
Yellowknife Inn, Fiftieth Street at Fiftieth Avenue, (867) 873–2601. Moderate to expensive.
Yellowknife has more than a dozen bed-and-breakfast establishments; for a complete list contact the Northern Frontier Visitors Centre at (877) 881–4262 or www.northernfrontiers.com.
A&H Great Slave Lake B&B, 87B Morrison Drive, (867) 920–7160. Lakefront house. Moderate.
Captain Ron's B&B, 8 Lessard Drive, (867) 873–3746. On the shores of Great Slave Lake and near the Wildcat Café. Moderate.
The Prospector B&B, 3306 Wiley Road, (867) 920–7620. In historic Old Town, across from the Wildcat. Moderate.
The Bayside B&B, 3505 McDonald Drive, (867) 920–4686, lakefront house. Moderate.

Key Communities and Accommodations

All the accommodations cited in this section have dining rooms and other amenities and are priced in the high-moderate to expensive range:
Fort McPherson (reached via Dempster Highway from Dawson City, Yukon) was the northern terminus for Northwest Mounted Police patrols from Dawson City during the early part of this century.
Inuvik means "place of man." Alexander Mackenzie canoed by here in 1789 on his way to the Arctic Ocean. Today the town is the government, commercial, and transportation center for the Western Arctic. It is also a supply base for oil and gas exploration in the Beaufort Sea and headquarters of the Inuvialuit, the first group to receive a land-claim settlement in the Northwest Territories. Accommodations are available at **Eskimo Inn,** (867)

Lodges in the Yellowknife Area

The following lodges are for anglers and those who want to get away from it all. The accommodations are comfortable, and the food is great. Fishing equipment, guides, and boats are provided as needed. Services and facilities vary; call ahead for full details and reservations.

Aylmer Lake Lodge, Aylmer Lake, (888) 832-2299

Blachford Lake Lodge, Blachford Lake, (867) 873-3303

Enodah Wilderness Travel, North Arm Great Slave Lake, (867) 873-4334

Frontier Fishing Lodge, on Great Slave Lake, (867) 465-6843

Mackay Lodge, on Mackay Lake, (867) 873-8533

Pilot Point Lodge, on Duncan Lake, (867) 669-7000

Plummers, on Great Slave Lake, (867) 665-0240

Prelude Lake Lodge, (867) 873-4776

Sandy Point Lodge, on Gordon Lake, (867) 920-2339

Trophy Lodge, on Great Slave Lake, (867) 873-5420

Watta Lake Lodge, (867) 872-5330

979-2801; **Finto Motor Inn,** (867) 979-2647; and **Mackenzie Hotel,** (867) 979-2861.

Tuktoyaktuk is a remote community on the shores of the Beaufort Sea, only 160 km/99 mi south of the polar ice cap. From here you can see Canada's famous pingos, hills pushed up by heaving permafrost. Visit *Our Lady of Lourdes* mission boat. Alaskan Inupiat descendants and whale-hunting Karngmalit people live the traditional life of hunting, trapping, sealing, fishing, and reindeer herding. **Hotel Tuk Inn,** (867) 977-2381, and **Pingo Park Lodge,** (867) 977-2155, are places to stay here.

Fort Simpson is the center for trips into Nahanni National Park. Established in 1804, it is the oldest continuously occupied community on the Mackenzie River. Pope John Paul II visited the people of Fort Simpson, fulfilling a promise made after a previous stop had to be canceled because of bad weather. **The Nahanni**

Inn, (867) 695–2201, is located here, as is the **Maroda Hotel,** (867) 695–2602.

Fort Smith provides road access to Wood Buffalo National Park (detailed in Chapter 7). Most of the park is in Alberta, but about one-third is in the Northwest Territories. Fort Smith is located on the eastern border parts, on the Northwest Territories–Alberta border. The town itself was once a part of a chain of fur-trading posts, and Alexander Mackenzie explored this area in his search for the Pacific Ocean. The **Thebacha Campus of Arctic College** is now part of Fort Smith's life. While in Fort Smith, visit the **Northern Life Museum,** (867) 872–2859, and **North of 60 Books,** (867) 872–2606, which has a large selection of books, maps, and charts of the North.

Pinecrest Hotel, (867) 872–2320, also provides accommodations.

Hay River is the southernmost port on the Mackenzie River system. Visit the Coast Guard headquarters in town. Sandy beaches are on Great Slave Lake, which is good for swimming in summer, and a golf course is in town. You can drive to Hay River from the south or take a flight from Edmonton, Alberta, on any day of the week. **Hay River Hotel,** (867) 874–6022, and **Ptarmigan Inn,** (867) 874–6781 or (800) 661–0842, provide accommodations.

Nunavut: Canada's True Arctic

On April 1, 1999, the map of Canada changed for the first time in fifty years (Newfoundland joined Canada in 1949) when the Northwest Territories were divided in two and the new territory of Nunavut was created.

This is a land of almost unimaginable diversity and memorable beauty. It is one of the last great unspoiled wilderness habitats on earth. You will discover towering mountain fortresses, an archipelago filled with icebergs, and an immense array of wildlife. Walruses, narwhals, beluga whales, musk-oxen, and polar bears call this awesome domain home.

Nunavut is also home to the Inuit—a remarkable people who are keepers of an ancient culture that stretches back thousands of years. Nunavut means "our land" in Inukitut, the Inuit language.

In size Nunavut encompasses about one-fifth the landmass of Canada. From north to south it stretches about as far as London to Beruit, and to travel east to west would be the equivalent of flying from Miami to Lima, Peru.

There is a sense of the eternal about the Inuit living in Nunavut. It seems as if they have always been here and always will be.

Physically the land is stark and beautiful in the same breath. The landscape ranges from mountains and fjords on the eastern shores of Baffin and Ellesmere Islands, through the many lakes and tundra of the empty lands on the mainland between the Hudson Bay coast and western territory boundary near the Manitoba border, to the plateaus and cliffs of the Arctic coast and the Coronation Gulf.

Nunavut is the result of years of negotiations between the Inuit, who have long yearned to govern their own land and future, and the Canadian government. This new territory will be governed by a commissioner, an elected legislative assembly, a cabinet, and a territorial court that will gradually assume the responsibilities formerly exercised by the Northwest Territories government.

Nunavut is bounded on the east by Davis Inlet and Baffin Bay, and to the south by Hudson Strait, Hudson Bay, and the northern border of Manitoba. To the north is the Arctic Ocean, and to the west the remainder of the Northwest Territories.

Nunavut is an exciting new frontier, waiting to be explored. Its exotic beauty is a dramatic contrast to the modern Western world. To live in an igloo, explore the frozen Arctic by dogsled or snowmobile, or simply gaze in awe at the nighttime spectacle of aurora borealis and clear skies is an adventure that will provide a lifetime of memories. Nunavut, the last frontier of Canada.

The new territory includes Baffin Island, Ellesmere Island, Southampton Island, Prince of Wales Island, Somerset Island, and the eastern half of Victoria Island. The North Magnetic Pole falls inside Nunavut.

The capital of Nunavut is Iqaluit, formerly called Frobisher Bay. The Inuit word means "place of fishes." At the northern tip of Ellesmere Island is Alert, the northernmost settlement in the world.

Nunavut has not always been part of the Great White North. Just above the eightieth parallel, on Axel Heiberg Island, are the remains of tree stumps and alligator bones, meaning that forty-five million years ago this part of the world had a climate similar to that of the Florida Everglades.

Nunavut Tourism

Contact Nunavut Tourism, P.O. Box 1450, Iqaluit, Nunavut X0A
0H0; (800) 491–7910 or www.nunatour.nt.ca.

Useful Information
Area code: 867
Time zones: Atlantic, Eastern, and Central
Climate: The winter temperature here can drop to –40°C (it's the
  same in Fahrenheit); add windchill and whiteout conditions
  and you have a difficult season. But some days are more like
  –15°C or 0°F, and with the sun shining and the snow crunch-
  ing under your feet, it's a good time for cross-country skiing.
In summer the mosquitoes will compete with the dust to aggravate
you. Keep a bug jacket on over your T-shirt.

How to Get to Nunavut
Air transportation to the larger communities in Nunavut, such as
Iqaluit, Franklin Inlet, Resolute Bay, and Cambridge Bay, is provided through scheduled jet service from most major cities in
Canada. From these points travelers connect to twin- or single-
engine propeller aircraft. Scheduled air service is operated by the
following airlines:

> Calm Air, www.calmair.com
> Canadian North, www.cdnair.ca
> First Air, www.firstair.ca
> NWT Air, www.nwtair.nt.ca

Baffin Island and Iqaluit
Baffin Island, named for the British sailor William Baffin, who explored the island's coastal waters in 1615 and 1616, is the largest,
most inhabited, and most scenicly spectacular in the Arctic archipelago. Almost two-thirds of the island lies north of the Arctic
Circle and in summer, with its continuous hours of daylight, the
tundra blooms with an astonishing variety of tiny colorful flowers.
Most who live here are Inuit, and they pursue their traditional
lifestyles in small communities. The administrative center and
largest community on the island is Iqaluit.

Early Exploration

With southern sea routes to Asia controlled by the Spanish and Portuguese in the sixteenth century, the British dreamed of a Northwest Passage to the riches of the Orient over the top of North America. The dream turned into an obsession for close to 300 years, despite the fact that no practical route was ever discovered.

In 1576 Sir Martin Frobisher was the first among many British sailors to venture into the icy Arctic waters. Their tiny ships were ill equipped for ice-clogged seas. The worst disaster was the third voyage of John Franklin in 1845: The entire expedition, 129 men, was lost. Not all expeditions were so ill-fated. Three hundred years after Martin Frobisher's voyages, Norwegian explorer Roald Amundsen, aboard the vessel *Gjoa,* finally navigated the Northwest Passage. And in 1944 the *St. Roch,* an RCMP Arctic supply and patrol ship, successfully navigated the Northwest Passage in both directions in one year. The *St. Roch* is now drydocked at the Maritime Museum in Vancouver, British Columbia.

Land expeditions on the whole were much more successful. In 1770 Samuel Hearne and his Chipewyan guide, Matonabbee, went from Prince of Wales Fort on Hudson Bay to the mouth of the Coppermine River—making Hearne the first European to travel overland to the Arctic coast of North America.

Originally known as Frobisher Bay, Iqaluit is regional seat of government for the newly formed territory of Nunavut and is the gateway for tourism to this vast region.

It is a modern settlement with a complete infrastructure of hotels, schools, hospitals, weather and radio stations, and even a camp site. The year-round population is approximately 3,500.

Iqaluit balances between the twenty-first century and a culture that has survived and thrived for thousands of years in a land of harsh realities. A simple stroll through the town reveals artists and carvers working at their traditional crafts and caribou grazing on the fringes of the settlement. You will see dog teams, but the preferred modes of transport are snowmobiles and ATVs. Igloos are still used, but you're more likely to see modern prebuilt constructions, complete with Internet connections.

The town includes banks, a post office, several churches, a theater, a swimming pool, a drugstore, restaurants, and several art galleries.

Sights and Attractions

Unikkaarvik Baffin Regional Visitor Information Centre, (867) 979–4636. Displays depict the life and culture of the southern Baffin, including a life-size diorama of the floe edge above and below the water, and a larger-than-life-size marble carving of a drum dancer. This is a good source of advice on activities, events, and attractions.

Qaummaarviit Historic Park, on an island in Frobisher Bay, 12 km/9 mi east of Iqaluit. Occupied for more than 1,000 years by the Thule Inuit, who lived in villages and hunted the bowhead whale. There are remains of house foundations, tent rings, and meat caches. Outfitters offer trips by snowmobile or dog team and by boat in summer.

Auyuittuq National Park Reserve, Pangnirtung, open year-round except national holidays; $15-per-day user fee. For information call (867) 473–8828. A stark and forbidding landscape of perpetual ice, jagged peaks, and glacier-scarred valleys. Auyuittuq means "land that never melts" in Inukitut, an appropriate name for Canada's first national park north of the Arctic Circle. Fully a quarter of its area is covered by the Penny Ice Cap. Since its creation in 1972, the park has drawn climbers from around the world to challenge its landscape.

Activities

Arts and crafts

The Inuit of Nunavut have long been associated with soapstone carvings, printmaking and woven wall hangings, caribou antler jewelry, and replicas of tools of skin or stone from a more traditional time. Summer courses in Quivviuq weaving, photography, and watercolor painting are offered in outdoor classrooms. For more information visit www.nunatour.nt.ca./artscrafts.html.

Wildlife Viewing

In Nunavut wildlife viewing is accomplished by trekking either by foot or boat in summer, or via dogsled or snow machine in spring to the edge of an ice floe. Musk oxen and caribou can be seen in herds, as can thousands of seabirds nesting in the cliff areas such as Bylot Island. Whales, seals, and walruses abound in selected areas.

Floe Edge Tours

One of the most astonishing events in the Arctic occurs in summer at a place where the land-fast ice meets the open sea—the floe edge. Plankton begins to bloom, and huge schools of shrimp and fish congregate to feast on it. The polar bears follow, haunting the ice floes in their quest for seals. If you want the thrill of seeing a polar bear, humpback whale, walrus, or narwhal, make this trek to the floe edge. Inuit guides take visitors on guided snowmobile or dogsled tours to search for this wildlife and icebergs.

For floe edge tours, mountain climbing, kayaking, river rafting, sport fishing, or dogsledding, Nunavut Tourism (www.nunatour.nt.ca) can provide a comprehensive list of licensed tour operators.

Accommodations

You can overnight in an igloo or a first-class hotel. Or both: Take an overnight trip to get a taste of life in an igloo and then return to your hotel and catch up with CNN, direct-dial phone, and indoor plumbing.

Navigator Inn, (867) 979–2601 or www.arctictravel.com/EVAZ/navigator.html. A modern hotel and conference center with executive suites, a licensed dining room, and a coffee shop. All rooms are equipped with cable TV, AM/FM radio, modem-ready telephones, and full baths with showers. Moderate to expensive.

Discovery Lodge Hotel, P. O. Box 387, (867) 979–4433 or www.arctictravel.com/DIS/covery.html. The hotel has comfortable rooms, an executive suite, and conference and banquet facilities. Internet access, voicemail, fax and copier services, laundry, room service, and airport pickup are a few of the amenities. Moderate to expensive.

Frobisher Inn, P. O. Box 4209, (867) 979–2222 or frobinn@nunanet.com. Iqaluit's largest hotel, with an award-winning restaurant and lounge, a coffee bar, and conference facilities. Rooms feature original Inuit art. Some deluxe rooms and suites feature fireplaces and Jacuzzi tubs. Moderate to expensive.

Dining

One taste of double-smoked Arctic char and you may abandon your smoked salmon and cream cheese forever. Try local specialties such as caribou steaks, musk ox or caribou jerky, or scallops and giant fresh shrimp from frozen Arctic waters. Most of the restaurants in Iqaluit are connected to a hotel.

Special Events

Festivals and events are held in most communities to herald the arrival of spring, the return of the sun after a prolonged season of darkness, special holidays, and sporting events.

March/April

Easter celebrations. In bygone days people came in off the land, bringing their white fox skins and other furs, to trade and attend services in the small missions at Easter. The tradition continues, but today the activities include snowmobile and dogsled races.

Hamlet Days. These special celebrations in numerous communities generally combine traditional and modern games, music, and community feasts. For information call the Hamlet office in the community you intend to visit.

Nunavut 200 Dogteam Race. This important long-distance dog-team race alternates starts in Rankin Inlet and Arviat. The 322-m/ 200-mi race along the sea ice from one community to the other lasts five days and draws about thirty entrants, mostly traditional teams. For information call (867) 645-3754.

May

Omingmak Frolics in Cambridge Bay. A four-day festival that includes northern games, a talent show, snowmobile races, and a fantastic community feast. For information call (867) 983-2337.

June

Kingalik Jamboree. The community of Holman on Victoria Island holds an annual celebration on Victoria Day weekend that includes traditional events such as tea-boiling, duck-plucking, fish-filleting, square-dancing, and jigging contests. For information call (867) 376-3511.

July

Canada Day celebrations. Most Nunavut communities conduct celebrations on or around Canada Day (July 1). These range from parades to traditional dress contests, Inuit games, and often a community feast or square dance.

Nunavut Day, July 9. Join the celebration of summer and the formation of Nunavut. Events takes place throughout the territory. The Elders are an important part of this celebration.

Midnight Sun Marathon. The world's northernmost marathon draws runners from Canada, the United States, Europe, and Australia. There are 10-, 32-, 42-, and 84-km races between Nanisivik Mine and Arctic Bay. The marathon is open to only a hundred runners. For information call (867) 436-7435.

Midnight Sun Golf Tournament, Pelly Bay. This all-night golf tournament features an original, homemade golf course, complete with rugs right out of the homes of local citizens. For information call (867) 769-6281.

Cape Dorset E.A. Music Festival. Drum dancing, throat singing, and dancing to the music of fiddle, accordion, guitar, and concertina are all part of this traditional and contemporary music festival held in Nunanvut's most famous art community. For information call (867) 897-8943.

August

Kitikmeot Northern Games, Gjoa Haven and Taloyoak. Join competitors in traditional games such as bannock making, tea boiling, and duck plucking. Events include Alaskan high-kick, one-arm-reach, and Good Man/Good Woman contests, along with a northern feast. For information call (867) 561-6541.

December

Christmas in Nunavut. Christmas festivals are held in virtually every community. Pageants at the schools, caroling, church services on Christmas Eve, traditional games, dog team and snowmobile races, and indoor games of a ridiculous nature highlight the festivities. Blizzards may come and go, but the season is celebrated with much enthusiasm.

Adventure Touring Services

If you are not planning and executing your own wilderness expedition, the best way to experience this region is through the services of a licensed Northwest Territories tour operator, who will provide transportation, lodging, meals, outfitters, and knowledgeable commentary. There are both standard packages and those tailored to your interests—hunting and fishing, aurora viewing, canoeing, dogsledding, camping, trekking, and so forth. Among the advantages of using professional services is that the guides usually know where such animals as caribou, musk oxen, wolves, buffalo, and bears (including polar bears) can be seen. These guides can take you to remote villages, where you can see something of a way of life existing without major change for thousands of years. They know where to go, how to get there, and what to see. These services maximize your vacation experience in an incredibly rich area that, a few years ago, seemed remote and inaccessible.

Adventure Canada, Toronto, (800) 363–7566. Canoe or raft adventure trips to Nahanni National Park via the South Nahanni River.

Arctic Touring Company, Tuktoyaktuk, Northwest Territories, (867) 977–2230; fax (867) 977–2276; auroranet.nt.ca. Mackenzie Delta naturalist tours, festival and cultural tours, town tours, Dempster Highway tours.

Arctic Nature Tours, Inuvik, Northwest Territories, (867) 777–3300; fax (867) 777–3400; arctic@permafrost.com; www.arcticnaturetours.com. Tour packages on Dempster Highway, Mackenzie Highway, Richardson Mountains, Banks and Herschel Islands.

Black Feather Wilderness Adventures of Toronto and Ottawa, (800) 574–8375. Guided canoe trips down the Nahanni, Natla-Keele, and Mountain Rivers.

Blachford Lake Lodge, Yellowknife, Northwest Territories, (867) 920–4013 or blachford@internorth.com/blachford. Birdwatching, wildlife viewing, hiking, nature trails, day and overnight canoe trips, summer and winter activities.

Canoe Arctic, Fort Smith, Northwest Territories, (867) 872–2308; canoearctic@auroranet.nt.ca. Fly-in canoe trips are guided by wildlife biologist Alex Hall.

Great Slave Sledging Company, Yellowknife, Northwest Territories, (867) 920–4542. Fishing and camping adventures on the remote western shore of Great Slave Lake. Also offers winter experiences: dogsled trips and skiing expeditions.

Hudson Bay Tour Company, Rankin Inlet, Nunavit, (867)

645–2618. Variety of tour packages from dog-team trips to fishing expeditions, art to history.

Northcott Tour Planning & Consulting, Iqaluit, Nunavit, (867) 979–6261. Custom-designed tours for groups and individuals—dogsledding, kayaking, hiking, fishing, hunting.

Northwinds Arctic Tours, Iqaluit, Nunavit, (867) 979–0551. Summer and winter package adventures that share the culture and beauty of Baffin Island.

Raven Tours, Yellowknife, Northwest Territories, (867) 873–4776. Several day-trip options: City of Gold tour, Cameron Falls hike, dog-team rides, fishing, bird-watching, cruises on Great Slave Lake, "flight-seeing," caribou-viewing, and aurora borealis tours.

Sub-Arctic Wilderness Adventures, Fort Smith, Northwest Territories, (867) 872–2467. Great Slave circle tour, boating the Slave, trip to Wood Buffalo National Park, dog-team wilderness trip, Tazin highlands, and subarctic spring experience.

Nahanni River Adventures, Whitehorse, Yukon, (867) 668–3180; (800) 287–6927. Trips on the Nahanni River by canoe.

Index

John Walter Museum,
    Alberta, 243

K

Kamloops, B.C., 63–64
Kamloops Museum and Archives,
    B.C., 64
Kamloops Waterslide and R.V.
    Park, B.C., 64
Kamloops Wildlife Park, B.C., 64
Kaposvar Historic Site Museum,
    Sask., 268
Kasugai Gardens, B.C., 67
Kelowna, B.C., 66–68
Kenderdine Gallery, Sask., 282
Kicking Horse Pass, B.C., 75
Kildonan Park, Manitoba, 305
Kildonan Presbyterian Church,
    Manitoba, 304
Kimberley, B.C., 81–82
Kimberley Heritage Museum,
    B.C., 82
Kitimat, B.C., 186
Kitimat Centennial Museum,
    B.C., 186
Kitwanga area, B.C., 187
Klondike Highway 2, Y.T., 333
Kluane National Park,
    Y.T., 331–33
Knox United Church,
    Manitoba, 304
Kootenay Gallery of Art, History
    & Science, B.C., 78
Kootenay Lake, B.C., 79
Kootenay National Park, B.C., 74
'Ksan Village, B.C., 187
Kwakiutl Museum, B.C., 180

L

Lac La Biche Mission,
    Alberta, 203
Ladysmith Arboretum, B.C., 171
Ladysmith area, B.C., 171
Lake Louise, Alberta, 221–32
Lake Winnipeg area, 317–18
Lakeland Provincial Park,
    Alberta, 203

Lakelse Provincial Park,
    B.C., 186
Leechtown Gold Rush Site,
    B.C., 170
Legislative Building,
    Manitoba, 300
Legislative Building, Sask., 273
Leo Moi Sculpture Garden,
    Manitoba, 301
Lesser Slave Lake, Alberta, 202
Lethbridge, Alberta, 198–99
Lighthouse Park, Vancouver, 118
Little Stone School House,
    Sask., 282
lodging, 19–20
Lower Fort Garry National His-
    toric Park, Manitoba, 316
Lynn Canyon Park,
    Vancouver, 121
Lyric Theatre, Manitoba, 302

M

MacBride Museum, Y.T., 336
MacKenzie Art Gallery, Sask., 274
MacMillan Bloedel Place,
    Vancouver, 118
MacMillan Provincial Park,
    B.C., 175
Maltwood Art Museum and
    Gallery, Victoria, 159
Manitoba, 289–319
    attractions, 313–19
    Churchill, 313–15
    events, 292–93
    history, 289–92
    Lake Winnipeg, 317–18
    Selkirk, 316–17
    Southern Manitoba, 318–19
    touring services, 293–94
    tourism information, 290
    useful information, 294
    Western Manitoba, 316
    Winnipeg, 294–313
Manitoba Children's
    Museum, 303
Manitoba Museum of Man and
    Nature, 298

About the Editor

Ann Carroll Burgess has lived in Vancouver, British Columbia, off and on since 1974. She has more than twenty years' experience in the travel industry as a writer, editor, broadcaster, and lecturer.

She currently hosts *Postcards,* a live call-in radio talk show featuring interviews with travel industry guests and reports on destinations.

Her work also appears in magazines such as *Easy Living, Woman to Woman, Elan,* and *Natural History,* as well as newspapers in the United States and Canada.

Ann is a member of the Canadian Consulate's advisory board on tourism in Atlanta, Georgia, where she recently lived. She was the recipient of the Florida Press Club's General Excellence in Criticism Award three times running.